# PLANNING AND COMPULSORY
# PURCHASE ACT 2004

Related titles by Law Society Publishing

**A Guide to the National Conveyancing Protocol, 5th edn**
The Law Society
1 85328 997 3

**Business Tenancies: A Guide to the New Law**
Jason Hunter
1 85328 956 6

**Conveyancing Handbook, 12th edn (Autumn 2005)**
General Editor: Frances Silverman
1 85328 928 0

**Environmental Law Handbook, 6th edn (Autumn 2005)**
Trevor Hellawell
1 85328 978 7

**Licensing for Conveyancers (August 2005)**
Tim Hayden
1 85328 966 3

Titles from Law Society Publishing can be ordered from all good bookshops or direct from our distributors, Marston Book Services (tel. 01235 465656 or email **law.society@marston.co.uk**). For further information or a catalogue, email our editorial and marketing office at **publishing@lawsociety.org.uk**.

# PLANNING AND COMPULSORY PURCHASE ACT 2004

A Guide to the New Law

*Stephen Tromans, Martin Edwards, Richard Harwood and Justine Thornton*

The Law Society

ISBN 1 85328 925 6

Published in 2005 by the Law Society
113 Chancery Lane, London WC2A 1PL

Typeset by J&L Composition, Filey, North Yorkshire

Printed by Antony Rowe Ltd, Chippenham, Wiltshire

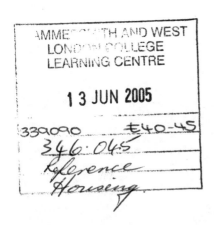

# CONTENTS

## 8    Compulsory Purchase                                      103

# Appendices

# ABOUT THE AUTHORS

**Stephen Tromans** is in practice as a barrister at 39 Essex Street Chambers. Prior to being called to the Bar in 1999, he was a solicitor, heading the Environmental Law Department at Simmons & Simmons from 1990–99, and before that was a partner with Hewitson, Becke & Shaw in Cambridge. He lectured at Cambridge University from 1981–88. His field of expertise is environmental and planning law, and associated areas of public, EC and commercial law. His books include titles on planning law, contaminated land and environmental impact assessment.

**Martin Edwards** qualified as a solicitor in 1981 and specialises in planning, environmental and public law. He has worked both in local government and private practice, being a partner and Head of Planning and Environmental Law at Titmuss Sainer Dechert. He is a case editor and commentator of the *Journal of Planning and Environmental Law* and of the *Planning Law Case Reports*. He is the joint author of the Estates Gazette's *Planning Notes* column, a Legal Associate of the RTPI and an Associate of the Chartered Institute of Arbitrators. He speaks regularly at conferences and training events and was legal adviser to the DoE's research team that produced the report *The Use of Planning Agreements*. Over the years he has been listed for his planning work in both the *Legal 500* and *Chambers & Partners* directories both as a solicitor and, more recently, at the Bar.

**Richard Harwood** is a barrister specialising in planning, environmental, parliamentary and public law at 39 Essex Street Chambers. He is Case Editor of the *Journal of Planning and Environment Law* and the author or co-author of several books on planning and environmental law. Richard is a member of the Advisory Panel on Standards for the Planning Inspectorate and the committee of the Planning and Environment Bar Association.

**Justine Thornton** is a senior associate at Allen & Overy specialising in environmental and planning litigation. She practised at the bar and worked for the European Commission Environment Department before moving to Allen & Overy. Justine is co-author of *Environmental Law*, published by Sweet and Maxwell. She is appointed by the Government to advise on biotechnology and the environment. She is also co-convenor of the United Kingdom Environmental Law Association (UKELA) working party on Environmental Litigation.

# FOREWORD

'Wait till it ain't broke any longer, then fix it' appears to be the rationale underlying the latest changes to the development plan system contained in the Planning and Compulsory Purchase Act 2004. It took many years before the network of Structure and Local Plans, introduced in 1968, achieved a comprehensive nationwide coverage, and the task of plan preparation was transformed into the more manageable process of review. Once this happy state of affairs had been achieved, Parliament decided that the time was ripe for a comprehensive overhaul of the development plan system. Pity the new Local Development Schemes, if they eventually turn out to be an improvement on Local Plans our legislators will be unable to resist tinkering with the procedures.

In a plan-led system there has long been a need for regional planning to be incorporated into the statutory development plan process. However, in the absence of directly elected Regional Assemblies, abolishing Structure Plans and replacing them with statements of the Secretary of State's own policies, incorporated into the development plan via Regional Spatial Strategies, represents a significant shift of power away from local government to Whitehall. Viewed in isolation, this particular example of centralisation may well be desirable, but what are the long-term implications for local government if the few remaining powers at local level continue to be eroded on an ad hoc basis?

Not that Whitehall's desire for central control is anything new. Sixty years ago we had a Minister of Town and Country Planning, charged with the duty of 'securing consistency and continuity in the framing and execution of a national policy with respect to the use and development of land throughout England and Wales.' Framing a national policy proved to be beyond the Minister's capabilities and his separate Ministry disappeared in 1951. Once there is a nationwide coverage of Spatial Strategies under Part 1 of the 2004 Act for all of the Regions, Greater London and Wales, the objective of having a national policy for the use and development of land will, at long last, have been achieved, albeit by a different procedural route.

Practitioners have had to grapple with planning legislation for nearly a century, since the Housing, Town Planning etc. Act 1909 first mentioned the subject and gave local authorities power to prepare planning schemes. There were, needless to say, considerable delays in the preparation of those schemes. Some things do not change. However, the intervening years have seen a constant process of legislative amendments to, and a huge increase in the complexity of, the planning code since the 14 sections devoted to Town Planning in the 1909 Act. This Guide should prove an invaluable aid to those seeking a pathway through the complexities of the latest changes.

*The Honourable Mr Justice Sullivan*
April 2005

# PREFACE

'The Government's "clearer, faster and more certain planning system" will be up and running by the beginning of 2004, it was announced this week at the unveiling of the Planning and Compulsory Purchase Bill

The ambitious timetable for reform means the Bill will get its second reading before the end of the year, go to the House of Lords before Easter and become law by the end of summer 2003. ODPM officials confirmed that local planning authorities will be required to work to the new system by 2004, regardless of whether the Bill has been passed or not.'

*Planning* magazine, 6 December 2002

The Bill finally received Royal Assent on 13 May 2004. It was the first Public Bill to be carried over from one Parliamentary session to the next. The Bill was disembowelled by the Lords and its entrails had to be stuffed back in by the Commons. At the last minute a government blunder almost lost it, but it was finally enacted. Implementation of the new legislation began in 2004 and is due to be complete in March 2006.

In 2001 the then Transport Secretary Stephen Byers called the planning system a 'banquet for barristers'. This point was reinforced by his Planning Minister, Lord Falconer QC, in a series of after-dinner speeches. A Green Paper was produced, only to be eviscerated by Parliamentary Select Committees. Lord Falconer moved on, Mr Byers moved out, his department was abolished and planning was transferred to Mr Prescott and the Office of the Deputy Prime Minister (OFFJOHN). Most of the Green Paper was dropped.

The Bill when it appeared in December 2002 was still the greatest change to the planning system since the Planning and Compensation Act 1991, if not the Town and Country Planning Act 1968. The Government had the Bill rushed through standing committee in the Commons by the end of January 2003. Sixty-four of the 90 clauses in the Bill were not debated. The Bill then disappeared, lost in some Parliamentary Bermuda Triangle. On 5 June the Planning Minister, Lord Rooker, announced that the Bill would be recommitted to a standing committee to 'enable us to bring forward provisions which will end the Crown's immunity from planning control'. Since the removal of the Crown exemption has been government policy since 1994, it seemed strange that this idea had only just occurred.

Ministers conceded that other amendments were required, including the correction of spelling mistakes in the Bill. Tony McNulty MP offered his 'final and grudging concession that "complusory" and "satisified" are not proper words'. The Bill returned to standing committee in the autumn of 2003. Ministers added planning contributions – the proposed replacement for planning obligations – to the Bill shortly before it left the Commons.

The Lords dismantled large parts of the Bill: Regional Spatial Strategies were to be delayed until there were elected regional assemblies; county councils had major roles to preparing regional policy; development plan inspector's reports were not to be binding; the current London Plan would not be part of the development plan; changes to simplified planning zones and the duration of planning permissions were rejected; statements of development principles were voted down; economic impact reports were required for major infrastructure schemes and site-specific elements of White Papers could be reopened by inspectors. Ministers also agreed to the 'Christmas-treeing' of the Bill, that is the Parliamentary practice of adding additional measures to a Bill. The Government produced amendments requiring design statements (to keep architects happy), access statements (to keep disability campaigners happy) and restrictions on mezzanine floors (to upset retailers). At Easter 2004, retail warehouse parks echoed to the sound of mezzanines being bolted into buildings in advance of the new controls. As the order is now expected in September 2005, they need not have rushed.

When the Bill returned to the Commons, the Government reversed most of their defeats. Statements of development principles (or as Sydney Chapman MP put it 'sod principles') were abandoned. Economic impact reports were retained and some concessions were made on the role of county councils. The Government then blundered. Both Houses are required to agree to the final text of a Bill. Amendments, acceptances and disagreements therefore shuttle between the Commons and the Lords in a process known as 'ping-pong'. The rally can continue indefinitely as long as the Houses offer 'amendments in lieu' of amendments they disagree with. However as the Companion to the Standing Orders says 'if one House insists on an amendment to which the other has disagreed, and the other insists on its disagreement, and neither has offered alternatives, the Bill is lost'. That is if one House rejects an amendment twice without proposing an amendment in lieu, Parliament has failed to agree the Bill. The Commons grouped Liberal Democrat and Conservative amendments to the Regional Spatial Strategies provisions together, offering an amendment in lieu of the Liberal Democrat amendment but twice rejecting the Conservative amendment. The Bill was technically and inadvertently lost.

However, as Erskine May said that there was no binding rule of order governing those proceedings the Lords could, by motion, excuse the error. That consent came at a price. After Lord Hanningfield, a Conservative spokesman, pointed out to Lord Rooker that he would otherwise be promoting the Planning and Compulsory Purchase (No.2) Bill 2004, ministers agreed that county councils and unitary authorities should have responsibility for preparing detailed proposals for different parts the regions. The strategic planning role of county councils was therefore maintained.

This book offers none of the rhetorical flourishes, procedural wheezes, lengthy pauses and (we hope) spelling mistakes of the Parliamentary process. We seek to explain how the provisions of the Bill came about, what they mean, the regulations, consultations and procedural guidance which have poured out of the Office of the Deputy Prime Minister and the National Assembly for Wales and the issues which will arise in practice. The Act and the important statutory instruments which have so far emerged are appended. In the interests of portability, the hefty planning policy statements and their companion guides are referred to, but not added to this volume.

The Planning and Compulsory Purchase Act 2004 is the most important Planning Act for over 30 years. It may take the rest of this decade for the procedures and documents it has spawned to fully emerge. However, despite its scale and breadth, the Bill always gave the impression of being behind events, rather than in front. The introduction of strategic environmental assessment of July 2004 will change all land-use policy making. The Act's changes to development control procedures are modest compared to the ODPM's current consideration of unification of development consents. The planning contribution proposals would be overtaken if the Barker Review on Housing Supply's proposals for a planning gain supplement are enacted. The Historic Environment Review proposes a complete re-write of heritage legislation, including the Planning (Listed Buildings and Conservation Areas) Act 1990. The Law Commission has proposed the codification and reform of compulsory purchase and compensation, the changes in Part 8 being mere appetizers for the feast.

Whether anyone has the stomach for further planning and compulsory purchase legislation remains to be seen.

This book has benefitted immensely from discussions at conferences and with professional colleagues. Some of the more printable views expressed have found their way into the commentary. We particularly wish to thank colleagues at 39 Essex Street and Allen & Overy for their help and collective wisdom.

*Stephen Tromans*
*Martin Edwards*
*Richard Harwood*
*Justine Thornton*
March 2005

# ABBREVIATIONS

| | |
|---|---|
| 1990 Act | Town and Country Planning Act 1990 (referred to as the principal Act in the 2004 Act) |
| 2004 Act | Planning and Compulsory Purchase Act 2004 |
| AONB | area of outstanding natural beauty |
| AAP | Area Action Plan |
| CS | core strategy |
| DPD | Development Plan Document |
| EIP | examination in public |
| GLC | Greater London Council |
| the Hazardous Substances Act | Planning (Hazardous Substances) Act 1990 |
| LDD | Local Development Document |
| LDF | Local Development Framework |
| LDS | Local Development Scheme |
| the Listed Buildings Act | Planning (Listed Buildings and Conservation Areas) Act 1990 |
| ODPM | Office of the Deputy Prime Minister |
| the Planning Acts | Town and Country Planning Act 1990, Planning (Listed Buildings and Conservation Areas) Act 1990, Planning (Hazardous Substances) Act 1990, Planning (Consequential Provisions) Act 1990 |
| PPS | Planning Policy Statement |
| the Regulations | Town and Country Planning (Local Development) (England) Regulations 2004, SI 2004/2204 |
| RDA | Regional Development Agency |
| RPB | Regional Planning Body |
| RPG | Regional Planning Guidance |
| RSDF | regional sustainable development framework |
| RSS | Regional Spatial Strategy |
| RTS | Regional Transport Strategy |
| SA | Sustainability Appraisal |
| SCI | Statement of Community Involvement |
| SEA Regulations | Environmental Assessment of Plans and Programmes Regulations 2004, SI 2004/6633 |

| | |
|---|---|
| SDS | Spatial Development Strategy |
| SEA | Strategic Environmental Assessment |
| SERPLAN | London and South East Regional Planning Conference |
| SPD | Supplementary Planning Document |
| TPO | Tree Preservation Order |
| UDC | Urban Development Corporation |
| UDP | unitary development plan |

# TABLE OF CASES

# TABLE OF STATUTES

# TABLE OF STATUTORY INSTRUMENTS

# TABLE OF EUROPEAN LEGISLATION

# 1 REGIONAL FUNCTIONS

## 1.1 PART 1 OF THE 2004 ACT

Part 1 of the Planning and Compulsory Purchase Act 2004 (the 2004 Act) deals with regional planning functions. It provides a framework under which each of the eight regions in England will have a regional spatial strategy (RSS) setting out policies for the use and development of land in the region. In each region, a regional planning body (RPB) will be charged with keeping the RSS under review and monitoring its implementation.

## 1.2 THE BACKGROUND TO REGIONAL PLANNING

### 1.2.1 Introduction

Regional planning has developed incrementally and has steadily assumed greater prominence as part of the development planning process, although without any statutory basis prior to the 2004 Act. Regional planning evolved originally as a response by planning authorities, particularly in the South East, to development pressures. The archetypal regional guidance was produced by the London and South East Regional Planning Conference (SERPLAN). Such arrangements were formalised by the issue of regional planning guidance by the Secretary of State from 1991, with Regional Planning Guidance notes (RPGs) for each region. RPGs are not part of the development plan, but were intended to provide a regional strategy within which development plans are prepared. Part 1 of the 2004 Act gives greater weight to regional guidance by making it a statutory part of the development plan, and by putting the arrangements for revising such guidance onto a statutory basis. Regional planning also needs to be seen in context with other regional initiatives, in particular economic regeneration and transport, and the development of devolved regional government. The Planning Policy Statement PPS11: *Regional Spatial Strategies* (2004) indicates that the intention is that the RSS will in future be better integrated with other regional strategies.

## 1.2.2   Regional Planning Guidance: previous arrangements

Until the introduction of the RSSs, regional guidance is to be found in 14 RPGs, covering the regions and conurbations such as London, Tyne & Wear, Manchester and the Thames Gateway. The guidance for each area was drafted by regional planning conferences formed by the local authorities concerned, or by regional chambers where these have been formed (see below).[1] Such guidance was published in draft for consultation, then considered by a public examination by a panel appointed by the Government Office for the Region.[2] It was then reviewed in the light of the panel's report and submitted as a final draft to the Government Office. The Secretary of State could propose changes (on which there was further consultation) and determined the final form of the guidance. The regional planning body was responsible for monitoring implementation of the guidance and for reviewing it. Guidance on the process was provided by the Planning Policy Guidance PPG11: *Regional Planning*, which was published in October 2000 together with a *Sustainability Appraisal of Regional Planning Guidance: Good Practice Guide*. This advised on the main areas to be covered in an RPG. The main purpose was stated as being to provide a regional, spatial strategy within which local development plans and transport plans were to be prepared. An RPG was to provide a broad development strategy for the region over a 15–20 year period and identify the scale and distribution of provision for new housing and priorities for the environment, transport, infrastructure, economic development, agriculture, minerals and waste management. PPG11 stressed a number of factors:

(1) the importance of environmental issues and the need for sustainable development appraisal of the regional policies;[3]
(2) the European context and the need for awareness of EU policies, programmes and regional funding regimes;[4] and
(3) economic objectives, with a focus on 'priority areas' and on 'clusters' of knowledge-driven industry.

In considering RPG as part of its 2002 study on *Environmental Planning*,[5] the Royal Commission on Environmental Pollution suggested that the most contentious issues in regional planning had been the amount and location of provision for new housing, and that the location of new growth areas and that in the South East decisions on housing provision had been largely imposed by the Secretary of State in the face of significant opposition from local authorities and the public. The Royal Commission also felt that there was a danger that RPG could be overshadowed by the regional economic strategy of the Regional Development Agency (see further below) and that regional planning guidance and regional economic strategies in their present form did not constitute integrated spatial strategies in the sense of complete synthesis of economic, social and environmental objectives 'considered in parallel rather than sequentially'.[6]

## 1.2.3    Regional economic development

The Regional Development Agencies Act 1998 established Regional Development Agencies (RDAs) for the nine English Regions, modelled to a degree on the national development agencies that already existed in Scotland and Wales. The 1998 Act has been said to constitute 'a significant step in the Labour Government's pursuit of its objective of regional devolution'.[7] The approach of creating statutory regional agencies to promote sustainable economic development and regeneration, and to facilitate local partnerships, was set out in the 1997 White Paper *Building Partnerships for Prosperity*.[8] Section 1 and Sched.1 to the 1998 Act divides England into nine regions (including Greater London) and provides that for each region there shall be an RDA. These nine regions are adopted in the 2004 Act for regional planning purposes: see s.12(1). Members of the RDAs are appointed by the Secretary of State (1998 Act, s.2). Under s.4 of the Regional Development Agencies Act 1998, RDAs have the following purposes:

(1)  to further the economic development and regeneration of the region;
(2)  to promote business efficiency, investment and competitiveness;
(3)  to promote employment;
(4)  to enhance the development and application of employment-related skills; and
(5)  to contribute to the achievement of sustainable development in the UK, where it is relevant to its area to do so.

By s.7 of the Regional Development Agencies Act 1998, RDAs are obliged to formulate and keep under review a strategy in relation to these purposes, and to have regard to that strategy in exercising their functions. The Secretary of State may give guidance and directions to RDAs in relation to the matters to be covered by the strategy and the issues to be taken into account in formulating it (s.7(2)).

The eight RDAs outside London were formally launched on 1 April 1999 and presented their strategies to Government on 26 October 1999. The Government responded on 12 January 2000 giving a broad welcome to the strategies. The ninth RDA, for London, was established in July 2000 following the establishment of the Greater London Authority; it presented its strategy in July 2001. Copies of the strategies (which are required to be reviewed in full every three years) may be found on the websites of the RDAs. The RDAs are as follows:

■  One NorthEast
■  North West Development Agency
■  Yorkshire Forward
■  Advantage West Midlands
■  East Midlands Development Agency
■  East of England Development Agency
■  South West of England Development Agency
■  South East England Development Agency
■  London Development Agency.

## 1.2.4    Regional Government Offices

In 1994 an integrated Government Office was created for each of the nine regions by merging the previously separate offices of the Departments of Environment, Transport, Employment, and Trade and Industry. They are seen as the leading element of central government in the regions and have played an important role in regional planning, which has increased to correspond with the enhanced role of regional planning.

## 1.2.5    Regional Chambers

Regional Chambers have been established by local authorities on a non-statutory, un-elected basis. As such, their constitution, role and membership are for the local councils to decide, on the basis of including representatives of the various sectors with an interest in the economic, social and environmental well-being of the region. The Government has not sought to impose a uniform framework for Regional Chambers, but the 1997 White Paper, *Building Partnerships for Prosperity*,[9] suggested desirable criteria. The reality is that their legal basis lacks consistency and clarity, some of them being unincorporated associations, funded and resourced on an ad hoc basis by local authorities, but each with an office in Brussels.

Under ss.8 and 18 of the Regional Development Agencies Act 1998, Regional Chambers were given at least some degree of statutory recognition, to the extent that Regional Chambers which were deemed sufficiently representative and 'suitable' could be designated by the Secretary of State, in which case the RDA is obliged to consult the Chamber and have regard to its views (s.8) and may be directed to answer questions put by the Chamber, supply information to it, and take other steps for the purpose of accountability to the Chamber (s.18). In September 1998 the Government issued guidance as to the general principles when considering Chambers for such designation, including matters such as political representativeness, the role of non-local government members, constitutional arrangements for debate and voting, and gender, disability and ethnic balance. By 1999 designated Chambers were in place in all regions, as follows:

- North West Regional Assembly
- North East Regional Assembly
- Regional Chamber for Yorkshire and the Humber
- West Midlands Regional Chamber
- East Midlands Regional Chamber
- East of England Regional Assembly
- South East of England Regional Assembly
- South West Regional Assembly.

The Government envisaged that Regional Chambers would play an important role in the formulation of RDA economic strategy, and potentially would also play a significant role in preparing RPG and regional sustainability frameworks. The December 2003 Planning Green Paper (see **section 1.3.3**) indicated (at para.4.44) that Regional Chambers were responsible for preparing draft RPG in the North West, South West, South East and Yorkshire and Humber Regions. Elsewhere, RPG continued to be prepared by regional planning conferences or associations of local authorities.

### 1.2.6   Elected Regional Assemblies

A further step towards formally devolved regional government was the proposed creation of elected Regional Assemblies, which was part of the Labour election manifesto, and was in part driven by EU regionalist tendencies. In May 2002, the White Paper *Your Region, Your Choice – Revitalising the English Regions*, put forward proposals for decentralisation of power by allowing the creation of elected Regional Assemblies, with specific responsibilities including land use and regional planning, economic development, housing, transport, environmental protection and public health. It envisaged that before an elected Assembly was established, there would have to be a referendum with a majority of those voting being in favour of having an Assembly. Such referendums would be held in those regions where it was considered there was sufficient public interest in an elected Assembly.[10] It envisaged that Assemblies would have between 25–35 members, with a leader and cabinet of up to six members. This led in turn to the passage of the Regional Assemblies (Preparations) Act 2003, to allow referendums to be held by order of the Secretary of State, and to provide for local government review by the Boundary Commission in considering whether a referendum should be held. The importance of having elected Regional Assemblies for the regional planning reforms is because there could clearly be potential difficulties in conferring power to create regional policy that forms part of the development plan on a non-elected body.[11] Hence the controversy, discussed below, as to whether regional functions should apply only if an elected assembly for the region had been established. The creation of elected regional assembles, however, ran into serious problems in 2004. Three referendums were proposed, for the North East, North West, and Yorkshire and Humber, and the rules were set.[12] Controversy over the method of a postal ballot was followed on 4 November 2004 by a decisive 'no' vote against an elected assembly in the North East (78 per cent against on a 48 per cent turnout). Within a couple of days, the Deputy Prime Minister announced the cancellation of the proposed referendums in the North West and Yorkshire and Humber, though continuing to state that it was clear Government policy to decentralise power and strengthen the regions. The result is the indefinite perpetuation of the ad hoc and legally insecure arrangements described above.

---

1   See B. Cullingworth and V. Nadin, *Town and Country Planning in the UK* (13th edn, 2002) p.78; also the summary in Royal Commission on Environmental Pollution 23rd Report, *Environmental Planning* (Cm.5459, 2002) para.2.50.

2   The examination is not intended to cover the whole of the submitted proposals; nor is it a hearing of objections. Rather it is to provide a public debate and testing of 'selected issues': see Annex A to PPG11. See S. Crow, *The Public Examination of Draft Regional Planning Guidance: Some Reflections on Process* [2000] JPL 990.

3 In addition to RPGs, regions have been encouraged by the Government to produce Regional Sustainability Frameworks, intended to provide a common vision and context for RPG and regional development strategies. See DETR, *Guidance on preparing Regional Sustainable Development Frameworks* (2000).

4 The European Spatial Development Perspective (ESDP), the Community Initiative on Trans-National Co-operation on Spatial Planning (Interreg Programmes) and EU Structural Funds are specifically mentioned in PPG11.

5 Cm.5459, para.10.36.

6 Ibid, paras.10.44 and 10.49.

7 See M. Grant, *The Encyclopedia of Planning Law*, para.2-3924.

8 Cm.3814.

9 Cm.3814.

10 In a speech to the English Regions Conference on 31 July 2002, the Minister for Local Government, Mr Nick Raynsford, indicated that this would be a matter for ministerial judgement. Such interest appeared greatest in the three northern regions, especially the North East, and lowest in the south and east.

11 See the 1998 consultation paper, *The Future of Regional Planning Guidance*, discussed at **section 1.3.1**.

12 The Regional Assembly and Local Government Referendums Order 2004, SI 2004/1962. See also HC Library Standard Note SN/PC/2922 *Referenda for Regional Assemblies* (1 July 2004).

## 1.3    DEVELOPMENT OF THE NEW REGIONAL PLANNING REGIME

### 1.3.1    The Future of Regional Planning Guidance

The consultation paper *The Future of Regional Planning Guidance* (February 1998) indicated the main criticisms of the then current RPG system, whereby local authorities in the region acting through the medium of a planning conference, submitted advice to the Secretary of State, who consulted on draft Guidance before formally issuing it.[1] These criticisms were:

- lack of truly regional focus and vision;
- lack of targets capable of being monitored (apart from those on housing);
- the process was too narrowly land-use orientated;
- lack of sufficient environmental objectives and appraisal;
- excessive time needed to produce RPG;
- failure to command commitment from regional stakeholders; and
- insufficiently transparent as a process.

The solution mooted in the 1998 consultation was not a root and branch reform, but a move towards a system where regional planning bodies would be given a greater role in producing RPG in partnership with the Government Office for the Region, whilst keeping the hands of the Secretary of State on the reins by the requirement of his ultimate endorsement and the ability to intervene during the process as the custodian of national policy. The paper stressed that the preparation of planning guidance or plans, which regulate the development and use of land in the public interest, should be the responsibility of democratically accountable bodies, with local authorities (as the principal delivery mechanism of such guidance through their development plans) having a central role. It was accordingly regarded as inappropriate for RDAs to take responsibility for such guidance, or for the Secretary of State to impose a statutory regional plan. The consultation paper also discussed the content of RPG, and in particular its broadening into a 'spatial strategy', i.e. the whole range of public activities intended to influence the future distribution of activities within the region. In particular, it stated that RPG must provide an effective basis for deciding regional or sub-regional issues that would be difficult to resolve if left to local authorities; be sufficiently prescriptive to determine the general location of regionally or sub-regionally significant development; and provide a sufficient framework to assist bids for EU Structural Funds and be sufficiently in tune with EU developments in spatial planning.

### 1.3.2    Planning Policy Guidance Note 11

In October 2000 the Government issued PPG11 *Regional Planning*, replacing guidance previously contained in the February 1992 version of PPG12. The guidance addressed the concerns expressed in the 1998 consultation, and in particular:

■  placed greater responsibility on regional planning bodies, working with the Government Offices and regional stakeholders, to resolve planning issues at regional level;

■  advised on measures to strengthen the role and effectiveness of RPG by a greater focus on strategic issues, the extension beyond purely land-use issues into a 'spatial strategy', the development of a sufficiently prescriptive strategy to determine the general location of regionally or sub-regionally significant development, and the adoption of a complementary approach to the economic strategies of the RDAs;

■  provided a streamlined timetable for the production of RPGs;

■  set out arrangements for the testing of an RPG at a non-statutory public examination, with a published report;

■  confirmed the need for sustainable development appraisal of the environmental, economic and social impacts of development options; and

■  established a new focus on outputs, with annual monitoring of performance against targets and indicators to ensure that RPG is kept up to date.

### 1.3.3    The Planning Green Paper

On 12 December 2001 the Government published its Green Paper *Planning: Delivering a Fundamental Change*. Paragraph 4.39 of the Green Paper provided a clear endorsement of the role of regional planning:

'We believe that there is a continuing need for effective planning at the regional level. Regionally-based policies are needed for issues such as planning the scale and distribution of provision for new housing, including setting a brownfield target and the growth of major urban areas. Additionally, there is a need for coastal planning, planning for regional transport and waste facilities, and for major inward investment sites and other aspects of the RDA's economic strategies. Regional planning provides a framework within which local authority development plans, local transport plans and other relevant plans and strategies can be prepared.'

It noted that many of the objectives of the 1998 Green Paper and of PPG11 remained to be achieved. Accordingly, it was proposed to:

- Replace RPG with new Regional Spatial Strategies (RSS).
- Give the RSS statutory status, so that Local Development Frameworks and Local Transport Plans[2] should be consistent with the RSS.
- Make the content of RSS more focused, outlining specific regional or sub-regional policies, address the broad location of major development proposals, set targets and indicators where necessary and cross refer to (rather than repeat) national policy.
- Ensure that each RSS reflected regional diversity and specific regional needs.
- Integrate the RSS more fully with other regional strategies.
- Promote the preparation of sub-regional strategies,[3] where necessary, through the RSS process.

What is clear from the Green Paper is that a step-change in the role and quality of regional guidance was envisaged (para.4.45):

'We are looking for significant improvements in the quality of regional guidance to match the importance we attach to effective regional strategic planning. There has been a tendency to avoid making the hard strategic choices, such as accommodating demand for new housing or the location of areas of key employment or retail growth. Instead a lowest common denominator approach is taken, which in the long term can damage development across the region.'

---

1  Although, as the paper acknowledged, there were significant regional variations in practice.
2  Local Transport Plans are required to be produced under s.108 of the Transport Act 2000; see further **section 1.7.7**.
3  Sub-regional strategies are envisaged for issues involving major conurbations, the strategic planning of major towns and their hinterland, and for areas straddling regional or county boundaries (e.g. the Thames Gateway and the growth of the Cambridge sub-region). See further below.

## 1.4    THE REGIONS

The regions for the purposes of Part 1 of the 2004 Act are the regions defined in Sched.1 to the Regional Development Agencies Act 1998, excluding London (see s.12(1)). These, together with their constituent local authorities, are as follows.

### 1.4.1    East Midlands

Derbyshire, Leicestershire, Lincolnshire, Northamptonshire, Nottinghamshire; the non-metropolitan districts of Derby, Leicester, Nottingham, and Rutland.

## 1.4.2   Eastern

Bedfordshire, Cambridgeshire, Essex, Hertfordshire, Norfolk, and Suffolk; the non-metropolitan districts of Luton, Peterborough, Southend-on-Sea, and Thurrock.

## 1.4.3   North East

Durham and Northumberland; the metropolitan districts of Gateshead, Newcastle upon Tyne, North Tyneside, South Tyneside, and Sunderland; the non-metropolitan districts of Darlington, Hartlepool, Middlesbrough, Redcar and Cleveland, and Stockton-on-Tees.

## 1.4.4   North West

Cheshire, Cumbria, Lancashire; the metropolitan districts of Bolton, Bury, Knowsley, Liverpool, Manchester, Oldham, Rochdale, St. Helens, Salford, Sefton, Stockport, Tameside, Trafford, Wigan, and Wirral; the non-metropolitan districts of Blackburn with Darwen, Blackpool, Halton, and Warrington.

## 1.4.5   South East

Buckinghamshire, East Sussex, Hampshire, Isle of Wight, Kent, Oxfordshire, Surrey, West Sussex; the non-metropolitan districts of Bracknell Forest, Brighton and Hove, the Medway Towns, Milton Keynes, Portsmouth, Reading, Slough, Southampton, West Berkshire, Windsor and Maidenhead, and Wokingham.

## 1.4.6   South West

Cornwall, Devon, Dorset, Gloucestershire, Somerset, and Wiltshire; the non-metropolitan districts of Bath and North East Somerset, Bournemouth, Bristol, North Somerset, Plymouth, Poole, South Gloucestershire, Swindon, and Torbay; the Isles of Scilly.

## 1.4.7   West Midlands

Shropshire, Staffordshire, Warwickshire, and Worcestershire; the metropolitan districts of Birmingham, Coventry, Dudley, Sandwell, Solihull, Walsall, and Wolverhampton; the non-metropolitan districts of Herefordshire, Stoke-on-Trent, and Telford and Wrekin.

## 1.4.8   Yorkshire and the Humber

North Yorkshire; the metropolitan districts of Barnsley, Bradford, Calderdale, Doncaster, Kirklees, Leeds, Rotherham, Sheffield, and Wakefield; the non-metropolitan districts of the East Riding of Yorkshire, Kingston upon Hull, North East Lincolnshire, North Lincolnshire, and York.

### 1.4.9    Special provision for National Parks

Provision is made for the boundaries of regions to be altered by the Secretary of State in order to accommodate National Park boundaries. By s.12(2) if the area of a National Park falls within more than one region, the Secretary of State may by order direct that it be treated as falling wholly within such region as is specified in the order. See the Town and Country Planning (Regions) (National Parks) (England) Order 2004, SI 2004/2207, which directs that the areas of the North York Moors National Park and the Yorkshire Dales National Park be treated as falling wholly within the Yorkshire and Humber Region, and that the area of the Peak District National Park be treated as falling wholly within the East Midlands Region.

## 1.5    PART 1 AND ELECTED ASSEMBLIES

As amended by the House of Lords in Committee, the Bill contained a clause 1 providing that Part 1 should apply only if an elected assembly for the region had been established. This clause represented a defeat by the Government on an amendment proposed by Baroness Hamwee, in order to address 'a loss of democracy' on the face of the Bill.[1] The Commons, however, disagreed to the amendment but proposed an amendment in lieu as to the required composition of RPBs, which became s.2(3) and (4), as to which see **section 1.6**.[2] Clearly, had the House of Lords amendment been maintained in the Act, Part 1 might have been a dead letter in view of the autumn 2004 referendum defeat of proposals for the first elected regional assembly (see **section 1.2.6**).

1   Hansard, HL, 20 January 2004, cols.919–921, 937 (amendment agreed to by a majority of 158 to 137).
2   For further Lords debate on this issue, see Hansard, HL, 11 May 2004, cols.155–160.

## 1.6    'REGIONS BY STEALTH', THE COUNTY 'GAP' AND SUB-REGIONAL POLICY

In opening the debate on the Bill in the Lords on behalf of the Opposition, Lord Hanningfield referred to the regionalisation programme of the Government as their 'regions by stealth' agenda and expressed concern about the gap left by the removal of county councils from the development planning process:[1]

'Without a key role for county councils, it is difficult to envisage how the gap between regional planning and local planning can be bridged. It is simply too large without an intervening mechanism. For example, South Buckinghamshire District Council's local development plan will be for an area with a population of 62,000 residents. But the next level of planning – the regional spatial strategy for the south east – will directly affect 8 million people, which is equivalent to the population of Austria. There will be nothing statutory in between to join up those plans.'

Lord Bradshaw referred to the loss of local accountability involved in the south east region, citing the example of decisions in Oxfordshire being 'sucked away and placed in Guildford'[2] whereas Lord Mayhew of Twysden was concerned about the lack of homogeneity of the region, stretching from north Oxfordshire to Thanet.[3]

This controversy continued to the bitter end of the Bill in May 2004. The Government was eventually forced to concede that at least 60 per cent of members of RPBs would be members of local authorities, subject to the threat to revisit and if necessary re-amend the arrangements if they proved unworkable.[4] In addition, the Bill was amended to require the RPB to seek the advice of county councils and other bodies with strategic planning experience on whether sub-regional frameworks are desirable. The continued significance of the sub-regional dimension is also stressed in the final versions of PPS11 and PPS12. The Government was far from happy at what it saw as the complication of the new two-tier system by the possible interposition of a county approach. However, the amendments mean that it is too soon to speak of the demise of strategic county planning.

---

1   Hansard, HL, 6 January 2004, cols.104–5.
2   Hansard, HL, 6 January 2004, col.119.
3   Hansard, HL, 6 January 2004, cols.124–5. The region was also referred to by Baroness Cumberlege as the 'banana republic' because of its shape, '. . . as it bends round London from north Oxford to east Kent.' (HL, 6 January 2004, col.135)
4   Hansard, HC, 12 May 2004, col.414.

## 1.7   REGIONAL SPATIAL STRATEGY

### 1.7.1   Introduction

Part 1 of the 2004 Act makes provision for RSSs to have statutory status, replacing county structure plans introduced in 1968. By s.24(1) the local development documents produced under Part 2 of the 2004 Act must be in general conformity with the RSS. Under s.38(3) the RSS is part of the statutory development plan, and plays a commensurately important role under the plan-led system.

### 1.7.2   Scope

By s.12(1) the provisions apply only to England, and not to London. For London, the Greater London Authority Act 1999 already makes provision for a Spatial Development Strategy (SDS) to be prepared by the Mayor (see Part VIII of that Act). Provision as to Wales is made by Part 6 of the 2004 Act: s.60 provides for a spatial plan for Wales, to be known as the Wales Spatial Plan, setting out policies of the National Assembly in relation to the development and use of land in Wales.

### 1.7.3   Commencement

Part 1 was brought into force in relation to England from 28 September 2004 by the Planning and Compulsory Purchase Act 2004 (Commencement No.1) Order 2004, SI 2004/2097, art.2. At the same time a package of regulations on Part 1 was introduced, together with PPS11 on Regional Planning.

### 1.7.4   Requirement for RSS

By s.1(1) for each region (except London) there is to be an RSS. The RSS must set out the Secretary of State's policies (however expressed) in relation to the development and use of land within the region (s.1(2)). For this purpose the references to a region include references to any area within a region which includes the area or part of the area of more than one local planning authority (s.1(3)). Note that the policy is that of the Secretary of State, not any other planning body. The 'Secretary of State' is the Secretary of State for the time being having general responsibility for policy in relation to the development and use of land (s.12(4)). This is reflected in the strong 'centralist' tenor of the provisions of Part 1, with the Secretary of State very much holding the whip hand in terms of policy formulation.

### 1.7.5   Content of RSS

The Act itself does not make provision as to the definition or content of an RSS beyond the fact that it must set out the Secretary of State's policies in relation to the development and use of land within the region.[1] The Explanatory Notes to the Act suggest that the policies need not be directly related to the grant or refusal of planning permission; they could include, for example, congestion charging policies. The point of spatial development strategy is that it goes beyond traditional development planning, as was put by Lord Rooker in debate:[2]

> 'Spatial planning goes beyond traditional land use planning to bring together and integrate policies for the development and use of land with other policies and programmes which influence the nature of places and how they function. That includes policies which impact on land use, for example by influencing the demands on or need for development but which are not capable of being delivered solely or mainly through the granting or refusal of planning permission and which may be implemented by other means.'

Guidance on the concept of spatial planning to similar effect was included in paras.1.29 and 1.30 of draft PPS1, *Creating Sustainable Communities* (2004), which again stresses the integrating, cross-cutting nature of spatial planning. More detailed but somewhat jargon-laden guidance on the purpose and scope of an RSS is provided at paras.1.2–1.8 of PPS11. Essentially, the RSS is to provide 'a broad development strategy for the region for a fifteen to twenty year period', taking into account the scale and distribution of provision for new housing, environmental priorities, transport, infrastructure and economic developments, mineral extraction and waste disposal. It will need to tread a fine line between being sufficiently specific to provide clear guidance for local development documents (LDDs), whilst avoiding inappropriate levels of detail or dealing with matters which are not of genuine regional significance. For example, it should provide housing figures at district or sub-regional level as appropriate, should be 'locationally but not site specific'[3] and should be 'focused on delivery mechanisms which make clear what is to be done by whom and by when'. One of the less helpful guidelines is that it 'should apply the test of adding value to the overall planning process'.

A statutory distinction is drawn between policies and other material in an RSS: by s.1(4) if to any extent a policy set out in the RSS conflicts with any other state-ment or information in the RSS the conflict must be resolved in favour of the policy. What clearly the RSS should not do is to '. . . stray into . . . site-specific proposals and thereby subvert these statutory procedures [planning, highways and transport and Works inquiry procedures] and the safeguards they provide'.[4]

Under the Town and Country Planning (Regional Planning) (England) Regulations 2004, SI 2004/2203, reg.7(2) and (3), the draft revision of an RSS must include a reasoned justification for the policies. As with structure plans, it must contain a key diagram, not on a map base, illustrating the policies, and may also contain an inset diagram drawn to a larger scale and illustrating the application of policies to part of the area (reg.9).

## 1.7.6    Relationship with other regional strategies

PPS11, paras.2.11–2.16, discusses the relationship of the RSS with the multitude of other regional strategies: 'It is essential that the RSS both shapes, and is shaped by, other regional strategies.' Apart from the regional economic strategy under s.7 of the Regional Development Agencies Act 1998, these strategies do not have a statutory basis. They may, for example, include strategies on biodiversity, air quality, culture, forestry, health, higher education, skills and housing. Action is being taken by the Government to improve integration in this respect,[5] and the Government expects similar action at regional level to join up the different strategies.[6]

## 1.7.7    Regional Transport Strategy (RTS)

The RTS is an integral part of the RSS, which is thus an integrated planning and transport spatial strategy: para.2.16 of PPS11. Annex B to the PPS provides more detailed procedural guidance on the RTS.[7] The RTS 'should provide regional objectives and priorities for transport investment and management across all modes to support the spatial strategy and delivery of sustainable national trans-port policies'. There should be 'strong analytical underpinning' and the estab-lishment of 'a coherent set of regional objectives', which lead into policies to meet those objectives. The RTS will then play an important role in providing the context for the preparation of LDDs and also Local Transport Plans by local authorities under the Transport Act 2000.

## 1.7.8 Regional Planning Guidance as the RSS

The initial RSS for each region will comprise existing Regional Planning Guidance (see **section 1.2**) to the extent prescribed by the Secretary of State in regulations. By s.1(5) with effect from the appointed day the RSS for a region is so much of the Regional Planning Guidance as the Secretary of State prescribes. 'Regional Planning Guidance' is defined as 'a document issued by the Secretary of State setting out his policies (however expressed) in relation to the development and use of land within the region'. The ability of the Secretary of State to 'pick and choose' which RPG will become the RSS is intended to allow the Secretary of State to decide, where there is a range of RPGs in a region, which should become the RSS.[8] The Government resisted amendments to provide simply that all parts of existing RPG should form the new RSS. The Town and Country Planning (Initial Regional Spatial Strategy) (England) Regulations 2004, SI 2004/2206 specify which existing RPG (or in some cases which parts) become the initial RSS for which regions (see Appendix 2). In most cases the relevant current RPG for the region simply becomes the RSS, the exceptions being East of England (where the RSS is made up in part of RPG 6 for East Anglia and parts of RPG 9 for the South East) and the South East (where RPG 9 excludes Greater London, Hertfordshire, Bedfordshire and Essex, but includes revisions made in 2004 by the Regional Transport Strategy and the Ashford Growth Area). Steps taken in connection with the preparation of existing RPGs may be treated as the revision of the RSS: see the Town and Country Planning (Regional Planning Guidance as Revision of Regional Spatial Strategy) Order 2004, SI 2004/2208, discussed further below.

## 1.7.9 Transitional Provisions for Structure Plans

PPS11 para.2.54 states that structure plans will be 'saved' for a period of three years from commencement of Parts 1 and 2 of the 2004 Act or from the adoption of the structure plan, whichever is later, unless during that period either:

(1) RSS revisions are published by the Secretary of State which replace the structure plan policies in whole or in part; or

(2) the Secretary of State directs under Sched.8, para.1(3), that the three-year period should be extended.

The PPS places the onus on RPBs either to identify which policies in the draft RSS replace which policies in the structure plan, or whether any policies in the structure plan need to be saved beyond the three-year period in order to avoid a policy vacuum. Para.2.57 of PPS11 sets out the criteria in accordance with which the case for saving a structure plan policy will be judged. Essentially these are:

(1) consistency with current national policy and general conformity with the RSS;

(2) addressing an existing strategic policy deficit and not duplicating national or local policy;

(3) operation not materially changed by virtue of other structure plan policies not being saved; and

(4) any other reasons why it is appropriate for the policy to be saved for more than three years.

On transitional provisions generally, see the Town and Country Planning (Transitional Arrangements) (England) Regulations 2004, SI 2004/2205 (Appendix 2).

---

1  For an unsuccessful attempt to introduce an amendment defining an RSS, see Hansard, HL, 20 January 2004, col.951 (Lord Greaves).

2  Hansard, HL, 20 January 2004, col.969. This definition is replicated in the Glossary section to PPS11.

3  It must not identify specific sites as suitable for development, but should establish the locational criteria appropriate to regionally or sub-regionally significant development, or the location of 'major new inward investment sites': see PPS11, paras.1.16 and 1.17.

4  See Lord Rooker, Hansard, HL, 20 January 2004, col.955.

5  See para.2.12 – for example, actions consequent upon the Barker Report, *Delivering Stability: Securing our Future Housing Needs* (March 2004) to create single bodies responsible for managing regional housing markets.

6  See para.2.13.

7  See also the DfT/ODPM *Guide to Producing Regional Transport Strategies*.

8  Lord Rooker stated in debate that all current RPGs would be converted into RSS, with the exception of those RPGs (3, 3A, 3B, 9A and 9B) relating to London and the Thames Gateway, which will be replaced in large part by the Mayor's London Plan: see Hansard, HL, 20 January 2004, col.965.

## 1.8    REGIONAL PLANNING BODIES

### 1.8.1    Introduction

Regional Planning Bodies (RPBs) are the bodies which will have the role of keeping under review and revising the RSS for their region. The RPB must be a body which satisfies such criteria as are prescribed (s.2(2)) and which is recognised as the RPB by direction of the Secretary of State (s.2(1)). The RPB need not be an incorporated body (s.1(2)) and if it is not incorporated, a change in its membership will not of itself affect the validity of its recognition (s.2(8)). Recognition may also be withdrawn by direction (s.2(5)).

By s.2(3) the Secretary of State must not give a direction recognising an RPB unless not less than 60 per cent of its members fall within subs.(4). Effectively this requires 60 per cent of members of the RPB to be members of a district, county or metropolitan district council, National Park or Broads authority within the region. As indicated above, this is an important concession, made unwillingly by the Government at a late stage.

The further criteria for recognition of RPBs are prescribed by reg.4(1) of the Town and Country Planning (Regional Planning) (England) Regulations 2004, SI 2004/2203 as follows.

(1) At least 30 per cent of the members of the RPB are not also members of a relevant authority. (Relevant authorities being district, county and metropolitan district councils, National Park and Broads Authorities, and the Council of the Isles of Scilly.)

(2) All of the members are entitled to vote when any decision relating to the exercise by the RPB of its functions under the 2004 Act is taken by the RPB.

(3) The membership includes at least one member from each type of relevant authority, if such an authority exists within the region.

In the absence of a recognised RPB, the Secretary of State may exercise such functions of the RPB as he thinks appropriate (s.2(6) and (7)).

## 1.8.2    General functions

Section 3 confers on the RPB the following general functions.

(1) Keeping under review the RSS. It needs to be borne firmly in mind, however, that the RSS is in law the policy of the Secretary of State; the role of the RBP is to formulate the Secretary of State's policies in this respect.

(2) Keeping under review the matters which may be expected to affect development in the region or part of the region and the planning of that development.

(3) Monitoring the implementation of the RSS throughout the region and considering whether such implementation is achieving the purposes of the RSS.[1] Guidance on monitoring is provided at paras.3.1–3.11 of PPS11, from which it is clear that the Government takes this aspect of the RPG's work very seriously: the RPB will have to provide the Secretary of State with details of the proposed monitoring arrangements, and the Secretary of State will need to be satisfied that there is a mechanism to respond sufficiently quickly to any adverse impact of the RSS.[2]

(4) Preparing an annual report on the implementation of the RSS, in prescribed form and according to a prescribed timetable. The details are prescribed by reg.5 of the Town and Country Planning (Regional Planning) (England) Regulations 2004, which requires the report to be prepared in respect of each year commencing on 1 April, and to be published by 28 February in the following year. Regulation 5(3) requires that the report must identify which policies, if any, in the RSS are not being implemented, the reasons why the RPB is of the opinion the policies are not being implemented, and the measures it intends to take to secure implementation, including draft amendments to the policy. In particular, if the RSS contains any policy specifying the number of dwellings to be built in any part of the region, the report must include details of how many have in fact been built since the policy was published and during the year of the report (see reg.5(3)(a) and 5(4)).

(5) Giving advice to any other body or person if it thinks to do so would help to achieve implementation of the RSS.

### 1.8.3    Advice from local planning authorities

In exercising its functions of reviewing, monitoring and revising the RSS, the RPB is required by s.4(1) to seek the advice of each authority within its region which is a county council, metropolitan district council, district council (only in cases where there is no county council in the area) and National Park authority. These authorities are placed under a reciprocal obligation to give the relevant advice (s.4(2)). The advice includes advice relating to the inclusion in the RSS of specific policies relating to any part of the region (s.4(3)). The context of these provisions is that the Act seeks to simplify the planning process by abolishing the middle tier of structure planning in those areas where structure plans still exist.[3] Concern was expressed in debate as to the fact that county councils provide the key local authority services such as education, social services and community safety, yet have no major role in strategic planning under the new system.[4] Thus the Government reluctantly accepted amendments which changed the original wording (which had simply permitted RPBs to obtain advice from local authorities if they thought it desirable to do so) to impose legal requirements for collaboration. As indicated above, this provision is an important means by which counties are secured an ongoing role in the strategic planning process, but creates an obvious source of tension with the underlying desire to give primacy to regional planning whilst retaining a two-tier structure.

### 1.8.4    Assistance

As well as the duties in relation to seeking advice, an RPB may under s.4(5) make arrangements with the authorities referred to in s.4(4) or with any district council in the region for the discharge by the authority or council of a function of the RPB, except for publication of draft revised RSS and its submission to the Secretary of State (s.4(7)). The RSS may reimburse the expenditure of the other authority (s.4(6)) and such arrangements are to be taken to be arrangements between local authorities for the purpose of s.101 of the Local Government Act 1972.[5] The distinction is that whereas the advice referred to in s.4(1) is simply the opinion of the authority concerned, 'arrangements' under s.4(5) relate to the commissioning of substantive work, which may be under contractual arrangements, to provide specified outputs (see PPS11, para.2.21). Examples of the types of work which may appropriately be the subject of such arrangements are given at para.2.25 of PPS11. Where formal arrangements are entered into, they should specify the work to be carried out, and the date by which it is to be carried out, proposed expenditure which may be charged to the RPB, and the relationship between the officers and members of the RPB undertaking the work: see para.2.26 of PPS11.

### 1.8.5    'Partnership working'

Annex D to PPS11 contains a section on partnership working between RPBs and local authorities, including county councils.It stresses that local authorities are the key bodies that can translate the vision of the RSS into reality and that through their monitoring activities they will also be the providers of data and information fundamental to the RSS monitoring and revision process. They are likely to have particularly important roles in sub-regional work, checking for general conformity of local development plan documents with the RSS, and in the technical work underpinning revisions of the RSS and any groups steering this work. Paragraph 2.24 of PPS11 also raises the possibility of joint studies as a matter to be considered by RPBs.

1  Implementation in this context presumably includes both the formulation of local development policy under Part II (which must by s.24(1) be in general conformity with the RSS) and actual development control decisions.
2  See also the ODPM Guidance, *Monitoring Regional Spatial Strategies: Good Practice Guidance*, containing a set of core output indicators.
3  See, for example, Lord Rooker, Hansard, HL, 6 January 2004, col.99.
4  See, for example, Baroness Cumberlege, HL, 6 January 2004, col.134.
5  These are the powers allowing local authorities to arrange for the discharge of their functions by committees, sub-committees, offices and other authorities, sometimes loosely referred to as 'agency' arrangements: see Arden, Manning and Collins, *Local Government Constitutional and Administrative Law* (Sweet & Maxwell, 1999) pp.239ff.

## 1.9    REVISION OF REGIONAL SPATIAL STRATEGIES

### 1.9.1    Duty to prepare draft revision of RSS

By s.5(1) the RPB is under a duty to prepare a draft revision of the RSS in three circumstances:

(1)  where it appears necessary or expedient to do so;[1]
(2)  at such a time as may be prescribed; and
(3)  if directed to do so.

Revision and draft revision include the revision of an RSS in part, or in relation to part of a region: s.12(6). Thus ostensibly the RPB has, in the absence of any prescribed frequency for review, discretion as to the timing of review. This is, however, subject to the reserve powers of the Secretary of State under s.10 to direct the RPB to undertake revision, and to prepare a draft revision himself if the RPB fails to comply.

### 1.9.2    The process of revision by the RPB

Section 5(3) contains a list of matters to which the RPB must have regard in preparing a draft revision of RSS. The RPB must also carry out a sustainability appraisal of the proposals and prepare a report on the findings of the appraisal: s.5(4). The draft revision, sustainability report and any other documents pre-scribed in regulations made under s.5(7) must be published and submitted to the Secretary of State: s.5(8). The RPB may withdraw a draft revision at any time before the draft is submitted to the Secretary of State: s.5(9).

The key stages in the RSS revision process are summarised in paras.2.31–2.53 of PPS11, together with a target timetable, and comprise the following.

(1) Drawing up a project plan.
(2) Developing options and policies.
(3) Submission of the draft revision to the Secretary of State.
(4) The Examination in Public.
(5) The Panel Report.
(6) Publication and consultation on proposed changes.
(7) Issue of final RSS.

## 1.9.3   Regulations

Under s.11 regulations may be made as to the procedures for the revision of RSS. Further, as to regulations and orders made under the 2004 Act, see s.122. The main procedural regulations are the Town and Country Planning (Regional Planning) (England) Regulations 2004, SI 2004/2203.

## 1.9.4   'Front-loading'

A recurrent theme of the procedures for RSS revision is what PPS11 terms 'front-loading', defined in the Glossary of the PPS as follows:

> 'Involving stakeholders, developers and landowners in the policy production process with an aim to develop consensus on significant issues early in the RSS process. The RPB in its Statement of Public Participation should set out how it intends to provide opportunities for participation in identifying issues and debating options from the earliest stages. Community involvement should happen at a point at which people recognise that they have the potential to make a difference and contribute to policy development.'

## 1.9.5   Matters to which the RPB must have regard

The breadth of the RSS concept is perhaps best illustrated by the huge and daunting range of the matters to which the RPB should have regard in formulating any draft revision. These derive from statute, regulations and guidance. In preparing revisions to an RSS, the RPB must have regard to the matters listed at s.5(3). One of these is the national policies and advice contained in guidance issued by the Secretary of State: s.5(3)(a).[2] Other matters include the RSS or equivalent guidance[3] for any adjoining region, the resources likely to be available for implementation of the RSS and the desirability of making different provision in relation to different parts of the region. Other matters are prescribed under the Town and Country Planning (Regional Planning) (England) Regulations 2004, reg.10. These include:

(1) the strategy for the region prepared under the Regional Development Agencies Act 1998 (see further above);

(2) the objectives of preventing major accidents and limiting their consequences, and the need to maintain appropriate distances between establishments presenting major accident hazards and residential areas and other potentially vulnerable land uses;[4] and

(3) the National Planning Framework for Scotland (April 2004) where the region adjoins Scotland.

In addition paras 2.5–2.8 of PPS11 refer to other matters to be considered:

(1) inter-Governmental and EU legislation, policies, programmes and funding regimes;[5]

(2) SEA requirements (see further below): and

(3) statutory duties to have regard to statutory purposes of the Broads, National Parks and areas of outstanding natural beauty (AONB) where relevant.[6]

Annex A to PPS11 contains a detailed, but non-exhaustive, list of EU, central government and central government agency guidance and other material to be taken into account by RPBs. An updated topic-based list, which RPBs are advised to consult, will be maintained on the Office of the Deputy Prime Minister (ODPM) website (**www.opdm.gov.uk**). The Annex importantly includes interim guidance, pending publication of PPS10, on waste management. A clear and deliverable strategy for managing waste should be included as an integral part of the RSS, including policies 'to enable the timely provision of sufficient facilities for waste management of an appropriate size and mix in the right locations'.

## 1.9.6    Sustainability Appraisal and Strategic Environmental Assessment

By s.5(3), in preparing a draft RSS the RPB must also carry out an appraisal of the sustainability of the proposals and prepare a report of the findings of the appraisal. As para.2.10 of PPS11 points out, the Regional Sustainable Development Framework or equivalent (RSDF)[7] should be the starting point for the RSS. The sustainability appraisal (SA) process is discussed at paras.2.36–2.39 of PPS11 and is based on the four aims for sustainable development outlined in PPS1:

(1) social progress which recognises the needs of everyone;

(2) effective protection of the environment;

(3) prudent use of natural resources; and

(4) maintenance of high and stable levels of economic growth and employment.

The SA should ensure these aims are tackled in an integrated way, at an early stage of the RSS process.

Separate requirements on the strategic environmental assessment (SEA) of the RSS apply under Directive 2001/42/EC, which came into force in July 2004.[8] Guidance on complying with the SEA Directive generally has been produced by the ODPM.[9] The objective is that the analysis of impacts under the SA process will be carried out on a comparable basis to that required by the SEA Directive.[10] The

Directive and its transposing regulations require that the RPB carry out an environmental assessment during the preparation of the RSS and before its adoption or submission to the legislative process. This will entail the preparation of an environmental report identifying, describing and evaluating the likely significant environmental effects of implementing the RSS and reasonable alternatives, and containing specified information. These include not only a description of the likely significant effects of implementing the plan or programme, but also the measures envisaged to prevent, reduce and offset any significant adverse effects, and an outline of the reasons for selecting the alternatives. Given that an RSS is intended to operate at a regional, non-site specific, level, it remains to be seen how rigorously these requirements will be applied in practice. It is clear, however, that SEA requirements may offer a potent ground for challenge to an RSS, if not complied with.

## 1.9.7    Sub-regional strategies

Another matter to which the RSS must have regard is the desirability of making different provision in relation to different parts of the region: s.5(3)(f). If it is decided to do so then the detailed proposals must first be made by a lower tier planning authority mentioned in s.4(4), subject to the ability to agree otherwise: see s.5(5) and (6). Lord Rooker for the Government indicated that sub-regional strategies are intended to be the exception rather than the rule, and to be confined to cases where they are needed.[11] Where they are needed then the authorities with strategic planning expertise in the area concerned will be expected to '. . . take the lead on, or participate in, that work'.

Where the RPB decides to make sub-regional provision, it must notify the s.4(4) authorities, and *may* give them information as to the geographical area to be covered, the broad subject matter of the detailed proposals, other bodies to be involved, and which authority should take the lead in making the detailed proposals: reg.8. By reg.8(3) the s.4(4) authorities must make the detailed proposals within 12 weeks of such notification, which seems an extraordinarily demanding timescale. It might be thought cynically that the very unhelpful (indeed probably impracticable) terms of reg.8 represent a way of discouraging s.4(4) authorities from taking up this role. As para.2.28 of PPS11 points out, it is possible for the RPB and s.4(4) authorities to agree that the RPB will take the lead in preparing proposals on a partnership basis. It will not necessarily be an attractive proposition for the s.4(4) authorities to take the lead, working within the RPB's brief, to an impossible timescale and without the possibility of recompense for work undertaken under a statutory duty.

## 1.9.8    Sub-regional controversies

In the House of Lords, an amendment moved by Lord Hanningfield (Leader of Essex County Council) was carried, requiring the RSS in all cases to include sub-regional plans for all parts of the region.[12] Lord Hanningfield made the point in cogent terms that in order to deliver appropriate regional developments, sub-regional schemes (concerning, for example, the A12 corridor, the expansion of Harlow, and Haven Gateway) would be necessary. The Commons disagreed with the amendment.[13] In the Commons the Minister for Housing and Planning (Keith Hill) indicated that the role of sub-regional authorities would be strengthened by amending PPS11 to require that the examination in public (EIP) should consider major issues of contention between the RPB and sub-regional authorities, and to make clear that in some parts of regions a sub-regional framework would be necessary, for example where important development or infrastructure proposals cross local authority boundaries.[14] Annex C, para.20 of PPS11 states that:

> '. . . on major issues of contention between an RPB and authorities with strategic planning expertise relevant to a matter to be examined at the EIP, the Panel will ensure that the issues are examined and the appropriate authority or authorities are invited compatible with having a manageable debate.'

### 1.9.9   Community involvement

Under s.6, the RPB must prepare and publish a statement of its policies as to the involvement of persons appearing to have an interest in the exercise of the RPB's revision functions. TheRPB must keep the policies under review and from time to time revise the statement. The RPB must comply with the statement in the exercise of its functions in revising the RSS, and will no doubt be vulnerable to legal challenge should it fail to do so. These duties are amplified by reg.6 of the Town and Country Planning (Regional Planning) (England) Regulations 2004, which requires policies to be included on how and when persons appearing to the RPB to have an interest in the revision of the RSS will be involved, and how other persons will be identified and involved.

These provisions were not originally in the Bill, but during its passage through the House of Lords, Lord Hanningfield introduced an amendment requiring a statement of community involvement for an RSS on the basis that such a requirement would:

(1) establish minimum standards that RPBs will have to meet in order to have democratic legitimacy;
(2) allow more general scrutiny and accountability of RPBs; and
(3) make the new system fairer and more consistent.[15]

In responding, Lord Rooker accepted that:

> 'The regional planning body should from the very beginning plan for community involvement throughout the process.'[16]

Community involvement is addressed in PPS11 at paras.2.17–2.19. This is not simply a 'one-off' consultation exercise, but an ongoing process of 'proactive involvement' of the public. Detailed guidance is given in paras.12–53 of Annex D to PPS11, covering a very wide range of issues and techniques for engagement.

## 1.9.10 Consultation

The consultation of other bodies by the RPB was left to be dealt with by regulations. In debate, Lord Rooker gave an indication of the list of bodies it was intended should be consulted, including local planning authorities, county councils, parish councils, the Countryside Agency, the Historic Buildings and Monuments Commission, English Nature, the Environment Agency, regional development agencies, telecoms and infrastructure providers, voluntary bodies, racial, religious and ethnic groups and representatives of business and of disabled persons.[17]

The Town and Country Planning (Regional Planning) (England) Regulations 2004, prescribe lists of both 'specific consultation bodies' and 'general consultation bodies' (reg.2). The specific bodies must be consulted in so far as the RPB thinks that the draft revision is likely to affect that body. The general consultation bodies are to be consulted as the RPB considers it appropriate. PPS11, para.2.30 states that the RPB should involve those bodies from each category of general consultation bodies which it feels will be sufficiently representative. The prescribed bodies are to be seen as a statutory minimum rather than an 'exhaustive baseline' (PPS11, para.2.30). Annex D, para.54 of PPS11 gives an extensive list of bodies which may need to be consulted, though pointing out that there may be other bodies specific to particular regions.

Under the Town and Country Planning (Regional Planning) (England) Regulations 2004, reg.11, before submitting a draft revision of RSS to the Secretary of State, the RPB must consult:

(1) such of the specific consultation bodies as are, in the opinion of the RPB, likely to be affected by the draft revision; and
(2) such of the general consultation bodies as the RPB considers appropriate.

Under reg.11(2) the RPB must prepare a statement setting out:

(1) which bodies it consulted;
(2) how they were consulted;
(3) a summary of the main issues raised in the consultation; and
(4) how these main issues were addressed in the draft revision.

This pre-submission consultation statement must be published when submitting the draft revision to the Secretary of State (reg.13). Despite the reference to consultation, the statement should not restrict itself to actual consultation *per se*, but should address the broader issues of stakeholder engagement and active participation (PPS11, para.2.18).

## 1.9.11 Submission of draft revisions to Secretary of State and representations

The draft revision of the RSS and related documents are to be published by the RPB and submitted to the Secretary of State (s.5(8)). Provision as to the form in which the documents are to be submitted and the publicity required is made by the Town and Country Planning (Regional Planning) (England) Regulations 2004. The draft revision documents must be sent to the Secretary of State in electronic form (reg.12). Copies must be made available for inspection at the RPB's principal office and other suitable locations, and published on the RPB's website (reg.13). Local planning authorities in the region fall under similar obligations.

Any person may make representations on the draft revision of the RSS received by the Secretary of State (s.7(2)). Under reg.13 of the Town and Country Planning (Regional Planning) (England) Regulations 2004, representation must be made within 12 weeks, although this period may be reduced to a period not less than six weeks where, in the Secretary of State's opinion, the draft revision constitutes a minor amendment to the RSS. By reg.13(6) the Secretary of State is not obliged to have regard to any representation made after this period.

## 1.9.12    Examination in public

The Secretary of State, having regard to the matters referred to in s.7(4),[18] may decide to arrange for an examination in public (EIP) to be held. If an EIP is held, s.8 applies. Whilst there is power to approve an RSS revision without an EIP (see s.9(1)), the Explanatory Notes to the Act state that the intention is that it will only be in exceptional circumstances of minor revision that there will not be an EIP. Essentially, as for structure plans, the EIP is held before a person appointed for that purpose, no person has a right to be heard, and a report of the EIP must be made to the Secretary of State. The procedure follows the already well-established format for structure plans, placing on a legislative footing the non-statutory arrangements for regional planning guidance introduced in 2000 (see **section 1.3.2**).

The decision to hold an EIP, together with the start date, venue and name of the person appointed to conduct it, must be published on the Secretary of State's website: reg.14 of the Town and Country Planning (Regional Planning) (England) Regulations 2004. The Panel, Panel Secretary and Panel Assistant should in fact have already been appointed on a shadow basis prior to submission of the draft RSS to the Secretary of State: see PPS11, para.2.46.

The basic task of the Panel at the EIP is to satisfy themselves that the RSS is sound, when tested against the criteria listed in PPS11, para.2.49.

(1)  Whether it is a spatial plan, taking account of related policy initiatives and programmes relevant to meeting regional needs where these directly impact on the use of land, and whether it contains policies which sufficiently link with those related policy initiatives to deliver the desired spatial change.
(2)  Whether it meets the objectives for an RSS, set out in para.1.7 of PPS11.
(3)  Whether it is consistent with national planning policy and, if not, whether the case for departing from national policy has been made.
(4)  Whether it is consistent with other relevant regional strategies for the region.
(5)  Whether its policies are consistent with one another.
(6)  Whether it is founded on a robust and credible evidence base.

(7) Whether community involvement and partnership working have been satisfactory.

(8) Whether it is realistic, including about the availability of resources, and is capable of implementation without compromising its objectives.

(9) Whether it is robust and able to deal with changing circumstances.

(10) Whether it has been subject to a satisfactory sustainability assessment and whether alternative options have been ruled out taking account of the SA findings.

(11) Whether it has been prepared following the proper procedures.

(12) Whether it has clear mechanisms for monitoring and implementation.

Detailed guidance on the preparation for the conduct of an EIP is provided at Annex C to PPS11, including the appointment of the Panel, the duties of the Panel Secretary and Panel Assistant, accommodation, timetabling and preliminary meetings.[19] This also covers the selection of participants invited to the EIP. Objecting to the proposals is not a guarantee of a place at the table: the selection will flow from the matters to be examined and ensuring an effective range of viewpoints on the strategic issues: '. . . the EIP is not a forum for hearing all representations'. Nor are lawyers welcomed with open arms: the EIP will be conducted in an informal 'round table' manner, in which formal legal advocacy and cross examination will be deemed inappropriate. Those intending to make set-piece speeches are also likely to be disappointed. As PPS11 puts it:[20] 'The Panel will . . . pursue "inquisitive chairing" rather than allow a general airing of views which would not be a productive use of examination time.'

The Panel will expect any alternative options put forward at the EIP to have been the subject of a sustainability appraisal, if not by the RPB then by those making the relevant representations (PPS11, para.2.51). This should be borne in mind by those putting forward such suggestions.

The report of the EIP panel must be published by the Secretary of State on his website as soon as is reasonably practicable (reg.15). This obligation cascades down to the RPB, county councils and local planning authorities, which must make the report available for inspection (see reg.15(2) and (3)).

## 1.9.13   Consideration by Secretary of State

If no EIP is held, the Secretary of State must simply consider any representations made; if an EIP is held the Secretary of State must in addition consider the report (s.9(1) and (2)). If the Secretary of State proposes to make any changes to the draft he must publish these, with reasons (s.9(3)). Any person may then comment, and having considered such representations the Secretary of State must publish his further revision and his reasons (s.9(4)–(6)). There is no power to reopen the EIP in such circumstances.

Processes for the notification and publication of such changes are prescribed by reg.16 of the Town and Country Planning (Regional Planning) (England) Regulations 2004. The word 'changes' is used rather than 'modifications', which was the term used for structure plans and which is still used in relation to local development frameworks. This may possibly indicate broader powers of intervention by the Secretary of State. Following consideration of representations made on the proposed changes, the Secretary of State will then publish the final RSS. It is contemplated that this will be between 2 years 6 months and 2 years 11 months from the inception of the RSS process (PPS11, para.2.51 and Table 1). As a matter of practice the Secretary of State will also publish a summary of the representations received (see PPS11, para.2.51 and Annex C). As soon as practicable thereafter the RPB should publish a consolidated SA report of the entire SA process covering all RSS revision stages, and including a statement agreed by the Secretary of State and the RPB, summarising information on how the SA results and opinions received were taken into account, reasons for choice of alternatives, and proposals for monitoring (see PPS11, para.2.52). This is legally important in order to comply with the post-adoption procedures required by the SEA Directive and implementing regulations.

### 1.9.14    Withdrawal of draft revisions

Draft revisions may be withdrawn by the RPB before being submitted to the Secretary of State (s.5(9)). Similarly the Secretary of State may withdraw draft revisions before he publishes them (s.9(7)). Procedures for use in this event are prescribed by reg.18 of the Town and Country Planning (Regional Planning) (England) Regulations 2004.

### 1.9.15    Additional and reserve powers

Section 10 contains a number of important additional and reserve powers of the Secretary of State. For example, he may direct an RPB to prepare a draft revision of an RSS, or aspects of the RSS. He may prepare a draft revision himself if the RPB fails to do so. He may revoke an RSS in whole or in part, and he may in certain circumstances provide that part of an RPG shall have effect as a revision of the RSS (see below). Where the Secretary of State uses these default powers to prepare a draft revision, the procedural requirements of the Regulations are applied so far as is practicable, with any necessary modifications: reg.23 of the Town and Country Planning (Regional Planning) (England) Regulations 2004.

### 1.9.16    Transition from RPG to RSS

An important power is given to the Secretary of State by s.10(7) and (8). This allows the Secretary of State to provide by order for parts of RPG (to have effect as a revision of the RSS) in cases where the steps taken in connection with the preparation of the RPB correspond to a step taken under Part 1 in connection with preparation and publication of a revision of an RSS. This power has been used in the Town and Country Planning (Regional Planning Guidance as Revision of Regional Spatial Strategy) Order 2004, SI 2004/2208 (see Appendix 2) by specifying certain detailed steps taken in connection with various RPG and providing that they have effect as the equivalent step in relation to the RSS. The type of steps treated in this way are, for example, development of proposed changes, preparation of draft revisions, publication of proposed changes, consideration of panel reports, and decisions to hold public examinations. In this way there can be a relatively seamless transition between the RPG and RSS processes. So, for example, the RSS for Yorkshire and Humber to 2016 was published by the Government Office for Yorkshire and the Humber in December 2004, following the selective review of RPG 12 (2001) and based on the draft revised RPG produced by the Regional Assembly in June 2003, representations on that draft, the report of the EIP panel and representations made in July to September 2004 in response to the proposed changes.

1 In this case the RPB must give notice of its intention to prepare a draft revision to the Secretary of State under s.5(2).
2 For this purpose the term 'Secretary of State' is not confined to the Secretary of State having responsibility for planning policy: s.12(4).
3 I.e. the London strategy and Wales Spatial Plan where the region adjoins either London or Wales.
4 Applying Directive 96/82/EC on the Control of Major Accident Hazards (COMAH).
5 EU Structural Funds Programmes, the European Spatial Development Perspective, and the INTERREG IIIB and ESPON Community Initiative Programmes.
6 See the Environment Act 1995, s.62(2) and the Countryside and Rights of Way Act 2000, ss.85 and 97.
7 See *Guidance on Preparing Regional Sustainable Development Frameworks* (DETR, February 2000).
8 Transposed by the Environmental Assessment of Plans and Programmes Regulations 2004, SI 2004/1633 (reproduced at Appendix 2) and the Environmental Assessment of Plans and Programmes (Wales) Regulations 2004, SI 2004/1656.
9 *Draft Practical Guide to the SEA Directive* (July 2004).
10 See PPS11, para.2.40 and consultation paper, *Sustainability Appraisal of Regional Spatial Strategies and Local Development Frameworks* (ODPM, September 2004).
11 Hansard, HL, 24 February 2004, col.152.  The example of south Midlands/Milton Keynes was given.
12 Hansard, HL, 24 February 2004, cols.146, 154 (160 votes to 108).
13 For further debate, see Hansard, HL, 11 May 2004, cols.160–163.
14 Hansard, HC, 12 May 2004, col.415.
15 Hansard, HL, 20 January 2004, col.940.
16 Hansard, HL, 20 January 2004, col.943.
17 Hansard, HL, 20 January 2004, col.947.
18 These are: (a) the extent of the proposed revisions; (b) the extent and nature of prior consultation on the draft; (c) the level of interest shown in the draft; and (d) such other matters as seem appropriate.
19 Provision for remuneration of persons appointed is made by the Town and Country Planning (Regional Spatial Strategies) (Examinations in Public) (Remuneration and Allowances) (England) Regulations 2004, SI 2004/2209.
20 Annex C, para.44.

# 2 LOCAL DEVELOPMENT

'to put it in the Government's own acronyms in a document entitled *Creating Local Development Frameworks*, the LDF shall be set out in an LDS, comprising LDDs, some of which are DPDs, namely the CS, AAPs and a proposals map. Other documents will be LDDs but not DPDs, namely SPDs, and the SCI, although the SCI will be treated as a DPD – sometimes. These documents will require SA and may need SEA. The DP will be the DPDs plus the RSS or SDS.'

(Opposition spokesman, Baroness Hanham's summary of the new local development policies, *Hansard*, 24 February 2004, Col 209)

## 2.1 PART 2 OF THE 2004 ACT

The 2004 Act provides for the wholesale change of local planning policy documentation and formulation. The existing structure plans, local plans, unitary development plans (UDPs) and supplementary planning guidance are to be replaced by Local Development Frameworks. The new arrangements were elegantly, neatly and accurately parodied by Lady Hanham. For those who do not speak Mandarin, she offered the following translation:

'The Government propose that the local development framework shall be set out in a local development plan scheme comprising local development documents, some of which are development plan documents; namely, the core strategy, area action plans and a proposals map. Other documents will be local development documents but not the development plan documents, namely supplementary planning documents. A statement of community involvement will be treated as a development plan document – sometimes.

These documents will require sustainability appraisal and may need strategic environmental assessment. The development plan will be the development plan documents plus the regional spatial strategy or spatial development strategy.'

This chapter seeks to explain the new system and how it will operate, and also why it has been introduced. Those concerned with development in Wales will be relieved to note that the Welsh system is more simple (see **Chapter 6**). Beyond changing the form of policy documents, the Bill provided for two fundamental shifts in power. The first was the removal of the role of county councils in making strategic policy. They were to be left solely with responsibilities for minerals and waste. The Government's objective was not ultimately achieved, as pressure from the counties and the Opposition combined with a near-fatal blunder by the Government in the final stages of the Bill, to give the counties a strategic role in the regional spatial strategy process. The second shift was to remove local democratic control from local planning policy. Local policies were to be in general conformity with the RSS or London Plan and inspector's reports were to be binding on local authorities. Government defeats in the House of Lords on these issues were reversed by the Commons and this objective was achieved.

Important transitional provisions are contained in Sched.8 to the 2004 Act. Part 2 of the Act on Local Development was brought into force on 28 September 2004.[1] The detailed regulations for its operation are the Town and Country Planning (Local Development) (England) Regulations 2004, SI 2004/2204 (the Regulations).[2] Local authorities are under a statutory duty to have regard to any guidance issued by the Secretary of State (s.34). Whilst the Act does not explicitly say it, the obligation must be to have regard to guidance as far as it is relevant to the particular decision being taken. The 2004 Act cannot be sensibly construed as requiring regard to irrelevant considerations.

Government guidance is provided by PPS12: *Local Development Frameworks* and *Creating Local Development Frameworks: A Companion Guide to PPS12*.

1    Planning and Compulsory Purchase Act 2004 (Commencement No.2, Transitional Provisions and Savings) Order 2004, SI 2004/2202.
2    References in this Chapter to regulations will be to SI 2004/2204.

## 2.2    THE REASONS FOR CHANGE

### 2.2.1    The evolution of development plans

Development plans had been introduced by the Town and Country Planning Act 1947, although they would only be adopted for identified parts of a local planning authority's area. County-wide structure plans providing strategic policy guidance and local plans in district areas were adopted following the Town and Country Planning Act 1968. Local plans could be district-wide, subject plans on particular issues, such as Green Belt, or action area plans for particular parts of the area. Local plan schemes set out the programme for making and amending local plans on a county-wide basis. There was no obligation to produce any local plan, let alone a district-wide plan. Consequently as planning entered the 1980s, a particular site would be governed by the structure plan and might be covered by an 'old' development plan or a local plan.

The abolition of the Greater London Council (GLC) and the metropolitan counties placed local planning control entirely in the hands of the district and borough councils. These councils were to prepare UDPs containing general and local policies for their whole area. Central government moved to fill the vacuum created by the removal of the counties and GLC by publishing strategic planning guidance (styled as Regional Planning Guidance: RPGs) for each metropolitan county and London.

The Planning and Compensation Act 1991 required the non-unitary district councils to prepare area-wide local plans. This was the corner-stone of the plan-led system introduced by the 1991 Act, the s.54A presumption in favour of the development plan arising later in that Bill's progress.

## 2.2.2   Difficulties with the plan-led system

The process of adopting area-wide local plans and UDPs was slow. By November 2001, 13 per cent of 362 local plans/unitary development plans had still to be put in place. The time-limited elements (for example, housing allocations) of 214 current plans (which were not necessarily 'new' plans) had expired (see Planning Green Paper, footnote 2). The Planning Green Paper claimed that the new system had never worked effectively, saying (para.4.5):

■   the system was over complex;
■   there were too many inconsistencies;
■   plans were too long;
■   preparation was slow and expensive; and
■   local plans were too inflexible.

It would be fair comment to say that in the 1990s the development plan system had failed. However, by the end of the decade, comprehensive development plans were largely in place and reviews were progressing more quickly. It is questionable whether requiring an entirely new set of documents to be prepared in the 2000s is a necessary or prudent approach to the issue. The adoption process envisaged in the Green Paper has been elongated by a recognition of the work involved and procedural changes, such as giving all objectors a right to be heard. It might be considered that the complaint does not justify the cure.

## 2.3   A GUIDE TO THE NEW STRUCTURE

### 2.3.1   Introduction

Each district, borough and unitary authority will adopt a Local Development Framework (LDF). LDF is a non-statutory term used by the government to refer to all the documents produced by an authority under Part 2 of the 2004 Act.

### 2.3.2   Local Development Scheme

The contents of the LDF are set out in the Local Development Scheme (LDS) (s.15), which also proposes a timetable for their adoption and review.

The documents proposed in the LDS will be Local Development Documents (LDDs). These will comprise:

(1) Development Plan Documents (DPDs) – which form part of the development plan (s.37(3));
(2) a Statement of Community Involvement (SCI);
(3) an adopted Proposals Map (which might be a DPD);
(4) a submission Proposals Map;
(5) other documents which will be Supplementary Planning Documents (SPDs).

### 2.3.3   Development Plan Documents

DPDs must include (reg.7):

(1) core strategies;
(2) area action plans;
(3) any other document which includes a site allocation policy.

The local planning authority may make other documents DPDs (s.15(2)(c)).

### 2.3.4   Core Strategy

A Core Strategy is any document containing statements of (reg.6(1)(a), (3)):

(1) the development and use of land which the local planning authority wish to encourage during any specified period;
(2) objectives relating to design and access that the local planning authority wish to encourage during any specified period;
(3) any environmental, social and economic objectives that are relevant to the attainment of the development and use of land mentioned in paragraph (1);
(4) the authority's general policies in respect of the matters referred to in paragraphs (1) to (3).

There may be more than one Core Strategy. *Sustainable Communities – Delivery Through Planning* (ODPM, 2002) proposed 'a core strategy: the core policies for delivering the spatial strategy and vision for the area. The policies should be location specific rather than site specific and may need to be illustrated by a key diagram' (para.34). PPS12 refers to one Core Strategy which 'should set out the key elements of the planning framework for the area. It should be comprised of a spatial vision and strategic objectives for the area; a spatial strategy; core policies; and a monitoring and implementation framework with clear objectives for achieving delivery' (para.2.9). Despite the policy aspirations for a single document, a Core Strategy is any document meeting the statutory test, and this may have unexpected consequences for other documents. The overarching purpose of a Core Strategy is at odds with the statutory requirement that it relate to the type of development and use of land which the authority wish to encourage. It would seem to exclude policies on development which the authority wish to *discourage*, and general protective policies (such as Green Belt) would be mentioned only insofar as they relate to encouraged development (say, housing) and not discouraged development (say, an airport).

### 2.3.5    Area Action Plan

An Area Action Plan (AAP) is any document which (reg.6(2)(a), (4)):

(1) relates to part of the area of the local planning authority;
(2) identifies that area as an area of significant change or special conservation; and
(3) contains the authority's policies relevant to areas of significant change or special conservation.

Significant change is viewed as growth or regeneration.[1]

### 2.3.6    Other Development Plan Documents

Other DPDs may include site specific allocations of land, which PPS12 discourages local authorities from including in Core Strategies,[2] and generic development control policies.[3] Whether development control policies are contained in a separate DPD or in the Core Strategy is important, as AAPs and site allocation DPDs cannot contravene those policies if they are in the Core Strategy, but can do so if they are separate.[4]

### 2.3.7    Statement of Community Involvement

Local planning authorities, including county councils, are required to prepare Statements of Community Involvement (SCI) (s.18(1)). The statement of community involvement is defined in s.18(2) as a 'statement of the authority's policy as to the involvement in the exercise of the authority's functions under sections 19, 26 and 28 of this Act and Part 3 of the principal Act of persons who appear to the authority to have an interest in matters relating to development in their area'. In the July 2002 statement it was stated that:

> 'In order to ensure that the community is more effectively engaged in the planning process, the core strategy will contain a Statement of Community Involvement which will set out benchmarks for community participation in the preparation of LDF documents and significant planning applications.'

In Standing Committee, the Minister explained[5] that regulations were proposed that would set out minimum standards for community engagement, in respect of both LDD preparation and development control functions. These standards would apply to all local planning authorities and would be based on current good practice. Local planning authorities will be free to set additional standards, to be defined in the SCI.

Whether an SCI can impose obligations on applicants for permission is uncertain. A Conservative amendment in the House of Lords proposed:

> 'A statement of community involvement shall not seek to impose any greater obligation upon an applicant for planning permission than that contained in or made

under the planning Acts, or support the refusal of planning permission because of a failure by an applicant to comply with any such obligation.'

The Minister responded saying:

'The point I must make is that the statement of community involvement is a statement of the local authority's policy. That is what it is about – the local authority's policy. The provisions of the Bill do not place any direct obligations on developers or other persons who wish to take part in the planning process. It is not a backdoor route to placing unnecessary burdens on those interested in the planning process. It is not intended to do that.'

Consequently the amendment was withdrawn.[6]

Local planning authorities would still undertake their own consultations. The Government's view is that prior consultation by developers would improve the quality of planning applications and might smooth the path to planning permission. What it may well do is give the impression of speeding up the process of obtaining planning permission by reducing the amount of post-application consultation but, in reality, it may lengthen the process by requiring more consultation before the application is submitted. Could this be the planning system equivalent of the hospital waiting list: a neat move for a government obsessed with setting targets and benchmarks?

## 2.3.8    Adopted Proposals Map

The adopted proposals map is the equivalent of the proposals maps adopted in the previous development plan system. It is prepared on an Ordnance Survey map base, and may include inset maps (reg.14(1)–(3)). When first adopted it must show the geographical extent of any DPDs adopted at the same time and any old policies which remain current (reg.14(4)).

## 2.3.9    Submission Proposals Map

Where a Core Strategy document is being produced and shows policies attaching to sites or areas by reference to an Ordnance Survey map, it must be accompanied by a submission proposals map showing the changes that will be made to the adopted proposals map if the new document is adopted (reg.6(1)(b)).

## 2.3.10    Supplementary Planning Document

A supplementary planning document (SPD) 'means an LDD which is not a DPD, but does not include the local planning authority's statement of community involvement' (reg.2(1)). These will include documents currently produced as supplementary planning guidance or as development briefs or planning briefs for individual sites. Part 5 of the Town and Country Planning (Local Development) (England) Regulations 2004 sets out the procedure for their adoption.

## 2.3.11 Reasoned justification

All local development documents, except the proposals maps, must contain a reasoned justification of the policies contained within them (reg.13(1)). The reasoned justification must be clearly identified (reg.13(2)). LDDs are therefore likely to resemble local plans or UDPs in layout. PPS12 says that the reasoned justification 'should not contain new policies or expand on the policy to which it applies and should not contain material which will itself be used for taking decisions on planning applications' (para.2.31). However, whilst policy ought to be separate from reasoned justification, the understanding of the meaning and application of policy will be informed by the reasoned justification. The reasoned justification will be part of the local development document and will often be relevant to a planning decision.

---

1  PPS12, para.2.17.
2  PPS12, para.2.16 and PPS12 Companion, para.8.8.
3  PPS12 Companion, para.8.9.
4  See the discussion on conformity at **Section 2.7.7**.
5  Standing Committee G, *Official Report*, col.232; 16 January 2003.
6  Hansard, 27 January 2004, cols.115–116. The PPS12 Companion Guide says that statements cannot require developers to carry out consultation: para.7.

## 2.4  SURVEY OF THE AREA

### 2.4.1  Duties of local planning authorities

Section 13 places a local planning authority under a duty to 'keep under review the matters which may be expected to affect the development of their area or the planning of its development' (s.13(1)). This is based on a longstanding obligation in the Town and Country Planning Acts. However, the obligation is confined to district councils, unitaries (including those county councils which are unitaries) and London Boroughs. The review need not be in any particular form and in the past has been dealt with by authorities as an obligation to be alert to the social, economic and physical environment rather than a requirement to produce a report on a periodic or any other basis. An annual monitoring report is now required under s.35 on the operation of the local development scheme and some material relevant to the survey may be contained in that report.

The matters to be reviewed include those set out in s.13(2):

(1)  the principal physical, economic, social and environmental characteristics of the authority's area;
(2)  the principal purposes for which land is used in the area;
(3)  the size, composition and distribution of the population of the area;
(4)  the communications, transport system and traffic of the area; and
(5)  any other considerations which may be expected to affect those matters.

Section 13(3) then provides that the authority should also consider any changes which they think may occur 'in relation to any other matter' and 'the effect such changes are likely to have on the development of the authority's area or the planning of such development'. The wording of this sub-section obscures its purpose of requiring authorities to consider the future as well as the present. The use of 'other' appears to be superfluous as the section requires consideration of changes to the sub-section (2) matters. The effect of the changes in sub-paragraph (b) is also unnecessary as the effect on development and planning must be considered under sub-section (1).

An authority may also keep under review and examine matters in a neighbouring area if those matters might affect its area but must consult the relevant local planning authority (s.13(4), (5), (6)). This seems a sensible approach and may prevent local development schemes becoming too parochial in the absence of the inherent consistency that county structure plans provided.

The Secretary of State is able to prescribe or direct other matters to be considered in the survey. The Regulations do not prescribe any matters for s.13 reviews but do make provision with respect to county councils under s.14 below.

### 2.4.2   Duties of county councils

County councils have two survey responsibilities. Firstly, they are required by s.14(1) to review the matters which may affect development or the planning of development which is a county matter.[1] In addition to waste and minerals, this will include the county council's own developments.

The Secretary of State is also empowered by s.14(3) to require counties by regulations or direction to keep under review s.13 matters which districts are also monitoring. The power is applied by the Regulations to require counties to keep under review (reg.5(1)):

(1) the principal physical, economic, social and environmental characteristics of the authority;[2]
(2) the size, composition and distribution of the population of the area;
(3) the communications, transport system and traffic of the area;
(4) any other considerations which may be expected to affect those matters.

The purposes of land use are left out of this obligation. The results of the review must be made available to those persons the Secretary of State prescribes or directs (s.14(5)). The persons prescribed are local planning authorities for the county's area and, if it requests, the regional planning body (reg.5(2)). The form or frequency of such reviews is not prescribed by the Act or the Regulations but the obligation to make results available indicates some frequency and formality in reviews. Counties are therefore required to retain some element of their strategic planning capability.

1  County matters are defined in the Town and Country Planning Act 1990, Sched.1, para.1, but exclude for the purposes of this section matters partly in and partly out of National Parks (s.14(6), 2004 Act).
2  The published regulation refers to 'the principal physical, economic, social and environmental characteristics of the authority' rather than the 'characteristics of the area of the authority' used in s.13(2)(a). This appears to be a drafting error as monitoring merely the characteristics of the authority is outside s.14(3), inconsistent in object with the remainder of the requirements and does not appear to have a planning purpose. PPS12 believes that the characteristics are those of the area not the authority (para.4.8).

## 2.5    THE LOCAL DEVELOPMENT SCHEME

### 2.5.1    Introduction

Section 15 requires local planning authorities to prepare and maintain a Local Development Scheme (LDS) setting out their proposed local planning policy documents and the timetable for their preparation.

### 2.5.2    Contents of the Local Development Scheme

The LDS will specify (s.15(2)):

(1)  which documents are to be local development documents;
(2)  their subject matter and the geographical area to which each document relates;
(3)  which documents are development plan documents;
(4)  which documents (if any) are to be prepared jointly with one or more other local planning authorities;
(5)  any matter or area in respect of which the authority have agreed (or proposed to agree) to the constitution of a joint committee under s.29;
(6)  the timetable for their preparation and for revision of those documents.

Further requirements for the LDS are specified by regs.8 and 9 of the Regulations. There is a superfluous requirement to set out the proposed title, subject matter and geographical area of local development documents (reg.8(a)).[1] The date on which DPDs are to be published for public representations and submitted to the Secretary of State for independent examination have to be included (reg.8(c)).[2] Greater temporal uncertainty is permitted for SPDs whose proposed month and year of public participation consultation and adoption is required (reg.8(b)). The LDS will also include the timetable, area and subject matter of any draft development plans which will proceed to adoption by reason of Sched.8 to the 2004 Act.

By reg.9 the LDS must provide that the proposals map (once it has been adopted) will be revised each time a DPD is adopted. The revision will show the geographical application of the DPD policies, i.e. the particular policies rather than the DPD area. The proposals map will therefore have to show the particular areas covered by general development policies (e.g. employment, housing), protection policies (e.g. green wedges, nature conservation) and site specific allocations.

The LDS will encompass the particular authority's planning responsibilities, so unitary authorities will include waste and mineral planning policies in their LDSs.

### 2.5.3   Submission of the LDS

The LDS has to be submitted to the Secretary of State and the relevant regional planning body or the Mayor of London (reg.15(3)). The deadline for submission of LDSs to the Secretary of State was 28 March 2005, six months after Part 2 came into force (reg.10(1)).

The Secretary of State is empowered to direct the local planning authority to amend the scheme (s.15(4)).[3] Given government concern at the time taken to adopt development plans under the 1991 legislation, this power could be expected to be used to speed up slow authorities. However, it may find more use preventing schemes from becoming over-elaborate and in pacing the production of DPDs and SCIs. As these documents will all require examination by an inspector, amending the LDS timetables will allow demands on the Planning Inspectorate to be managed. However, the ability of the Secretary of State to make directions further distances the scheme from the public in the area that it will cover.

The Secretary of State has four weeks to decide whether to make a direction but he can give notice that he requires more time (reg.11(3), (6)). If no direction is given in time, the Secretary of State says he does not intend to make a direction, or a direction is given and complied with or is withdrawn, the local planning authority may then give effect to the scheme. They will then resolve that the LDS has effect from a specified date (reg.11).

The local planning authority must revise the LDS when they consider it appropriate or when directed to do so by the Secretary of State (s.15(8)). As LDDs must be prepared in accordance with the LDS (s.19(1)), the LDS must be revised if the authority wishes to add new LDDs or change proposed LDDs, or even to change the name of a proposed LDD. Revisions to local development schemes must go through the same statutory procedures, including notification to the Secretary of State, as the original LDS (s.15(9)).

The Regulations provide that LDSs brought into effect must be available for inspection at the authority's principal office and placed on the council website (reg.12(1)).

### 2.5.4   Minerals and waste development schemes

County councils will not prepare LDSs[4] but s.16 requires them to prepare and maintain minerals and waste development schemes. The LDS provisions in the Act and Regulations apply to the production of the minerals and waste development scheme, except that the scheme is not subject to the joint committee provisions and notice of the taking effect of the scheme or revisions to it must be given to the local planning authorities in the county's area (reg.12(3)).

1   This is unnecessary as the obligation is already contained in s.15(2)(a),(b).
2   A publication date, rather than a month of publication is required.
3   Any direction must contain the reasons for making it: s.15(5).
4   Unless they are a unitary authority.

## 2.6   THE COMPREHENSIVE NATURE OF LDF DOCUMENTS

The authority's land use and development policies must be contained within the local development framework. Section 17(3) provides that 'the local development documents must (taken as a whole) set out the authority's policies (however expressed) relating to the development and use of land in their area'. This means that policies cannot be contained in non-statutory documents. Non-statutory supplementary planning guidance is replaced by statutory supplementary planning documents. The flexibility of the LDF process means that a proposal for a new document, for example a planning brief on a windfall site, can be made and given effect to with reasonable despatch. The use of non-statutory processes cannot bypass the consultation and conformity requirements placed on SPDs. This approach is consistent with the approach of the House of Lords in *Westminster City Council v. Great Portland Estates plc*[1] to the omission of policies from a local plan.

Each local development document is not expected to deal with all the authority's policies, which is why the obligation is that the documents as a whole set out the policies.[2]

The s.17(3) duty creates difficulties for supplementary planning guidance in existence on 28 September 2004 when Part 2 was brought into effect. Plans or documents relating to an old policy are development plan documents under the local development scheme (Sched.8, para.15). This appears simply to be development plans, as supplementary planning guidance is otherwise converted to development plan status. There is no other potential saving provision for the (non-statutory) supplementary planning guidance. PPS12 assumes that supplementary planning guidance can be retained by reference in the LDS, but it is not a local development document, and so cannot meet the requirement that all policies are in LDDs.

1   [1985] AC 661. See also *Kingsley v. Secretary of State and Cheshire County Council* (2001) 82 P & CR 9 and *R(on the application of JA Pye(Oxford) Limited) v. Oxford City Council* [2001] EWHC Admin 870, [2002] PLCR 19; [2002] EWCA Civ 1116.
2   For an alternative view of s.17(3) see M. Grant *Planning Encyclopedia*, Monthly Bulletin, June 2004.

## 2.7    THE PREPARATION OF LDDs

### 2.7.1    Introduction

Certain elements of the procedure for preparing and adopting a local development document are set out in ss.19–24 of the 2004 Act. There are a number of common elements in the preparation of LDDs and these are considered first.

### 2.7.2    Content

The content and process of preparing LDDs is set out in s.19. In preparing an LDD the authority must have regard to the documents set out in s.19(2):

■    national policies and guidance issued by the Secretary of State;
■    the RSS (or where appropriate the London Plan or Wales Spatial Plan) for their region or for any adjoining region;
■    the community strategy prepared under s.4 of the Local Government Act 2000 by the local planning authority and any other local authority for its area;
■    other adopted local development documents; and
■    the resources likely to be available for implementing the proposals in the document.

Additionally, the Secretary of State has prescribed that regard must be had to the following (reg.15(1)):

■    the regional development agency's strategy;[1]
■    any local transport plan or other relevant policies under s.108(1) and (2) of the Transport Act 2000 which affect the authority's area;[2]
■    the requirements of Articles 5 and 12 of the European Union Council Directive 96/82/EC on the control of major accident hazards involving dangerous substances (known as 'SEVESO II');
■    the national waste strategy;
■    if the local planning authority's area adjoins Scotland, the National Planning Framework for Scotland.[3]

In preparing the LDDs the authority must also comply with its SCI (s.19(3)) from the time of adopting the SCI (s.19(4)).

### 2.7.3    Sustainability appraisal

The local planning authority must also carry out a sustainability appraisal of the proposals in each local development document and publish a report on its findings (s.19(5)). This report is referred to in the Regulations as a 'sustainability appraisal' report (reg.2(1)).

The Government view is that sustainability appraisals are not carried out on SCIs,[4] however, the SCI is a local development document (s.17(1)) and the sustainability appraisal requirement is not excluded under the 2004 Act. Sustainability appraisal can only be avoided on an SCI if it can be said that it does not involve any 'proposals'.

A sustainability appraisal report must be produced before a DPD is submitted to the Secretary of State (reg.28(1)(a)), and before a supplementary planning document is consulted upon (reg.17).

Sustainability appraisal is not explained further in the Act or Regulations but PPS12 says 'the purpose of sustainability appraisal is to appraise the social, environmental and economic effects of the strategies and policies in a local development document from the outset of the preparation process' (para.3.17). This includes consideration of sustainable development principles as required by s.39 of the 2004 Act.[5] A consultation paper *Sustainability Appraisal of Regional Spatial Strategies and Local Development Frameworks* was issued by the ODPM in September 2004.

### 2.7.4    Strategic Environmental Assessment

LDDs will require Strategic Environmental Assessment under the Environmental Assessment of Plans and Programmes Regulations 2004, SI 2004/1633 (SEA Regulations) where they:

(1)  set the framework for future development consent of projects which are listed in Annex I or II of the EIA Directive;[6]
(2)  require appropriate assessment under the Birds or Habitats Directive[7]; or
(3)  set the framework for future development consent of projects and the plan or programme is likely to have significant environmental effects;

subject in the first two cases to limited exceptions.[8]

The EIA Directive projects do not take account of the thresholds and criteria in Sched.2 to the Town and Country Planning (Environmental Impact Assessment) (England and Wales) Regulations 1999, SI 1999/293. However, smaller plans may be excepted under reg.5(6) of the SEA Regulations. The acknowledgement that appropriate assessment may be required of plans reverses guidance in PPG9 that the Habitats Directive 'does not include development plans, since the plan itself cannot authorise development that would affect the site'.[9]

The SEA Regulations, reg.5(6) exception applies to plans:

(1)  in the EIA Directive categories or which require appropriate assessment; which
(2)  determine the use of a small area at a local level or are for a minor modification of a plan or programme in the EIA Directive/appropriate assessment categories; and

(3) have been determined not to be likely to have significant environmental effects.[10]

This exception will be important for supplementary planning documents in the style of development briefs. In those cases strategic environmental assessment will only be required if the project is likely to have significant effects on the environment. The size of a 'small area' is undefined and will be a matter of judgement for the decision-maker, subject to correctly understanding the law and reaching a rational view.[11] It is possible, although in practice unlikely, that a plan might fall outside the 'small area' exception and require SEA even if it is not likely to have a significant effect on the environment.

Where the 'first formal preparatory act' of the plan takes place before 21 July 2004 then no SEA is required if it is adopted before 22 July 2006. However, if the plan is not adopted by that later date, SEA is required if it was likely to have significant environmental effects unless the responsible authority decides that SEA is not feasible.[12]

The SEA process requires the preparation of an Environmental Report, its sending to statutory consultees and making available to the public, the receipt of responses and their evaluation in a reasoned fashion. The SEA Regulations apply to all plans and programmes subject to the Directive and so impose obligations in a generalist fashion. The sequence of steps required ought not to conflict with the Town and Country Planning (Local Development) (England) Regulations. The detail of assessment is, however, greater and local authorities will need to ensure that their processes are carried out in accordance with both sets of Regulations. A breach of the SEA Regulations which is not completely corrected before the plan is adopted can only be excused by the court if it is *de minimis*.[13]

### 2.7.5    The DPD process

Part 6 of the Regulations provides more procedural requirements. This part of the Regulations also applies to SCIs and submission proposals maps, unless otherwise provided (reg.24(1), (2)). Where an SCI is in place, the process must comply with its requirements in addition to those of the Regulations.

The Regulations require the following process to be adopted:

(1) pre-submission consultation with particular bodies;
(2) pre-submission public participation;
(3) submission of the development plan document to the Secretary of State;
(4) representations on the DPD;
(5) representations on the site allocation representations which have been made;
(6) the examination;
(7) adoption of the DPD.

## Pre-submission consultation

The first statutory stage is for the local planning authority to consult various public and voluntary bodies (reg.25). The authority must consult those of the 'specific consultation bodies' which are affected by the proposed subject matter of the DPD. These bodies are the regional planning body or the Mayor of London, the Countryside Agency, the Environment Agency, English Heritage, English Nature, the Strategic Rail Authority, the Highways Agency, any other local planning authority, county council or parish council in or adjoining the authority's area, Regional Development Agencies, electronic communications code operators, electricity and gas licensees, sewerage and water undertakers and the Strategic Health Authority (reg.2(1)).[14]

The authority must also consult such of the 'general consultation bodies' it considers appropriate. These are voluntary bodies benefiting the authority's area, bodies representing the interests of different racial, ethnic or national groups, religious groups or disabled persons in the area and those representing the interests of businesses in the area (reg.2(1)).

The Regulations are silent as to what the consultation involves, and PPS12 is unclear whether this is consultation on preferred options or part of the identification of such options (para.4.12). It does say that an initial sustainability appraisal should be published at this time. The PPS12 Companion suggests this is a continuous process of informal discussion about issues and alternative options (para.4.3).

## Pre-submission public participation

The next stage is a formal consultation of the proposals for the development plan document. The authority is required to make available for public inspection in person and on its website the proposals for the DPD, any relevant supporting documents and details of how to make representations. The supporting documents are expected to include the sustainability appraisal report (PPS12, para.4.13). Copies of this material must be sent to all the bodies consulted at the pre-submission consultation stage (reg.26).

PPS12 states that local authorities should 'build consensus through continuous community involvement' (para.4.13). However, this does not take into account the fact that planning is an immensely important and political subject where opinions and interests vary wildly. There are many issues on which there is, and will be, no consensus.

Representations can be made within a six-week period (reg.27(2)). A person may request to be notified of the submission of the DPD to the Secretary of State (see reg.28(3)(e)). The authority must consider the representations before proceeding to prepare and submit the DPD (reg.27(3)).

## Submission of the DPD to the Secretary of State

Having considered the first-stage representations, the authority must prepare the DPD itself. The DPD is then sent to the Secretary of State (s.20(1)) along with the sustainability appraisal report, any SCI which has been adopted and statements setting out how the previous consultations were carried out, the main issues raised and how these have been addressed in the DPD and any supporting documents (reg.28(1)). Where the DPD is a core strategy containing site or area policies the supporting documents should include a submission proposals map.[15] The authority must think that the DPD is ready for the examination (s.20(2)).

## Representations on the DPD

The local planning authority must make the DPD available to the public with an explanation of how to make representations. Representations have to be made within six weeks of the date of submission of the DPD to the Secretary of State (reg.29(1). This will not necessarily be six weeks after the DPD is made available to the public although that should be 'as soon as reasonably practicable' after submission (reg.28(3)). The authority will also publish the sustainability appraisal and a 'pre-submission consultation statement'. This statement explains how presubmission consultation was carried out with the consultation bodies under reg.25 (reg.24(4)). Strangely, it does not include a statement of the formal consultation with the public and those bodies under reg.26. Copies of all these documents are to be sent to the bodies originally consulted and a local advertisement published (reg.28(3)).

Representations are to be made available for inspection and placed on the Council's website as they are received (reg.31(2)(a), (b)). Copies of the representations and a summary of the main issues must also be sent to the Secretary of State (reg.31(2)(c)).[16]

## Representations on the site allocation representations which have been made

Representations will often be to particular sites rather than particular policies. The old development plan system would allow objectors to the deposit plan to be heard at inquiry, but supporters would usually not be allowed to appear even if they were aware the site was in issue. If the objectors were successful and a modification for the site was proposed, the disgruntled supporters ('counter-objectors') would have to persuade the authority to hold a modifications inquiry.

The Regulations seek to enable all persons interested in a contested site to make representations, even though supporters are not given a right to be heard. Where a 'site allocation representation' is made which seeks to add or alter a 'site allocation policy' notice must be given by the authority and a further period of six weeks allowed for representations on the site allocation representation (regs.32 and 33).

'Site allocation policy' is given a restrictive meaning as 'a policy which allocates a site for a particular use or development' (reg.2(1)). It is debatable whether a general policy of restriction (such as Green Belt) is a site allocation policy, and a policy which might affect how a development could take place (such as an archaeological priority area) would be outside it entirely. So to take three examples:

(1) a representation to delete a site from the proposed Green Belt and allocate it for housing would be a site allocation representation;
(2) it is questionable whether a representation to delete a site from the Green Belt but to leave it within the countryside would be a site allocation representation;
(3) a representation to delete a local nature conservation designation will not be a site allocation representation unless the designation requires particular uses of the land.

## The examination

Section 20 provides that each DPD has to be submitted to the Secretary of State for independent examination by a person appointed by him.[17] In practice this will be a planning inspector.

The Government originally proposed that the right to be heard, currently enjoyed by objectors in unitary development plan and local plan inquiries, should not apply to Local Development Framework examinations.[18] In July 2002, ministers bowed to the public and Parliamentary opposition, giving all objectors a right to be heard but suggesting this would be in informal hearings.[19] Section 20(6) provides that a person who makes representations seeking to change a development plan document must, if he so requests, be given the opportunity to appear before and be heard by the person carrying out the examination. The Act and Regulations refer to a person requesting an opportunity to be heard, leaving the possibility that the opportunity is not automatically offered (reg.34(1)). It is therefore prudent for people who may want to be heard to request an opportunity to do so when making their initial representations.

Four procedures for considering representations are proposed in PPS12 (para.D15).

(1) *Written representations* – with exchange of statements. 'Where necessary, the inspector can seek clarification of matters raised in written representations during his or her examination of the development plan document by writing to the parties and inviting further comments on specific issues.'
(2) *Round table discussions* – with a number of participants representing different viewpoints.
(3) *Informal hearing sessions* – which are a 'reasonably informal and relaxed setting'. The PPS suggests this 'may be the most appropriate method for considering site specific issues, including any requests for boundary changes to sites identified in the development plan document'.

(4) *Formal hearing sessions* – PPS12 states 'The existing traditional inquiry procedure has been adapted to form the formal hearing, where the inspector leads the process in an inquisitorial manner and advocates are permitted to be present to assist in the proper testing of evidence.' It is not apparent how the traditional procedure has been adapted, as further guidance is deferred to a proposed Planning Inspectorate *Guide to Development Plan Examinations*.[20]

The PPS envisages that the inspector will decide the procedure to be adopted (para.D20), subject to the right to be heard.

## The examination tests – lawfulness and soundness

The examination will consider whether the development plan document satisfies the requirements of s.19 (preparation in accordance with the LDS, regard to particular policies, compliance with the SCI, sustainability appraisal), s.24(1) (general conformity with the RSS or SDS) and the Regulations, and whether it is 'sound' (s.20(5)). The examination is not confined, as local plan inquiries were, to considering objections to the plan. The inspector must give a judgement on the document as a whole, even on parts where representations have not been made.

'Sound' is not defined in the Act or Regulations. The critical question is whether it is a review of process or a judgement on the merits of individual proposals. PPS12 sets out the following tests in para.4.24:

> 'The presumption will be that the development plan document is sound unless it is shown to be otherwise as a result of evidence considered at the examination. The criteria for assessing whether a development plan document is sound will apply individually and collectively to policies in the development plan document. A development plan document will be sound if it meets the following tests:
>
> Procedural
>
> i.    it has been prepared in accordance with the local development scheme;
> ii.   it has been prepared in compliance with the statement of community involvement, or with the minimum requirements set out in the Regulations where no statement of community involvement exists;
> iii.  the plan and its policies have been subjected to sustainability appraisal;
>
> Conformity
>
> iv    it is a spatial plan which is consistent with national planning policy and in general conformity with the regional spatial strategy for the region or, in London, the spatial development strategy and it has properly had regard to any other relevant plans, policies and strategies relating to the area or to adjoining areas;
> v.    it has had regard to the authority's community strategy;
>
> Coherence, consistency and effectiveness
>
> vi    the strategies/policies/allocations in the plan are coherent and consistent within and between development plan documents prepared by the authority and by neighbouring authorities, where cross boundary issues are relevant;

vii.   the strategies/policies/allocations represent the most appropriate in all the circumstances, having considered the relevant alternatives, and they are founded on a robust and credible evidence base;

viii.   there are clear mechanisms for implementation and monitoring; and

ix.   the plan is reasonably flexible to enable it to deal with changing circumstances.'

The first five tests relate to the specific statutory requirements. The final four tests are elements of soundness. Test (vii) asks whether the strategies, policies and allocations are 'the most appropriate in all the circumstances', that is, whether they are right.

## The binding inspector's report

The person carrying out the examination will make recommendations and give reasons (s.20(7)). The term 'recommendations' is a linguistic hang-over from the previous regime, as the report is binding on the local planning authority.

An authority may only adopt a DPD as originally prepared if the inspector recommends it is adopted in that form (s.23(2), (4)). Similarly, the authority may only adopt a DPD with modifications if those modifications are recommended by the inspector (s.23(3), (4)).

The change from inspectors making recommendations which need not be followed to making binding reports was one of the most controversial in the Bill. Local authorities wished to preserve the power to reject recommendations. Professional opinion was divided, with the Town and Country Planning Association supporting the change. The House of Lords agreed with Opposition proposals to remove the binding nature of the reports; however, the amendments were rejected by the House of Commons and the Bill finally passed with the 'binding' provisions intact.

There were also concerns that there should be mechanisms for correcting errors. An alternative Opposition amendment proposed that the local planning authority should be able to require the inspector to reconsider his report if the authority considered that:[21]

'(a)   there has been a change in material circumstances;

(b)   the recommendation or its reasoning contains a substantial error of fact or error in the interpretation of policy;

(c)   the recommendation or its reasoning contains a legal error or the conduct of the examination contained a procedural error or was unfair with respect to that matter;

(d)   a recommendation lacks clarity.'

The minister, Lord Rooker, replied:[22]

'if a problem is raised there should always be a way of addressing it. There is no question about that. We believe that serious mistakes will rarely happen but, if they do, we have put in place a number of safeguards.

If people believe that an inspector has made a simple error of fact or omission, they can ask the local planning authority to bring the matter to the attention of the planning inspectorate, which will obtain the inspector's views. If necessary, the inspector will issue an addendum report to correct the error or omission.

Under [section 21], the Secretary of State will have the power to direct changes to a development plan document or call in the document before it is adopted and make modifications to it if needed. If a local planning authority felt that the inspector's recommendations were unreasonable it could ask the Secretary of State to consider using these powers.'

The Secretary of State's power to direct changes or call in the document is in the Act (s.21) and provides the local planning authority with an informal avenue of appeal. Section 21 gives the Secretary of State wide powers of intervention and supervision in that if he considers an LDD to be unsatisfactory he may direct that it should be modified before adoption. The Secretary of State may also direct that the whole or a part of the document should be submitted to him for his approval (a 'call-in').[23] This power can also be used when the Secretary of State disagrees with the local authority and the inspector.

The Regulations give no comfort with respect to the minister's first suggestion, that the local planning authority may be asked to contact the Planning Inspectorate and seek reconsideration of errors of fact or omission. Whilst the Act obliges local planning authorities to publish the Inspector's report (s.20(8)) the Regulations provide that this must be done as soon as possible after the DPD is adopted or the Secretary of State makes a s.21 direction (reg.35(1)). In the former situation it would be too late for a third party to comment on the report. In practice the report is likely to be disclosed before the document is adopted, including when the document is reported to councillors for adoption.

The proposal for an addendum report was not included in the Act or Regulations. As the recommendations are binding, it is at least possible that the inspector has no power to amend or supplement his report after it has been sent to the local planning authority. PPS12 proposes instead that the report will be sent in draft to the local planning authority for a 'fact check'. The authority will have two weeks to raise factual errors or seek clarifications of conclusions. The inspector will respond and the report will then be issued, incorporating any changes (para.4.29).

## 2.7.6    Withdrawal of LDDs

An LDD can be withdrawn by the authority at any time before adoption (s.22(1)).[24] However, the authority cannot withdraw a DPD once it has been submitted for independent examination unless either the inspector recommends withdrawal (and the Secretary of State does not overrule the inspector) or the Secretary of State directs that the DPD be withdrawn (s.22(2)). Consequently, a local planning authority cannot unilaterally withdraw a DPD because it does not agree with the inspector's recommendations.

## 2.7.7   Conformity

### The general conformity obligation

Under s.24 the LDDs must be in general conformity with the relevant Regional Spatial Strategy or the London Plan (s.24(1)). The obligation already existed with respect to UDPs and the London Plan;[25] however, the requirement to be in general conformity with regional policy is entirely new. It also makes a fundamental change in the relationship between local and central government. The previous general conformity requirement was between different tiers of local government (county structure plans and district local plans, the London Plan and London unitary development plans). The requirement on non-London authorities is now to be in general conformity with the Secretary of State's RSS.

### Opinions on general conformity

The local planning authority must request an opinion as to general conformity of a DPD from the Regional Planning Body (RPB) or the Mayor (s.24(2)(a), (4)(a)). This request should be made at the same time as the DPD is sent to the Secretary of State (reg.30(1)). The RPB is required to give its opinion on a DPD request to the local planning authority and the Secretary of State within six weeks.[26] Curiously, the Mayor is not required to respond. The 2004 Act provides that the local planning authority may request an opinion from the RPB or Mayor with respect to any other LDD (s.24(2)(b), (4)(b)). However, the Local Development Regulations purport to require authorities to request opinions on supplementary planning documents (reg.17(2)(d)). It is questionable whether regulations, which do not have power to amend the Act, can change a statutory power into a statutory duty.

If the RPB (or Mayor) is of the opinion that the document is not in general conformity then they are taken as having made representations seeking a change in the document (s.24(6), (7)). The Secretary of State can direct that an RPB (but not the Mayor) is not to be taken to have made such representations (s.24(8)) although it is not apparent why he should have this power.[27]

### Conformity within Local Development Frameworks

Conformity is required within LDF documents. A DPD (other than a core strategy or a proposals map) must be in conformity with the policies of an adopted core strategy, or if no core strategy has been adopted, the old development plan (reg.13(6), (9), (10)).[28] A DPD need not be in conformity with the old development plan if it is intended to supersede an old development plan policy (reg.13(7)). It is not required to be in conformity with another DPD.

The policies in a supplementary planning document must be in conformity with the policies in the core strategy and other DPDs, or if none have been adopted, the old development plan (reg.13(8)). This is an important change. Under the previous regime, non-statutory supplementary planning guidance or planning briefs could be adopted which were inconsistent with the development plan.[29] For example, this might arise where a major development proposal came forward outside the plan or changes to housing policy in PPG3 were reflected in supplementary policy before the development plan was changed. Whilst PPG12 discouraged such policies (para.3.15), they were lawful. Policy changes must now be made by amendments to DPDs where they are inconsistent with the new policy, rather than relying on an informal policy. As LDDs, SPDs must also be in general conformity with the RSS or London Plan (s.24(1)).

## The meaning of general conformity and conformity

The meaning of 'general conformity' and 'conformity' has not been defined clearly. 'General conformity' has previously arisen in development plan inquiries and allows some departure from the overall policy. The Minister explained:

> 'it is the Government's policy that it is only where a local development document would cause significant harm to the implementation of the regional spatial strategy that the local development document should be considered not to be in general conformity'.[30]

'Conformity' certainly prohibits SPDs which are inconsistent with the wording of a DPD. An issue does arise as to whether a SPD which does not seek to achieve the aims and objectives of the DPDs can be in conformity with them.

## The hierarchy of conformity

Consequently the following rules apply:

(1) the core strategy must be in general conformity with the RSS/London Plan;
(2) other DPDs must be in general conformity with the RSS/London Plan and in conformity with the core strategy or the old development plan (unless it supersedes old policies);
(3) supplementary planning documents must be in general conformity with the RSS/London Plan and in conformity with the core strategy and DPDs or the old development plan.

## 2.7.8    Preparation of Supplementary Planning Documents

Part 5 of the Regulations sets out the procedure for preparing Supplementary Planning Documents (SPDs) in addition to the requirements for non-DPD LDDs in the 2004 Act itself. The process is much more straightforward than the adoption of DPDs.

The local planning authority may consult any persons when preparing the draft SPD. The Regulations do not oblige it to do so, but they do require a consultation statement of the consultation undertaken, the main issues raised and how they are addressed in the SPD. This statement is to be produced when the draft SPD is published for formal consultation (reg.17(1)(b)). Consultation will have to comply with any SCI.

Formal public participation requires the publication of the SPD, the sustainability appraisal and consultation statement. The document must be placed on the council's website, and sent to the specific and general consultation bodies affected or interested, and a local advertisement must be published (reg.17).

A period for representations will be announced, which must be between four and six weeks from the SPD being made available (reg.18(3)). Prior to adoption, the local planning authority is required to consider any duly made representations and prepare a statement summarising the main issues raised and how these have been addressed in the SPD (reg.18(4)). There is no obligation to give reasons for accepting or not accepting each representation. This statement is to be published as soon as reasonably practicable after adoption of the SPD (reg.19), but in practice it should be produced in draft with any report to the council recommending adoption.

The Secretary of State can direct modifications to an SPD (s.21(1))[31] but he does not have a power to call in the document.

## 2.7.9    Final adoption of LDDs

An LDD is adopted by the local planning authority by a resolution of the authority (s.23(5)). This seems to require a decision of the full Council, rather than an executive decision. That is a change in responsibilities for non-development plan documents, as approval of supplementary planning guidance has been an executive responsibility.

---

1 Prepared under s.7, Regional Development Agencies Act 1998.
2 The local transport plan is prepared by the county council, unitary authority or passenger transport authority under s.108 of the Transport Act 2000. The reference in the Regulations to other policies prepared under that section is curious as s.108(3) requires the local transport plan to contain those policies.
3 Scottish Executive, April 2004.
4 See Town and Country Planning (Local Development) (England) Regulations 2004, footnote to reg.2(1)(b).
5 Considered in more detail under Part 3 of the 2004 Act.
6 Directive 85/337/EEC as amended by Council Directive 97/11/EC.
7 Council Directives 79/409/EEC and 92/43/EEC.
8 Environmental Assessment of Plans and Programmes Regulations 2004, reg.5.
9 PPG9, Annex A, para.A15, footnote 1.
10 The determination is either that of the responsible authority under reg.9(1) or the Secretary of State under reg.10(3).
11 R(on the application of Goodman) v. Lewisham LBC [2003] EWCA Civ 130, [2003] JPL 1309.
12 SEA Regulations, reg.6.
13 Berkeley v. Secretary of State for the Enviroment [2001] 2 AC 603.

14 For the statement of community involvement only the regional planning body/Mayor, councils and, curiously, the Highways Agency need to be consulted as 'specific consultation bodies': reg.25(2).

15 Regulation 6(1)(b) requires this to be produced as an LDD but there is no explicit reference to submission proposals maps in Part 6.

16 Whilst poorly drafted, it appears this obligation arises when the six-week period for making representations has expired.

17 An examination is a statutory inquiry under the Tribunals and Inquiries Act 1992 and so subject to the supervisory jurisdiction of the Council on Tribunals: s.114, 2004 Act.

18 Green Paper.

19 *Sustainable Communities*, para.38.

20 At the time of writing, the Planning Inspectorate had produced guidance on examinations for transitional development plans but withdrawn draft guidance on DPD examinations.

21 House of Lords Committee Stage, amendment 106ZA.

22 Hansard, 27 January 2004, cols.147–148.

23 The Secretary of State may direct that a DPD is not adopted whilst he considers whether to make a direction under s.21: reg.38. The procedure for call-ins is contained in regs.40 to 44.

24 Notice of withdrawal must be given under reg.37.

25 Greater London Authority Act 1999.

26 Section 24(3) and reg.30(2). Although s.24(3) allows a period to be prescribed for requests for opinions on non-DPD LDDs, no period has been set.

27 Lord Rooker explained 'I hope that there will not be a case where a regional planning body acts irresponsibly in its consideration of general conformity. But there could be cases where it tries to tie down the local planning authority to too great a detail of conformity, perhaps to the letter of some out-of-date policy which has not yet been amended by revision of the regional spatial strategy. In such instances, [section 24] allows the Secretary of State to override the opinion of the regional planning body.' Hansard, 27 January 2004, col.159. He did not address why the Mayor could not act in the same fashion.

28 An old development plan is the plan in force before commencement of the 2004 Act (see Sched.8, para.1, 2004 Act).

29 *R(on the application of Bedford)* v. *Islington LBC* [2002] EWHC 2044 Admin at paras.51–64.

30 Lord Rooker, Hansard, 27 January 2004, col.155.

31 Procedural requirements are at ss.22 and 23.

## 2.8    REVOCATION OF ADOPTED DOCUMENTS

An adopted document may only be revoked:

(1) by the Secretary of State at the request of the local planning authority; or

(2) by the local planning authority in limited circumstances prescribed by the Regulations (s.25).

Those prescribed circumstances are where an SPD ceases to be in conformity with the core strategy, any other DPD or an old policy, or where it contains policies relating to the development of a site specified in the SPD, and that development has been completed (reg.21).

However, a policy in an LDD can be superseded by the adoption of another LDD.

## 2.9    REVISION OF ADOPTED DOCUMENTS

Section 26 provides that a local planning authority may revise an LDD at any time or when directed to do so by the Secretary of State (s.26(1), (2)). The Secretary of State may then specify a timetable for the revision. The relationship between the power to revise 'at any time' in s.26(1) and the LDS is unclear. By s.19(1) preparation of an LDD must take place in accordance with the LDS and s.26 applies Part 2 of the 2004 Act to revision as it does to preparation (s.26(3)). The authority will usually have included the proposed revision in its LDS (or a revision of it) but it may be that s.26(1) simply authorises the revision of documents and the procedure which must be followed under Part 2 involves first of all revising the LDS.

The local planning authority is also obliged to review every LDD if an enterprise zone scheme is made and prepare modifications as required (s.26(4)–(7)).

## 2.10    SECRETARY OF STATE'S DEFAULT POWERS

Section 27 contains the Secretary of State's default powers in relation to DPDs. If he considers that a local planning authority are 'failing or omitting to do anything it is necessary for them to do in connection with the preparation, revision or adoption of a development plan document' (s.27(1)) then he must hold an independent examination and publish the recommendations and reasons of the person appointed (s.27(2), (3)). This examination is into the suggested failure or omission.

The Secretary of State then has power (irrespective of the outcome of the examination but subject to the usual controls on discretion) to prepare or revise the DPD and adopt it (s.27(4)). In preparing or revising the DPD he must comply with the relevant provisions of Part 2 (reg.45), which will include holding an independent examination into his proposed document.

The authority must reimburse the Secretary of State for his costs of preparing or revising the document (s.27(6)). No provision is made for the costs of the independent examination into the alleged default.

## 2.11    JOINT DOCUMENTS AND COMMITTEES

### 2.11.1    Joint LDDs

Section 28 enables two or more local planning authorities to prepare joint LDDs. These documents will need to be specified in each authority's local development scheme. As each authority will have many LDDs it is more practical for authorities to prepare joint documents than previously. For example, an action area plan or supplementary planning document could be prepared for a development area which crosses administrative boundaries or all district councils within a county could prepare common policies on housing design.

## 2.11.2   Joint committees

However, s.28 does not permit the involvement of non-unitary county councils. The counties can only be involved in a joint committee under s.29. A joint committee may be formed following an agreement between one or more local planning authorities and one or more county councils that the joint committee should be the local planning authority for a particular area in respect of agreed matters (s.29(1)). If agreement is reached, the Secretary of State may by order constitute the joint committee as the local planning authority (s.29(2)). The Secretary of State still has discretion whether to make the order and it is subject to the negative resolution procedure in Parliament. Having secured the order, the constitutent authorities can extend the joint committee's geographical and subject remit by agreement (s.30). It is a curiosity of what are obscurely drafted provisions that an order is required to set up the local planning authority for a particular area and matters, but its remit can be extended by agreement. However, the rules governing the joint committee, such as composition, can be prescribed in the order and further authorities cannot be added to the joint committee by agreement alone. The Secretary of State may dissolve a joint committee at the request of a constituent authority.

## 2.12    TRANSITIONAL PROVISIONS

Many development plans will have been in the process of review or alteration when the 2004 Act came into force. Schedule 8 allows the adoption of deposited plans, although some of the new Act's procedures are applied.

If proposals for a structure plan replacement or alteration were deposited (under s.33(2) of the 1990 Act) before 28 September 2004, the 1990 Act continues to apply and they can be adopted. The report of the examination in public will not bind the county council. Any proposals at an earlier stage cannot be adopted and 'have no effect' (Sched.8, para.2). The 2004 Act is not explicit whether 'no effect' means that the emerging plan is not a material consideration for development control purposes.

UDP or local plan proposals which were not placed on deposit by 28 September 2004 cannot be adopted and again have no effect (Sched.8, paras.3 and 8 respectively). Where these proposals had been placed on deposit and there are no objections or an inspector had been appointed to hold an inquiry prior to 28 September 2004, the UDP or local plan can proceed to adoption in accordance with the 1990 Act (Sched.8, paras.4 and 9 respectively).

Where UDPs or local plans have reached first deposit stage but either there are objections and no inspector has been appointed, the plans may proceed under revised 1990 Act procedures (Sched.8, para. 5(1) and 10(1) respectively).[1] The plan must be put on deposit again before proceeding to an inquiry. The local planning authority is required to follow the recommendations of the inspector and may not promote changes after the inquiry (Sched.8, para.5(4), (5) and 10(4), (5) respectively). The Secretary of State's powers to intervene under the 1990 Act remain and the local planning authority may ask him to overrule the inspector.

The Secretary of State may disapply the general conformity requirement between local plans and structure plans where this may cause inconsistency with national policies or the RSS (Sched.8, para.11). That is, the Secretary of State's own policies may be given precedence over the structure plan when local plans are being adopted.

During the transitional period (i.e. to 28 September 2007) local development schemes and minerals and waste development schemes must include any plan or document relating to an old development plan policy (which has not been superseded) and any old-style plan which continues towards adoption (Sched.8, para.15).

---

1  R(on the application of Martin Grant Homes Limited) v. Wealden District Council [2005] EWHC 453 (Admin) held that the pleas should proceed unless there was very good reason not to.

## 2.13   URBAN DEVELOPMENT CORPORATIONS

Urban Development Corporations (UDCs) have in the past been given development control powers but not powers to prepare development plans. This distinction is maintained in the 2004 Act. The local authorities remain responsible for preparing the LDF. However, the Secretary of State may direct under s.33 that Part 2 does not apply to the area of a UDC. In those cases, the local planning authorities will not be able to produce LDDs for those areas.

Opposition amendments proposed that UDCs be responsible for preparing SCIs for the exercise of their development control functions.[1] The Government resisted those proposals. The minister explained that PPSs would expect UDCs to apply relevant community involvement principles and that UDCs would be expected by government to follow the relevant local authority's SCI for consulting on planning applications.[2]

---

1  See Hansard, HL, 24 February 2004, cols.220–223.
2  Letter from Rt Hon Jeff Rooker to Baroness Hanham, 22 March 2004.  A copy is in the House of Lords Library.

## 2.14   ANNUAL MONITORING REPORT

Section 35 requires each local planning authority[1] to make an annual report to the Secretary of State (s.35(1)).

The report must cover the period from 1 April to 31 March for the relevant year (reg.48(1)) and be produced within nine months of the end of the period, that is by 31 December (reg.48(2)).

The report will set out the documents in the LDS, the timetable for their adoption and the stage reached. If documents are behind the timetable an explanation of the reasons must be given and a timetable, which may be revised, given for the remaining steps in the process (reg.48(3)(a)–(c)). The Government's expectation is that a timetable revision will necessitate a revision to the LDS and a timetable for that process should also be given.[2] The date and title of any documents approved or adopted with the period will also be identified (reg.48(3)(c)).

The Act provides no sanction for failure to adhere to the LDS timetable. However, it is likely that government funding will be based on meeting the timetable, as Planning Delivery Grant is determined, in part, on how up-to-date the development plan is.[3]

If the local planning authority 'are not implementing a policy' in a DPD or an old policy they should say so in the report, give reasons why not and explain whether a DPD or DPD revision will amend or replace the policy (reg.48(4), (5)). As the local planning authority has no power to simply disapply or ignore the development plan, non-implementation would seem to relate to positive policies of steps the authority will take, rather than development control policies controlling other persons.

The Regulations require the authority to report on compliance in the year with any policy containing numbers for net additional housing units (reg.48(6), (7)). Beyond this essentially formal, factual material, PPS12 seeks an assessment of the effect of the LDF policies, how they meet other policy targets and whether changes are required in the light of national or regional policy (para.4.48).

The annual report will also set out the title of any local development order adopted, with the reasons for making the order and a statement of the effect of the order with a comparison with the reasons for making it (reg.48(3)(e), (f)). PPS12 understands this to ask for an assessment of whether the order is achieving its purposes and reasons for it not doing so (para.4.48iii, iv). Further guidance on the content and preparation of the annual monitoring report will be included in the Government's *Local Development Framework Monitoring Guide*. The authority must also publish the report on its website (reg.48(8)).

---

1   Including county councils with respect to their waste and minerals responsibilities: s.16(3).
2   PPS12, para.4.47iii.
3   See *Sustainable Communities – Delivery through planning*, paras.73, 84

## 2.15    CHALLENGES TO THE NEW DEVELOPMENT PLANS

### 2.15.1    Section 113 applications

A further statutory appeal route is added for development plans by s.113 of the 2004 Act. Section 287 of the Town and Country Planning Act 1990 is amended to refer only to simplified planning zones and highways orders under the 1990

Act.[1] Challenges to the new development plans, including revisions of the RSS or the SDS and DPDs, and the Wales Spatial Plan are now brought by an application to the High Court under s.113. The application may be made by a person aggrieved. The validity of these documents may not be questioned in any other legal proceedings (s.113(2)).

The grounds of the application are that the document is not within the appropriate power or that a procedural requirement has not been complied with (s.113(3)). This is in substance the same test as for s.287 applications. The court has again power to quash the plan in whole or part if the document is outside the appropriate powers or the interests of the applicant have been substantially prejudiced by a failure to comply with a procedural requirement. The application must be made within six weeks of the adoption or publication of the document (s.113(4), (11)). As a statutory time limit, this period cannot be extended by the court.

The effect of a quashing under s.287 is that the affected part of the plan would have to be reconsidered by means of a revision or alteration to the plan.[2] It is not possible for the local planning authority to simply re-trace its steps to the point where an error was made in the process and resume consideration. This has caused a degree of judicial concern. In *First Corporate Shipping Ltd* v. *North Somerset Council*[3] the central question in that case was whether the decision of a local planning authority not to hold a further inquiry into objections to proposed modifications to a local plan was reasonable. The judge at first instance held that it was. The Court of Appeal took the same view and dismissed the appeal. In addition, however, Buxton LJ made observations *obiter*, with which the other members of the court agreed, concerning the need for caution in the exercise of discretion to quash parts of a local plan (para.38):

'To grant a remedy in terms of quashing may be a logical remedy attached to a complaint made where the investigative process has come to an end and the error complained of is irrationality or unfairness of a public law nature in the actual proposals adopted, that is to say an error in the rational process of thinking of the local authority; but here the irrationality is said to be not in the result that the local authority produced but in its failure to take a particular procedural step. It is very much more difficult to see how quashing can be a justified response to such an error. It is even more difficult to see how a justified response to such an error can be to quash a part of the plan in respect of which no actual complaint was made by the applicant. If I thought, which I have already indicated that I do not, that there had been public law error in this case in terms of not requiring a public inquiry, by far the most obvious remedy for that error in public law terms would be either a declaration on the part of this court or a remission of the matter to the local authority. Neither of those remedies is available under section 287. That means (and I say this only as a matter of comment) that if a court found itself in a position where there had been such an error it would have to consider very carefully in terms of its discretion whether, nonetheless, it was appropriate to articulate that error and give relief in terms of quashing part of the plan. I mention this point because it was a matter of some concern, certainly to me and I think also to my Lords, as to how this jurisdiction could properly be administered.'

Parliament (or more accurately the Secretary of State) has chosen not to widen the range of remedies available to the court. That may ameliorate some of the judicial concerns about the consequences of successful applications.

## 2.15.2    The potential for challenge before a DPD is adopted

The other particular problem is whether a challenge can be brought by judicial review before a DPD is adopted. Under the Town and Country Planning Act 1990, old development plans could not be challenged 'before or after the plan . . . has been approved or adopted'.[4] The effectiveness of these words to prevent pre-adoption challenges was established by the Court of Appeal in *R v. Cornwall County Council ex p Huntingdon*.[5] The sole case where judicial review proceedings have been allowed is *R v. Hinckley and Bosworth Borough Council ex p F.L. Fitchett and J.S. Bloor (Services) Limited*.[6] In that case the High Court quashed the council's decision to refuse to exercise its discretion to consider an objection to the deposit plan which was received four minutes late. Whilst the court's decision is readily understandable, its compatibility with *Huntingdon* is not.

Section 113 does not contain the 'before or after' formulation. The effect of this and the intention behind the change is unclear.[7] The section, for example, refers to a 'development plan document'. This expression is used in Part 2 of the 2004 Act to refer to both adopted and draft documents.[8] Even if the ouster provision protects draft documents, proceedings might be possible to challenge another person's action which could otherwise affect the document. The inspector will make modifications which may require the local planning authority to modify the document, but which are not themselves changes to the document. It may be that the inspector's report or his conduct of the examination could be subject to judicial review without contravening s.113(2). Similarly, the intervention or non-intervention of the Secretary of State in DPDs might also be open to challenge.

## 2.15.3    Challenges by a local planning authority

The problems of early challenge arise in their most acute form if the local planning authority considers an inspector's recommendation on a DPD to be unlawful. If the recommendation can only be challenged once the document has been adopted, the potential options are undesirable, artificial and expensive, if not impossible.

The council would have to challenge its own decision to adopt the document in the courts. A body could not be both claimant and defendant, but might be capable of making an application to the court. However, it would be strange for a body to apply to quash its own decision, and it is questionable whether the council could be a 'person aggrieved'. It would be 'aggrieved' in one sense by its own decision to adopt, but would have been compelled to act by the inspector's recommendation.

The council could put up a councillor to bring proceedings[9] against the adoption. Again this is artificial and the councillor may well not be a person aggrieved if the councillor voted in favour of the adoption. If the councillor could vote against, it is hard to see why the remainder of the council should vote for the document.

The council could wait for a third party to bring proceedings, or even encourage a third party to do so, making clear that it would not defend the proceedings. However, other parties might then be drawn into defending the decision.

The local planning authority cannot simply adopt the document without what it considers to be the inspector's legal errors, as a positive recommendation for the document as originally produced or as recommended to be modified is required before it can be adopted (s.23(2)–(4)). Nor may the authority withdraw the document at that stage (s.22(2)). If the Secretary of State is unwilling to intervene, the authority's options are to seek to persuade the Planning Inspectorate to reopen the examination, decline to adopt the document (without formally withdrawing it) on the basis that a lawful examination has not taken place or to judicially review the inspector's recommendations. This latter option, which enables the issues to be resolved, is dependent upon s.113 not barring such proceedings. The presently unclear nature of s.113 may therefore cause real difficulties.

### 2.15.4   Challenges to LDDs which are not DPDs

LDDs which are not DPDs are outside the scope of s.113 entirely. These documents include the SCI. Any legal challenge should be brought by judicial review promptly, and in any event within three months of the adoption of the document.[10]

### 2.15.5   The relevance of earlier case-law

The 2004 Act will mean that the decisions causing most challenges in the old development plan system (such as consideration of the inspector's report, post-report modifications and consideration whether to hold a modifications inquiry) will no longer occur. However, the issues underlying those challenges will not go away. The reasoning under scrutiny will be that of the inspector rather than the local authority. The fairness issues underpinning modifications inquiries will arise on the inspector's examination. Have people who might be affected by the acceptance of an objection or the inspector raising a fresh option had a 'fair crack of the whip'?[11] An inspector might have to publicly invite representations on particular issues during the course of the examination if a properly informed and fair decision is to be made.

Challenges might also be brought against a decision of the Secretary of State to intervene under s.21 or his failure to overrule an inspector and do so.

The existing development plan case-law therefore needs to be considered with care. Their underlying principles may still be of assistance in development plan litigation on the 2004 Act.

---

1   Schedule 6, para.9, 2004 Act.

2 *Charles Church Developments Limited* v. *South Northamptonshire District Council* [2000] PLCR 46.

3 [2001] EWCA Civ 693, [2002] PLCR 7.

4 Town and Country Planning Act 1990, s.284(1)(a).

5 [1994] 1 All ER 694, concerning similar provisions of the Wildlife and Countryside Act 1981. Applied to development plan challenges in R v. *Test Valley Borough Council ex p Peel Estates* [1990] 3 PLR 14.

6 (1996) 74 P. & C.R. 52.

7 See also the discussion in *Challenges to Development Plans – new plans, new problems; the Planning and Compulsory Purchase Bill* [2003] JPL 1384, Alice Robinson and Joanne Clement.

8 For example, s.20(1), 2004 Act.

9 See judicial review of a planning permission in R v. *Bassetlaw District Council ex p Oxby* [1998] PLCR 283.

10 The adoption statement for a supplementary planning document should refer to this timescale: reg.16(2).

11 *Fairmount Limited* v. *Secretary of State for the Environment* [1976] 1 WLR 1255 at 1265H–1266A per Lord Russell of Killowen.

## 2.16   ACRONYMS

A final thought. Anyone suffering from an overload of acronyms brought on by excessive use of LDF, LDS, LDD, DPD and SCI in this chapter will find comfort from the following exchange involving the Planning Minister, Lord Rooker, during the Bill's Committee Stage:[1]

> **Lord Rooker:** . . . Without a general conformity requirement which exists at present in relation to the strategic –
>
> Hang on a minute. I have an acronym in my notes which I refuse to read out.
>
> **Noble Lords:** Oh!
>
> **Lord Rooker:** I have not done that once, yet, and I am not going to now. I apologise. I shall have to get around this. The acronym must refer to the –
>
> **Baroness Hanham:** Have a break.
>
> **Lord Rooker:** I cannot.'

1    Hansard, 27 January 2004, cols.122–123

# 3 DEVELOPMENT

'We have been particularly concerned during our enquiry to find the term sustainable used in a blanket way to refer to just about anything which the witness supports.'

Select Committee on Environment, Transport and Regional Affairs, 10th Report 1998, *Housing*, para 237

## 3.1 PART 3 OF THE 2004 ACT

Part 3 is very short and is concerned with two matters: the meaning of 'development plan'; and a limited duty to have regard to sustainable development.

### 3.1.1 The development plan

Section 38 defines the development plan.[1] In Greater London this is the Spatial Development Strategy (the London Plan) and the DPDs adopted for the particular area (s.38(2)). In other parts of England the development plan is the Regional Spatial Strategy and the DPDs adopted for the particular area (s.38(3)). During the transitional period of three years, these will include any adopted structure plan, local plan or unitary development plan whose policies have not been expressly replaced (Sched.8, para.1). Any waste or minerals development plan document will be part of the development plan.

These definitions contain an important shift in policy and operation. When the Greater London Authority Act 1999 was enacted the Spatial Development Strategy (SDS) was purposefully left out of the development plan. The Mayor's views were to have effect as a material consideration, by the general conformity obligation and his power to direct refusal of strategic applications. As the London Plan had just been adopted without being seen as a development plan, this prompted a Liberal Democrat amendment to exclude it from the development plan until a new SDS had been adopted. The amendment was passed by the House of Lords but rejected by the Commons.

The change in the treatment of regional policy is perhaps even more important. For the first time government policy, in the form of the RSS, will be part of the development plan.

In Wales the position is simpler. The development plan is the local development plan adopted for the particular area (s.38(4)). The Wales Spatial Plan is not part of the development plan.

Where development plan policies are in conflict, the conflict must be resolved in favour of the policy which is contained in the last document to be adopted, approved or published (s.38(5)). This provision is of immediate importance in England. The London Plan was adopted on 14 February 2004. Conflicting policies in earlier unitary development plans (or their reviews) are now overridden. A common example is the level of affordable housing proposed in a development. So the London Plan will prevail over conflicts in the Merton UDP Review (adopted autumn 2003) but the Bexley UDP Review (adopted spring 2004) will override the London Plan. It is questionable whether the earlier policy can survive as another material consideration.

The presumption in favour of the development plan is re-enacted as s.38(6):[2]

> 'If regard is to be had to the development plan for the purpose of any determination to be made under the planning Acts the determination must be made in accordance with the plan unless material considerations indicate otherwise.'

The wording is slightly changed from s.54A of the 1990 Act but the meaning is unaltered. Consequently, the existing authorities on s.54A will continue to be applicable.[3]

### 3.1.2    Sustainable development

As planning reform and the Bill were being debated there was discussion as to whether a statutory purpose should be established for the planning system. The attenuated outcome of this debate was the inclusion of a duty in policy making to promote sustainable development.

Section 39 imposes a duty on bodies exercising functions with respect to regional spatial strategies, the Welsh Spatial Plan and LDDs[4] to 'exercise the function with the objective of contributing to the achievement of sustainable development' (s.39(2)). The tortuous expression 'the objective of contributing to the achievement' distances the provision from a requirement that each decision be sustainable. The function-exercising bodies include the Secretary of State, the National Assembly for Wales, regional planning bodies and local planning authorities. The Mayor of London's duty to have regard to 'the achievement of sustainable development in the United Kingdom' when preparing the SDS is unaffected by the new provision.[5] The duty does not apply to other decisions under the Planning Acts, in particular development control.

The Government resisted all attempts to define sustainable development during the Bill's passage. In complying with the sustainable development duty, bodies are required to have regard to national guidance and advice issued by the Secretary of

State or the National Assembly for Wales, as appropriate (s.39(3)). In England this guidance is mainly contained in PPS1.

## PPS1: Delivering sustainable development

The principal government guidance on sustainable development in the planning system is contained in *PPS1: Delivering Sustainable Development*.[6] It says that 'at the heart of sustainable development is the simple idea of ensuring a better quality of life for everyone, now and for future generations' (para.3). The PPS repeats the four aims for sustainable development in the 1999 strategy *A Better Quality of Life – A Strategy for Sustainable Development for the UK*:

- social progress which recognizes the needs of everyone.
- effective protection of the environment.
- the prudent use of natural resources.
- the maintenance of high and stable levels of economic growth and employment.

The PPS then explains sustainable development in various contexts. However, as explained, the combination of environmental, social and economic matters means that almost any project, falling short of wanton vandalism, is capable of being described as sustainable. The Select Committee's concern about the use of the term will not have been dispelled.

---

1   The definition is for the purposes of the 2004 Act, the Planning Acts, 'any other enact-ments relating to town and country planning', the Acquisition of Land Act 1981 and the Highways Act 1980: s.38(7).
2   Section 54A of the 1990 Act is repealed with the rest of Part 2 of that Act.
3   The leading authority is *City of Edinburgh* v. *Secretary of State for Scotland* [1997] 1 WLR 1447, HL.
4   That is, under Parts 1, 2 and 6 of the 2004 Act.
5   Section 41, Greater London Authority Act 1999.
6   ODPM, February 2005.

# 4 DEVELOPMENT CONTROL

## 4.1 PART 4 OF THE 2004 ACT

Part 4 of the 2004 Act contains some fairly controversial provisions that could well have a significant bearing on the planning system. These provisions are the ones most likely to affect developers and landowners. However, at the end of November 2004, the ODPM issued a consultation paper regarding the power to decline to determine applications in s.43, the duration of permission and consent in s.51, the duty to respond to consultation in s.54, the designation of regional planning bodies as statutory consultees brought about by para.16(4) of Sched.6 to the Act (which inserts a new para.7 into Sched.1 to the 1990 Act) and economic impact reports for major infrastructure projects introduced by s.44. The consultation period expired on 22 February 2005. More importantly, the consultation paper also stated that a further round of consultation could be expected in 2005 on local development orders, mezzanines, outline planning permissions and reserved matters, design and access statements, standard application forms, the criteria for consulting statutory consultees, the determination of major applications and E-fees. It is clear, therefore, that there is a degree of fluidity surrounding the details and implementation of this part of the 2004 Act. Furthermore a consultation draft of a revised circular on planning obligations was also issued, with responses required by 25 January 2005. Further details of this are set out at **section 4.7** below.

## 4.2 LOCAL DEVELOPMENT ORDERS

Section 40 enables local planning authorities to expand on existing permitted development rights by making a local development order. This is achieved by inserting ss.61A–C and Sched.4A into the 1990 Act. Whilst these orders have significant potential in encouraging development at the local level, the Act provides for a considerable degree of central control and supervision which only reinforces the centralising nature of the 2004 Act as a whole.

Section 61A(1) provides that these orders can be made for the purpose of implementing policies in one or more DPD in England or in a local development plan in Wales. The order can grant planning permission for development specified in the order or for any development of any class specified in the order. The order can relate to all or part of the land in the authority's area or it could relate to a specific site. Further, the order can make different provisions for different descriptions of land. However, sub-section (5) appears to retain for the Secretary of State the ability to use the power in s.59 of the 1990 Act so as to enable him to specify in a development order any area or class of development in respect of which a local development order must not be made. Therefore central government may well exert control over the general scope of local development orders. An authority may revoke a local development order at any time.

Section 61B(1) of the 1990 Act enables the Secretary of State (or the National Assembly in Wales) to step in before a local development order is made and direct that the whole or part of the order should be submitted to him (or it) for prior approval. If such a direction is made the authority must not take any steps towards adoption and the order remains of no effect unless and until it has been approved. It would appear from the wording of sub-section (3) that the powers of review given to the Secretary of State or the National Assembly are extremely wide. Reasons have to be given by the Secretary of State or the Assembly for its decision. It may approve or reject an order in whole or in part. Sub-section (6) gives the Secretary of State or the Assembly the power to modify by direction any order before it is adopted if they think that the order is unsatisfactory. Reasons have to be given for taking this course of action and the local planning authority is obliged to comply with the direction.

The Secretary of State or the National Assembly may revoke a local development order at any time if they think it expedient to do so, and are obliged to give reasons for doing so. The provisions in s.100(3)–(6) of the 1990 Act regarding the revocation of planning permission apply. Consequently, an order may not be revoked without consultation with, and notice being served on, the local planning authority, which will have at least 28 days to require an opportunity to be heard by a person appointed by the Secretary of State or the National Assembly.

Section 61C(1) of the 1990 Act provides that permission granted by a local development order may be granted unconditionally or subject to conditions and limitations. If permission is granted for development of a specified description the order may direct that the permission does not apply in relation to development in a particular area or any particular development.

For some reason not readily apparent, the provisions for revising development orders are set out in s.41 which merely inserts a new s.61D into the 1990 Act. This provides that a development order or a local development order may include a provision permitting the completion of development if a planning permission is granted by the order in respect of the development, and the permission is withdrawn after the development has started but before it is completed. A planning permission granted by development order is withdrawn if the order is revoked, or amended so that it ceases to grant permission in respect of the development or materially changes any condition or limitation subject to which the permission was granted, or by a direction issued under powers conferred by the order. Similarly, planning permission granted by a local development order is withdrawn if the order is revoked under s.61A(6) (by the local planning authority at any time) or s.61B(8) (by the Secretary of State or the National Assembly), or if the order is revised under para.2 of Sched.4A so that it ceases to grant permission in respect of the development or materially changes any condition or limitation subject to which the permission was granted, or by a direction issued under powers conferred by the order.

## 4.3    THE CONTENT OF PLANNING APPLICATIONS

Section 42 is a particularly detailed and important provision. Sub-section (1) heralds the dawn of a uniform national planning application form by substituting a new s.62 into the 1990 Act. This enables the Secretary of State to make provision as to planning applications made to local planning authorities, which will include the form and content of planning applications. Whether or not the process of applying for planning permission will become easier or more involved will only become clear once the necessary regulations have been made. The intention was to speed up the decision-making process, but the proposals were eventually watered down and may prove to be counterproductive because of the mandatory nature of the new provisions. Furthermore, s.62(3) enables local planning authorities to require such additional information as they think necessary provided that it is not inconsistent with the development order requirements, which may also introduce delay.

Under s.62(5) the development order will require a planning application to be accompanied by (as opposed to incorporated within the application) a statement of developments' design principles and concepts and a further statement about how access issues have been dealt with. Both of these may be more complicated than they first seem and have the potential to introduce further areas of dispute into the planning application process. It is possible that this will result in further cost and delay to developers. Much will depend upon the precise content of the development order. However, as there is no definition in the Act of 'access', it is unclear what this means. Does it simply mean means of access or does it go much wider? Could it include disability access (probably) but also wider sustainable transport issues including green transport plan proposals or public transport subsidies? Consistent with this, s.42(2) removes s.73(3) which governs the form and content of applications to develop land without compliance with conditions previously attached.

On a purely grammatical note, as with other parts of the Act, s.42(2) refers to s.73(3) being 'omitted'. However, as that sub-section was always there until s.42(2) came into force, it would appear to be more accurate to refer to it having been 'deleted'. 'Omit' means to leave out or not include: that sub-section was in the Act originally so it is hard to see how 'omitted' could be appropriate.

Section 42(3) makes similar provisions for applications for consent under tree preservation orders and sub-section (3) does likewise for applications for advertisement consent.

Section 42(5) introduces into the 1990 Act a new s.327A which includes a provision whereby a local planning authority must not entertain any planning application which does not comply with these new requirements. The mandatory nature of this provision may unwittingly open the door for third party challenges where there have been procedural failings, similar to some of the challenges seen in recent years where there have been failures to comply with the regulations regarding environmental impact assessment.

## 4.4   POWER TO DECLINE TO DETERMINE APPLICATIONS

Section 43 gives planning authorities a new power to decline to determine certain applications. Sub-section (1) removes from the 1990 Act s.70A and replaces it with new ss.70A and 70B. The consultation paper states that the new powers are intended to inhibit the use of repeated applications that are submitted with the intention of, over time, reducing opposition to undesirable developments. They are not intended to prevent the submission of a similar application which has been altered in order to address objections to a previous application. However, it emphasises that applicants should be encouraged to enter into pre-application discussions to minimise the likelihood of the application being rejected. Of course, it should be borne in mind that s.53 of the Act amends s.303 of the 1990 Act so as to enable charges to be brought in for pre-application discussions. Therefore, taken together, these provisions may increase the cost of obtaining planning permissions.

Similar provisions apply to listed building and conservation area consent applications by inserting ss.81A and 81B into the Listed Buildings Act and applications for prior approval by the local planning authority for development which is permitted under the Town and Country Planning (General Permitted Development) Order 1995, SI 1995/418.

Section 70A(1) now gives the local planning authority the power (as opposed to a duty) to decline to determine a relevant application (which is defined by sub-section (5) as an application for planning permission for the development of any land or an application under s.60(2)) provided that any of certain specified conditions are met. These are set out in sub-sections (2) to (4). The first condition is that in the period of two years ending with the date on which the relevant application is received the Secretary of State has refused a similar application referred to him under s.76A of the 1990 Act (a provision inserted into that Act by s.44 and relating to major infrastructure projects) or an application called-in under s.77 of the 1990 Act. The second condition is that the Secretary of State had refused an appeal in respect of a similar application. The third and new condition is that the local planning authority has refused a similar application within the preceding two years and there had been no appeal against that refusal. If any of these conditions are met and the local planning authority thinks there has been no significant change in the relevant considerations since the relevant event, the authority may decline to determine the application.

'Similar application' is defined in s.70A(8) of the 1990 Act. An application will be 'similar' if the local planning authority thinks that the development and the land to which the applications relate are the same or substantially the same. Section 81A(7) defines a 'similar' application for listed building consent or conservation area consent in similar terms.

The consultation paper suggests that where the local planning authority considers that an application is similar it does not have to decline to determine it but that it should be mindful of the intention behind the power. It goes on to assert that it can be a major cause of frustration to members of the public and the local community to have to deal with a repeat application when they have already dealt with the original application and seen the development refused.

The consultation paper suggests that a 'significant change' in a DPD or other material consideration will exist if it is likely to alter the weight given to any planning consideration in the determination of an application. If 'significant change' is interpreted that widely, it is possible that the impact of this provision will be lessened as, more often than not, the determination of a planning application will involve a host of development plan policy and other material considerations.

Furthermore, the consultation paper suggests that in doubtful cases the local planning authority should give the benefit of the doubt to the applicant and determine the application.

In theory, the practice known as 'twin tracking' is also to be prevented by the introduction of a new s.70B into the 1990 Act. However, the consultation paper states that this provision will not be introduced 'until the development control performance of local planning authorities' improves. The Act uses the expression 'overlapping applications' so that it applies not just to identical but also similar applications. This could prove to be a tricky area in practice. Developers will need to tread carefully and arguments may arise over whether a fresh application is substantially the same as a previous one. A two-year delay may be sufficiently long to justify the relatively cheap cost of judicially reviewing an authority's decision. In Parliament the minister did not refer to the abolition of twin-tracking but to adding a degree of discretion by using the word 'may' as opposed to 'must'. However, how long will it be before discretion becomes habit?

## 4.5   MAJOR INFRASTRUCTURE PROJECTS

Originally the Government had intended to promote wide-scale reforms to the procedure for dealing with major infrastructure projects in the wake of the Heathrow Terminal 5 inquiry. However, these reforms were abandoned in the face of criticism by the House of Commons Select Committee on Transport, Local Government and the Regions, and the Act therefore is far less ambitious.

These new provisions relating to major infrastructure projects apply to England only. By s.44, ss.76A and 76B are inserted into the 1990 Act. These allow the Secretary of State to call in any application (and other related applications) for his approval which relates to development of national or regional importance. The Secretary of State must appoint an inspector (and in some instances a team of inspectors operating under a lead inspector) to consider the application. However, the Act is silent on whether the application will go to an inquiry, although the Standing Committee's debate proceeded on the basis that it would. The position may become clearer once the regulations have been made, but there must be a concern at the potentially undemocratic nature of this provision. If no inquiry is to be held (or, if one is held but real debate is stifled procedurally) then such developments may well become the target for 'eco-warriors'. At first sight these proposals appear to be a retreat from the original idea of making such projects subject to Parliamentary approval. However, as drafted, the Act's provisions are even less democratic than that, as the decision whether or not to approve the development will be left to the Secretary of State alone.

Following a difference of opinion between the House of Commons and the House of Lords over whether or not there should be a statutory requirement for an economic impact assessment of such projects a compromise was reached whereby s.76A(5) and (6) of the 1990 Act give the Secretary of State a discretion on whether to direct that an economic impact report should be prepared.

## 4.6   SIMPLIFIED PLANNING ZONES

Initially, the Government had intended to introduce what were called 'Business Planning Zones' in the Green Paper. However, the proposal looked remarkably similar to the existing concept of the simplified planning zone which, over the years, had proven to be a little-used tool in the local planning authorities' box.

The existing law regarding simplified planning zones is therefore modified by s.45. This removes sub-section 83(1) from the 1990 Act and inserts a new sub-section (1A), so that a zone can only be made where the RSS identifies a need for such a zone. The local planning authority must make a zone if they consider it desirable or if directed to do so by the Secretary of State. Sub-section 83(2) is replaced by new sub-sections (2)–(2B). Unfortunately, many issues are as yet undetermined in relation to these zones. For example, the temporary nature of the zones does not easily lend itself to a fast-changing development climate, so that a zone could rapidly become out of date. There also seems to be a degree of overlap with local development orders. Furthermore, given that the essence of these zones is to lift the requirement for specific grants of planning permission for certain types of development, there must be some doubt as to how they will relate to the requirement for environmental impact assessment, even though the position appears to be covered by reg.23 of the Town and Country Planning (Environmental Impact Assessment) (England and Wales) Regulations 1999, SI 1999/293 which, of course, pre-dates these provisions.

## 4.7   PLANNING CONTRIBUTIONS

There is an air of unfinished business regarding the proposals for planning contributions. This is not surprising given the odd and lengthy history behind these
provisions but it is most unfortunate because this is an area that has the potential
to be highly controversial. Furthermore, the lack of clarity with regard to the
Government's intentions and the resulting uncertainty will make it difficult for
those who have to advise clients. For example, solicitors drafting option agreements with a life span of 10 years or so may have to contemplate the possibility
and effect of the existing regime of planning obligations either remaining or being
replaced by the new planning contributions provisions in the 2004 Act, and the
possible introduction of planning gain supplements within a few years. These
measures, whether taken individually or collectively, could change the bargaining
strengths of the parties and may have not been contemplated when negotiations
were concluded. The continuing uncertainty surrounding these provisions and
overall government policy make it necessary to examine the evolution of the debate
over planning contributions in order to divine precisely what the Government's
long-term intentions might be for planning contributions.

### 4.7.1   The consultation paper

Sections 46–48 contain the provisions relating to planning contributions. Some
might be surprised to note that the Act has anything to say at all on the subject
of planning contributions. This is because the Bill as originally introduced into
Parliament did not contain any mention of planning contributions even though
the Government had issued a consultation paper *Reforming Planning Obligation:
A Consultation Paper* in January 2002.

Ten years after the introduction of the planning obligation in ss.106–106B of the
Town and Country Planning Act 1990 as amended by s.12 of the Planning and
Compensation Act 1991, it appeared to the Government that significant problems
still remained. According to the January 2002 consultation paper, planning obligations were seen by the Government to be operating in a way that was inconsistent, unfair and lacking in transparency. Consequently, the consultation paper
suggested that radical changes needed to be made rather than merely tinkering
once more at the edges.

Refreshingly, the consultation paper made no attempt to hide from the fact that
planning obligations are increasingly used as economic instruments, securing
private sector provision of a wide range of infrastructure and other community
benefits. Indeed, in recent years successive governments have expanded the policy
areas where planning obligations may be sought when determining planning
applications. These were helpfully summarised in Annex C and confirmed that
government thinking had moved a long way from the days when planning gain
was frowned upon. The consultation paper, therefore, acknowledged the revenue-
generating function underlying many planning obligations and nowhere was this
clearer than in the passages dealing with tariffs. To adopt the words of the paper it

did not seek to reopen the debate over betterment tax 'other than to acknowledge the nature of the relationship between planning obligations and land betterment'.

A far more positive approach towards planning obligations was advocated. Their purpose was to be 'refocused'. They should no longer be seen as simply a means of restricting or controlling development. Thus the paper stated 'we believe that planning obligations should be used to achieve a wider range of objectives than is permitted under current policy as set out in Circular 1/97'. In reality, following the House of Lords' decision in *Tesco Stores Limited* v. *Secretary of State for the Environment* [1995] 1 WLR 759, that policy has only been of relevance to developments that were subject to scrutiny by the Secretary of State on appeal or call-in. Thus many developers and local authorities have been content to pay only lip service to the Circular. The consultation paper acknowledged this at para.1.10 when it stated 'The Government believes that a new approach to planning obligations is required that regularises what are currently very uncertain procedures and which gives a clear purpose to planning obligations.'

Whilst some may have viewed this as being a fundamental shift in policy direction it should, nevertheless, have come as no surprise. In the last 20 years, with privatisation and private finance initiatives, the boundary between the public and private sectors has become blurred to the point of obscurity. Much of the emphasis in the planning Green Paper was centred on providing what the Government considered to be an essential need for the business sector: a faster, more efficient and more effective planning system. That is what the 2004 Act is supposed to deliver. But there may be a price to pay: developers may expect to be called upon to fund a wider range of community benefits which may appear to be more remote from the proposed development under consideration. However, the Government appears to recognise that there are dangers inherent in this approach. Consequently, the paper talked of a need to ensure that planning obligations do not impose unacceptable burdens on developers, which would ultimately result in desirable development not taking place.

The paper set out in Annex A three alternatives to the Government's preference for a tariff-based system, on which views were solicited. The other alternatives can be loosely described as either a beefed up 'necessity' test which would certainly prevent the system achieving the new objectives that the Government has set for it, a complete free-for-all, or a system of US-style impact fees which Government-commissioned research suggests would be less flexible than a tariff system.

The Government's preferred solution was to set standardised tariffs for different types of development through the plan-making process. The tariffs would only be supplemented or substituted by negotiated agreements where they were clearly justified; for example, site-specific requirements. In principle, this tariff-based approach is commendable. It could potentially ensure far greater transparency because local authorities, developers and the public will all know what benefits are associated with a particular development.

However, there are problems with this approach. Whilst negotiated agreements are intended to be the exception, it is conceivable that the exception could become the norm. Were that to happen, the Government will have achieved the worst of both worlds. The consultation paper recognised this danger and has attempted to tackle it in a variety of ways. First, both the current and proposed systems would require details of all planning obligations to be made available for public inspection on the statutory register. Thus there ought to be an end to secret deals done in smoke-filled rooms. This proposal reflects one suggested 10 years ago in research commissioned by the then Department of the Environment ('The Use of Planning Agreements' HMSO, para.7.27). Second, there should be an increased use of standard contractual terms for negotiated planning obligations. Third, a dispute resolution procedure should be established to cover situations where the developer and local authority fail to agree on the value of on-site costings.

The paper recognised that any move to a tariff-based system would require primary legislation to give the Secretary of State the powers to oversee the system, and this has now been enacted. New national policy guidance will also have to be issued to cover the workings of the system and requiring local authorities to set clear policies in their development plans or LDFs dealing with the use of planning obligations and their approach to setting tariff schedules. However, local authorities will have discretion to determine the types, sizes and location of development on which the tariff would be charged and how it would apply in different circumstances. Furthermore, it is proposed that a wider range of developments will be subject to a tariff than that currently caught by planning obligations. Thus, effectively, tariffs might amount to a tax on development. This could be seen in the proposal to extend the affordable housing supporting tariff to both residential and commercial developments. This element could be satisfied in cash or kind or a mixture of both.

What was not clear is whether the setting of tariffs by individual planning authorities could result in the distortion of development pressures within particular areas. If one authority sets a level of tariff far lower than that of neighbouring authorities, this could skew development to that authority's area rather than those of its neighbours. Equally, a nimby-minded authority might use tariffs to choke off development by setting exorbitant tariff levels. The Government, understandably, sought views on whether tariffs should be set nationally, regionally or locally. It was suggested in the paper that the only way of testing tariffs will be through the plan-making process. Once an authority has set a tariff it is envisaged that there would be a dispute resolution mechanism that could be used to challenge valuation issues only. No details were given regarding the proposed mechanism and the paper implies that the usual s.78 appeal process will remain an option for disgruntled developers, although the outcome of independent valuations will be a material consideration in determining an appeal.

The consultation paper set out a number of options on which the Government sought the views of developers, planning authorities and the public. It is clear that the Government proposed radical reform. The paper acknowledged some, but not all, of the potential drawbacks and, whilst adopting a more honest approach to the debate over the real world use of planning obligations, it falls short of promoting US-style impact fees or betterment levies.

However, following criticism by the House of Commons Select Committee the ODPM announced in July 2002 that the original proposals were to be abandoned and replaced by a more modest set of procedural reforms.

## 4.7.2    The Bill

It was no surprise, therefore, that when the Planning and Compulsory Purchase Bill was first introduced into Parliament in December 2002 there were no provisions dealing with the reform of planning obligations. Following resubmission of the Bill into the 2003/04 Parliamentary session, the Government published in November 2003 a new consultation paper *Contributing to sustainable communities – a new approach to planning obligations* with a short consultation period that expired on 8 January 2004. It wanted to hear the views of all stakeholders on how a flexible and responsive system of planning contributions could act so as to encourage all participants in the development process to be more pro-active and positive in the delivery of urban regeneration projects. In order to expedite matters the Government tabled the new clauses for the Bill before the consultation period expired. Taken together the clauses would replace ss.106, 106A and 106B in the 1990 Act.

The key principles of the new policy for negotiated planning obligations was stated to be clarifying the relationship between the contribution and development; providing greater transparency, predictability and accountability, promoting flexibility to meet the needs of sustainable communities and reducing delays.

The new clauses are now ss.46, 47 and 48 of the 2004 Act. As is so common these days, they leave the reader with very little idea of what they are intended to achieve. They simply provide a rudimentary framework with the details to be provided eventually by subordinate legislation and policy.

Section 48 provides the mechanism by which ss.46 and 47 apply to Wales.

Under s.120 of, and Sched.9 to, the Act, ss.106, 106A and 106B are to be repealed. When this will happen depends on the wider proposals regarding planning gain supplements.

On 17 June 2004 the Government announced the timetable for the implementation of the Act. It stated that the regulations on planning obligations will not be made until early 2006. However, on the same day, the Minister for Housing and Planning (Keith Hill MP) set out a slightly different time horizon. He stated that the Government had taken on board the recommendation of the Barker Report that there should be introduced a planning gain supplement tied to the grant of planning permission so that part of a landowner's development gains could contribute to wider benefits for the community. It also recommended that, if the

Government were minded to do this, planning obligations should be scaled back to cover direct impacts and mitigation along with affordable and social housing requirements.

Consequently, the Government agreed that it was acceptable to fund social housing and other measures out of the uplift in land values associated with the development process and the Chancellor of the Exchequer said in his Budget Report of 17 March 2004 that he would consider proposals for a national planning gain supplement and make a decision by the end of 2005. This sounds suspiciously like the return of some form of betterment levy, even though the history of such tax raising measures is not a happy one.

It was reported in *Planning* on 13 August 2004 that planning consultancy Tetlow King had undertaken an investigation into the operation of the planning obligations system for the Association of London Government and had found that there was 'considerable unease' among authorities over the introduction of the planning contribution. The *Estates Gazette* reported on 31 July 2004 that there was considerable unease at the prospect of a return to some form of betterment levy or tax. As the editor, Peter Bill, observed in his leader column 'What the Treasury will make of the bones of five failed attempts in 100 years to tax the increase in value of land is anyone's guess'. In May 2004 the Treasury (whose position on this tax, it is reported, has created a rift with the ODPM) set up a separate property tax division under the auspices of Edward Troup, a former partner at Simmons & Simmons to look not only at the proposals for real estate investment trusts (REITs), but also to consider development land tax plans. It is expected that the Chancellor was to signal his intentions in his autumn statement with a view to bringing forward legislation in the spring of 2005.

Therefore, the Government has decided to press ahead with identifying and implementing changes to the current arrangements for negotiated agreements. It will do this by revising the current advice in Circular 1/97 and publishing good practice guidance for local authorities and developers. A revised draft circular was issued for consultation in November 2004 with a view to putting the new arrangements in place in early 2005. The consultation period expired on 25 January 2005.

However, whatever changes may result from the new circular, they may prove to be stop-gap measures for it is made clear that any changes are 'to be made in advance of potentially more major reforms to the system that may come forward in the next 2–3 years' in response to the recommendations of the Barker Review of Housing Supply; i.e. the introduction of the planning gain supplement or some other form of tax on the uplift in development value resulting from the grant of planning permission.

It is also made clear that the regulation-making powers for planning contributions in ss.46 and 47 of the 2004 Act will not be used for the time being. Therefore, any changes introduced at the moment will be subject to the existing legislative framework. (It is certainly arguable that the new provisions, whilst flexible, do not provide the necessary legislative tools for the introduction of a planning gain supplement and that further primary legislation may be required before such a system could be introduced.)

The Government's main aim is to make changes to the current system to promote speed, certainty, transparency and accountability. These are laudable objectives and the draft circular also aims to clarify existing policy. Overall, 13 main changes are mooted, of which the most significant is the retention in a simplified form of the policy tests by placing greater emphasis on the requirement for planning obligations to be necessary in order to make the development 'acceptable in planning terms'. Thus a link will be needed between the contribution sought and the presence of a relevant policy in local or national planning policy. As we have seen in recent years, for example with affordable housing and green transport plans, the boundaries of acceptability in planning terms has widened considerably. Whilst the overriding requirement of reasonableness remains, this 'simplification' could result in an explosion in the use of planning obligations. In order to limit this it is proposed that the planning obligation should remain an impact mitigation or positive planning measure linked to planning necessity rather than being used for tax-like purposes. It is also stated that the intention is to 'discourage the offering by developers of facilities that are not required by the development, in order to make clear that planning permission is not being bought or sold'. Despite these reassuring words, defining the boundary of acceptability has dogged the planning system for years and it is debatable whether this policy revision will make matters better or worse.

The issue of affordable housing provision was one of the earliest signs of a widening of the scope of planning obligations. The consultation paper acknowledges that there was a perceived lack of clarity in Circular 1/97. Therefore it is proposed to separate out affordable housing policy from impact mitigation or compensation policies, which the paper tellingly admits is 'legitimising current practice'.

Another area of difficulty has been maintenance contributions by developers. A balanced approach is advocated whereby planning authorities can require such contributions but only for a limited period and with payments agreed in advance.

A major departure from the current guidance is the proposal that there should no longer be any examples of appropriate uses of planning obligations. Instead it will be made clear that if a local community has decided, through its development planning processes, that development should comply with certain agreed policies, it will be acceptable to require development to contribute to the matters contained within those policies through planning obligations, if they cannot be addressed through the planning application itself and cannot be dealt with by conditions. In our view, for this to work effectively it may require policing, possibly by much closer scrutiny by central government of planning gain policies in emerging development plan documents.

Other changes are aimed at speeding up the process of negotiating planning obligations. Consequently, the use of standard formulae and charges within clear parameters is to be encouraged. Similarly, new guidance is to be given on the use of standard forms of agreements and undertakings. Both of these seem eminently sensible, as does the new encouragement to developers to use unilateral undertakings in conjunction with applications in the interest of speed. Thus the unilateral undertaking may lose its unfortunate hostile connotation and be viewed as a more positive instrument.

With the possible exception of the revised policy tests, the proposed changes appear practical, welcome and workable. Whether they will be a stop-gap measure or acquire more permanency may eventually depend on how successful the reforms brought about by the new Act prove to be.

## 4.8 DEVELOPMENT TO INCLUDE CERTAIN INTERNAL OPERATIONS

Section 49 makes a potentially significant change. It was brought about following a late amendment to the Bill. A survey of local planning authorities had shown that supermarkets and other large retailers were building large internal extensions, including mezzanine floors, in out-of-town stores in apparent contradiction of the policy in PPG6. Although such extensions do not affect the footprint of the store, they do increase its floorspace thereby intensifying the use of the site and generating other pressures such as car parking and increased traffic.

When brought into force, it will effectively outlaw the insertion of additional floorspace into buildings without planning permission by bringing this within the meaning of development in s.55 of the 1990 Act. This was introduced as a direct response to the popularity of mezzanine floors in retail stores. Subordinate legislation is required so there is, currently, a window of opportunity to be exploited. In introducing this amendment into the Bill on 25 March 2004 in the House of Lords the Minister responsible, Lord Rooker, said:

> 'We envisage that the development order will specify the type of floor space to which it applies and the scale of additional floor space which will require permission. It could, for example, specify that additional retail floor space above a certain threshold would be defined as "development". Our aim is to bring forward draft secondary legislation as soon as possible. Naturally, as a listening Government, we will consult widely before finalising the order.'

In reply to a comment by Lord Lucas about the prospect of 'the noble Lord's favourite retailers calling in the builders to get something started' Lord Rooker said: 'it is true that the provisions cannot be brought in overnight. We accept that; there is not much that we can do about it'. The clear inference from the Minister's statement is that there will be a period during which the exception in s.55(2)(a) can still be relied on. The November 2004 consultation paper did not include any proposals for this provision and it stated that it was likely to be the subject of a consultation exercise during 2005.

Certificates of Lawfulness of Proposed Use or Development issued before the Secretary of State makes the Order cannot be relied on if the development has not been commenced before the Order comes into force.

## 4.9    DUAL JURISDICTION IN THE EVENT OF AN APPEAL

Section 50 makes a sensible but rather limited change which applies when appeals have been made to the Secretary of State against the non-determination of an application. For a short period (likely to be 14 days) the local planning authority would retain jurisdiction concurrently with the Secretary of State so that the authority would still be able to issue its decision even though the appeal has been lodged. Presently, the moment the appeal is lodged the authority loses all jurisdiction over the application.

## 4.10    DURATION OF PERMISSION AND CONSENT

An important change is made by s.51 which amends ss.73, 91 and 92 of the 1990 Act and ss.18 and 19 of the Planning (Listed Buildings and Conservation Areas) Act 1990 and reduces the life of planning permissions and consents from five to three years, although authorities may still direct that longer or shorter periods should apply where appropriate. Furthermore a new sub-section (5) is inserted into s.73 of the 1990 Act to prevent s.73 applications being used to extend the life of a planning permission by varying the time limit condition. These two changes could potentially create major difficulties for developers.

The highly controversial proposal to replace outline planning permissions with statements of development principles were eventually dropped by the Government after an Opposition amendment to omit the relevant clause was carried at the Report stage in the House of Lords.

## 4.11    TEMPORARY STOP NOTICES

Section 52 contains a new power for planning authorities to serve temporary stop notices. It adds to the already powerful enforcement armoury available to local planning authorities in the 1990 Act by making stop notices more powerful. It provides that where a local planning authority 'thinks':

(1)  that there has been a breach of planning control; and
(2)  that it is expedient that the activity (or any part of the activity) which amounts to the breach is stopped immediately

it may issue a temporary stop notice. The notice must be in writing and must specify the activity considered to be the breach, prohibit its continuance and set out the authority's reasons for issuing the notice. It can be served on any of the following:

(1) the person carrying on the activity;
(2) the occupier of the land;
(3) any person with an interest in the land.

A copy of the notice must be displayed on the land together with a statement of the effect of the notice and of the effect of provisions of s.171G which deals with offences for breaches of temporary stop notices. The notice has effect from the time a copy of it is first displayed. Thus if a disgruntled landowner rips it down – tough! A temporary stop notice lasts for a maximum of 28 days.

There are some restrictions, set out in s.171F. A temporary stop notice will not prohibit:

(1) the use of a building as a dwelling house; or
(2) the carrying out of an activity of such a description or in such circumstances as is prescribed.

It will not be able to prohibit the carrying on of any activity which has been carried on (whether continuously or not) for a period of four years ending with the day on which the copy notice was first displayed. A temporary stop notice can prohibit any activity which is incidental to building, engineering, mining or other operations or the deposit of refuse or waste materials. A second or subsequent temporary stop notice must not be issued in respect of the same activity unless the authority has first taken some other enforcement action in relation to the breach including the grant of an injunction.

The fines for a breach of a temporary stop notice are similar to those for failing to comply with an enforcement notice, and are a maximum of £20,000 in the magistrates' court and an unlimited fine in the Crown Court. Similarly, the court must have regard to the financial benefit which has accrued to the defendant in failing to comply with the notice. This formulation is differently worded to that which applies to a failure to comply with an enforcement notice.

Section 171H deals with the issue of compensation. If a notice is issued and at least one of the following applies then the compensation provisions set out in s.186(3) to (7) will be engaged:

(1) the activity specified in the notice is authorized by a pre-existing planning permission or a development order;
(2) a lawful development certificate is issued. (It appears that the certificate, which can be one issued on application or appeal, does not have to be pre-existing. This is because existing lawfulness is presupposed before a certificate can be issued.);
(3) the authority withdraws the notice unless it is withdrawn following the grant of planning permission.

Section 53 contains new provisions regarding fees and other charges. Previously, local planning authorities only had the power to charge for determining planning applications. Over the years, partly in response to funding shortfalls, some planning authorities began the practice of charging for pre-application discussions with developers. This practice was successfully challenged in the courts when the House of Lords ruled in *R v. Richmond upon Thames Borough Council ex p. McCarthy & Stone (Developments) Ltd* [1992] 1 PLR 131 that, in the absence of any express or implied statutory power, there was no power for a public body to levy charges for its services and that s.111 of the Local Government Act 1972 did not extend as far as permitting such charges to be made. This section therefore undoes the limitations of that decision.

The section will allow regulations to be made that will enable fees to be charged by planning authorities in respect of any of their functions or anything else done by them that relates to such a function. It is to be noted that the section covers both fees and charges. Therefore it is possible that certain matters may be covered by fees where the level is fixed by regulations whereas other matters may be subject to charges levied on an ad hoc basis, e.g. negotiating planning obligations, where the level of charges might need to reflect the amount of time spent by the authority and the complexity of the matter.

Section 54 sets out a framework for the introduction of a legal duty on certain consultees to respond to a consultation within a prescribed time limit. However, the section is silent on the issue of sanctions.

Section 55 provides that Sched.2 will apply and therefore requires the Secretary of State to take decisions in relation to called-in applications and planning appeals (under ss.77 and 78 of the 1990 Act) within certain timetables. It is not a legally binding duty and therefore it will remain to be seen if this provision is merely cosmetic or whether the Secretary of State leads by example by setting effective timetables and sticking to them.

# 5 CORRECTION OF ERRORS

## 5.1 PART 5 OF THE 2004 ACT

Part 5 deals with the correction of errors in appeal decisions by the Secretary of State or an inspector. It had long been recognised that the Secretary of State lacked the power to correct errors in decision letters. Whilst such errors occurred very infrequently, the only route available to correct such errors was via an application to the High Court. Section 56 therefore allows errors to be corrected without the need to resort to such a measure. Only certain types of 'correctable error' will be covered by this proposal and these are set out in s.59(5). A correctable error is one which is contained in any part of the decision document which records the decision but which is not part of the reasons given for the decision. This suggests that it will be limited to errors of fact or inference from a fact, but only if it is not central to the decision. In the House of Lords, the Minister suggested that its purpose was to correct only minor errors such as 'obvious clerical errors, typographical errors, omissions or accidental slips, which are obvious to the parties concerned'. Furthermore it was said that it 'would not enable the Secretary of State or an inspector to alter or vary a decision'.

One drawback is that a correction can only be made within six weeks of the date of the decision letter. As this is the same period as that for statutory challenges it is possible that unless prompt action is taken to notify the Secretary of State or inspector of the possible error and for that error to be examined and, if necessary, corrected, an affected party may still have to protect its position by mounting a statutory challenge in the High Court. Section 57 provides that any error is to be corrected by serving a 'correction notice'.

# 6 WALES

'So why is there broad support in Wales for the proposals dealing with Welsh plans? Why do the Welsh feel that they are making the necessary changes without going to such radical lengths as we are in England? It is because a single development plan at the local level as proposed for Wales would deliver greater simplicity and efficiency for the benefit of the public and developers alike in England.'

Opposition Spokesman Lord Hanningfield, Hansard, 5 February 2004, col.888.

## 6.1 PART 6 OF THE 2004 ACT

Part 6 of the 2004 Act introduces a Wales Spatial Plan and a new development plan system for Wales. After the bewildering number of documents required in England under Part 2 of the Act, a trip west of Offa's Dyke becomes restful and straightforward. There will be one Wales Spatial Strategy. Each unitary authority will have a local development plan.

The attractive simplicity of the Welsh system prompted a slightly tongue-in-cheek series of amendments from the Opposition at Lords Committee stage to apply the English system to Wales. The intention was to prompt the Government to explain why what was good for the Welsh was not good for the English. At Report stage the Conservative benches moved a more serious set of amendments (adapted from Town and Country Planning Association drafts) to apply the Welsh system to England. Neither proposal found favour with the Government and England and Wales remain two nations, divided by walls of local development frameworks.

This chapter will be able to address the Welsh legislation relatively briefly, for three reasons. Firstly, it is more simple. Secondly, it is otherwise closely based on the English provisions in the 2004 Act and the reader is directed to the discussion of those measures earlier in this book. Finally, the Welsh procedural regulations required under the 2004 Act have not been made at the time of writing.[1]

---

1 The regulation-making powers came into force on 1 August 2004: Planning and Compulsory Purchase Act 2004 (Commencement No.2) (Wales) Order 2004, SI 2004/1813.

## 6.2    WALES SPATIAL PLAN

The National Assembly for Wales is required by s.60 to approve a Wales Spatial Plan containing such of its policies as it thinks appropriate in relation to the development and use of land in Wales. The power to approve is given to the Assembly itself and cannot be delegated (s.60(5), (6)).

The Assembly is obliged to consult as it considers appropriate in preparing or reviewing the Wales Spatial Plan but there are otherwise no procedures imposed by the Act. Section 60 was brought into force on 14 July 2004.[1] By order, any step taken by the Assembly before that date on the Plan was treated as having been taken under s.60.[2] One effect of commencing the provisions on 14 July was that the Strategic Environmental Assessment Directive does not apply to the Plan, although any review or revision will be subject to it.

A consultation draft of the *Wales Spatial Plan – People, Places, Futures* was published in September 2003, and the approved plan was published in November 2004.

1   Article 2, Planning and Compulsory Purchase Act 2004 (Commencement No.1 and Transitional Provision) (Wales) Order 2004, SI 2004/1814.
2   Article 3.

## 6.3    LOCAL DEVELOPMENT POLICIES

Welsh local planning authorities are required to keep under review matters which may affect the development of their area or its planning (s.61). National park authorities are local planning authorities for their area (s.78(3)).

They must also produce a local development plan for their area (s.62(1)). The plan will set out the authority's objectives for the development and use of land in their area, general policies for the implementation of those objectives and may include specific policies for parts of their area (s.62(2), (3)). The form of the plan is a matter for regulations and a sustainability appraisal is required (s.62(4) and (6) respectively).

Authorities must first prepare a community involvement scheme as to how they will consult people in preparing their plan (s.63(1)). Unlike SCIs in England, the schemes do not address consultation in development control. They must also prepare a timetable for the preparation and adoption of the local development plan. The community involvement scheme and timetable must be agreed with the National Assembly and, in the absence of agreement, the Assembly can direct the terms of those documents (s.63(4)–(6)). The procedure for preparing these documents can also be prescribed by the Assembly (s.63(7)).

Binding independent examination takes place in a similar form to England (s.64) but there is no requirement that the local development plan be in general conformity with the Wales Spatial Plan. The Assembly may direct modifications to the plan or call it in for approval (s.65). Provisions for adoption, revocation and revision of local development plans are similar to Part 2 (ss.67, 68 and 70).[1] A provision unique to Wales is that local planning authorities are required to review their local development plan at such times as the Assembly prescribes (s.69).

The Assembly has default powers (s.71) and local authorities may agree to prepare joint local development plans (s.72). The Assembly may direct that the local development plan does not extend to the area of an urban development corporation (s.74). Matching the English provisions, local planning authorities must have regard to any guidance issued by the Assembly in exercising Part 6 powers (s.75) and must make an annual monitoring report to the Assembly (s.76).

---

1   There is, however, no provision for authorities to revoke local development plans themselves (cf. s.25) perhaps because the Welsh regime applies only to the local development plan not other subsidiary documents.

# 7 APPLICATION OF THE PLANNING ACTS TO THE CROWN

## 7.1 PART 7 OF THE 2004 ACT

Part 7 of the 2004 Act fulfills a longstanding policy commitment to end the Crown's immunity from the planning system. It makes the Crown subject to the requirements of the Town and Country Planning Act 1990, the Planning (Listed Buildings and Conservation Areas) Act 1990 and the Planning (Hazardous Substances) Act 1990 (together referred to as the 'Planning Acts').

Government departments and other Crown bodies can now be treated like any other developer or landowner for the purposes of planning permissions, listed building consent, hazardous substance consent and other planning controls. The removal of immunity is, however, subject to exceptions in relation to planning applications which raise issues of national security or security of property or where urgent works are required on Crown land or to listed buildings on Crown land. In addition Crown bodies remain, in the main, immune from the enforcement of planning controls.

## 7.2 CROWN IMMUNITY

### 7.2.1 The background

It has been a longstanding constitutional principle that an Act of Parliament is presumed not to bind the Crown in the absence of express provision or necessary implication. The Court of Appeal in *Ministry of Agriculture, Fisheries and Food* v. *Jenkins*[1] and the House of Lords in *Lord Advocate* v. *Dumbarton District Council*[2] confirmed this general constitutional principle in the context of planning matters. Thus to date, the Planning Acts have been held not to apply to the Crown or those acting as servants or agents of the Crown. The Crown does not, for example, need planning permission to develop its own land or land elsewhere.[3] However, to the extent that any interest is held in Crown land other than by the Crown, such as by a tenant, development in respect of that privately held interest, which is not by or on behalf of the Crown, is subject to planning control in the normal way.[4]

The potentially wide ranging extent of the immunity, had it remained, is apparent from the decision by the Court of Appeal in *R (on the application of Cherwell District Council)* v. *First Secretary of State*.[5] Construction and operation of an asylum centre on Crown land by the private sector under a public private partnership with the Home Office was held to be development by or on behalf of the Crown and did not therefore require planning permission.

### 7.2.2    Previous arrangements

Whilst the Planning Acts may not have bound the Crown, this has not meant that Crown development has been unregulated. Government departments, Crown Estate Commissioners and the Duchies of Cornwall and Lancaster have followed a non-statutory procedure, laid down in Part IV of Circular 18/84, whereby they have consulted with local planning authorities about proposals which would, absent the immunity, otherwise require permission or consent. Pursuant to this procedure, objections to the proposal could be considered and any controversial or major developments assessed by a planning inspector. If the local planning authority was not content with the proposal, the development could be referred to the Secretary of State for his determination.[6]

It has always been open to Crown bodies to bring themselves within the Planning Acts, should they so choose. A Crown body might, for example, apply for planning permission in anticipation of disposal of the land.[7] Disposal of the land with the benefit of planning permission might increase the value of the land. Similarly, where a government department wished to dispose of its interest in land containing a listed building, it could always seek listed building consent from the local planning authority to demolish/carry out works to a listed building.[8]

### 7.2.3    Removal of Crown immunity

In 1992, the then Department of the Environment issued a consultation paper setting out proposals for bringing Crown exemption from the planning system to an end. Whilst the non-statutory procedures for Crown development were considered to have worked well in practice, the Government believed that, in the interests of greater accountability and openness, a more formal system was now appropriate. Legislation would be introduced 'when a suitable legislative opportunity occurred' to subject Crown bodies to planning control in the same circumstances as private individuals.

In March 1994, the Government announced that the proposals to remove Crown immunity in planning and conservation matters had received overwhelming support, but as yet no such 'suitable legislative opportunity' had presented itself. This approach was endorsed by the present Government in 1998 in response to a parliamentary question and again in its 2001 Green Paper, *Planning: Delivering a Fundamental Change*:

'We remain committed to the principle of removing Crown immunity from planning control, subject to certain safeguards relating to the national interest, such as security and defence. We will introduce legislation when an opportunity arises.'[9]

However, despite the repeated policy commitment to ending Crown immunity, the Planning and Compulsory Purchase Bill, as originally published in December 2002, made no mention of any reform of the position on Crown immunity. Provisions were only introduced in October 2003 when the Bill returned to Standing Committee in the House of Commons, by way of 21 new clauses, three new schedules and 10 other amendments.

---

1   [1963] 2 QB 317.
2   [1990] 2 AC 580.
3   *Lord Advocate* v. *Dumbarton District Council* [1990] 2 AC 580.
4   *Ministry of Agriculture, Fisheries and Food* v. *Jenkins* [1963] 2 QB 317 and *R (on the application of Cherwell District Council)* v. *First Secretary of State)* [2004] EWCA Civ 1420.
5   [2004] EWCA Civ 1420.
6   See Pt. IV of Circular 18/84 Crown Land and Crown Development. Trunk roads including motorways have not been within the procedures as they have been subject to the provisions of the Highways Act 1980. The other exception relates to major transportation projects which since 1992 have been subject to the Transport and Works Act 1992.
7   Under s.299 of the Town and Country Planning Act 1990 (now repealed by the 2004 Act).
8   Section 84 of the Planning (Listed Buildings and Conservation Areas) Act 1990 (repealed by the 2004 Act).
9   *Planning: Delivering for Wales* (February 2002) contained the same promise.

## 7.3   PART 7 AND SCHEDULES 3, 4 AND 5

### 7.3.1   Introduction

The way in which Crown immunity is brought to an end and then reinstated for certain aspects of planning control, is complicated. The basic principle (that immunity is at an end), and exceptions to the basic principle, are set out in Part 7 of the 2004 Act. Part 7 is divided into two chapters: Chapter 1 applies to England and Wales and Chapter 2 applies to Scotland. In Chapter 1 relevant amendments are made to the Town and Country Planning Act 1990 (referred to as the 'Principal Act'). By and large, the same provisions and changes are made to the Planning (Hazardous Substances) Act 1990 and the Planning (Listed Buildings and Conservation Areas) Act 1990 (referred to in this chapter as the Hazardous Substances Act and the Listed Buildings Act). A further long list of exceptions, provisos and other special provisions for the Crown are set out in Scheds.3 and 5 (Scotland) to the 2004 Act.[1] Transitional arrangements for the change from non-statutory to statutory control over the Crown in planning matters are dealt with in Sched.4.

In Standing Committee debate, the Minister for Housing and Planning acknowledged and sought to explain the complexities of bringing Crown immunity to an end:

'Let me make a general observation about Crown exemption and the Crown's response to the planning and compulsory purchase process. There is an opaqueness to various aspects of the Bill, which I believe will remain a moot point throughout our consideration of it, about the way in which Crown institutions respond to aspects of planning law. The point is that the Crown may not be compelled to comply, but it is, above all, the custodian of the law, and we expect it to pursue the requirements of the law as extensively and in as many circumstances as possible. There is no body higher than the Crown upon which it is more incumbent to pursue the law.'[2]

### 7.3.2   The general principle: 'the Crown is bound'

Express provision makes clear that the Planning Acts bind the Crown. A new section, inserted into the 1990 Act, states confidently: 'This Act binds the Crown.'[3] Similar provisions are added to the Listed Buildings Act and the Hazardous Substances Act.[4] Thus the Crown will have to obtain planning consents, in the normal way.

### 7.3.3   Definition of the Crown

The 'Crown' is not expressly defined in the Planning Acts although revised definitions of Crown land and Crown interest provide an indication of the scope of the term.[5] As a matter of constitutional principle, the Crown means the sovereign acting in a public or official capacity. In practice the Crown's legal powers are exercised by ministers, since convention requires that the Crown should act as its ministers advise on all constitutional affairs.[6]

In the Planning Acts, references to the Crown or Crown land may now refer to land owned by the Monarch privately,[7] the Duchies and the Crown Estate, government departments and the Palace of Westminster.[8] Certain provisions also apply to private interests in Crown Land (e.g. leases).[9]

### 7.3.4   Appropriate authority

As a matter of practice, the various Crown interests have a designated appropriate authority which acts, in effect, as the Crown's representative and is the body on which notices and other documents must be served. It is this body which gives any necessary consents and varies according to the nature of the Crown interest. It will usually be the Secretary of State of the government department that holds the property involved, but it may be the Crown Estate Commissioners. In one or two cases it will be Her Majesty in relation to her private estates, except in the case of land belonging to the Duchy of Cornwall or Lancaster or in relation to the Palace of Westminster where other provisions apply. 'Appropriate authority' is not a new concept but is widened by the 2004 Act to include appropriate representatives in relation to Her Majesty's private estates, Westminster Hall and the Palace of Westminster.[10]

## 7.3.5   Exceptions and provisos to the general principle

Various exceptions and provisos to the general principle that the Crown is bound by the Planning Acts are introduced, not all of which apply to all three Acts.

The mechanics of introducing the exceptions are different for the 1990 Act than for the Listed Buildings and Hazardous Substances Acts. Because the 1990 Act is so large and complex (337 sections and 17 schedules), the approach taken is to qualify the general principle that the 1990 Act binds the Crown by means of a statement that the general principle is subject to express provision made by the Act.[11] The other two Acts are much shorter and less complex so a list of provisions which do not apply to the Crown is set out.[12]

In Standing Committee debate, Mr Clifton Brown for the Opposition expressed concern about the exemptions and provisos which detracted from the general principle that the Crown is bound.[13] In response the Minister for Housing and Planning made the point that whilst the Crown may not be compelled to comply, it is the custodian of the law and can be expected to pursue the requirements of the law as extensively and in as many circumstances as possible.[14]

## 7.3.6   National security and security of premises or property

As a general rule, all oral evidence at local inquiries must be heard in public and documents must be open to public inspection.[15] The general rule does not apply, however, when the information in question relates to national security or to the security of any premises or property and public disclosure of the information would be contrary to the national interest. In these circumstances, the Secretary of State may direct that the relevant evidence is disclosed only to specific individuals (known as a 's.321 direction').[16]

In Standing Committee debate, the Minister for Housing and Planning explained the need for new provisions in light of the ending of Crown immunity. The ability to make a s.321 direction has been part of planning legislation since 1982, but does not appear to have been exercised. However, with the Crown to be made bound by the Planning Acts, there was thought to be the distinct prospect of planning applications being made with national security implications. A procedure was necessary for dealing with sensitive material subject to a s.321 direction which would not be generally accessible, without creating an injustice to those unable to see the information.[17]

### The appointment of special advocates

The solution, introduced by Part 7, provides for the appointment of so-called 'special advocates' to represent the interests of the people who are prevented from seeing the sensitive material.

Where the Secretary of State is considering making a direction restricting the disclosure of evidence, the Attorney General may appoint a person to represent the interests of anyone who would be prevented from hearing or inspecting any evidence at a local inquiry if the direction is given.[18] A special advocate can also be appointed after the direction is given. In Wales, the Counsel General to the National Assembly for Wales (the Assembly's chief legal adviser) will appoint the special advocate.

Provision is made for payment of the fees and expenses of the special advocate whether or not any inquiry is held, by a person nominated by the Secretary of State.[19] The Lord Chancellor may make rules to govern the procedure to be followed by the Secretary of State in making a direction and the functions of the special advocate.[20] If any such rules are made in Wales, rules made by the Lord Chancellor do not have effect.[21]

In Scotland, the Scottish Ministers or the Secretary of State are given the concurrent power to make directions restricting disclosure of specified evidence at any inquiry. However, before the Scottish Ministers make such a direction, they are required to consult the Secretary of State. The concurrent power and consultation requirement reflect the fact that national security functions are reserved to Westminster and the UK Government whilst planning functions are devolved to the Scottish Parliament and Executive. The Secretary of State and the Scottish Ministers are given powers to make rules as to the procedure to be followed by them before giving a direction. In addition, the power to appoint special advocates in Scotland is conferred on the Lord Advocate to reflect differences in the Scottish legal system.[22]

As originally drafted, those who could be special advocates was limited to qualified lawyers with specified rights of audience.[23] In its representations on the Bill the Law Society took the view that it was unduly restrictive to exclude others and, in particular, planning consultants. The merit of this point was accepted by the Government and there are now no restrictions on who the Attorney General may appoint, save that any person appointed will need to be cleared for security purposes.

## Special Advocates: the background[24]

Special advocates are a novel feature of English law. They were first introduced in 1997 for special immigration appeals and are now used in at least seven different tribunals. Their origin stems from a decision of the European Court of Human Rights in *Chahal* v. *United Kingdom*. Mr Chahal challenged a decision to deport him as a threat to national security, made by way of an internal Home Office advisory panel on the basis of sensitive intelligence material which Mr Chahal had no opportunity to challenge.[25] In its judgment, the court made the following statement:

'The Court recognises that the use of confidential material may be unavoidable where national security is at stake. This does not mean, however, that the national authorities can be free from effective control by the domestic courts whenever they choose to assert that national security and terrorism are involved . . . *[T]here are techniques which can be employed which both accommodate legitimate security concerns about the nature and sources of intelligence information and yet accord the individual a substantial measure of procedural justice.'* (author's emphasis)

The developing jurisprudence in relation to special advocates in the UK in the Special Immigration Appeals Commission has identified the following key features of the role of a special advocate.[26] The role of the special advocate should be to represent the interests of the person in those parts of the proceedings from which he and his legal representative are excluded. To ensure the independence of a special advocate, the advocate should be appointed by the Attorney-General. The special advocate will probably need to be present throughout the proceedings. An important feature of the role is that the special advocate should not have a client relationship with the person he represents. The advocate does not take instructions from the client and he is not obliged to do what the client says.[27] The advocate must make a judgement about the way in which the person he represents would have wanted the case to be argued.[28] Having seen the sensitive material, the special advocate is not entitled to communicate with the client, save in a form approved by the relevant public body. The client is, however, free to continue to send the special advocate any further instructions even after the advocate has seen the relevant material. The role of the special advocate role is twofold: to test whether or not the material should in fact remain 'closed' and secondly, to make submissions on the closed material. A summary of the closed proceedings is made available to the person represented and his lawyers to ensure that as much information as possible is available to that person.[29]

## Special advocates in the planning context

In discussions in Standing Committee, which focused on applications for planning permission, the Minister for Housing and Planning set out two scenarios in which it was envisaged that a special advocate might be necessary:[30]

(1) The Ministry of Defence or one of the security and intelligence services might submit a planning application which omitted to specify the use of the building because to reveal such information could compromise national security. If as a result of pre-application discussions with the local planning authority the expectation of the applicant department was that the local planning authority would not be able to determine the application because it needed information that the applicant department could not reveal, the department might ask the Secretary of State to call in the application and to make a s.321 direction for the subsequent planning inquiry.[31]

(2) A private person's planning application might interfere with some aspect of national security. For example, a proposed tall building might overlook a restricted site or interfere with a communications system. The Crown would be an objector to the planning application and it could ask the Secretary of State to call in the application.

The scope of the power to withhold information on grounds of national security was discussed in debate. The question was asked, but not answered, as to whether the power extended to security arrangements in a prison, or the configuration of buildings within the curtilage of a prison or other premises provided for custody.[32] In relation to information withheld to 'ensure the security of any premises or property',[33] the question was asked as to whether this extended to arrangements for the security of other premises or property to prevent people from getting in rather than out.[34]

Whilst the 2004 Act provides the framework for special advocates, no detailed rules have, as at the time of writing, been made by the Lord Chancellor and it remains to be seen how closely any rules will be based on the procedures for the Special Immigration Appeals Commission. During Standing Committee debate the Minister indicated that the rules would cover the procedure for showing the classified material to the special advocate and the procedure for representations by the advocate as well as a procedure for both the applicant and the special advocate to make representations if the Secretary of State is minded not to make a s.321 direction.[35] In debate the Minister also indicated that further secondary legislation will need to be made under existing powers including amendments to existing inquiries procedure rules (or even new ones), for planning inquiries that require a special advocate. Provision would need to be made in the Town and Country Planning (General Development Procedure) Order 1995, SI 1995/418, for the Crown to withhold information subject to a s.321 direction.[36] New regulations would also be necessary to cover the situation in which the existence of development could not be admitted. For example, where a house was to be converted into an operational building for the security and intelligence services (whilst it would still appear to be a house, the conversion would constitute a development). The Minister indicated that these would be dealt with by the creation of a new permitted development right in the 1995 order.[37]

### 7.3.7 Urgent Crown development and urgent works to listed buildings on Crown land

*Overview*

Development by Crown bodies considered to be of national importance and required more quickly than permitted by the usual procedures is exempt from an application to the local planning authority. Instead any application is made directly to the Secretary of State and the application is to be treated as if it were a 'called-in' application.[38] The effect is to short-circuit the often lengthy period taken by a local planning authority to reach a decision in circumstances where the development is expected to be referred to the Secretary of State or might be expected to lead to a local inquiry on appeal.

The Crown, as the developer, must certify that the proposed development is of such national importance and urgency that the change in procedure is justified. An almost identical procedure is introduced for urgent work to a listed building on Crown land.[39] The same changes are made to the equivalent Scottish legislation.[40]

The Inquiries Procedure Rules (SI 2000/1624) will be amended to provide a shorter period than the 22 weeks currently allowed between the date when the Secretary of State announces the date of the inquiry and the date when it actually starts. During debate the Minister indicated that Government would consult on the length of the shorter period but that 14 weeks was the Government's current thinking. The aim is:

> 'to have the shortest period consistent with giving the objector sufficient time to consider the appropriate authority's case and to prepare his own case . . . the new clauses could deliver a decision on a controversial application in about seven months, rather than 11 months, from the start date to the conclusion of the inquiry'.[41]

The Minister also indicated that for Crown development required more or less immediately, the Government was minded to introduce, and would consult on, a new permitted development right to enable development to take place with the proviso that it should be followed by a planning application within a certain period. This suggestion was characterised in Standing Committee debate as 'naive' on the basis that any application considered retrospectively would be unlikely to be turned down.[42] The Minister did not give any examples of urgent development but the burial pits dug on Crown land during the foot and mouth crisis were discussed in debate as an example of development in this category.[43] Examples of urgent works to listed buildings given by the Minister included barriers installed immediately after 11 September 2001 in the Palace of Westminster.[44]

During Standing Committee debate, concerns expressed included that these procedures would be used by the Crown for all controversial applications and that the Government's proposal for a permitted development right for urgent development might deprive local people of the opportunity to make representations. In addition, the distinction to be drawn between urgent Crown development which would benefit from permitted development rights and development of slightly lesser urgency which would benefit from the exemptions from the need to apply to the local planning authority was not clear or necessary.[45]

## Procedures for urgent developments/works

The Crown is required to advertise the application for urgent development or repair work in one or more local newspapers giving details of the development proposed and stating that a planning application will be made directly to the Secretary of State.

The application to the Secretary of State will need to be supported by the necessary documentation, including an environmental statement where required and a statement of the case for seeking permission. Copies of the relevant documents will be made public in the area of the proposed development and the local planning authority and interested third parties will then have the opportunity to put forward views. The Secretary of State must consult certain prescribed persons as well as the local planning authority. Decisions on these applications can only be challenged under s.288 of the 1990 Act.[46]

### 7.3.8    Enforcement in relation to Crown land

It has long been considered inappropriate for the enforcement provisions of planning legislation to apply to the Crown, particularly those which contain criminal sanctions or permit the local planning authority to enter land. This policy is reflected in Part 7. The Crown remains immune from prosecution for any offence under the Planning Acts. Nothing it does or omits to do will constitute an offence under the Planning Acts.[47]

Local planning authorities will now, however, be able to initiate enforcement action by serving enforcement notices or issuing revocation orders, but they will not be able to enforce them by entering onto Crown land, bringing proceedings or making applications to the court without the permission of the appropriate authority. The Crown's consent is therefore still required before any step towards enforcement action can be taken.[48] Immunity from enforcement extends to land within the estates of the Duchies of Cornwall and Lancaster as well as to land in which there is a Crown interest. Similar provisions are made in Scotland.[49]

The effect of disapplying the relevant provision on offences in the Listed Buildings Act[50] as regards the Crown is that the defences to the offence listed in the Act are also disapplied. These include the need to carry out urgent repair works to a building in the interests of health or safety or for the preservation of the building. A new section introduced into the Listed Buildings Act ensures that these statutory defences are available to the Crown.[51] As the Minister explained in Standing Committee debate, the Government wanted the Crown to have the same freedom of action in these circumstances as a private person. To have no power to carry out emergency works in these types of situation was, in the words of the Minister, 'clearly unsatisfactory':

> 'We therefore have a principle that where offences have been disapplied, we have to add back in any statutory defences as a positive right for the Crown so that the Crown has the same freedom of action as a private person. It may sound complicated but it does make sense.'[52]

### 7.3.9    Rights of entry onto land for reasons other than enforcement

In addition to enforcement, local planning authorities may have other reasons to enter property including the need to survey the land in connection with the development planning process.[53] Permission is required to do so in the case of entry onto Crown land (including land within the estates of the Duchies of Cornwall and Lancaster) by 'a person appearing to be entitled to give it' or by the appropriate authority.[54] As expressed in Standing Committee debate, the expectation is that the local planning authority will be able to arrange entry to sites locally – generally by approaching the person in charge of the site, e.g. the site manager or his deputy or the head of accommodation services. If entry is refused, the local planning authority can then ask permission of the appropriate authority.[55]

## 7.3.10    Other provisions

### Trees

Tree preservation orders can be made by local planning authorities in respect of trees on Crown land without the prior consent of the relevant Crown body, subject to two modifications.[56]

(1)  The provisions in the 1990 Act relating to tree preservation orders (TPOs) are amended to ensure that forestry operations or woodland management carried out by the Forestry Commissioners (usually on Crown land) are not subject to the controls of the TPO system. This is on the basis that the Forestry Commissioners make their felling and other management decisions in accordance with their duty under the Forestry Act 1967 to achieve a reasonable balance between forestry and conservation.[57]

(2)  Protection for trees in conservation areas which are not subject to tree preservation orders are adapted to include a declaratory and consent procedure for the Crown. The Crown is prohibited from doing any act to a tree in a conservation area which might be prohibited by a TPO, unless it serves notice of its intention on the local planning authority and does the act either with the consent of the authority or between six weeks and two years after the date of the notice.[58] In effect this gives the local planning authority six weeks to respond. If it wishes to prevent the work or attach conditions to it, it will need to make a TPO. The provisions in Scotland are similarly amended.[59]

### Old mining permissions

Crown bodies holding old mining permissions granted pursuant to wartime interim development orders in the period 1943–1948 that were subsequently validated by the Town and Country Planning Act 1947 have the opportunity to register such permissions and apply for the determination of appropriate new operating conditions on the same terms that applied to all other permissions when the Planning and Compensation Act 1991 was implemented.[60] Because Crown immunity applied to the 1991 Act, there was thought to be a possibility, albeit a remote one, that there may be permissions granted on Crown land which have not been registered. The 2004 Act therefore restarts the clock for this limited category of permissions.[61] The changes to Scottish planning legislation are similar.[62]

## Subordinate legislation

The Secretary of State will be able to make an order defining which existing subordinate legislation is to apply to the Crown, either as it stands or with modifications.[63] This provision is necessary as existing subordinate legislation is not automatically binding on the Crown because the enabling Acts did not allow for it to be so when adapted. A similar power is given to the Scottish Ministers.[64]

### 7.3.11   Transitional provisions

Transitional arrangements are made for the transition from a non-statutory to a statutory planning system for the Crown.[65]

## Planning applications

Where notice of proposed development has been submitted by the Crown to the local planning authority pursuant to the arrangements in Circular 11/84 before 6 August 2004, the following provisions apply:

(1) where the notice was approved before 6 August 2004, the approval is to be treated as if it was a grant of planning permission;[66]
(2) where a notice is in dispute and has been referred to the Secretary of State, who has not made a determination before 6 August 2004, the notice shall be treated as a recovered appeal;[67] and
(3) for pending proposals, i.e. where a development notice has been submitted to the local planning authority but was still being considered as at 6 August 2004, this should be treated as an application for planning permission.[68]

## Listed building works[69]

The same procedures apply in respect of works to listed buildings where the Crown submitted a notice of proposed works to the local planning authority before 6 August 2004:

(1) where the notice has been approved, it is to be treated as if it is a listed building consent granted under the Listed Buildings Act;
(2) if the notice is in dispute (i.e. it has been referred to but not decided by the Secretary of State), it is to be treated as if it is a recovered appeal; and
(3) where the proposal is pending, it should be treated as if it were an application for listed building consent.

## The Hazardous Substances Act

If, for the year immediately preceding 6 August 2004, a hazardous substance was present on, over or under Crown land, the relevant Crown body has six months in which to claim a deemed consent for the presence of the substances.[70] The

Scottish Executive intend that corresponding transitional provisions will be made by subordinate legislation in Scotland.

### 7.3.12   Compulsory acquisition of Crown land

Crown land cannot be acquired compulsorily unless 'it is an interest which is for the time being held otherwise than by or on behalf of the Crown' and the appropriate authority consents.[71] Similar provision is made for the Listed Buildings Act.

### 7.3.13   Purchase notices

Crown bodies are not generally able to serve a purchase notice or listed building purchase notice requiring a local authority to purchase their interest in the land, following an adverse planning or listed building control decision.

A purchase notice can only be served in relation to Crown land in two sets of circumstances. Firstly, an owner of a private interest on Crown land may serve a purchase notice if the owner has offered his interest to the appropriate authority on equivalent terms and that offer has been refused.[72] Secondly, an appropriate authority can serve a purchase notice in relation to the Queen's private estates and land belonging to the Duchies of Lancaster and Cornwall and land forming part of the Crown Estate. There are similar provisions for listed building purchase notices.

In Standing Committee debate the Minister explained that purchase notices exist to protect the private and commercial interests of landowners. The Crown, in general, does not have such interests. As the Crown maintains immunity from compulsory purchase under the Planning Acts, it is not generally appropriate for it to be able to enforce a quasi-compulsory purchase on a local planning authority. However, Her Majesty's private estates are private. The Duchies of Lancaster and Cornwall and the Crown Estates operate in the private sector similarly to other landed estates, and have commercial interests that could be adversely affected by refusal of planning permission. It is therefore appropriate that they should have the ability to serve purchase notices as private interests do.[73]

### 7.3.14   Applications for planning permissions and listed building/hazardous substance consents

The Secretary of State can make regulations modifying or excluding any statutory provision relating to the making and determination of applications.[74]

A hazardous substance consent is not revoked if there is a change in the person in control of the land provided the control changes from one emanation of the Crown to another.[75]

## 7.3.15    Provision of information

The Crown has limited immunity from the powers available under the Planning Acts to the Secretary of State or local authority to require information about land. The appropriate authority must comply with a request by the Secretary of State for information on specified matters unless to do so will disclose information on national security or security of premises or property.[75] Crown bodies do not, however, have to provide information to a local planning authority or to an urban development corporation. This provision does not apply to private interests on Crown land which will therefore be subject to the general provisions.

1 The Minister for Housing and Planning in Standing Committee debate described Sched.3 (then Sched.1) as 'a varied and complex set of provisions': House of Commons Standing Committee A(pt3) 14 October 2003, col.016.

2 Ibid, col.023.

3 See s.79 of the 2004 Act inserting s.292A in to the 1990 Act. Section 292A appears in Part 13 of the 1990 Act. Part 13 covers the application of the Act to Crown land. Its role to date has been to indicate how the Crown is affected by the 1990 Act given the general principle of immunity.

4 Section 79 of the 2004 Act also adds s.82A to the Planning (Listed Buildings and Conservation Areas) Act 1990 and s.30A to the Planning (Hazardous Substances) Act 1990.

5 See Sched.3 paras.6, 7 and 8 of the 2004 Act amending the relevant definitions in the Planning Acts.

6 See Wade & Forsyth, *Administrative Law*, 9th ed (OUP, 2005), p.45.

7 As the Minister for Housing and Planning pointed out in Standing Committee debate (14 October 2003 (col.030)), the Queen will have to obtain planning permission if she wants to undertake any development at Sandringham.

8 Certain portions of the Palace of Westminster are owned by Her Majesty.

9 E.g. Sched.3, para.1 to the 2004 Act.

10 Ibid, paras.6 and 7.

11 Section 79 of the 2004 Act, inserting s.292A into the 1990 Act.

12 Section 79 of the 2004 Act inserts new s.82A(2) into the Listed Buildings Act and new s.30A(2) into the Hazardous Substances Act.

13 House of Commons Standing Committee A (pt 5), 14 October 2003, cols.017–020.

14 Ibid, col.023.

15 Section 321 of the 1990 Act. The rule also applies to appeals against decisions about hazardous substance or listed building consent (see Sched.3 to the Listed Buildings Act and the Schedule to the Hazardous Substances Act).

16 Section 321 of the 1990 Act.

17 In particular without breaching Article 6 of the European Convention on Human Rights.

18 Section 80(1) of the 2004 Act adds s.321(5) to the 1990 Act.

19 New s.321(9), 1990 Act.

20 New s.321(7), 1990 Act.

21 Section 81 of the 2004 Act inserts new s.321B into the 1990 Act.

22 Section 91 of the 2004 Act introduces a new s.265A to the Scottish Planning Act 1997 and applies it to the Scottish Listed Buildings and Hazardous Substances Acts 1997.

23 Rights of audience in any part of the Supreme Court or in all proceedings in county courts or magistrates' courts.

24 See the informative papers written by Dr Eric Metcalfe, Barrister and Director of Human Rights Policy, JUSTICE 'Representative but not Responsible – the use of special advocates in English law' and by Thomas de la Mere, Blackstone Chambers, 'The Proper and

Fair Use of Special Advocates in Civil and Criminal Proceedings – Getting a grip on a slippery slope'.

25 *Chahal v. United Kingdom* 23 EHRR 413 (November 1996).

26 Pursuant to the Special Immigration Appeals Commission Act 1997.

27 Hansard, HC Debates, 26 November 1997, cols.1070–1071. See also 3rd reading, HC Debates, 26 November 1997, col.1039: 'the special advocate has an obligation to seek to represent the appellant's interests without taking instructions from him. As I have mentioned in previous debates, that is not completely unprecedented. Perhaps it has never been done on this scale and in this way, but it happens in cases involving people with psychiatric problems and with minors. Their lawyer sometimes had to exercise independent judgment in the way in which he represents that person'.

28 Hansard, HC Debates, 3rd reading, 26 November 1997, col.1039.

29 Ibid, col.1070.

30 House of Common Standing Committee 4 (pt 9), 14 October 2003, col.36.

31 The Minister noted that even if the local planning authority rejected or failed to determine an application on the ground of lack of information, the s.321 procedure could be applied to a recovered appeal.

32 Ibid, col.039.

33 Section 321(4) of the 1990 Act.

34 Ibid, col.039.

35 Ibid, col.037.

36 Ibid, col.037.

37 Ibid, col.037.

38 Section 82 of the 2004 Act adding in s.293A to the 1990 Act.

39 Section 82 of the 2004 Act adding in s.82B to the Listed Buildings Act.

40 Section 92 and 93 of the 2004 Act.

41 Ibid, cols.47 and 48.

42 Sir Sydney Chapman, col.51.

43 Ibid, col.50.

44 Ibid, col.53.

45 Ibid, cols.49 and 50.

46 Section 82 which inserts s.293A into the 1990 Act.

47 Section 84 introduces ss.296A (enforcement in relation to the Crown) and 296B (References to an interest in land) to the 1990 Act, ss.82D and 82E to the Listed Buildings Act and ss.30C and 30D to the Hazardous Substances Act.

48 Sections 294 and 295 of the 1990 Act which relate to special enforcement notices are omitted.

49 Section 94 introduces new ss.245A (Enforcement in relation to the Crown) and 245B (References to an interest in land) to the 1997 Scottish Planning Act. It also introduces equivalent amendments to the Scottish Listed Buildings Act 1997 (new sections 73D and 73E) and the Scottish Hazardous Substances Act 1997 (new ss.30B and 30C). The amendments to Scottish legislation take account of differences in Scotland, such as the absence of Duchy land.

50 Section 9 of the Listed Buildings Act.

51 See s.79 of the 2004 Act which inserts s.82A(3) into the Listed Buildings Act.

52 Ibid, col.015. See s.79 of the 2004 Act which inserts s.82A(3) into the Listed Buildings Act.

53 Those reasons are governed by s.324 of the 1990 Act, with supplementary provisions being made in s.325.

54 Schedule 3 to the 2004 Act, paras.13, 14 and 15.

55 Ibid, col.027.

56 Sections 85 and 86 of the 2004 Act. In addition to the two modifications, s.300 of the 1990 Act is repealed as it is no longer necessary.

57 Ibid, col.062.

58 Section 86 of the 2004 Act amends s.211 of the 1990 Act.

59 Section 96 of the 2004 Act amends s.172 of the Principal Scottish Planning Act.
60 Section 87 of the 2004 Act.
61 Ibid, col.067.
62 Section 97 of the 2004 Act makes the relevant changes to the Scottish Planning Legislation.
63 Section 89 of the 2004 Act.
64 Section 98 of the 2004 Act.
65 Section 89, Sched.4 to the 2004 Act and Planning and Compulsory Purchase Act 2004 (Commencement No.1) Order 2004, SI 2004/2097.
66 Part I, para.3.
67 I.e. an appeal by an applicant for planning permission under s.78 of the 1990 Act; ibid para.5(3) of Part I.
68 Ibid, para.6 of Part 1.
69 See Part 2 of Sched.4 and SI 2004/2097.
70 See s.30B of the Hazardous Substances Act inserted by s.79 of the 2004 Act.
71 See Sched.3 to the 2004 Act, paras.3, 4 and 5.
72 See Sched.3, paras.1 and 2 equivalent terms are those that would be repayable were it acquired in pursuance of a purchase notice.
73 Ibid, col.025.
72 Schedule 3, para.10 to the 2004 Act.
75 Schedule 3, para.20.
76 Schedule 3, paras.17, 19 and 21.

## 7.4    COMMENCEMENT ORDERS

The following provisions of the 2004 Act came into force on 6 August 2004:[1]

- Section 79: Crown application of the Planning Acts.
- Section 80: Special provision relating to national security.
- Section 81: Special provision relating to national security: Wales.
- Section 82: Urgent Crown development.
- Section 83: Urgent works relating to Crown land.
- Section 88: Subordinate legislation.
- Section 91: Special provision for certain circumstances where disclosure of information as to national security may occur: Scotland.

1 Planning and Compulsory Purchase Act 2004 (Commencement No.I) Order 2004, SI 2004/2097.

# 8 COMPULSORY PURCHASE

## 8.1 PART 8 OF THE 2004 ACT

Whilst the main parts of the 2004 Act deal with reforms to the development plan system and changes to certain aspects of development control, Part 8 of the Act introduces some important changes in the area of compulsory purchase law.

The need for major reforms to the complex law and procedure governing compulsory purchase and compensation has long been recognised. These reforms stemmed from recommendations made to Ministers in 2000 by the Compulsory Purchase Policy Review Advisory Group, which also proposed that the Law Commission should prepare a new legislative code that would simplify the law. In December 2003 the Law Commission published its final report, *Towards a Compulsory Purchase Code: (1) Compensation* (Law Com No.286) and a further report on compulsory purchase procedure was to be produced. The Law Commission's proposals will build upon the reforms in the Act which are aimed at increasing the ability of local authorities to promote regeneration projects. Unlike the planning parts of the Act, the changes to the compulsory purchase regime are more definite and so there is less of a dependency upon regulation-making powers.

## 8.2 ACQUIRING LAND FOR COMPULSORY PURCHASE

Section 99 amends s.226(1) and (2) of the 1990 Act which contain the general planning powers under which a local authority may acquire land compulsorily for the carrying out of development, redevelopment or improvement. The amended wording of s.226(1) greatly increases the powers of acquiring local authorities and diminishes the ability of landowners to object to compulsory purchase orders by restricting the scope of objections. The requirement for local authorities to demonstrate that the land is both suitable and required for its purposes is replaced by a simple requirement to show that the authority thinks that the land might facilitate its desired purpose. Furthermore the local authority is no longer required to have regard to the development plan, planning permissions in force and other material considerations. A new sub-section (1A) allows the local planning authority to exercise its compulsory purchase power if it thinks that the carrying out of the development, redevelopment or improvement is likely to contribute to the achievement or promotion of the economic, social or environmental well-being of its area.

At the Report Stage of the Bill in the House of Lords the Minister stated that a local planning authority seeking to use these powers would need to show that the proposals were in accordance with its up-to-date planning policies prepared in full consultation with those living and working in the area. Ideally those policies would have been included in the authority's DPDs but acquisition might not be delayed where there had not been time yet to update the documents to reflect the current proposals for the land in question. Given the democratic deficit elsewhere in the Act, this widening of the scope of the powers of compulsory acquisition is significant. However, the compulsory acquisition of land represents a fundamental interference with property rights. Therefore the interplay between the amended power and the protection afforded by Articles 8 and 1 of the First Protocol of the European Convention on Human Rights may prove to be a fertile ground for litigation.

A local authority is defined by s.226(8) of the 1990 Act as a council of a county, county borough, district or London borough. Joint planning boards and National Park authorities may also exercise the same power.

Section 100 amends various provisions of the Acquisition of Land Act 1981 in relation to orders confirmed other than by the Minister. Section 13 is replaced and ss.13A–C introduced. Similarly, s.15 is replaced. The effect of these changes to the procedure for making and confirming compulsory purchase orders is to extend the categories of people entitled to be served, and to object, to the order. It also introduces a written representations procedure for considering objections as an alternative to public local inquiries or hearings. Furthermore, orders can now be confirmed in stages. Section 101 makes corresponding amendments where orders are to be authorised by a Minister.

Section 102 introduces a new s.14A into the Acquisition of Land Act 1981 which deals with the situations when there can be confirmation of orders by the acquiring authority as opposed to the confirming authority. Sub-section (1) provides that this will only apply where the confirming authority has notified the acquiring authority that the order can be confirmed by the acquiring authority and the notice to that effect has not been revoked. Furthermore, it will only apply when there is no objection to the proposed confirmation of the order or when all objections have been withdrawn and the whole order (as opposed to only part) is capable of being confirmed without modification.

## 8.3   COMPENSATION

Section 103 inserts a new s.5A into the Land Compensation Act 1961. Where the value of the land is to be assessed on the basis of open market value and a notice to treat has been served, the valuation date is the earlier of the date of entry and the date of assessment. If the land is subject to a general vesting declaration, the relevant valuation date is the earlier of the vesting date and the date of assessment. No adjustments are to be made to the valuation in respect of anything that happens after the relevant valuation date. Thus this confirms the position following the House of Lords' decision in *Birmingham Corporation* v. *West Midlands Baptist (Trust) Association* [1970] AC 874. However, this section does not affect valuations based on equivalent reinstatement.

Section 104 amends s.52 of the Land Compensation Act 1973 so that it now contains specific provisions in relation to land subject to a mortgage which are now to be found in new ss.52ZA and 52ZB. The former relates to land where the compensation payment amounts to less than 90 per cent of the mortgage principal and the latter to payments in excess of 90 per cent.

Section 105 inserts s.5A into the Acquisition of Land Act 1981 and gives acquiring authorities the power to require information regarding land in relation to which they are entitled to exercise a power of compulsory purchase.

## 8.4   LOSS PAYMENTS

Sections 106–109 introduce new provisions in relation to basic loss payments. The intention is to provide a new statutory scheme in the Land Compensation Act 1973 for those with an interest in an acquired property who would not be entitled to home loss payments under the scheme currently set out in ss.29–33 of the 1973 Act. The current home loss payment scheme is retained but the farm loss payments scheme is to be repealed. The stated intention of the new scheme is to make some allowance for the upset, discomfort and inconvenience of being required to leave a property (or give up an interest in it) against the owner's or occupier's wishes. Those professionals who act for property owners and occupiers of residential properties will be only too familiar with the considerable distress that compulsory purchase can cause. The new payments are to act as inducements to encourage the co-operation of owners and occupiers in land assembly projects that involve the potential use of compulsory purchase powers, thus sweetening what can sometimes be a bitter pill to swallow.

Section 106 inserts a new s.33A into the Land Compensation Act 1973. Claimants will be entitled to claim a basic loss payment in addition to the compensation paid for the value of their interest in the property and disturbance costs to the extent that they are not entitled to a home loss payment. To qualify for the payment a claimant must be either the freehold owner or a tenant for at least a year before the earliest of the date the acquiring authority takes possession, entry, vesting, the compensation is agreed or determined by the Lands Tribunal. For the purposes of this scheme compulsory acquisition includes the acquisition of an interest under either a blight or purchase notice. The claimant is entitled to a payment of 7.5 per cent of his interest up to a maximum of £75,000. Where part of the interest acquired includes a dwelling to which the person is entitled to a home loss payment, the amount of the value represented by that dwelling is offset against the payment. The new section will only apply to compulsory purchase orders made on or after the date the section comes into force.

New ss.33B and 33C are inserted into the Land Compensation Act 1973 by s.107. Section 33B provides in relation to agricultural land for the payment of an occupier's loss payment in addition to the basic loss payment. The payment is subject to the same conditions as apply to the basic loss payment. There is a maximum payment of £25,000. The payment is calculated on the basis of the greater of either 2.5 per cent of the value of the interest or, where it would be more advantageous, a formula based on the land or floor space of the building from which he is being displaced. The 'land amount' formula is £100 per hectare or part hectare up to 100 hectares and then £50 per hectare up to 300 hectares. The 'buildings amount' is £25 per square metre of the gross floor space (measured externally). Section 33C relates to non-agricultural land. The payment basis of 2.5 per cent of the value of the interest and the £25,000 ceiling apply but the land amount is £2.50 per square metre, subject to a maximum of £2,500. However, if only part of the land is acquired, the £2,500 maximum is replaced by a £300 maximum. The buildings amount remains at £25 per square metre.

The new loss payments are subject to a number of important exclusions set out in s.33D. These are where the claimant has been served with a notice or order relating to one of the following:

(1) derelict land, where a notice has been served under s.215 of the 1990 Act;
(2) a house unfit for human habitation, where a notice has been served under s.189 of the Housing Act 1985;
(3) a dwelling in disrepair, where a notice has been served under s.190 of the Housing Act 1985;
(4) a listed building in disrepair, where a repairs notice has been served prior to compulsory acquisition; or
(5) a closing order under s.264 or demolition order under s.265 of the Housing Act 1985.

There are various supplementary provisions relating to matters such as the arrangements for making claims, insolvent claimants, and claims where the claimant dies before the claim is submitted. Overall, however, the reforms introduced by the Act are relatively straightforward and ought not to attract much controversy, except in relation to the powers of acquisition. Whilst local authorities' powers are widened, they will still need to exercise those powers with sensitivity and care if litigation from disgruntled owners and occupiers is to be avoided.

# Appendix 1
# PLANNING AND COMPULSORY PURCHASE ACT 2004

## CONTENTS

## PART 1    REGIONAL FUNCTIONS

## PART 2    LOCAL DEVELOPMENT

## PART 3    DEVELOPMENT

## PART 4    DEVELOPMENT CONTROL

## PART 7    CROWN APPLICATION OF PLANNING ACTS

### CHAPTER 1    ENGLAND AND WALES

### CHAPTER 2    SCOTLAND

## PART 8   COMPULSORY PURCHASE

## PART 9   MISCELLANEOUS AND GENERAL

# PLANNING AND COMPULSORY PURCHASE ACT 2004

An Act to make provision relating to spatial development and town and country planning; and the compulsory acquisition of land.

[13 May 2004]

BE IT ENACTED by the Queen's most Excellent Majesty, by and with the advice and consent of the Lords Spiritual and Temporal, and Commons, in this present Parliament assembled, and by the authority of the same, as follows:–

## PART 1   REGIONAL FUNCTIONS

### *Spatial strategy*

#### 1 Regional Spatial Strategy

(1)   For each region there is to be a regional spatial strategy (in this Part referred to as the 'RSS').

(2)   The RSS must set out the Secretary of State's policies (however expressed) in relation to the development and use of land within the region.

(3)   In subsection (2) the references to a region include references to any area within a region which includes the area or part of the area of more than one local planning authority.

(4)  If to any extent a policy set out in the RSS conflicts with any other statement or information in the RSS the conflict must be resolved in favour of the policy.

(5)  With effect from the appointed day the RSS for a region is so much of the regional planning guidance relating to the region as the Secretary of State prescribes.

(6)  The appointed day is the day appointed for the commencement of this section.

## Planning bodies

### 2  Regional planning bodies

(1)  The Secretary of State may give a direction recognising a body to which subsection (2) applies as the regional planning body for a region (in this Part referred to as the 'RPB').

(2)  This subsection applies to a body (whether or not incorporated) which satisfies such criteria as are prescribed.

(3)  The Secretary of State must not give a direction under subsection (1) in relation to a body unless not less than 60%; of the persons who are members of the body fall within subsection (4).

(4)  A person falls within this subsection if he is a member of any of the following councils or authorities and any part of the area of the council or authority (as the case may be) falls within the region to which the direction (if given) will relate –

    (a)  a district council;

    (b)  a county council;

    (c)  a metropolitan district council;

    (d)  a National Park authority;

    (e)  the Broads authority.

(5)  The Secretary of State may give a direction withdrawing recognition of a body.

(6)  Subsection (7) applies if the Secretary of State –

    (a)  does not give a direction under subsection (1) recognising a body, or

    (b)  gives a direction under subsection (5) withdrawing recognition of a body and does not give a direction under subsection (1) recognising any other body.

(7)  In such a case the Secretary of State may exercise such of the functions of the RPB as he thinks appropriate.

(8)  A change in the membership of a body which is not incorporated does not (by itself) affect the validity of the recognition of the body.

### 3  RPB: general functions

(1)  The RPB must keep under review the RSS.

(2)  The RPB must keep under review the matters which may be expected to affect –

    (a)  development in its region or any part of the region;

    (b)  the planning of that development.

(3)  The RPB must –

    (a)  monitor the implementation of the RSS throughout the region;

    (b)  consider whether the implementation is achieving the purposes of the RSS.

(4)  The RPB must for each year prepare a report on the implementation of the RSS in the region.

(5)  The report –

    (a)  must be in respect of such period of 12 months as is prescribed;

    (b)  must be in such form and contain such information as is prescribed;

    (c)  must be submitted to the Secretary of State on such date as is prescribed.

(6)  The RPB must give advice to any other body or person if it thinks that to do so will help to achieve implementation of the RSS.

**4 Assistance from certain local authorities**

(1)  For the purpose of the exercise of its functions under sections 3(1) and (3)(a) and 5(1) the RPB must seek the advice of each authority in its region which is an authority falling within subsection (4).

(2)  The authority must give the RPB advice as to the exercise of the function to the extent that the exercise of the function is capable of affecting (directly or indirectly) the exercise by the authority of any function it has.

(3)  The advice mentioned in subsection (1) includes advice relating to the inclusion in the RSS of specific policies relating to any part of the region.

(4)  Each of the following authorities fall within this subsection if their area or any part of their area is in the RPB's region –

  (a)  a county council;
  (b)  a metropolitan district council;
  (c)  a district council for an area for which there is no county council;
  (d)  a National Park authority.

(5)  The RPB may make arrangements with an authority falling within subsection (4) or with any district council the whole or part of whose area is in the region for the discharge by the authority or council of a function of the RPB.

(6)  The RPB may reimburse an authority or council which exercises functions by virtue of such arrangements for any expenditure incurred by the authority or council in doing so.

(7)  Subsection (5) does not apply to a function of the RPB under section 5(8).

(8)  Any arrangements made for the purposes of subsection (5) must be taken to be arrangements between local authorities for the purposes of section 101 of the Local Government Act 1972 (c. 70).

(9)  Nothing in this section affects any power which a body which is recognised as an RPB has apart from this section.


## RSS revision

**5  RSS: revision**

(1)  The RPB must prepare a draft revision of the RSS –

  (a)  when it appears to it necessary or expedient to do so;
  (b)  at such time as is prescribed;
  (c)  if it is directed to do so under section 10(1).

(2)  But the RPB must give notice to the Secretary of State of its intention to prepare a draft revision under subsection (1)(a).

(3)  In preparing a draft revision the RPB must have regard to –

  (a)  national policies and advice contained in guidance issued by the Secretary of State;
  (b)  the RSS for each adjoining region;
  (c)  the spatial development strategy if any part of its region adjoins Greater London;
  (d)  the Wales Spatial Plan if any part of its region adjoins Wales;
  (e)  the resources likely to be available for implementation of the RSS;
  (f)  the desirability of making different provision in relation to different parts of the region;
  (g)  such other matters as are prescribed.

(4)  In preparing a draft revision the RPB must also –

  (a)  carry out an appraisal of the sustainability of the proposals in the draft, and
  (b)  prepare a report of the findings of the appraisal.

(5) If the RPB decides to make different provision for different parts of the region the detailed proposals for such different provision must first be made by an authority which falls within section 4(4).

(6) But if the RPB and the authority agree, the detailed proposals may first be made –

   (a) by a district council which is not such an authority, or
   (b) by the RPB.

(7) The Secretary of State may by regulations make provision as to –

   (a) the subject matter of a draft revision prepared in pursuance of subsection (1)(b);
   (b) any further documents which must be prepared by the RPB in connection with the preparation of a draft revision;
   (c) the form and content of any draft, report or other document prepared under this section.

(8) When the RPB has prepared a draft revision, the report to be prepared under subsection (4)(b) and any other document to be prepared in pursuance of subsection (7)(b) it must –

   (a) publish the draft revision, report and other document;
   (b) submit them to the Secretary of State.

(9) But the RPB may withdraw a draft revision at any time before it submits the draft to the Secretary of State under subsection (8)(b).

## 6 RSS: community involvement

(1) For the purposes of the exercise of its functions under section 5, the RPB must prepare and publish a statement of its policies as to the involvement of persons who appear to the RPB to have an interest in the exercise of those functions.

(2) The RPB must keep the policies under review and from time to time must –

   (a) revise the statement;
   (b) publish the revised statement.

(3) The RPB must comply with the statement or revised statement (as the case may be) in the exercise of its functions under section 5.

(4) The documents mentioned in section 5(7)(b) and (c) include the statement and revised statement.

## 7 RSS: Secretary of State's functions

(1) This section applies when the Secretary of State receives a draft revision of the RSS.

(2) Any person may make representations on the draft.

(3) The Secretary of State may arrange for an examination in public to be held into the draft.

(4) In deciding whether an examination in public is held the Secretary of State must have regard to –

   (a) the extent of the revisions proposed by the draft;
   (b) the extent and nature of the consultation on the draft before it was published;
   (c) the level of interest shown in the draft;
   (d) such other matters as he thinks appropriate.

## 8 RSS: examination in public

(1) This section applies if the Secretary of State decides that an examination in public is to be held of a draft revision of the RSS.

(2) The examination must be held before a person appointed by the Secretary of State.

(3) No person has a right to be heard at an examination in public.

(4) The Secretary of State may, after consultation with the Lord Chancellor, make regulations with respect to the procedure to be followed at an examination in public.

(5) The person appointed under subsection (2) must make a report of the examination to the Secretary of State.

(6) The Secretary of State may by regulations make provision as to the procedure to be followed in connection with the recommendations of the person appointed under subsection (2).

(7) An examination in public –

    (a) is a statutory inquiry for the purposes of section 1(1)(c) of the Tribunals and Inquiries Act 1992 (c. 53) (report on administrative procedures);

    (b) is not a statutory inquiry for any other purpose of that Act.

## 9 RSS: further procedure

(1) If no examination in public is held the Secretary of State must consider any representations made on the draft revision of the RSS under section 7(2).

(2) If an examination in public is held the Secretary of State must consider –

    (a) the report of the person appointed to hold the examination;

    (b) any representations which are not considered by the person appointed to hold the examination.

(3) If after proceeding under subsection (1) or (2) the Secretary of State proposes to make any changes to the draft he must publish –

    (a) the changes he proposes to make;

    (b) his reasons for doing so.

(4) Any person may make representations on the proposed changes.

(5) The Secretary of State must consider any such representations.

(6) The Secretary of State must then publish –

    (a) the revision of the RSS incorporating such changes as he thinks fit;

    (b) his reasons for making the changes.

(7) But the Secretary of State may withdraw a draft revision of an RSS at any time before he publishes the revision of the RSS under subsection (6).

## 10 Secretary of State: additional powers

(1) If the Secretary of State thinks it is necessary or expedient to do so he may direct an RPB to prepare a draft revision of the RSS.

(2) Such a direction may require the RPB to prepare the draft revision –

    (a) in relation to such aspects of the RSS as are specified;

    (b) in accordance with such timetable as is specified.

(3) The Secretary of State may prepare a draft revision of the RSS if the RPB fails to comply with –

    (a) a direction under subsection (1),

    (b) section 5(1)(b), or

    (c) regulations under section 5(7) or 11.

(4) If the Secretary of State prepares a draft revision under subsection (3) –

    (a) section 7 applies as it does if the Secretary of State receives a draft revision from the RPB, and

    (b) sections 8 and 9 apply.

(5) If the Secretary of State thinks it necessary or expedient to do so he may at any time revoke –

    (a) an RSS;

    (b) such parts of an RSS as he thinks appropriate.

(6) The Secretary of State may by regulations make provision as to the procedure to be followed for the purposes of subsection (3).

(7) Subsection (8) applies if –

    (a) any step has been taken in connection with the preparation of any part of regional planning guidance, and

    (b) the Secretary of State thinks that the step corresponds to a step which must be taken under this Part in connection with the preparation and publication of a revision of the RSS.

(8) The Secretary of State may by order provide for the part of the regional planning guidance to have effect as a revision of the RSS.

## Supplementary

### 11 Regulations

(1) The Secretary of State may by regulations make provision in connection with the exercise by any person of functions under this Part.

(2) The regulations may in particular make provision as to –

    (a) the procedure to be followed for the purposes of section 5;

    (b) the procedure to be followed by the RPB in connection with its functions under section 6;

    (c) requirements about the giving of notice and publicity;

    (d) requirements about inspection by the public of a draft revision or any other document;

    (e) the nature and extent of consultation with and participation by the public in anything done under this Part;

    (f) the making of representations about any matter to be included in an RSS;

    (g) consideration of any such representations;

    (h) the remuneration and allowances payable to a person appointed to carry out an examination in public under section 8;

    (i) the determination of the time at which anything must be done for the purposes of this Part;

    (j) the manner of publication of any draft, report or other document published under this Part;

    (k) monitoring the exercise by RPBs of their functions under this Part;

    (l) the making of reasonable charges for the provision of copies of documents required by or under this Part.

### 12 Supplementary

(1) A region is a region (except London) specified in Schedule 1 to the Regional Development Agencies Act 1998 (c. 45).

(2) But the Secretary of State may by order direct that if the area of a National Park falls within more than one region it is treated as falling wholly within such region as is specified in the order.

(3) Regional planning guidance for a region is a document issued by the Secretary of State setting out his policies (however expressed) in relation to the development and use of land within the region.

(4) The Secretary of State is the Secretary of State for the time being having general responsibility for policy in relation to the development and use of land.

(5) Subsection (4) does not apply for the purposes of section 5(3)(a).

(6) References to a revision or draft revision of an RSS include references to a revision or draft revision –

    (a) of any part of an RSS;

    (b) of the RSS as it relates to any part of a region.

(7) This section has effect for the purposes of this Part.

## PART 2    LOCAL DEVELOPMENT

### *Survey*

### 13  Survey of area

(1)  The local planning authority must keep under review the matters which may be expected to affect the development of their area or the planning of its development.

(2)  These matters include –

    (a)  the principal physical, economic, social and environmental characteristics of the area of the authority;

    (b)  the principal purposes for which land is used in the area;

    (c)  the size, composition and distribution of the population of the area;

    (d)  the communications, transport system and traffic of the area;

    (e)  any other considerations which may be expected to affect those matters;

    (f)  such other matters as may be prescribed or as the Secretary of State (in a particular case) may direct.

(3)  The matters also include –

    (a)  any changes which the authority think may occur in relation to any other matter;

    (b)  the effect such changes are likely to have on the development of the authority's area or on the planning of such development.

(4)  The local planning authority may also keep under review and examine the matters mentioned in subsections (2) and (3) in relation to any neighbouring area to the extent that those matters may be expected to affect the area of the authority.

(5)  In exercising a function under subsection (4) a local planning authority must consult with the local planning authority for the neighbouring area in question.

(6)  If a neighbouring area is in Wales references to the local planning authority for that area must be construed in accordance with Part 6.

### 14  Survey of area: county councils

(1)  A county council in respect of so much of their area for which there is a district council must keep under review the matters which may be expected to affect development of that area or the planning of its development in so far as the development relates to a county matter.

(2)  Subsections (2) to (6) of section 13 apply for the purposes of subsection (1) as they apply for the purposes of that section; and references to the local planning authority must be construed as references to the county council.

(3)  The Secretary of State may by regulations require or (in a particular case) may direct a county council to keep under review in relation to so much of their area as is mentioned in subsection (1) such of the matters mentioned in section 13(1) to (4) as he prescribes or directs (as the case may be).

(4)  For the purposes of subsection (3) –

    (a)  it is immaterial whether any development relates to a county matter;

    (b)  if a matter which is prescribed or in respect of which the Secretary of State gives a direction falls within section 13(4) the county council must consult the local planning authority for the area in question.

(5)  The county council must make available the results of their review under subsection (3) to such persons as the Secretary of State prescribes or directs (as the case may be).

(6)  References to a county matter must be construed in accordance with paragraph 1 of Schedule 1 to the principal Act (ignoring sub-paragraph (1)(i)).

## Development schemes

### 15 Local development scheme

(1) The local planning authority must prepare and maintain a scheme to be known as their local development scheme.

(2) The scheme must specify –

   (a) the documents which are to be local development documents;

   (b) the subject matter and geographical area to which each document is to relate;

   (c) which documents are to be development plan documents;

   (d) which documents (if any) are to be prepared jointly with one or more other local planning authorities;

   (e) any matter or area in respect of which the authority have agreed (or propose to agree) to the constitution of a joint committee under section 29;

   (f) the timetable for the preparation and revision of the documents;

   (g) such other matters as are prescribed.

(3) The local planning authority must –

   (a) prepare the scheme in accordance with such other requirements as are prescribed;

   (b) submit the scheme to the Secretary of State at such time as is prescribed or as the Secretary of State (in a particular case) directs;

   (c) at that time send a copy of the scheme to the RPB or (if the authority are a London borough) to the Mayor of London.

(4) The Secretary of State may direct the local planning authority to make such amendments to the scheme as he thinks appropriate.

(5) Such a direction must contain the Secretary of State's reasons for giving it.

(6) The local planning authority must comply with a direction given under subsection (4).

(7) The Secretary of State may make regulations as to the following matters –

   (a) publicity about the scheme;

   (b) making the scheme available for inspection by the public;

   (c) requirements to be met for the purpose of bringing the scheme into effect.

(8) The local planning authority must revise their local development scheme –

   (a) at such time as they consider appropriate;

   (b) when directed to do so by the Secretary of State.

(9) Subsections (2) to (7) apply to the revision of a scheme as they apply to the preparation of the scheme.

### 16 Minerals and waste development scheme

(1) A county council in respect of any part of their area for which there is a district council must prepare and maintain a scheme to be known as their minerals and waste development scheme.

(2) Section 15 (ignoring subsections (1) and (2)(e)) applies in relation to a minerals and waste development scheme as it applies in relation to a local development scheme.

(3) This Part applies to a minerals and waste development scheme as it applies to a local development scheme and for that purpose –

   (a) references to a local development scheme include references to a minerals and waste development scheme;

   (b) references to a local planning authority include references to a county council.

(4) But subsection (3) does not apply to –

   (a) section 17(3);

   (b) section 24(1)(b), (4) and (7);

   (c) the references in section 24(5) to subsection (4) and the Mayor;

   (d) sections 29 to 31.

## *Documents*

### 17  Local development documents

(1)  Documents which must be specified in the local development scheme as local development documents are –

(a)  documents of such descriptions as are prescribed;

(b)  the local planning authority's statement of community involvement.

(2)  The local planning authority may also specify in the scheme such other documents as they think are appropriate.

(3)  The local development documents must (taken as a whole) set out the authority's policies (however expressed) relating to the development and use of land in their area.

(4)  In the case of the documents which are included in a minerals and waste development scheme they must also (taken as a whole) set out the authority's policies (however expressed) in relation to development which is a county matter within the meaning of paragraph 1 of Schedule 1 to the principal Act (ignoring sub-paragraph (1)(i)).

(5)  If to any extent a policy set out in a local development document conflicts with any other statement or information in the document the conflict must be resolved in favour of the policy.

(6)  The authority must keep under review their local development documents having regard to the results of any review carried out under section 13 or 14.

(7)  Regulations under this section may prescribe –

(a)  which descriptions of local development documents are development plan documents;

(b)  the form and content of the local development documents;

(c)  the time at which any step in the preparation of any such document must be taken.

(8)  A document is a local development document only in so far as it or any part of it –

(a)  is adopted by resolution of the local planning authority as a local development document;

(b)  is approved by the Secretary of State under section 21 or 27.

### 18  Statement of community involvement

(1)  The local planning authority must prepare a statement of community involvement.

(2)  The statement of community involvement is a statement of the authority's policy as to the involvement in the exercise of the authority's functions under sections 19, 26 and 28 of this Act and Part 3 of the principal Act of persons who appear to the authority to have an interest in matters relating to development in their area.

(3)  For the purposes of sections 19(2) and 24 the statement of community involvement is not a local development document.

(4)  Section 20 applies to the statement of community involvement as if it were a development plan document.

(5)  But in section 20(5)(a) –

(a)  the reference to section 19 must be construed as if it does not include a reference to subsection (2) of that section;

(b)  the reference to section 24(1) must be ignored.

(6)  In the following provisions of this Part references to a development plan document include references to the statement of community involvement –

(a)  section 22;

(b)  section 23(2) to (5).

**19  Preparation of local development documents**

(1)  Local development documents must be prepared in accordance with the local development scheme.

(2)  In preparing a local development document the local planning authority must have regard to –

    (a)  national policies and advice contained in guidance issued by the Secretary of State;

    (b)  the RSS for the region in which the area of the authority is situated, if the area is outside Greater London;

    (c)  the spatial development strategy if the authority are a London borough or if any part of the authority's area adjoins Greater London;

    (d)  the RSS for any region which adjoins the area of the authority;

    (e)  the Wales Spatial Plan if any part of the authority's area adjoins Wales;

    (f)  the community strategy prepared by the authority;

    (g)  the community strategy for any other authority whose area comprises any part of the area of the local planning authority;

    (h)  any other local development document which has been adopted by the authority;

    (i)  the resources likely to be available for implementing the proposals in the document;

    (j)  such other matters as the Secretary of State prescribes.

(3)  In preparing the other local development documents the authority must also comply with their statement of community involvement.

(4)  But subsection (3) does not apply at any time before the authority have adopted their statement of community involvement.

(5)  The local planning authority must also –

    (a)  carry out an appraisal of the sustainability of the proposals in each document;

    (b)  prepare a report of the findings of the appraisal.

(6)  The Secretary of State may by regulations make provision –

    (a)  as to any further documents which must be prepared by the authority in connection with the preparation of a local development document;

    (b)  as to the form and content of such documents.

(7)  The community strategy is the strategy prepared by an authority under section 4 of the Local Government Act 2000 (c. 22).

**20  Independent examination**

(1)  The local planning authority must submit every development plan document to the Secretary of State for independent examination.

(2)  But the authority must not submit such a document unless –

    (a)  they have complied with any relevant requirements contained in regulations under this Part, and

    (b)  they think the document is ready for independent examination.

(3)  The authority must also send to the Secretary of State (in addition to the development plan document) such other documents (or copies of documents) and such information as is prescribed.

(4)  The examination must be carried out by a person appointed by the Secretary of State.

(5)  The purpose of an independent examination is to determine in respect of the development plan document –

    (a)  whether it satisfies the requirements of sections 19 and 24(1), regulations under section 17(7) and any regulations under section 36 relating to the preparation of development plan documents;

    (b)  whether it is sound.

(6) Any person who makes representations seeking to change a development plan document must (if he so requests) be given the opportunity to appear before and be heard by the person carrying out the examination.

(7) The person appointed to carry out the examination must –

    (a)  make recommendations;

    (b)  give reasons for the recommendations.

(8) The local planning authority must publish the recommendations and the reasons.

## 21  Intervention by Secretary of State

(1) If the Secretary of State thinks that a local development document is unsatisfactory –

    (a)  he may at any time before the document is adopted under section 23 direct the local planning authority to modify the document in accordance with the direction;

    (b)  if he gives such a direction he must state his reasons for doing so.

(2) The authority –

    (a)  must comply with the direction;

    (b)  must not adopt the document unless the Secretary of State gives notice that he is satisfied that they have complied with the direction.

(3) But subsection (2) does not apply if the Secretary of State withdraws the direction.

(4) At any time before a development plan document is adopted by a local planning authority the Secretary of State may direct that the document (or any part of it) is submitted to him for his approval.

(5) The following paragraphs apply if the Secretary of State gives a direction under subsection (4) –

    (a)  the authority must not take any step in connection with the adoption of the document until the Secretary of State gives his decision;

    (b)  if the direction is given before the authority have submitted the document under section 20(1) the Secretary of State must hold an independent examination and section 20(4) to (7) applies accordingly;

    (c)  if the direction is given after the authority have submitted the document but before the person appointed to carry out the examination has made his recommendations he must make his recommendations to the Secretary of State;

    (d)  the document has no effect unless it or (if the direction relates to only part of a document) the part has been approved by the Secretary of State.

(6) The Secretary of State must publish the recommendations made to him by virtue of subsection (5)(b) or (c) and the reasons of the person making the recommendations.

(7) In considering a document or part of a document submitted under subsection (4) the Secretary of State may take account of any matter which he thinks is relevant.

(8) It is immaterial whether any such matter was taken account of by the authority.

(9) In relation to a document or part of a document submitted to him under subsection (4) the Secretary of State –

    (a)  may approve, approve subject to specified modifications or reject the document or part;

    (b)  must give reasons for his decision under paragraph (a).

(10) In the exercise of any function under this section the Secretary of State must have regard to the local development scheme.

## 22  Withdrawal of local development documents

(1) A local planning authority may at any time before a local development document is adopted under section 23 withdraw the document.

(2)  But subsection (1) does not apply to a development plan document at any time after the document has been submitted for independent examination under section 20 unless –

(a)  the person carrying out the examination recommends that the document is withdrawn and that recommendation is not overruled by a direction given by the Secretary of State, or

(b)  the Secretary of State directs that the document must be withdrawn.

### 23  Adoption of local development documents

(1)  The local planning authority may adopt a local development document (other than a development plan document) either as originally prepared or as modified to take account of –

(a)  any representations made in relation to the document;

(b)  any other matter they think is relevant.

(2)  The authority may adopt a development plan document as originally prepared if the person appointed to carry out the independent examination of the document recommends that the document as originally prepared is adopted.

(3)  The authority may adopt a development plan document with modifications if the person appointed to carry out the independent examination of the document recommends the modifications.

(4)  The authority must not adopt a development plan document unless they do so in accordance with subsection (2) or (3).

(5)  A document is adopted for the purposes of this section if it is adopted by resolution of the authority.

### 24  Conformity with regional strategy

(1)  The local development documents must be in general conformity with –

(a)  the RSS (if the area of the local planning authority is in a region other than London);

(b)  the spatial development strategy (if the local planning authority are a London borough).

(2)  A local planning authority whose area is in a region other than London –

(a)  must request the opinion in writing of the RPB as to the general conformity of a development plan document with the RSS;

(b)  may request the opinion in writing of the RPB as to the general conformity of any other local development document with the RSS.

(3)  Not later than the end of the period prescribed for the purposes of this section the RPB must send its opinion to –

(a)  the Secretary of State;

(b)  the local planning authority.

(4)  A local planning authority which are a London borough –

(a)  must request the opinion in writing of the Mayor of London as to the general conformity of a development plan document with the spatial development strategy;

(b)  may request the opinion in writing of the Mayor as to the general conformity of any other local development document with the spatial development strategy.

(5)  Whether or not the local planning authority make a request mentioned in subsection (2) or (4) the RPB or the Mayor (as the case may be) may give an opinion as to the general conformity of a local development document with the RSS or the spatial development strategy (as the case may be).

(6) If in the opinion of the RPB a document is not in general conformity with the RSS the RPB must be taken to have made representations seeking a change to the document.

(7) If in the opinion of the Mayor a document is not in general conformity with the spatial development strategy the Mayor must be taken to have made representations seeking a change to the document.

(8) But the Secretary of State may in any case direct that subsection (6) must be ignored.

(9) If at any time no body is recognised as the RPB under section 2 the functions of the RPB under this section must be exercised by the Secretary of State and subsections (3)(a), (6) and (8) of this section must be ignored.

## 25 Revocation of local development documents

The Secretary of State –

(a) may at any time revoke a local development document at the request of the local planning authority;

(b) may prescribe descriptions of local development document which may be revoked by the authority themselves.

## 26 Revision of local development documents

(1) The local planning authority may at any time prepare a revision of a local development document.

(2) The authority must prepare a revision of a local development document –

(a) if the Secretary of State directs them to do so, and

(b) in accordance with such timetable as he directs.

(3) This Part applies to the revision of a local development document as it applies to the preparation of the document.

(4) Subsection (5) applies if any part of the area of the local planning authority is an area to which an enterprise zone scheme relates.

(5) As soon as practicable after the occurrence of a relevant event –

(a) the authority must review every local development document in the light of the enterprise zone scheme;

(b) if they think that any modifications of the document are required in consequence of the scheme they must prepare a revised document containing the modifications.

(6) The following are relevant events –

(a) the making of an order under paragraph 5 of Schedule 32 to the Local Government, Planning and Land Act 1980 (c. 65) (designation of enterprise zone);

(b) the giving of notification under paragraph 11(1) of that Schedule (approval of modification of enterprise zone scheme).

(7) References to an enterprise zone and an enterprise zone scheme must be construed in accordance with that Act.

## 27 Secretary of State's default power

(1) This section applies if the Secretary of State thinks that a local planning authority are failing or omitting to do anything it is necessary for them to do in connection with the preparation, revision or adoption of a development plan document.

(2) The Secretary of State must hold an independent examination and section 20(4) to (7) applies accordingly.

(3) The Secretary of State must publish the recommendations and reasons of the person appointed to hold the examination.

(4) The Secretary of State may –

(a) prepare or revise (as the case may be) the document, and

(b) approve the document as a local development document.

(5) The Secretary of State must give reasons for anything he does in pursuance of subsection (4).

(6) The authority must reimburse the Secretary of State for any expenditure he incurs in connection with anything –

    (a)  which is done by him under subsection (4), and

    (b)  which the authority failed or omitted to do as mentioned in subsection (1).

## 28 Joint local development documents

(1) Two or more local planning authorities may agree to prepare one or more joint local development documents.

(2) This Part applies for the purposes of any step which may be or is required to be taken in relation to a joint local development document as it applies for the purposes of any step which may be or is required to be taken in relation to a local development document.

(3) For the purposes of subsection (2) anything which must be done by or in relation to a local planning authority in connection with a local development document must be done by or in relation to each of the authorities mentioned in subsection (1) in connection with a joint local development document.

(4) Any requirement of this Part in relation to the RSS is a requirement in relation to the RSS for the region in which each authority mentioned in subsection (1) is situated.

(5) If the authorities mentioned in subsection (1) include one or more London boroughs the requirements of this Part in relation to the spatial development strategy also apply.

(6) Subsections (7) to (9) apply if a local planning authority withdraw from an agreement mentioned in subsection (1).

(7) Any step taken in relation to the document must be treated as a step taken by –

    (a)  an authority which were a party to the agreement for the purposes of any corresponding document prepared by them;

    (b)  two or more other authorities who were parties to the agreement for the purposes of any corresponding joint local development document.

(8) Any independent examination of a local development document to which the agreement relates must be suspended.

(9) If before the end of the period prescribed for the purposes of this subsection an authority which were a party to the agreement request the Secretary of State to do so he may direct that –

    (a)  the examination is resumed in relation to the corresponding document;

    (b)  any step taken for the purposes of the suspended examination has effect for the purposes of the resumed examination.

(10) A joint local development document is a local development document prepared jointly by two or more local planning authorities.

(11) The Secretary of State may by regulations make provision as to what is a corresponding document.

## *Joint committees*

## 29 Joint committees

(1) This section applies if one or more local planning authorities agree with one or more county councils in relation to any area of such a council for which there is also a district council to establish a joint committee to be, for the purposes of this Part, the local planning authority-

    (a)  for the area specified in the agreement;

    (b)  in respect of such matters as are so specified.

(2) The Secretary of State may by order constitute a joint committee to be the local planning authority –

    (a)  for the area;

    (b)  in respect of those matters.

(3) Such an order –

    (a)  must specify the authority or authorities and county council or councils (the constituent authorities) which are to constitute the joint committee;

    (b)  may make provision as to such other matters as the Secretary of State thinks are necessary or expedient to facilitate the exercise by the joint committee of its functions.

(4) Provision under subsection (3)(b) –

    (a)  may include provision corresponding to provisions relating to joint committees in Part 6 of the Local Government Act 1972 (c. 70);

    (b)  may apply (with or without modifications) such enactments relating to local authorities as the Secretary of State thinks appropriate.

(5) If an order under this section is annulled in pursuance of a resolution of either House of Parliament –

    (a)  with effect from the date of the resolution the joint committee ceases to be the local planning authority as mentioned in subsection (2);

    (b)  anything which the joint committee (as the local planning authority) was required to do for the purposes of this Part must be done for their area by each local planning authority which were a constituent authority of the joint committee;

    (c)  each of those local planning authorities must revise their local development scheme accordingly.

(6) Nothing in this section or section 30 confers on a local planning authority constituted by virtue of an order under this section any function in relation to section 13 or 14.

(7) The policies adopted by the joint committee in the exercise of its functions under this Part must be taken for the purposes of the planning Acts to be the policies of each of the constituent authorities which are a local planning authority.

(8) Subsection (9) applies to any function –

    (a)  which is conferred on a local planning authority (within the meaning of the principal Act) under or by virtue of the planning Acts, and

    (b)  which relates to the authority's local development scheme or local development documents.

(9) If the authority is a constituent authority of a joint committee references to the authority's local development scheme or local development documents must be construed as including references to the scheme or documents of the joint committee.

(10) For the purposes of subsection (4) a local authority is any of the following –

    (a)  a county council;

    (b)  a district council;

    (c)  a London borough council.

## 30  Joint committees: additional functions

(1) This section applies if the constituent authorities to a joint committee agree that the joint committee is to be, for the purposes of this Part, the local planning authority for any area or matter which is not the subject of –

    (a)  an order under section 29, or

    (b)  an earlier agreement under this section.

(2) Each of the constituent authorities and the joint committee must revise their local development scheme in accordance with the agreement.

(3)  With effect from the date when the last such revision takes effect the joint committee is, for the purposes of this Part, the local planning authority for the area or matter mentioned in subsection (1).

### 31  Dissolution of joint committee

(1)  This section applies if a constituent authority requests the Secretary of State to revoke an order constituting a joint committee as the local planning authority for any area or in respect of any matter.

(2)  The Secretary of State may revoke the order.

(3)  Any step taken by the joint committee in relation to a local development scheme or a local development document must be treated for the purposes of any corresponding scheme or document as a step taken by a successor authority.

(4)  A successor authority is –

(a)  a local planning authority which were a constituent authority of the joint committee;

(b)  a joint committee constituted by order under section 29 for an area which does not include an area which was not part of the area of the joint committee mentioned in subsection (1).

(5)  If the revocation takes effect at any time when an independent examination is being carried out in relation to a local development document the examination must be suspended.

(6)  But if before the end of the period prescribed for the purposes of this subsection a successor authority falling within subsection (4)(a) requests the Secretary of State to do so he may direct that –

(a)  the examination is resumed in relation to the corresponding document;

(b)  any step taken for the purposes of the suspended examination has effect for the purposes of the resumed examination.

(7)  The Secretary of State may by regulations make provision as to what is a corresponding scheme or document.

## Miscellaneous

### 32  Exclusion of certain representations

(1)  This section applies to any representation or objection in respect of anything which is done or is proposed to be done in pursuance of –

(a)  an order or scheme under section 10, 14, 16, 18, 106(1) or (3) or 108(1) of the Highways Act 1980 (c. 66);

(b)  an order or scheme under section 7, 9, 11, 13 or 20 of the Highways Act 1959 (c. 25), section 3 of the Highways (Miscellaneous Provisions) Act 1961 (c. 63) or section 1 or 10 of the Highways Act 1971 (c. 41) (which provisions were replaced by the provisions mentioned in paragraph (a));

(c)  an order under section 1 of the New Towns Act 1981 (c. 64).

(2)  If the Secretary of State or a local planning authority thinks that a representation made in relation to a local development document is in substance a representation or objection to which this section applies he or they (as the case may be) may disregard it.

### 33  Urban development corporations

The Secretary of State may direct that this Part does not apply to the area of an urban development corporation.

### 34 Guidance

In the exercise of any function conferred under or by virtue of this Part the local planning authority must have regard to any guidance issued by the Secretary of State.

### 35 Annual monitoring report

(1) Every local planning authority must make an annual report to the Secretary of State.
(2) The annual report must contain such information as is prescribed as to –

(a) the implementation of the local development scheme;
(b) the extent to which the policies set out in the local development documents are being achieved.

(3) The annual report must –

(a) be in respect of such period of 12 months as is prescribed;
(b) be made at such time as is prescribed;
(c) be in such form as is prescribed;
(d) contain such other matter as is prescribed.

## General

### 36 Regulations

(1) The Secretary of State may by regulations make provision in connection with the exercise by any person of functions under this Part.
(2) The regulations may in particular make provision as to –

(a) the procedure to be followed by the local planning authority in carrying out the appraisal under section 19;
(b) the procedure to be followed in the preparation of local development documents;
(c) requirements about the giving of notice and publicity;
(d) requirements about inspection by the public of a local development document or any other document;
(e) the nature and extent of consultation with and participation by the public in anything done under this Part;
(f) the making of representations about any matter to be included in a local development document;
(g) consideration of any such representations;
(h) the remuneration and allowances payable to a person appointed to carry out an independent examination under section 20;
(i) the determination of the time at which anything must be done for the purposes of this Part;
(j) the manner of publication of any draft, report or other document published under this Part;
(k) monitoring the exercise by local planning authorities of their functions under this Part;
(l) the making of reasonable charges for the provision of copies of documents required by or under this Part.

### 37 Interpretation

(1) Local development scheme must be construed in accordance with section 15.
(2) Local development document must be construed in accordance with section 17.
(3) A development plan document is a document which –

(a) is a local development document, and
(b) forms part of the development plan.

(4) Local planning authorities are –

(a)   district councils;

(b)   London borough councils;

(c)   metropolitan district councils;

(d)   county councils in relation to any area in England for which there is no district council;

(e)   the Broads Authority.

(5)   A National Park authority is the local planning authority for the whole of its area and subsection (4) must be construed subject to that.

(6)   RSS and RPB must be construed in accordance with Part 1.

(7)   This section applies for the purposes of this Part.

## PART 3   DEVELOPMENT

### Development plan

#### 38   Development plan

(1)   A reference to the development plan in any enactment mentioned in subsection (7) must be construed in accordance with subsections (2) to (5).

(2)   For the purposes of any area in Greater London the development plan is –

(a)   the spatial development strategy, and

(b)   the development plan documents (taken as a whole) which have been adopted or approved in relation to that area.

(3)   For the purposes of any other area in England the development plan is –

(a)   the regional spatial strategy for the region in which the area is situated, and

(b)   the development plan documents (taken as a whole) which have been adopted or approved in relation to that area.

(4)   For the purposes of any area in Wales the development plan is the local development plan adopted or approved in relation to that area.

(5)   If to any extent a policy contained in a development plan for an area conflicts with another policy in the development plan the conflict must be resolved in favour of the policy which is contained in the last document to be adopted, approved or published (as the case may be).

(6)   If regard is to be had to the development plan for the purpose of any determination to be made under the planning Acts the determination must be made in accordance with the plan unless material considerations indicate otherwise.

(7)   The enactments are –

(a)   this Act;

(b)   the planning Acts;

(c)   any other enactment relating to town and country planning;

(d)   the Land Compensation Act 1961 (c. 33);

(e)   the Highways Act 1980 (c. 66).

(8)   In subsection (5) references to a development plan include a development plan for the purposes of paragraph 1 of Schedule 8.

### Sustainable development

#### 39   Sustainable development

(1)   This section applies to any person who or body which exercises any function –

(a)  under Part 1 in relation to a regional spatial strategy;

(b)  under Part 2 in relation to local development documents;

(c)  under Part 6 in relation to the Wales Spatial Plan or a local development plan.

(2)  The person or body must exercise the function with the objective of contributing to the achievement of sustainable development.

(3)  For the purposes of subsection (2) the person or body must have regard to national policies and advice contained in guidance issued by –

(a)  the Secretary of State for the purposes of subsection (1)(a) and (b);

(b)  the National Assembly for Wales for the purposes of subsection (1)(c).

## PART 4   DEVELOPMENT CONTROL

### Local development orders

#### 40  Local development orders

(1)  In the principal Act after section 61 (supplementary provision about development orders) there are inserted the following sections-

### 'Local development orders

#### 61A  Local development orders

(1)  A local planning authority may by order (a local development order) make provision to implement policies –

(a)  in one or more development plan documents (within the meaning of Part 2 of the Planning and Compulsory Purchase Act 2004);

(b)  in a local development plan (within the meaning of Part 6 of that Act).

(2)  A local development order may grant planning permission –

(a)  for development specified in the order;

(b)  for development of any class so specified.

(3)  A local development order may relate to –

(a)  all land in the area of the relevant authority;

(b)  any part of that land;

(c)  a site specified in the order.

(4)  A local development order may make different provision for different descriptions of land.

(5)  But a development order may specify any area or class of development in respect of which a local development order must not be made.

(6)  A local planning authority may revoke a local development order at any time.

(7)  Schedule 4A makes provision in connection with local development orders.

#### 61B  Intervention by Secretary of State or National Assembly

(1)  At any time before a local development order is adopted by a local planning authority the appropriate authority may direct that the order (or any part of it) is submitted to it for its approval.

(2)  If the appropriate authority gives a direction under subsection (1) –

(a)  the authority must not take any step in connection with the adoption of the order until the appropriate authority gives its decision;

(b)  the order has no effect unless it (or, if the direction relates to only part of an order, the part) has been approved by the appropriate authority.

(3) In considering an order or part of an order submitted under subsection (1) the appropriate authority may take account of any matter which it thinks is relevant.

(4) It is immaterial whether any such matter was taken account of by the local planning authority.

(5) The appropriate authority –

    (a)    may approve or reject an order or part of an order submitted to it under subsection (1);

    (b)    must give reasons for its decision under paragraph (a).

(6) If the appropriate authority thinks that a local development order is unsatisfactory –

    (a)    it may at any time before the order is adopted by the local planning authority direct them to modify it in accordance with the direction;

    (b)    if it gives such a direction it must state its reasons for doing so.

(7) The local planning authority –

    (a)    must comply with the direction;

    (b)    must not adopt the order unless the appropriate authority gives notice that it is satisfied that they have complied with the direction.

(8) The appropriate authority –

    (a)    may at any time by order revoke a local development order if it thinks it is expedient to do so;

    (b)    must, if it revokes a local development order, state its reasons for doing so.

(9) Subsections (3) to (6) of section 100 apply to an order under subsection (8) above as they apply to an order under subsection (1) of that section and for that purpose references to the Secretary of State must be construed as references to the appropriate authority.

(10) The appropriate authority is –

    (a)    the Secretary of State in relation to England;

    (b)    the National Assembly for Wales in relation to Wales.

**61C Permission granted by local development order**

(1) Planning permission granted by a local development order may be granted –

    (a)    unconditionally, or

    (b)    subject to such conditions or limitations as are specified in the order.

(2) If the permission is granted for development of a specified description the order may enable the local planning authority to direct that the permission does not apply in relation to –

    (a)    development in a particular area, or

    (b)    any particular development.'

(2) In each of the following provisions of the principal Act in each place where it occurs after 'development order' there is inserted 'or a local development order' –

    (a)    section 56(5)(a) (definition of material development);

    (b)    section 57(3) (extent of permission granted by development order);

    (c)    section 58(1)(a) (grant of planning permission by development order);

    (d)    section 77(1) (certain applications to be referred to the Secretary of State);

    (e)    section 78(1)(c) (right of appeal in relation to certain planning decisions);

    (f)    section 88(9) (grant of planning permission in enterprise zone);

    (g)    section 91(4)(a) (no limit to duration of planning permission granted by development order);

    (h)    section 108 (compensation for refusal of planning permission formerly granted by development order);

    (i)    section 109(6) (apportionment of compensation for depreciation);

(j)  section 253(2)(c) (cases in which certain procedures may be carried out in anticipation of planning permission);

(k)  section 264(5)(b) (land treated not as operational land);

(l)  section 279(1)(a)(i) (compensation for certain decisions and orders).

(3)  Section 333 of the principal Act (regulations and orders) is amended as follows –

    (a)  in subsection (4) after '55(2)(f),' there is inserted '61A(5)';

    (b)  in subsection (5)(b) after '28,' there is inserted '61A(5) (unless it is made by the National Assembly for Wales),'.

(4)  Schedule 1 further amends the principal Act.


## Revision of development orders

### 41  Effect of revision or revocation of development order on incomplete development

In the principal Act after section 61C (planning permission granted by local development orders) (inserted by section 40 of this Act) there is inserted the following section –

#### '61D  Effect of revision or revocation of development order on incomplete development

(1)  A development order or local development order may include provision permitting the completion of development if –

    (a)  planning permission is granted by the order in respect of the development, and

    (b)  the planning permission is withdrawn at a time after the development is started but before it is completed.

(2)  Planning permission granted by a development order is withdrawn –

    (a)  if the order is revoked;

    (b)  if the order is amended so that it ceases to grant planning permission in respect of the development or materially changes any condition or limitation to which the grant of permission is subject;

    (c)  by the issue of a direction under powers conferred by the order.

(3)  Planning permission granted by a local development order is withdrawn –

    (a)  if the order is revoked under section 61A(6) or 61B(8);

    (b)  if the order is revised in pursuance of paragraph 2 of Schedule 4A so that it ceases to grant planning permission in respect of the development or materially changes any condition or limitation to which the grant of permission is subject;

    (c)  by the issue of a direction under powers conferred by the order.

(4)  The power under this section to include provision in a development order or a local development order may be exercised differently for different purposes.'


## Applications

### 42  Applications for planning permission and certain consents

(1)  In the principal Act for section 62 (form and content of applications for planning permission) there is substituted the following section –

#### '62  Applications for planning permission

(1)  A development order may make provision as to applications for planning permission made to a local planning authority.

(2)  Provision referred to in subsection (1) includes provision as to –

> (a)   the form and manner in which the application must be made;
> (b)   particulars of such matters as are to be included in the application;
> (c)   documents or other materials as are to accompany the application.
>
> (3)  The local planning authority may require that an application for planning permission must include –
>
> (a)   such particulars as they think necessary;
> (b)   such evidence in support of anything in or relating to the application as they think necessary.
>
> (4)  But a requirement under subsection (3) must not be inconsistent with provision made under subsection (1).
>
> (5)  A development order must require that an application for planning permission of such description as is specified in the order must be accompanied by such of the following as is so specified –
>
> (a)   a statement about the design principles and concepts that have been applied to the development;
> (b)   a statement about how issues relating to access to the development have been dealt with.
>
> (6)  The form and content of a statement mentioned in subsection (5) is such as is required by the development order.'

(2)  In section 73 of the principal Act (determination of applications to develop land without compliance with conditions previously attached) subsection (3) is omitted.

(3)  In section 198 of that Act (tree preservation orders) after subsection (7) there is inserted –

> '(8)  In relation to an application for consent under a tree preservation order the appropriate authority may by regulations make provision as to –
>
> (a)   the form and manner in which the application must be made;
> (b)   particulars of such matters as are to be included in the application;
> (c)   the documents or other materials as are to accompany the application.
>
> (9)  The appropriate authority is –
>
> (a)   the Secretary of State in relation to England;
> (b)   the National Assembly for Wales in relation to Wales,
>
> and in the case of regulations made by the National Assembly for Wales section 333(3) must be ignored.'

(4)  In section 220 of that Act (regulations controlling display of advertisements) after subsection (2) there is inserted the following subsection –

> '(2A)  The regulations may also make provision as to –
>
> (a)   the form and manner in which an application for consent must be made;
> (b)   particulars of such matters as are to be included in the application;
> (c)   any documents or other materials which must accompany the application.'

(5)  In the principal Act before section 328 (settled land and land of universities and colleges) there is inserted the following section –

### '327A  Applications: compliance with requirements

> (1)  This section applies to any application in respect of which this Act or any provision made under it imposes a requirement as to –
>
> (a)   the form or manner in which the application must be made;
> (b)   the form or content of any document or other matter which accompanies the application.
>
> (2)  The local planning authority must not entertain such an application if it fails to comply with the requirement.'

(6)  In section 10(2) of the listed buildings Act (applications for listed buildings consent) the words from 'shall be made' to 'require and' are omitted.

(7)  In section 10(3) of that Act for paragraph (a) there are substituted the following paragraphs –

'(a)   the form and manner in which such applications are to be made;
(aa)  particulars of such matters as are to be included in such applications;
(ab)  the documents or other materials as are to accompany such applications;'.

(8)  In section 10 of that Act after subsection (3) there are inserted the following subsections –

'(4)  The regulations must require that an application for listed building consent of such description as is prescribed must be accompanied by such of the following as is prescribed –

(a)   a statement about the design principles and concepts that have been applied to the works;
(b)   a statement about how issues relating to access to the building have been dealt with.

(5)  The form and content of a statement mentioned in subsection (4) is such as is prescribed.'

(9)  In section 89(1) of that Act (application of certain provisions of the principal Act) after the entry relating to section 323 there is inserted –

'section 327A (compliance with requirements relating to applications),'.

### 43  Power to decline to determine applications

(1)  For section 70A of the principal Act (power of local planning authority to decline to determine application) there are substituted the following sections –

'**70A  Power to decline to determine subsequent application**

(1)  A local planning authority may decline to determine a relevant application if –

(a)   any of the conditions in subsections (2) to (4) is satisfied, and
(b)   the authority think there has been no significant change in the relevant considerations since the relevant event.

(2)  The condition is that in the period of two years ending with the date on which the application mentioned in subsection (1) is received the Secretary of State has refused a similar application referred to him under section 76A or 77.

(3)  The condition is that in that period the Secretary of State has dismissed an appeal –

(a)   against the refusal of a similar application, or
(b)   under section 78(2) in respect of a similar application.

(4)  The condition is that –

(a)   in that period the local planning authority have refused more than one similar application, and
(b)   there has been no appeal to the Secretary of State against any such refusal.

(5)  A relevant application is –

(a)   an application for planning permission for the development of any land;
(b)   an application for approval in pursuance of section 60(2).

(6)  The relevant considerations are –

(a)   the development plan so far as material to the application;
(b)   any other material considerations.

(7) The relevant event is –

    (a)    for the purposes of subsections (2) and (4) the refusal of the similar application;

    (b)    for the purposes of subsection (3) the dismissal of the appeal.

(8) An application for planning permission is similar to another application if (and only if) the local planning authority think that the development and the land to which the applications relate are the same or substantially the same.

### 70B Power to decline to determine overlapping application

(1) A local planning authority may decline to determine an application for planning permission for the development of any land which is made at a time when any of the conditions in subsections (2) to (4) applies in relation to a similar application.

(2) The condition is that a similar application is under consideration by the local planning authority and the determination period for that application has not expired.

(3) The condition is that a similar application is under consideration by the Secretary of State in pursuance of section 76A or 77 or on an appeal under section 78 and the Secretary of State has not issued his decision.

(4) The condition is that a similar application –

    (a)    has been granted by the local planning authority,

    (b)    has been refused by them, or

    (c)    has not been determined by them within the determination period,

and the time within which an appeal could be made to the Secretary of State under section 78 has not expired.

(5) An application for planning permission is similar to another application if (and only if) the local planning authority think that the development and the land to which the applications relate are the same or substantially the same.

(6) The determination period is –

    (a)    the period prescribed by the development order for the determination of the application, or

    (b)    such longer period as the applicant and the authority have agreed for the determination of the application.'

(2) In section 78(2)(aa) of that Act after '70A' there is inserted 'or 70B'.

(3) After section 81 of the listed buildings Act (authorities with functions under the Act) there are inserted the following sections –

## 'Power to decline to determine application

### 81A Power to decline to determine subsequent application

(1) A local planning authority may decline to determine an application for a relevant consent if –

    (a)    one or more of the conditions in subsections (2) to (4) is satisfied, and

    (b)    the authority think there has been no significant change in any material considerations since the relevant event.

(2) The condition is that in the period of two years ending with the date on which the application mentioned in subsection (1) is received the Secretary of State has refused a similar application referred to him under section 12.

(3) The condition is that in that period the Secretary of State has dismissed an appeal –

(a)   against the refusal of a similar application, or

(b)   under section 20(2) in respect of a similar application.

(4)   The condition is that –

(a)   in that period the local planning authority have refused more than one similar application, and

(b)   there has been no appeal to the Secretary of State against any such refusal.

(5)   Relevant consent is –

(a)   listed building consent, or

(b)   conservation area consent.

(6)   The relevant event is –

(a)   for the purposes of subsections (2) and (4) the refusal of the similar application;

(b)   for the purposes of subsection (3) the dismissal of the appeal.

(7)   An application for relevant consent is similar to another application if (and only if) the local planning authority think that the building and works to which the applications relate are the same or substantially the same.

(8)   For the purposes of an application for conservation area consent a reference to a provision of this Act is a reference to that provision as excepted or modified by regulations under section 74.

### 81B  Power to decline to determine overlapping application

(1)   A local planning authority may decline to determine an application for a relevant consent which is made at a time when any of the conditions in subsections (2) to (4) applies in relation to a similar application.

(2)   The condition is that a similar application is under consideration by the local planning authority and the determination period for that application has not expired.

(3)   The condition is that a similar application is under consideration by the Secretary of State in pursuance of section 12 or on an appeal under section 20 and the Secretary of State has not issued his decision.

(4)   The condition is that a similar application –

(a)   has been granted by the local planning authority,

(b)   has been refused by them, or

(c)   has not been determined by them within the determination period,

and the time within which an appeal could be made to the Secretary of State under section 20 has not expired.

(5)   Relevant consent is –

(a)   listed building consent, or

(b)   conservation area consent.

(6)   An application for relevant consent is similar to another application if (and only if) the local planning authority think that the building and works to which the applications relate are the same or substantially the same.

(7)   The determination period is –

(a)   the period prescribed for the determination of the application, or

(b)   such longer period as the applicant and the authority have agreed for the determination of the application.

(8)   For the purposes of an application for conservation area consent a reference to a provision of this Act is a reference to that provision as excepted or modified by regulations under section 74.'

(4)  Section 20(2) of that Act (appeals) is amended as follows –

    (a)  for 'neither' there is substituted 'done none of the following';

    (b)  after paragraph (a) for 'nor' there is substituted –

        '(aa)  given notice to the applicant that they have exercised their power under section 81A or 81B to decline to determine the application;'.

(5)  This section has effect only in relation to applications made under the principal Act or the listed buildings Act which are received by the local planning authority after this section comes into force.

## Major infrastructure projects

### 44  Major infrastructure projects

In the principal Act the following sections are inserted before section 77 (Reference of applications to the Secretary of State) –

#### '76A  Major infrastructure projects

(1) This section applies to –

    (a)  an application for planning permission;

    (b)  an application for the approval of a local planning authority required under a development order,

if the Secretary of State thinks that the development to which the application relates is of national or regional importance.

(2) The Secretary of State may direct that the application must be referred to him instead of being dealt with by the local planning authority.

(3) If the Secretary of State gives a direction under subsection (2) he may also direct that any application –

    (a)  under or for the purposes of the planning Acts, and

    (b)  which he thinks is connected with the application mentioned in subsection (1),

must also be referred to him instead of being dealt with by the local planning authority.

(4) If the Secretary of State gives a direction under this section –

    (a)  the application must be referred to him;

    (b)  he must appoint an inspector to consider the application.

(5) If the Secretary of State gives a direction under subsection (2) the applicant must prepare an economic impact report which must –

    (a)  be in such form and contain such matter as is prescribed by development order;

    (b)  be submitted to the Secretary of State in accordance with such provision as is so prescribed.

(6) For the purposes of subsection (5) the Secretary of State may, by development order, prescribe such requirements as to publicity and notice as he thinks appropriate.

(7) A direction under this section or section 76B may be varied or revoked by a subsequent direction.

(8) The decision of the Secretary of State on any application referred to him under this section is final.

(9) Regional relates to a region listed in Schedule 1 to the Regional Development Agencies Act 1998 (c. 45).

(10) The following provisions of this Act apply (with any necessary modifications) to an application referred to the Secretary of State under this section as they apply to an application which falls to be determined by a local planning authority –

  (a)   section 70;
  (b)   section 72(1) and (5);
  (c)   section 73;
  (d)   section 73A.

(11) A development order may apply (with or without modifications) any requirements imposed by the order by virtue of section 65 or 71 to an application referred to the Secretary of State under this section.

(12) This section does not apply to an application which relates to the development of land in Wales.

### 76B  Major infrastructure projects: inspectors

(1) This section applies if the Secretary of State appoints an inspector under section 76A(4)(b) (the lead inspector).

(2) The Secretary of State may direct the lead inspector –

  (a)   to consider such matters relating to the application as are prescribed;
  (b)   to make recommendations to the Secretary of State on those matters.

(3) After considering any recommendations of the lead inspector the Secretary of State may –

  (a)   appoint such number of additional inspectors as he thinks appropriate;
  (b)   direct that each of the additional inspectors must consider such matters relating to the application as the lead inspector decides.

(4) An additional inspector must –

  (a)   comply with such directions as to procedural matters as the lead inspector gives;
  (b)   report to the lead inspector on the matters he is appointed to consider.

(5) A copy of directions given as mentioned in subsection (4)(a) must be given to –

  (a)   the person who made the application;
  (b)   the local planning authority;
  (c)   any other person who requests it.

(6) If the Secretary of State does not act under subsection (3) he must direct the lead inspector to consider the application on his own.

(7) In every case the lead inspector must report to the Secretary of State on –

  (a)   his consideration of the application;
  (b)   the consideration of the additional inspectors (if any) of the matters mentioned in subsection (3)(b).

(8) The function of the lead inspector in pursuance of subsection (2) –

  (a)   may be exercised from time to time;
  (b)   includes making recommendations as to the number of additional inspectors required from time to time.

(9) The power of the Secretary of State under subsection (3) to appoint an additional inspector includes power to revoke such an appointment.'


## Simplified planning zones

### 45  Simplified planning zones

(1) In section 83 of the principal Act (making simplified planning zone schemes) subsection (1) is omitted.

(2) Before section 83(2) of that Act there are inserted the following subsections –

'(1A) This section applies if –

(a) the regional spatial strategy for the region in which the area of a local planning authority in England is situated identifies the need for a simplified planning zone in that area (or any part of it);

(b) the criteria prescribed by the National Assembly for Wales for the need for a simplified planning zone are satisfied in relation to the area (or any part of the area) of a local planning authority in Wales.

(1B) The local planning authority must consider the question for which part or parts of their area a simplified planning zone scheme is desirable.

(1C) The local planning authority must keep under review the question mentioned in subsection (1B).'

(3) For section 83(2) of that Act there are substituted the following subsections –

'(2) A local planning authority must make a simplified planning zone scheme for all or any part of their area –

(a) if as a result of the consideration mentioned in subsection (1B) or the review mentioned in subsection (1C) they decide that it is desirable to do so;

(b) if they are directed to do so by the Secretary of State or the National Assembly for Wales (as the case may be).

(2A) A local planning authority may at any time –

(a) alter a scheme adopted by them;

(b) with the consent of the Secretary of State alter a scheme made or altered by him under paragraph 12 of Schedule 7 or approved by him under paragraph 11 of that Schedule;

(c) with the consent of the National Assembly for Wales alter a scheme made or altered by it under paragraph 12 of Schedule 7 or approved by it under paragraph 11 of that Schedule.

(2B) A simplified planning zone scheme for an area in England must be in conformity with the regional spatial strategy.'

(4) In section 83 of that Act after subsection (3) there is inserted the following subsection –

'(4) In this section and in Schedule 7–

(a) a reference to the regional spatial strategy must be construed in relation to any area in Greater London as a reference to the spatial development strategy;

(b) a reference to a region must be construed in relation to such an area as a reference to Greater London.'

(5) In section 85(1) of that Act (duration of simplified planning zone scheme) for the words from 'period' to the end there is substituted 'specified period'.

(6) After section 85(1) of that Act there is inserted the following subsection –

'(1A) The specified period is the period not exceeding 10 years –

(a) beginning with the date when the scheme is adopted or approved, and

(b) which is specified in the scheme.'

(7) In Schedule 7 of that Act in paragraph 2 (notification of proposal to make scheme) for 'decide under section 83(2) to make or' there is substituted 'are required under section 83(2) to make or decide under section 83(2A) to'.

(8) In Schedule 7 of that Act paragraphs 3 and 4 are omitted.

(9) In Schedule 7 of that Act in paragraph 12 (default powers of Secretary of State) for sub-paragraph (1) there are substituted the following sub-paragraphs –

'(1)    This paragraph applies if each of the following conditions is satisfied.

(1A)   The first condition is that –

(a) the regional spatial strategy for the region in which the area of a local planning authority is situated identifies the need for a simplified planning zone in any part of their area, or

(b) the criteria prescribed by the National Assembly for Wales for the need for a simplified planning zone are satisfied in relation to the area of a local planning authority in Wales.

(1B)   The second condition is that the Secretary of State or the National Assembly for Wales (as the case may be) is satisfied after holding a local inquiry or other hearing that the authority are not taking within a reasonable period the steps required by this Schedule for the adoption of proposals for the making or alteration of a scheme.

(1C)   The Secretary of State or the National Assembly for Wales (as the case may be) may make or alter the scheme.'

## *Planning contribution*

### 46  Planning contribution

(1) The Secretary of State may, by regulations, make provision for the making of a planning contribution in relation to the development or use of land in the area of a local planning authority.

(2) The contribution may be made –

(a) by the prescribed means,

(b) by compliance with the relevant requirements, or

(c) by a combination of such means and compliance.

(3) The regulations may require the local planning authority to include in a development plan document (or in such other document as is prescribed) –

(a) a statement of the developments or uses or descriptions of development or use in relation to which they will consider accepting a planning contribution;

(b) a statement of the matters relating to development or use in relation to which they will not consider accepting a contribution by the prescribed means;

(c) the purposes to which receipts from payments made in respect of contributions are (in whole or in part) to be put;

(d) the criteria by reference to which the value of a contribution made by the prescribed means is to be determined.

(4) The regulations may make provision as to circumstances in which –

(a) except in the case of a contribution to which subsection (3)(b) applies, the person making the contribution (the contributor) must state the form in which he will make the contribution;

(b) the contribution may not be made by compliance with the relevant requirements if it is made by the prescribed means;

(c) the contribution may not be made by the prescribed means if it is made by compliance with the relevant requirements;

(d) a contribution must not be made.

(5) The prescribed means are –

(a) the payment of a sum the amount and terms of payment of which are determined in accordance with criteria published by the local planning authority for the purposes of subsection (3)(d),

(b) the provision of a benefit in kind the value of which is so determined, or

(c) a combination of such payment and provision.

(6) The relevant requirements are such requirements relating to the development or use as are –

(a) prescribed for the purposes of this section, and

(b) included as part of the terms of the contribution,

and may include a requirement to make a payment of a sum.

(7) Development plan document must be construed in accordance with section 37(3).

### 47 Planning contribution: regulations

(1) This section applies for the purpose of regulations made under section 46.

(2) Maximum and minimum amounts may be prescribed in relation to a payment falling within section 46(5)(a).

(3) Provision may be made to enable periodic adjustment of the criteria mentioned in section 46(3)(d).

(4) The local planning authority may be required to publish an annual report containing such information in relation to the planning contribution as is prescribed.

(5) If a document is prescribed for the purposes of section 46(3) the regulations may prescribe –

(a) the procedure for its preparation and the time at which it must be published;

(b) the circumstances in which and the procedure by which the Secretary of State may take steps in relation to the preparation of the document.

(6) Provision may be made for the enforcement by the local planning authority of the terms of a planning contribution including provision –

(a) for a person obstructing the taking of such steps as are prescribed to be guilty of an offence punishable by a fine not exceeding level 3 on the standard scale;

(b) for a person deriving title to the land from the contributor to be bound by the terms of the contribution;

(c) for a condition to be attached to any planning permission relating to the land requiring the contribution to be made before any development is started;

(d) for the enforcement of a planning contribution in respect of land which is Crown land within the meaning of section 293(1) of the principal Act.

(7) The regulations may –

(a) require the local planning authority to apply receipts from planning contributions made by the prescribed means only to purposes mentioned in section 46(3)(c);

(b) make provision for setting out in writing the terms of the planning contribution;

(c) make provision in relation to the modification or discharge of a planning contribution.

(8) The regulations may –

(a) make different provision in relation to the areas of different local planning authorities or different descriptions of local planning authority;

(b) exclude their application (in whole or in part) in relation to the area of one or more local planning authorities or descriptions of local planning authority.

### 48 Planning contribution: Wales

In relation to land in Wales, sections 46 and 47 apply subject to the following modifications –

(a) references to the Secretary of State must be construed as references to the National Assembly for Wales;

(b) the reference to a development plan document must be construed as a reference to a local development plan (within the meaning of section 62).

## Miscellaneous

### 49 Development to include certain internal operations

(1) In the principal Act in section 55 (meaning of development) after subsection (2) there are inserted the following subsections –

'(2A) The Secretary of State may in a development order specify any circumstances or description of circumstances in which subsection (2) does not apply to operations mentioned in paragraph (a) of that subsection which have the effect of increasing the gross floor space of the building by such amount or percentage amount as is so specified.

(2B) The development order may make different provision for different purposes.'

(2) This subsection applies if –

(a) section 55(2) of the principal Act is disapplied in respect of any operations by virtue of a development order under section 55(2A) of that Act,

(b) at the date the development order comes into force a certificate under section 192 of the principal Act (certificate of lawfulness of proposed use or development) is in force in respect of the operations, and

(c) before that date no such operations have been begun.

(3) If subsection (2) applies the certificate under section 192 of the principal Act is of no effect.

(4) A development order made for the purposes of section 55(2A) of the principal Act does not affect any operations begun before it is made.

### 50 Appeal made: functions of local planning authority

(1) In the principal Act after section 78 (right to appeal) there is inserted the following section –

'78A Appeal made: functions of local planning authorities

(1) This section applies if a person who has made an application mentioned in section 78(1)(a) appeals to the Secretary of State under section 78(2).

(2) At any time before the end of the additional period the local planning authority may give the notice referred to in section 78(2).

(3) If the local planning authority give notice as mentioned in subsection (2) that their decision is to refuse the application –

(a) the appeal must be treated as an appeal under section 78(1) against the refusal;

(b) the Secretary of State must give the person making the appeal an opportunity to revise the grounds of the appeal;

(c) the Secretary of State must give such a person an opportunity to change any option the person has chosen relating to the procedure for the appeal.

(4) If the local planning authority give notice as mentioned in subsection (2) that their decision is to grant the application subject to conditions the Secretary of State must give the person making the appeal the opportunity –

(a) to proceed with the appeal as an appeal under section 78(1) against the grant of the application subject to conditions;

(b) to revise the grounds of the appeal;

(c) to change any option the person has chosen relating to the procedure for the appeal.

(5) The Secretary of State must not issue his decision on the appeal before the end of the additional period.

(6) The additional period is the period prescribed by development order for the purposes of this section and which starts on the day on which the person appeals under section 78(2).'

(2) In the listed buildings Act after section 20 (right to appeal) there is inserted the following section –

**'20A Appeal made: functions of local planning authorities**

(1) This section applies if a person who has made an application mentioned in section 20(1)(a) appeals to the Secretary of State under section 20(2).

(2) At any time before the end of the additional period the local planning authority may give the notice referred to in section 20(2).

(3) If the local planning authority give notice as mentioned in subsection (2) that their decision is to refuse the application –

    (a) the appeal must be treated as an appeal under section 20(1) against the refusal;

    (b) the Secretary of State must give the person making the appeal an opportunity to revise the grounds of the appeal;

    (c) the Secretary of State must give such a person an opportunity to change any option the person has chosen relating to the procedure for the appeal.

(4) If the local planning authority give notice as mentioned in subsection (2) that their decision is to grant the application subject to conditions the Secretary of State must give the person making the appeal the opportunity –

    (a) to proceed with the appeal as an appeal under section 20(1) against the grant of the application subject to conditions;

    (b) to revise the grounds of the appeal;

    (c) to change any option the person has chosen relating to the procedure for the appeal.

(5) The Secretary of State must not issue his decision on the appeal before the end of the additional period.

(6) The additional period is the period prescribed for the purposes of this section and which starts on the day on which the person appeals under section 20(2).'

(3) This section has effect only in relation to relevant applications which are received by the local planning authority after the commencement of this section.

(4) The following are relevant applications –

    (a) an application mentioned in section 78(1)(a) of the principal Act;

    (b) an application mentioned in section 20(1)(a) of the listed buildings Act;

    (c) an application mentioned in section 20(1)(a) of the listed buildings Act as given effect by section 74(3) of that Act (application of certain provisions to the control of demolition in conservation areas).

**51 Duration of permission and consent**

(1) Section 91 of the principal Act (limit on duration of planning permission) is amended as follows –

    (a) in subsections (1)(a) and (3) for the words 'five years' there is substituted 'three years';

    (b) after subsection (3) there are inserted the following subsections –

        '(3A) Subsection (3B) applies if any proceedings are begun to challenge the validity of a grant of planning permission or of a deemed grant of planning permission.

(3B)   The period before the end of which the development to which the planning permission relates is required to be begun in pursuance of subsection (1) or (3) must be taken to be extended by one year.

(3C)   Nothing in this section prevents the development being begun from the time the permission is granted or deemed to be granted.'

(2)   In section 92 of that Act (outline planning permission) –

(a)   in subsection (2)(b) sub-paragraph (i) is omitted;

(b)   in subsection (2)(b) in sub-paragraph (ii) the words 'if later' are omitted;

(c)   in subsection (4) 'five years' is omitted.

(3)   In section 73 of the principal Act (applications to develop land without compliance with existing conditions) after subsection (4) there is inserted the following subsection –

'(5)   Planning permission must not be granted under this section to the extent that it has effect to change a condition subject to which a previous planning permission was granted by extending the time within which –

(a)   a development must be started;

(b)   an application for approval of reserved matters (within the meaning of section 92) must be made.'

(4)   Section 18 of the listed buildings Act (limit of duration of listed buildings consent) is amended as follows –

(a)   in subsections (1)(a) and (2) for the words 'five years' there is substituted 'three years';

(b)   after subsection (2) there are inserted the following subsections –

'(2A)   Subsection (2B) applies if any proceedings are begun to challenge the validity of a grant of listed building consent or of a deemed grant of listed building consent.

(2B)   The period before the end of which the works to which the consent relates are required to be begun in pursuance of subsection (1) or (2) must be taken to be extended by one year.

(2C)   Nothing in this section prevents the works being begun from the time the consent is granted.'

(5)   In section 19 of that Act (variation or discharge of conditions) after subsection (4) there is inserted the following subsection –

'(5)   But a variation or discharge of conditions under this section must not –

(a)   vary a condition subject to which a consent was granted by extending the time within which the works must be started;

(b)   discharge such a condition.'

(6)   This section has effect only in relation to applications made under the principal Act or the listed buildings Act which are received by the local planning authority after the commencement of the section.

## 52   Temporary stop notice

After section 171D of the principal Act (penalties for non-compliance with planning contravention notice) there are inserted the following sections –

### 'Temporary stop notices

#### 171E   Temporary stop notice

(1)   This section applies if the local planning authority think –

(a)    that there has been a breach of planning control in relation to any land, and

(b)    that it is expedient that the activity (or any part of the activity) which amounts to the breach is stopped immediately.

(2)    The authority may issue a temporary stop notice.

(3)    The notice must be in writing and must –

(a)    specify the activity which the authority think amounts to the breach;

(b)    prohibit the carrying on of the activity (or of so much of the activity as is specified in the notice);

(c)    set out the authority's reasons for issuing the notice.

(4)    A temporary stop notice may be served on any of the following –

(a)    the person who the authority think is carrying on the activity;

(b)    a person who the authority think is an occupier of the land;

(c)    a person who the authority think has an interest in the land.

(5)    The authority must display on the land –

(a)    a copy of the notice;

(b)    a statement of the effect of the notice and of section 171G.

(6)    A temporary stop notice has effect from the time a copy of it is first displayed in pursuance of subsection (5).

(7)    A temporary stop notice ceases to have effect –

(a)    at the end of the period of 28 days starting on the day the copy notice is so displayed,

(b)    at the end of such shorter period starting on that day as is specified in the notice, or

(c)    if it is withdrawn by the local planning authority.

## 171F  Temporary stop notice: restrictions

(1)    A temporary stop notice does not prohibit –

(a)    the use of a building as a dwelling house;

(b)    the carrying out of an activity of such description or in such circumstances as is prescribed.

(2)    A temporary stop notice does not prohibit the carrying out of any activity which has been carried out (whether or not continuously) for a period of four years ending with the day on which the copy of the notice is first displayed as mentioned in section 171E(6).

(3)    Subsection (2) does not prevent a temporary stop notice prohibiting –

(a)    activity consisting of or incidental to building, engineering, mining or other operations, or

(b)    the deposit of refuse or waste materials.

(4)    For the purposes of subsection (2) any period during which the activity is authorised by planning permission must be ignored.

(5)    A second or subsequent temporary stop notice must not be issued in respect of the same activity unless the local planning authority has first taken some other enforcement action in relation to the breach of planning control which is constituted by the activity.

(6)    In subsection (5) enforcement action includes obtaining the grant of an injunction under section 187B.

## 171G  Temporary stop notice: offences

(1)    A person commits an offence if he contravenes a temporary stop notice –

(a)    which has been served on him, or

(b)    a copy of which has been displayed in accordance with section 171E(5).

(2)   Contravention of a temporary stop notice includes causing or permitting the contravention of the notice.

(3)   An offence under this section may be charged by reference to a day or a longer period of time.

(4)   A person may be convicted of more than one such offence in relation to the same temporary stop notice by reference to different days or periods of time.

(5)   A person does not commit an offence under this section if he proves –

(a)   that the temporary stop notice was not served on him, and

(b)   that he did not know, and could not reasonably have been expected to know, of its existence.

(6)   A person convicted of an offence under this section is liable –

(a)   on summary conviction, to a fine not exceeding £20,000;

(b)   on conviction on indictment, to a fine.

(7)   In determining the amount of the fine the court must have regard in particular to any financial benefit which has accrued or has appeared to accrue to the person convicted in consequence of the offence.

### 171H   Temporary stop notice: compensation

(1)   This section applies if and only if a temporary stop notice is issued and at least one of the following paragraphs applies –

(a)   the activity which is specified in the notice is authorised by planning permission or a development order or local development order;

(b)   a certificate in respect of the activity is issued under section 191 or granted under that section by virtue of section 195;

(c)   the authority withdraws the notice.

(2)   Subsection (1)(a) does not apply if the planning permission is granted on or after the date on which a copy of the notice is first displayed as mentioned in section 171E(6).

(3)   Subsection (1)(c) does not apply if the notice is withdrawn following the grant of planning permission as mentioned in subsection (2).

(4)   A person who at the time the notice is served has an interest in the land to which the notice relates is entitled to be compensated by the local planning authority in respect of any loss or damage directly attributable to the prohibition effected by the notice.

(5)   Subsections (3) to (7) of section 186 apply to compensation payable under this section as they apply to compensation payable under that section; and for that purpose references in those subsections to a stop notice must be taken to be references to a temporary stop notice.'

### 53   Fees and charges

(1)   Section 303 (fees for planning applications, etc) of the principal Act is amended as follows.

(2)   The following subsections are substituted for subsections (1) and (2) –

'(1)   The appropriate authority may by regulations make provision for the payment of a charge or fee to a local planning authority in respect of –

(a)   the performance by the local planning authority of any function they have;

(b)   anything done by them which is calculated to facilitate or is conducive or incidental to the performance of any such function.

(2)   The regulations may prescribe –

(a)   the person by whom the charge or fee is payable;

(b)   provision as to the calculation of the charge or fee (including the person by whom it is to be calculated);

(c)   circumstances in which no charge or fee is to be paid;

(d)   circumstances in which a charge or fee is to be transferred from one local planning authority to another.

(2A) The appropriate authority is –

(a)   the Secretary of State in relation to England;

(b)   the National Assembly for Wales in relation to Wales,

and in the case of regulations made by the National Assembly for Wales section 333(3) must be ignored.'

(3)   In subsection (4) after the first 'prescribed' there is inserted 'charge or'.

(4)   After subsection (5) there are inserted the following subsections –

'(5A)   If the local planning authority calculate the amount of fees or charges in pursuance of provision made by regulations under subsection (1) the authority must secure that, taking one financial year with another, the income from the fees or charges does not exceed the cost of the performance of the function or doing of the thing (as the case may be).

(5B)   A financial year is the period of 12 months beginning with 1 April.'

(5)   Subsection (6) is omitted.

## 54   Duty to respond to consultation

(1)   This section applies to a prescribed requirement to consult any person or body (the consultee) which exercises functions for the purposes of any enactment.

(2)   A prescribed requirement to consult is a requirement –

(a)   with which the appropriate authority or a local planning authority must comply before granting any permission, approval or consent under or by virtue of the planning Acts;

(b)   which is prescribed for the purposes of this subsection.

(3)   At any time before an application is made for any permission, approval or consent mentioned in subsection (2) any person may in relation to a proposed development consult the consultee on any matter in respect of which the appropriate authority is or the local planning authority are required to consult the consultee.

(4)   The consultee must give a substantive response to any consultation mentioned in subsection (2) or by virtue of subsection (3) before the end of –

(a)   the period prescribed for the purposes of this subsection, or

(b)   such other period as is agreed in writing between the consultee and the appropriate authority or the local planning authority (as the case may be).

(5)   The appropriate authority may also prescribe –

(a)   the procedure to be followed for the purposes of this section;

(b)   the information to be provided to the consultee for the purposes of the consultation;

(c)   the requirements of a substantive response.

(6)   Anything prescribed for the purposes of subsections (1) to (5) must be prescribed by development order.

(7)   A development order may –

(a)   require consultees to give the appropriate authority a report as to their compliance with subsection (4);

(b)   prescribe the form and content of the report;

(c)   prescribe the times at which the report is to be made.

(8)   The appropriate authority is –

(a)   the Secretary of State in relation to England;

(b)   the National Assembly for Wales in relation to Wales.

**55 Time in which Secretary of State to take decisions**

(1) Schedule 2 contains provisions about the time in which the Secretary of State must take certain decisions.

(2) But Schedule 2 does not apply in relation to any decision taken in the exercise of a function in relation to Wales if the function is exercisable in relation to Wales by the National Assembly for Wales by virtue of an order under section 22 of the Government of Wales Act 1998 (c. 38).

## PART 5   CORRECTION OF ERRORS

**56 Correction of errors in decisions**

(1) This section applies if the Secretary of State or an inspector issues a decision document which contains a correctable error.

(2) The Secretary of State or the inspector (as the case may be) may correct the error –

    (a) if he is requested to do so in writing by any person;

    (b) if he sends a statement in writing to the applicant which explains the error and states that he is considering making the correction.

(3) But the Secretary of State or inspector must not correct the error unless –

    (a) not later than the end of the relevant period he receives a request mentioned in subsection (2)(a) or sends a statement mentioned in subsection (2)(b),

    (b) he informs the local planning authority of that fact, and

    (c) he obtains the appropriate consent.

(4) The relevant period –

    (a) is the period within which an application or appeal may be made to the High Court in respect of the decision recorded in the decision document;

    (b) does not include any time by which such a period may be extended by the High Court.

(5) It is immaterial whether any such application or appeal is made.

(6) The appropriate consent is –

    (a) the consent in writing of the applicant;

    (b) if the applicant is not the owner of the land in respect of which the decision was made, the consent in writing of both the applicant and the owner.

(7) But consent is not appropriate consent if it is given subject to a condition.

**57 Correction notice**

(1) If paragraph (a) or (b) of section 56(2) applies the Secretary of State or the inspector must as soon as practicable after making any correction or deciding not to make any correction issue a notice in writing (a correction notice) which –

    (a) specifies the correction of the error, or

    (b) gives notice of his decision not to correct such an error.

(2) The Secretary of State or the inspector (as the case may be) must give the correction notice to –

    (a) the applicant;

    (b) if the applicant is not the owner of the land in respect of which the original decision was made, the owner;

    (c) the local planning authority for the area in which the land in respect of which the decision was made is situated;

    (d) if the correction was requested by any other person, that person.

(3) The Secretary of State may by order specify any other person or description of persons to whom the correction notice must be given.

**58  Effect of correction**

(1)  If a correction is made in pursuance of section 56–

    (a)  the original decision is taken not to have been made;

    (b)  the decision is taken for all purposes to have been made on the date the correction notice is issued.

(2)  If a correction is not made –

    (a)  the original decision continues to have full force and effect;

    (b)  nothing in this Part affects anything done in pursuance of or in respect of the decision.

(3)  Section 288 of the principal Act (proceedings for questioning the validity of certain decisions) applies to the correction notice as if it were an action on the part of the Secretary of State to which that section applies, if the decision document in respect of which the correction notice is given records a decision mentioned in –

    (a)  paragraph (a) of section 59(4) below, or

    (b)  paragraph (b) of that section, if it is a decision mentioned in section 177 of the principal Act (grant or modification of planning permission on appeal against enforcement notice).

(4)  Section 289 of the principal Act (appeals to the High Court relating to enforcement notices and notices under section 207 of that Act) applies to the correction notice as if it were a decision of the Secretary of State mentioned in –

    (a)  subsection (1) of that section, if the decision document in respect of which the correction notice is given records a decision mentioned in paragraph (b) of section 59(4) below (not being a decision mentioned in section 177 of the principal Act), or

    (b)  subsection (2) of that section, if the decision document in respect of which the correction notice is given records a decision mentioned in paragraph (c) of section 59(4) below.

(5)  Section 63 of the listed buildings Act (proceedings for questioning the validity of certain decisions) applies to the correction notice as if it were a decision of the Secretary of State to which that section applies, if the decision document in respect of which the correction notice is given records a decision mentioned in any of paragraphs (d) to (f) of section 59(4) below.

(6)  Section 22 of the hazardous substances Act (proceedings for questioning the validity of certain decisions) applies to the correction notice as if it were a decision of the Secretary of State under section 20 or 21 of that Act, if the decision document in respect of which the correction notice is given records a decision mentioned in paragraph (g) of section 59(4) below.

(7)  If the decision document in respect of which the correction notice is given records a decision mentioned in paragraph (h) of section 59(4) the Secretary of State must by order make provision for questioning the validity of the notice which corresponds to the provisions of the planning Acts mentioned in subsections (3) to (6) above.

(8)  Except to the extent provided for by virtue of this section a correction notice must not be questioned in any legal proceedings.

**59  Supplementary**

(1)  This section applies for the purposes of this Part.

(2)  An inspector is a person appointed under any of the planning Acts to determine appeals instead of the Secretary of State.

(3)  In the case of a decision document issued by an inspector any other inspector may act under this Part.

(4)  A decision document is a document which records any of the following decisions –

(a)  a decision of any description which constitutes action on the part of the Secretary of State under section 284(3) of the principal Act (decisions which are not to be questioned in legal proceedings);

(b)  a decision in proceedings on an appeal under Part 7 of that Act (enforcement notices);

(c)  a decision in proceedings on an appeal under section 208 of that Act (appeals against enforcement notices relating to trees);

(d)  a decision mentioned in section 62(2) of the listed buildings Act (decisions which are not to be questioned in legal proceedings);

(e)  a decision on an appeal under section 39 of that Act (appeals against listed building enforcement notices);

(f)  a decision relating to conservation area consent within the meaning of section 74(1) of that Act (consent required for demolition of certain buildings);

(g)  a decision under section 20 or 21 of the hazardous substances Act (certain applications referred to and appeals determined by the Secretary of State);

(h)  a decision under any of the planning Acts which is of a description specified by the Secretary of State by order.

(5)  A correctable error is an error –

(a)  which is contained in any part of the decision document which records the decision, but

(b)  which is not part of any reasons given for the decision.

(6)  The applicant is –

(a)  in the case of a decision made on an application under any of the planning Acts, the person who made the application;

(b)  in the case of a decision made on an appeal under any of those Acts, the appellant.

(7)  The owner in relation to land is a person who –

(a)  is the estate owner in respect of the fee simple;

(b)  is entitled to a tenancy granted or extended for a term of years simple of which not less than seven years remain unexpired;

(c)  is entitled to an interest in any mineral prescribed by a development order, in the case of such applications under the principal Act as are so prescribed.

(8)  Error includes omission.

(9)  For the purposes of the exercise of any function under this Part in relation to Wales references to the Secretary of State must be construed as references to the National Assembly for Wales.


## PART 6   WALES

### Spatial plan

#### 60  Wales Spatial Plan

(1)  There must be a spatial plan for Wales to be known as the 'Wales Spatial Plan'.

(2)  The Wales Spatial Plan must set out such of the policies (however expressed) of the National Assembly for Wales as it thinks appropriate in relation to the development and use of land in Wales.

(3)  The Assembly must –

(a)  prepare and publish the Plan;

(b)  keep under review the Plan;

(c)  consider from time to time whether it should be revised.

(4)  If the Assembly revises the Plan, it must publish (as it considers appropriate) –

    (a)  the whole Plan as revised, or

    (b)  the revised parts.

(5)  The Assembly must consult such persons or bodies as it considers appropriate in preparing or revising the Plan.

(6)  The Plan and any revision of it must be approved by the Assembly.

(7)  The Assembly must not delegate its function under subsection (6).

## Survey

### 61 Survey

(1)  The local planning authority must keep under review the matters which may be expected to affect the development of their area or the planning of its development.

(2)  These matters include –

    (a)  the principal physical, economic, social and environmental characteristics of the area of the authority;

    (b)  the principal purposes for which land is used in the area;

    (c)  the size, composition and distribution of the population of the area;

    (d)  the communications, transport system and traffic of the area;

    (e)  any other considerations which may be expected to affect those matters;

    (f)  such other matters as may be prescribed or as the Assembly in a particular case may direct.

(3)  These matters also include –

    (a)  any changes which the authority think may occur in relation to any other matter;

    (b)  the effect such changes are likely to have on the development of the authority's area or on the planning of such development.

(4)  The local planning authority may also keep under review and examine the matters mentioned in subsections (2) and (3) in relation to any neighbouring area to the extent that those matters may be expected to affect the area of the authority.

(5)  In exercising a function under subsection (4) a local planning authority must consult the local planning authority for the neighbouring area in question.

(6)  If a neighbouring area is in England references to the local planning authority for that area must be construed in accordance with Part 2.

## Plans

### 62 Local development plan

(1)  The local planning authority must prepare a plan for their area to be known as a local development plan.

(2)  The plan must set out –

    (a)  the authority's objectives in relation to the development and use of land in their area;

    (b)  their general policies for the implementation of those objectives.

(3)  The plan may also set out specific policies in relation to any part of the area of the authority.

(4)  Regulations under this section may prescribe the form and content of the plan.

(5)  In preparing a local development plan the authority must have regard to –

    (a)  current national policies;

    (b)  the Wales Spatial Plan;

    (c)  the RSS for any region which adjoins the area of the authority;

    (d)  the community strategy prepared by the authority;

(e)  the community strategy for any other authority whose area comprises any part of the area of the local planning authority;

(f)  the resources likely to be available for implementing the plan;

(g)  such other matters as the Assembly prescribes.

(6)  The authority must also –

(a)  carry out an appraisal of the sustainability of the plan;

(b)  prepare a report of the findings of the appraisal.

(7)  The community strategy is the strategy prepared by an authority under section 4 of the Local Government Act 2000 (c. 22).

(8)  A plan is a local development plan only in so far as it –

(a)  is adopted by resolution of the local planning authority as a local development plan;

(b)  is approved by the Assembly under section 65 or 71.

## 63  Preparation requirements

(1)  A local development plan must be prepared in accordance with –

(a)  the local planning authority's community involvement scheme;

(b)  the timetable for the preparation and adoption of the authority's local development plan.

(2)  The authority's community involvement scheme is a statement of the authority's policy as to the involvement in the exercise of the authority's functions under this Part of the persons to which subsection (3) applies.

(3)  The persons mentioned in subsection (2) –

(a)  must include such persons as the Assembly prescribes;

(b)  may include such other persons as appear to the authority to have an interest in matters relating to development in the area of the authority.

(4)  The authority and the Assembly must attempt to agree the terms of the documents mentioned in paragraphs (a) and (b) of subsection (1).

(5)  But to the extent that the Assembly and the authority cannot agree the terms the Assembly may direct that the documents must be in the terms specified in the direction.

(6)  The authority must comply with the direction.

(7)  The Assembly may prescribe –

(a)  the procedure in respect of the preparation of the documents mentioned in paragraphs (a) and (b) of subsection (1);

(b)  the form and content of the documents;

(c)  the time at which any step in the preparation of the documents must be taken;

(d)  publicity about the documents;

(e)  making the documents available for inspection by the public;

(f)  circumstances in which the requirements of the documents need not be complied with.

## 64  Independent examination

(1)  The local planning authority must submit their local development plan to the Assembly for independent examination.

(2)  But the authority must not submit a plan unless –

(a)  they have complied with any relevant requirements contained in regulations under this Part, and

(b)  they think the plan is ready for independent examination.

(3)  The authority must also send to the Assembly (in addition to the local development plan) such other documents (or copies of documents) and such information as is prescribed.

(4) The examination must be carried out by a person appointed by the Assembly.

(5) The purpose of the independent examination is to determine in respect of a local development plan –

(a)   whether it satisfies the requirements of sections 62 and 63 and of regulations under section 77;

(b)   whether it is sound.

(6) Any person who makes representations seeking to change a local development plan must (if he so requests) be given the opportunity to appear before and be heard by the person carrying out the examination.

(7) The person appointed to carry out the examination must –

(a)   make recommendations;

(b)   give reasons for the recommendations.

(8) The local planning authority must publish the recommendations and the reasons.

## 65  Intervention by Assembly

(1) If the Assembly thinks that a local development plan is unsatisfactory –

(a)   it may at any time before the plan is adopted by the local planning authority direct them to modify the plan in accordance with the direction;

(b)   if it gives such a direction it must state its reasons for doing so.

(2) The authority –

(a)   must comply with the direction;

(b)   must not adopt the plan unless the Assembly gives notice that it is satisfied that they have complied with the direction.

(3) But subsection (2) does not apply if the Assembly withdraws the direction.

(4) At any time before a local development plan is adopted by a local planning authority the Assembly may direct that the plan is submitted to it for its approval.

(5) The following paragraphs apply if the Assembly gives a direction under subsection (4) –

(a)   the authority must not take any step in connection with the adoption of the plan until the Assembly gives its decision;

(b)   if the direction is given before the authority have submitted the plan under section 64(1) the Assembly must hold an independent examination and section 64(4) to (7) applies accordingly;

(c)   if the direction is given after the authority have submitted the plan the person appointed to carry out the examination must make his recommendations to the Assembly;

(d)   the plan has no effect unless it has been approved by the Assembly.

(6) The Assembly must publish the recommendations made to it by virtue of subsection (5)(b) or (c) and the reasons of the person making the recommendations.

(7) In considering a plan submitted under subsection (4) the Assembly may take account of any matter which it thinks is relevant.

(8) It is immaterial whether any such matter was taken account of by the authority.

(9) The Assembly –

(a)   may approve, approve subject to specified modifications or reject a plan submitted to it under subsection (4);

(b)   must give reasons for its decision under paragraph (a).

(10) In the exercise of any function under this section the Assembly must have regard to the documents mentioned in paragraphs (a) and (b) of section 63(1).

### 66  Withdrawal of local development plan

(1)  A local planning authority may at any time before a local development plan is adopted under section 67 withdraw the plan.

(2)  But subsection (1) does not apply to a local development plan at any time after the plan has been submitted for independent examination under section 64 unless –

    (a)  the person carrying out the examination recommends that the plan is withdrawn and that recommendation is not overruled by a direction given by the Assembly, or

    (b)  the Assembly directs that the plan must be withdrawn.

### 67  Adoption of local development plan

(1)  The local planning authority may adopt a local development plan as originally prepared if the person appointed to carry out the independent examination of the plan recommends that the plan as originally prepared is adopted.

(2)  The authority may adopt a local development plan with modifications if the person appointed to carry out the independent examination of the plan recommends the modifications.

(3)  A plan is adopted for the purposes of this section if it is adopted by resolution of the authority.

(4)  But the authority must not adopt a local development plan if the Assembly directs them not to do so.

### 68  Revocation of local development plan

The Assembly may at any time revoke a local development plan at the request of the local planning authority.

### 69  Review of local development plan

(1)  A local planning authority must carry out a review of their local development plan at such times as the Assembly prescribes.

(2)  The authority must report to the Assembly on the findings of their review.

(3)  A review must –

    (a)  be in such form as is prescribed;

    (b)  be published in accordance with such requirements as are prescribed.

### 70  Revision of local development plan

(1)  The local planning authority may at any time prepare a revision of a local development plan.

(2)  The authority must prepare a revision of a local development plan –

    (a)  if the Assembly directs them to do so;

    (b)  if, following a review under section 69, they think that the plan should be revised.

(3)  This Part applies to the revision of a local development plan as it applies to the preparation of the plan.

### 71  Assembly's default power

(1)  This section applies if the Assembly thinks that a local planning authority are failing or omitting to do anything it is necessary for them to do in connection with the preparation, revision or adoption of a local development plan.

(2)  The Assembly must hold an independent examination and section 64(4) to (7) applies accordingly.

(3)  The Assembly must publish the recommendations and reasons of the person appointed to hold the examination.

(4)  The Assembly may –

  (a)  prepare or revise (as the case may be) the plan, and
  (b)  approve the plan as a local development plan.

(5)  The Assembly must give reasons for anything it does in pursuance of subsection (4).
(6)  The authority must reimburse the Assembly for any expenditure it incurs in connection with anything –

  (a)  which is done by it under subsection (4), and
  (b)  which the authority failed or omitted to do as mentioned in subsection (1).

### 72  Joint local development plans

(1)  Two or more local planning authorities may agree to prepare a joint local development plan.
(2)  This Part applies for the purposes of the preparation, revision, adoption, withdrawal and revocation of a joint local development plan as it applies for the purposes of the preparation, revision, adoption, withdrawal and revocation of a local development plan.
(3)  For the purposes of subsection (2) anything which must be done by or in relation to a local planning authority in connection with a local development plan must be done by or in relation to each of the authorities mentioned in subsection (1) in connection with a joint local development plan.
(4)  Subsections (5) to (7) apply if a local planning authority withdraw from an agreement mentioned in subsection (1).
(5)  Any step taken in relation to the plan must be treated as a step taken by –

  (a)  an authority which was a party to the agreement for the purposes of any corresponding plan prepared by them;
  (b)  two or more other authorities who were parties to the agreement for the purposes of any corresponding joint local development plan.

(6)  Any independent examination of a local development plan to which the agreement relates must be suspended.
(7)  If before the end of the period prescribed for the purposes of this subsection an authority which was a party to the agreement requests the Assembly to do so it may direct that –

  (a)  the examination is resumed in relation to the corresponding plan;
  (b)  any step taken for the purposes of the suspended examination has effect for the purposes of the resumed examination.

(8)  A joint local development plan is a local development plan prepared jointly by two or more local planning authorities.

## Miscellaneous

### 73  Exclusion of certain representations

(1)  This section applies to any representation or objection in respect of anything which is done or is proposed to be done in pursuance of –

  (a)  an order or scheme under section 10, 14, 16, 18, 106(1) or (3) or 108(1) of the Highways Act 1980 (c. 66);
  (b)  an order or scheme under section 7, 9, 11, 13 or 20 of the Highways Act 1959 (c. 25), section 3 of the Highways (Miscellaneous Provisions) Act 1961 (c. 63) or section 1 or 10 of the Highways Act 1971 (c. 41) (which provisions were replaced by the provisions mentioned in paragraph (a));
  (c)  an order under section 1 of the New Towns Act 1981 (c. 64).

(2) If the Assembly or a local planning authority thinks that a representation made in relation to a local development plan is in substance a representation or objection to which this section applies it or they (as the case may be) may disregard it.

### 74  Urban development corporations

The Assembly may direct that this Part (except section 60) does not apply to the area of an urban development corporation.

### 75  Guidance

In the exercise of any function conferred under or by virtue of this Part the local planning authority must have regard to any guidance issued by the Assembly.

### 76  Annual monitoring report

(1) Every local planning authority must make an annual report to the Assembly.
(2) The annual report must contain such information as is prescribed as to the extent to which the objectives set out in the local development plan are being achieved.
(3) The annual report must –
    (a) be made at such time as is prescribed;
    (b) be in such form as is prescribed;
    (c) contain such other matter as is prescribed.

## General

### 77  Regulations

(1) The Assembly may by regulations make provision in connection with the exercise of functions conferred by this Part on any person.
(2) The regulations may in particular make provision as to –
    (a) the procedure to be followed by the local planning authority in carrying out the appraisal under section 62(6);
    (b) the procedure to be followed in the preparation of local development plans;
    (c) requirements about the giving of notice and publicity;
    (d) requirements about inspection by the public of a plan or any other document;
    (e) the nature and extent of consultation with and participation by the public in anything done under this Part;
    (f) the making of representations about any matter to be included in a local development plan;
    (g) consideration of any such representations;
    (h) the remuneration and allowances payable to the person appointed to carry out an independent examination under section 64;
    (i) the time at which anything must be done for the purposes of this Part;
    (j) the manner of publication of any draft, report or other document published under this Part;
    (k) monitoring the exercise by local planning authorities of their functions under this Part.

### 78  Interpretation

(1) Local development plan must be construed in accordance with section 62.
(2) Local planning authorities are –
    (a) county councils in Wales;
    (b) county borough councils.
(3) A National Park authority is the local planning authority for the whole of its area and subsection (2) must be construed subject to that.

(4)  The Assembly is the National Assembly for Wales.

(5)  RSS must be construed in accordance with Part 1.

(6)  This section applies for the purposes of this Part.

## PART 7    CROWN APPLICATION OF PLANNING ACTS

## CHAPTER 1    ENGLAND AND WALES

### *Crown application*

### 79  Crown application of planning Acts

(1)  In Part 13 of the principal Act before section 293 (preliminary definitions for Part 13) there is inserted the following section –

'292A  Application to the Crown

(1)  This Act binds the Crown.

(2)  But subsection (1) is subject to express provision made by this Part.'

(2)  In the listed buildings Act after section 82 there is inserted the following section –

'82A    Application to the Crown

(1)  This Act (except the provisions specified in subsection (2)) binds the Crown.

(2)  These are the provisions –

    (a)    section 9;

    (b)    section 11(6);

    (c)    section 21(7);

    (d)    section 42(1), (5) and (6);

    (e)    section 43;

    (f)    section 44A;

    (g)    section 54;

    (h)    section 55;

    (i)    section 59;

    (j)    section 88A.

(3)  But subsection (2)(a) does not have effect to prohibit the doing of anything by or on behalf of the Crown which falls within the circumstances described in section 9(3)(a) to (d) and the doing of that thing does not contravene section 7.'

(3)  In the hazardous substances Act after section 30 there are inserted the following sections –

'30A  Application to the Crown

(1)  This Act (except the provisions specified in subsection (2)) binds the Crown.

(2)  The provisions are –

    (a)    section 8(6);

    (b)    section 23;

    (c)    section 26AA;

    (d)    section 36A;

    (e)    section 36B(2).

30B  Crown application: transitional

(1)  This section applies if at any time during the establishment period a hazardous substance was present on, over or under Crown land.

(2) The appropriate authority must make a claim in the prescribed form before the end of the transitional period.

(3) The claim must contain the prescribed information as to –

    (a)   the presence of the substance during the establishment period;

    (b)   how and where the substance was kept and used.

(4) Unless subsection (5) or (7) applies, the hazardous substances authority is deemed to have granted the hazardous substances consent claimed in pursuance of subsection (2).

(5) This subsection applies if the hazardous substances authority think that a claim does not comply with subsection (3).

(6) If subsection (5) applies, the hazardous substances authority must, before the end of the period of two weeks starting with the date they received the claim –

    (a)   notify the claimant that they think the claim is invalid;

    (b)   give their reasons.

(7) This subsection applies if at no time during the establishment period was the aggregate quantity of the substance equal to or greater than the controlled quantity.

(8) Hazardous substances consent which is deemed to be granted under this section is subject –

    (a)   to the condition that the maximum aggregate quantity of the substance that may be present for the purposes of this subsection at any one time must not exceed the established quantity;

    (b)   to such other conditions (if any) as are prescribed for the purposes of this section and are applicable in the case of the consent.

(9) A substance is present for the purposes of subsection (8)(a) if –

    (a)   it is on, over or under land to which the claim for consent relates,

    (b)   it is on, over or under other land which is within 500 metres of it and is controlled by the Crown, or

    (c)   it is in or on a structure controlled by the Crown any part of which is within 500 metres of it,

and in calculating whether the established quantity is exceeded a quantity of a substance which falls within more than one of paragraphs (a) to (c) must be counted only once.

(10) The establishment period is the period of 12 months ending on the day before the date of commencement of section 79(3) of the Planning and Compulsory Purchase Act 2004.

(11) The transitional period is the period of six months starting on the date of commencement of that section.

(12) The established quantity in relation to any land is the maximum quantity which was present on, over or under the land at any one time within the establishment period.'

(4)  Schedule 3 amends the planning Acts in relation to the application of those Acts to the Crown.


## National security

### 80 Special provision relating to national security

(1)  In section 321 of the principal Act (planning inquiries to be held in public subject to certain exceptions) after subsection (4) there are inserted the following subsections –

    '(5)  If the Secretary of State is considering giving a direction under subsection (3) the Attorney General may appoint a person to represent the interests of any person who will be prevented from hearing or inspecting any evidence at a local inquiry if the direction is given.

(6) If before the Secretary of State gives a direction under subsection (3) no person is appointed under subsection (5), the Attorney General may at any time appoint a person as mentioned in subsection (5) for the purposes of the inquiry.

(7) The Lord Chancellor may by rules make provision –

    (a)    as to the procedure to be followed by the Secretary of State before he gives a direction under subsection (3) in a case where a person has been appointed under subsection (5);

    (b)    as to the functions of a person appointed under subsection (5) or (6).

(8) Rules made under subsection (7) must be contained in a statutory instrument subject to annulment in pursuance of a resolution of either House of Parliament.

(9) If a person is appointed under subsection (5) or (6) (the appointed representative) the Secretary of State may direct any person who he thinks is interested in the inquiry in relation to a matter mentioned in subsection (4) (the responsible person) to pay the fees and expenses of the appointed representative.

(10) If the appointed representative and the responsible person are unable to agree the amount of the fees and expenses, the amount must be determined by the Secretary of State.

(11) The Secretary of State must cause the amount agreed between the appointed representative and the responsible person or determined by him to be certified.

(12) An amount so certified is recoverable from the responsible person as a civil debt.'

(2)    After section 321 of the principal Act (planning inquiries to be held in public subject to certain exceptions) there is inserted the following section –

### '321A Appointed representative: no inquiry

(1) This section applies if –

    (a)    a person is appointed under subsection (5) or (6) of section 321, but

    (b)    no inquiry is held as mentioned in subsection (1) of that section.

(2) Subsections (9) to (12) of section 321 apply in respect of the fees and expenses of the person appointed as if the inquiry had been held.

(3) For the purposes of subsection (2) the responsible person is the person to whom the Secretary of State thinks he would have given a direction under section 321(9) if an inquiry had been held.

(4) This section does not affect section 322A.'

(3)    In Schedule 3 to the listed buildings Act (determination of certain appeals by person appointed by the Secretary of State) after paragraph 6 there is inserted the following paragraph –

  '6A    (1)    If the Secretary of State is considering giving a direction under paragraph 6(6) the Attorney General may appoint a person to represent the interests of any person who will be prevented from hearing or inspecting any evidence at a local inquiry if the direction is given.

        (2)    If before the Secretary of State gives a direction under paragraph 6(6) no person is appointed under sub-paragraph (1), the Attorney General may at any time appoint a person as mentioned in sub-paragraph (1) for the purposes of the inquiry.

        (3)    The Lord Chancellor may by rules make provision –

            (a)    as to the procedure to be followed by the Secretary of State before he gives a direction under paragraph 6(6) in a case where a person has been appointed under sub-paragraph (1);

            (b)    as to the functions of a person appointed under sub-paragraph (1) or (2).

    (4) If a person is appointed under sub-paragraph (1) or (2) (the appointed representative) the Secretary of State may direct any person who he thinks is interested in the inquiry in relation to a matter mentioned in paragraph 6(7) (the responsible person) to pay the fees and expenses of the appointed representative.

    (5) If the appointed representative and the responsible person are unable to agree the amount of the fees and expenses, the amount must be determined by the Secretary of State.

    (6) The Secretary of State must cause the amount agreed between the appointed representative and the responsible person or determined by him to be certified.

    (7) An amount so certified is recoverable from the responsible person as a civil debt.

    (8) Rules made under sub-paragraph (3) must be contained in a statutory instrument subject to annulment in pursuance of a resolution of either House of Parliament.

    (9) Sub-paragraph (10) applies if –

        (a)   a person is appointed under sub-paragraph (1) or (2), but

        (b)   no inquiry is held as mentioned in paragraph 6(1).

    (10) Sub-paragraphs (4) to (7) above apply in respect of the fees and expenses of the person appointed as if the inquiry had been held.

    (11) For the purposes of sub-paragraph (10) the responsible person is the person to whom the Secretary of State thinks he would have given a direction under sub-paragraph (4) if an inquiry had been held.

    (12) Sub-paragraphs (9) to (11) do not affect paragraph 6(8).'

(4) In the Schedule to the hazardous substances Act (determination of certain appeals by person appointed by the Secretary of State) after paragraph 6 there is inserted the following paragraph –

  '6A   (1) If the Secretary of State is considering giving a direction under paragraph 6(6) the Attorney General may appoint a person to represent the interests of any person who will be prevented from hearing or inspecting any evidence at a local inquiry if the direction is given.

    (2) If before the Secretary of State gives a direction under paragraph 6(6) no person is appointed under sub-paragraph (1), the Attorney General may at any time appoint a person as mentioned in sub-paragraph (1) for the purposes of the inquiry.

    (3) The Lord Chancellor may by rules make provision –

        (a)   as to the procedure to be followed by the Secretary of State before he gives a direction under paragraph 6(6) in a case where a person has been appointed under sub-paragraph (1);

        (b)   as to the functions of a person appointed under sub-paragraph (1) or (2).

    (4) If a person is appointed under sub-paragraph (1) or (2) (the appointed representative) the Secretary of State may direct any person who he thinks is interested in the inquiry in relation to a matter mentioned in paragraph 6(7) (the responsible person) to pay the fees and expenses of the appointed representative.

    (5) If the appointed representative and the responsible person are unable to agree the amount of the fees and expenses, the amount must be determined by the Secretary of State.

    (6) The Secretary of State must cause the amount agreed between the appointed representative and the responsible person or determined by him to be certified.

(7) An amount so certified is recoverable from the responsible person as a civil debt.

(8) Rules made under sub-paragraph (3) must be contained in a statutory instrument subject to annulment in pursuance of a resolution of either House of Parliament.

(9) Sub-paragraph (10) applies if –

    (a)    a person is appointed under sub-paragraph (1) or (2), but

    (b)    no inquiry is held as mentioned in paragraph 6(1).

(10) Sub-paragraphs (4) to (7) above apply in respect of the fees and expenses of the person appointed as if the inquiry had been held.

(11) For the purposes of sub-paragraph (10) the responsible person is the person to whom the Secretary of State thinks he would have given a direction under sub-paragraph (4) if an inquiry had been held.

(12) Sub-paragraphs (9) to (11) do not affect paragraph 6(8).'

## 81 Special provision relating to national security: Wales

(1) After section 321A of the principal Act (inserted by section 80 above) there is inserted the following section –

### '321B Special provision in relation to planning inquiries: Wales

(1) This section applies if the matter in respect of which a local inquiry to which section 321 applies is to be held relates to Wales.

(2) The references in section 321(5) and (6) to the Attorney General must be read as references to the Counsel General to the National Assembly for Wales.

(3) The Assembly may by regulations make provision as mentioned in section 321(7) in connection with a local inquiry to which this section applies.

(4) If the Assembly acts under subsection (3) rules made by the Lord Chancellor under section 321(7) do not have effect in relation to the inquiry.

(5) The Counsel General to the National Assembly for Wales is the person appointed by the Assembly to be its chief legal adviser (whether or not he is known by that title).

(6) Section 333(3) does not apply to regulations made under subsection (4).'

(2) In Schedule 3 to the listed buildings Act (determination of certain appeals by person appointed by the Secretary of State), after paragraph 7 there is inserted the following paragraph –

### '8 Local inquiries: Wales

(1) This paragraph applies in relation to a local inquiry held in pursuance of this Schedule if the matter in respect of which the inquiry is to be held relates to Wales.

(2) The references in paragraph 6A(1) and (2) to the Attorney General must be read as references to the Counsel General to the National Assembly for Wales.

(3) The Assembly may by regulations make provision as mentioned in paragraph 6A(3) in connection with a local inquiry to which this section applies.

(4) If the Assembly acts under sub-paragraph (3) rules made by the Lord Chancellor under paragraph 6A(3) do not have effect in relation to the inquiry.

(5) The Counsel General to the National Assembly for Wales is the person appointed by the Assembly to be its chief legal adviser (whether or not he is known by that title).

(6) Section 93(3) does not apply to regulations made under this paragraph.'

(3) In the Schedule to the hazardous substances Act, after paragraph 7 there is inserted the following paragraph –

'8 Local inquiries: Wales

(1) This paragraph applies in relation to a local inquiry held in pursuance of this Schedule if the matter in respect of which the inquiry is to be held relates to Wales.

(2) The references in paragraph 6A(1) and (2) to the Attorney General must be read as references to the Counsel General to the National Assembly for Wales.

(3) The Assembly may by regulations make provision as mentioned in paragraph 6A(3) in connection with a local inquiry to which this section applies.

(4) If the Assembly acts under sub-paragraph (3) rules made by the Lord Chancellor under paragraph 6A(3) do not have effect in relation to the inquiry.

(5) The Counsel General to the National Assembly for Wales is the person appointed by the Assembly to be its chief legal adviser (whether or not he is known by that title).

(6) Section 40(3) does not apply to regulations made under this paragraph.'

## Urgent development and works

### 82 Urgent Crown development

(1) Before section 294 of the principal Act (special enforcement notices in relation to development on Crown land) there is inserted the following section –

'293A Urgent Crown development: application

(1) This section applies to a development if the appropriate authority certifies –

(a) that the development is of national importance, and

(b) that it is necessary that the development is carried out as a matter of urgency.

(2) The appropriate authority may, instead of making an application for planning permission to the local planning authority in accordance with Part 3, make an application for planning permission to the Secretary of State under this section.

(3) If the appropriate authority proposes to make the application to the Secretary of State it must publish in one or more newspapers circulating in the locality of the proposed development a notice –

(a) describing the proposed development, and

(b) stating that the authority proposes to make the application to the Secretary of State.

(4) For the purposes of an application under this section the appropriate authority must provide to the Secretary of State –

(a) any matter required to be provided by an applicant for planning permission in pursuance of regulations made under section 71A;

(b) a statement of the authority's grounds for making the application.

(5) If the appropriate authority makes an application under this section subsections (6) to (9) below apply.

(6) The Secretary of State may require the authority to provide him with such further information as he thinks necessary to enable him to determine the application.

(7) As soon as practicable after he is provided with any document or other matter in pursuance of subsection (4) or (6) the Secretary of State must make a copy of the document or other matter available for inspection by the public in the locality of the proposed development.

(8) The Secretary of State must in accordance with such requirements as are contained in a development order publish notice of the application and of the fact that such documents and other material are available for inspection.

(9) The Secretary of State must consult –

    (a)    the local planning authority for the area to which the proposed development relates, and

    (b)    such other persons as are specified or described in a development order,

about the application.

(10) Subsection (7) does not apply to the extent that the document or other matter is subject to a direction under section 321(3) (matters related to national security).

(11) Subsections (4) to (7) of section 77 apply to an application under this section as they apply to an application in respect of which a direction under section 77 has effect.'

(2)    In section 284 of the principal Act (validity of certain matters) in subsection (3) at the end there is inserted the following paragraph –

'(i)    any decision on an application for planning permission under section 293A.'

### 83  Urgent works relating to Crown land

(1)    After section 82A of the listed buildings Act (inserted by section 79(2)) there is inserted the following section –

#### '82B  Urgent works relating to Crown land: application

(1) This section applies to any works proposed to be executed in connection with any building which is on Crown land if the appropriate authority certifies –

    (a)    that the works are of national importance, and

    (b)    that it is necessary that the works are carried out as a matter of urgency.

(2) The appropriate authority may, instead of making an application for consent to the local planning authority in accordance with this Act, make an application for consent to the Secretary of State under this section.

(3) If the appropriate authority proposes to make the application to the Secretary of State it must publish in one or more newspapers circulating in the locality of the building a notice –

    (a)    describing the proposed works, and

    (b)    stating that the authority proposes to make the application to the Secretary of State.

(4) For the purposes of an application under this section the appropriate authority must provide to the Secretary of State a statement of the authority's grounds for making the application.

(5) If the appropriate authority makes an application under this section subsections (6) to (9) below apply.

(6) The Secretary of State may require the authority to provide him with such further information as he thinks necessary to enable him to determine the application.

(7) As soon as practicable after he is provided with any document or other matter in pursuance of subsection (4) or (6) the Secretary of State must make a copy of the document or other matter available for inspection by the public in the locality of the proposed development.

(8) The Secretary of State must in accordance with such requirements as may be prescribed publish notice of the application and of the fact that such documents and other material are available for inspection.

(9) The Secretary of State must consult –

    (a)    the local planning authority for the area to which the proposed development relates, and

    (b)    such other persons as may be prescribed,

about the application.

(10) Subsection (7) does not apply to the extent that the document or other matter is subject to a direction under paragraph 6(6) of Schedule 3 (matters related to national security).

(11) Subsections (4) and (5) of section 12 apply to an application under this section as they apply to an application in respect of which a direction under section 12 has effect.'

(2) In section 62 of the listed buildings Act (validity of certain matters) in subsection (2) at the end there is inserted the following paragraph –

'(d) any decision on an application for listed building consent under section 82B.'

## Enforcement

### 84   Enforcement in relation to Crown land

(1) Section 296 of the principal Act (exercise of powers in relation to Crown land) is omitted.

(2) After section 296 there are inserted the following sections –

#### '296A   Enforcement in relation to the Crown

(1) No act or omission done or suffered by or on behalf of the Crown constitutes an offence under this Act.

(2) A local planning authority must not take any step for the purposes of enforcement in relation to Crown land unless it has the consent of the appropriate authority.

(3) The appropriate authority may give consent under subsection (2) subject to such conditions as it thinks appropriate.

(4) A step taken for the purposes of enforcement is anything done in connection with the enforcement of anything required to be done or prohibited by or under this Act.

(5) A step taken for the purposes of enforcement includes –

(a)   entering land;

(b)   bringing proceedings;

(c)   the making of an application.

(6) A step taken for the purposes of enforcement does not include –

(a)   service of a notice;

(b)   the making of an order (other than by a court).

#### 296B   References to an interest in land

(1) Subsection (2) applies to the extent that an interest in land is a Crown interest or a Duchy interest.

(2) Anything which requires or is permitted to be done by or in relation to the owner of the interest in land must be done by or in relation to the appropriate authority.

(3) An interest in land includes an interest only as occupier of the land.'

(3) After section 82C of the listed buildings Act (inserted by Schedule 3) there are inserted the following sections –

#### '82D   Enforcement in relation to the Crown

(1) No act or omission done or suffered by or on behalf of the Crown constitutes an offence under this Act.

(2) A local planning authority must not take any step for the purposes of enforcement in relation to Crown land unless it has the consent of the appropriate authority.

(3) The appropriate authority may give consent under subsection (2) subject to such conditions as it thinks appropriate.

(4) A step taken for the purposes of enforcement is anything done in connection with the enforcement of anything required to be done or prohibited by or under this Act.

(5) A step taken for the purposes of enforcement includes –

    (a) entering land;

    (b) bringing proceedings;

    (c) the making of an application.

(6) A step taken for the purposes of enforcement does not include –

    (a) service of a notice;

    (b) the making of an order (other than by a court).

### 82E References to an interest in land

(1) Subsection (2) applies to the extent that an interest in land is a Crown interest or a Duchy interest.

(2) Anything which requires or is permitted to be done by or in relation to the owner of the interest in land must be done by or in relation to the appropriate authority.

(3) An interest in land includes an interest only as occupier of the land.'

(4) After section 30B of the hazardous substances Act (inserted by section 79(3)) there are inserted the following sections –

### '30C Enforcement in relation to the Crown

(1) No act or omission done or suffered by or on behalf of the Crown constitutes an offence under this Act.

(2) A local planning authority must not take any step for the purposes of enforcement in relation to Crown land unless it has the consent of the appropriate authority.

(3) The appropriate authority may give consent under subsection (2) subject to such conditions as it thinks appropriate.

(4) A step taken for the purposes of enforcement is anything done in connection with the enforcement of anything required to be done or prohibited by or under this Act.

(5) A step taken for the purposes of enforcement includes –

    (a) entering land;

    (b) bringing proceedings;

    (c) the making of an application.

(6) A step taken for the purposes of enforcement does not include –

    (a) service of a notice;

    (b) the making of an order (other than by a court).

### 30D References to an interest in land

(1) Subsection (2) applies to the extent that an interest in land is a Crown interest or a Duchy interest.

(2) Anything which requires or is permitted to be done by or in relation to the owner of the interest in land must be done by or in relation to the appropriate authority.

(3) An interest in land includes an interest only as occupier of the land.'

## *Trees*

### 85 Tree preservation orders: Forestry Commissioners

For section 200 of the principal Act (Orders affecting land where Forestry Commissioners interested) there is substituted the following section –

### '200 Tree preservation orders: Forestry Commissioners

(1) A tree preservation order does not have effect in respect of anything done –

    (a) by or on behalf of the Forestry Commissioners on land placed at their disposal in pursuance of the Forestry Act 1967 or otherwise under their management or supervision;

    (b) by or on behalf of any other person in accordance with a relevant plan which is for the time being in force.

(2) A relevant plan is a plan of operations or other working plan approved by the Forestry Commissioners under –

    (a) a forestry dedication covenant within the meaning of section 5 of the Forestry Act 1967, or

    (b) conditions of a grant or loan made under section 1 of the Forestry Act 1979.

(3) A reference to a provision of the Forestry Act 1967 or the Forestry Act 1979 includes a reference to a corresponding provision replaced by that provision or any earlier corresponding provision.'

### 86 Trees in conservation areas: acts of Crown

After section 211(4) of the principal Act (preservation of trees in conservation areas) there are inserted the following subsections –

'(5) An emanation of the Crown must not, in relation to a tree to which this section applies, do an act mentioned in subsection (1) above unless –

    (a) the first condition is satisfied, and

    (b) either the second or third condition is satisfied.

(6) The first condition is that the emanation serves notice of an intention to do the act (with sufficient particulars to identify the tree) on the local planning authority in whose area the tree is situated.

(7) The second condition is that the act is done with the consent of the authority.

(8) The third condition is that the act is done –

    (a) after the end of the period of six weeks starting with the date of the notice, and

    (b) before the end of the period of two years starting with that date.'

## *Miscellaneous*

### 87 Old mining permissions

(1) Subsection (2) applies if –

    (a) an old mining permission relates to land which is Crown land, and

    (b) the permission has not been registered in pursuance of Schedule 2 to the Planning and Compensation Act 1991.

(2) Section 22 of and Schedule 2 to that Act apply to the old mining permission subject to the following modifications –

    (a) in section 22(3) for 'May 1, 1991' there is substituted 'the date of commencement of section 87(2) of the Planning and Compulsory Purchase Act 2004';

(b)    in paragraph 1(3) of Schedule 2 for 'the day on which this Schedule comes into force' there is substituted 'the date of commencement of section 87(2) of the Planning and Compulsory Purchase Act 2004'.

(3)    Old mining permission must be construed in accordance with section 22 of the Planning and Compensation Act 1991.

(4)    Crown land must be construed in accordance with Part 13 of the principal Act.

## 88  Subordinate legislation

(1)    The Secretary of State may by order provide that relevant subordinate legislation applies to the Crown.

(2)    The order may modify such subordinate legislation to the extent that the Secretary of State thinks appropriate for the purposes of its application to the Crown.

(3)    Relevant subordinate legislation is an instrument which –

(a)    is made under or (wholly or in part) for the purposes of any of the planning Acts,

(b)    is made before the commencement of section 79 of this Act, and

(c)    is specified in the order.

## 89  Crown application: transitional

Schedule 4 (which makes transitional provisions in consequence of the application to the Crown of the planning Acts) has effect.

## CHAPTER 2    SCOTLAND

*******

## PART 8    COMPULSORY PURCHASE

### *Acquisition of land for development*

## 99  Compulsory acquisition of land for development etc

(1)    Section 226 of the principal Act (compulsory acquisition of land for development and other planning purposes) is amended as follows.

(2)    In subsection (1) –

(a)    the first 'which' is omitted;

(b)    for paragraph (a) there is substituted the following paragraph –

'(a)    if the authority think that the acquisition will facilitate the carrying out of development, re-development or improvement on or in relation to the land,';

(c)    in paragraph (b) at the beginning there is inserted 'which'.

(3)    After subsection (1) there is inserted the following subsection –

'(1A)  But a local authority must not exercise the power under paragraph (a) of subsection (1) unless they think that the development, re-development or improvement is likely to contribute to the achievement of any one or more of the following objects –

(a)    the promotion or improvement of the economic well-being of their area;

(b)    the promotion or improvement of the social well-being of their area;

(c)    the promotion or improvement of the environmental well-being of their area.'

(4)    Subsection (2) is omitted.

(5)    Nothing in this section affects a compulsory purchase order made before the commencement of this section.

## *Authorisation of compulsory acquisition*

### 100  Procedure for authorisation by authority other than a Minister

(1)  The Acquisition of Land Act 1981 (c. 67) (the '1981 Act') is amended as follows.

(2)  In section 6 (service of documents), in subsection (4) –

   (a)  after 'lessee' in each place there is inserted ', tenant';
   (b)  after ''lessee' there is inserted', 'tenant''.

(3)  In section 7 (interpretation), after subsection (2) there is added –

   '(3)  But an instrument containing regulations made for the purposes of section 13A or paragraph 4A of Schedule 1 is subject to annulment in pursuance of a resolution of either House of Parliament.'

(4)  In section 11 (notices in newspapers), after subsection (2) there is added –

   '(3)  In addition, the acquiring authority shall affix a notice in the prescribed form to a conspicuous object or objects on or near the land comprised in the order.
   (4)  The notice under subsection (3) must –

      (a)  be addressed to persons occupying or having an interest in the land, and
      (b)  set out each of the matters mentioned in subsection (2) (but reading the reference there to first publication of the notice as a reference to the day when the notice under subsection (3) is first affixed).'

(5)  In section 12 (notices to owners, lessees and occupiers) –

   (a)  in subsection (1), for the words from 'owner' to 'order' (where it first appears) there is substituted 'qualifying person';
   (b)  for subsection (2) there is substituted –

      '(2)  A person is a qualifying person, in relation to land comprised in an order, if –

         (a)  he is an owner, lessee, tenant (whatever the tenancy period) or occupier of the land, or
         (b)  he falls within subsection (2A).

      (2A)  A person falls within this subsection if he is –

         (a)  a person to whom the acquiring authority would, if proceeding under section 5(1) of the Compulsory Purchase Act 1965, be required to give a notice to treat, or
         (b)  a person the acquiring authority thinks is likely to be entitled to make a relevant claim if the order is confirmed and the compulsory purchase takes place, so far as he is known to the acquiring authority after making diligent inquiry.

      (2B)  A relevant claim is a claim for compensation under section 10 of the Compulsory Purchase Act 1965 (compensation for injurious affection).'

(6)  For section 13 (confirmation of compulsory purchase order) there are substituted the following sections –

### '13  Confirmation of order: no objections

(1)  The confirming authority may confirm a compulsory purchase order with or without modifications if it is satisfied –

   (a)  that the notice requirements have been complied with, and
   (b)  that one of the conditions in subsection (2) is satisfied.

(2)  The conditions are –

   (a)  no relevant objection is made;
   (b)  every relevant objection made is either withdrawn or disregarded.

(3) The confirming authority may require every person who makes a relevant objection to state the grounds of the objection in writing.

(4) If the confirming authority is satisfied that an objection relates exclusively to matters which can be dealt with by the tribunal by whom the compensation is to be assessed it may disregard the objection.

(5) The notice requirements are the requirements under sections 11 and 12 to publish, affix and serve notices in connection with the compulsory purchase order.

(6) A relevant objection is an objection by a person who is a qualifying person for the purposes of section 12(2), but if such a person qualifies only by virtue of section 12(2A)(b) and the confirming authority thinks that he is not likely to be entitled to make a relevant claim his objection is not a relevant objection.

(7) Disregarded means disregarded under subsection (4) or under any other power to disregard a relevant objection contained in the enactment providing for the compulsory purchase.

### 13A  Confirmation of order: remaining objections

(1) This section applies to the confirmation of a compulsory purchase order if a relevant objection is made which is neither –

(a) withdrawn, nor
(b) disregarded,

(a remaining objection).

(2) The confirming authority may proceed under the written representations procedure –

(a) if the order is not subject to special parliamentary procedure,
(b) in the case of an order to which section 16 applies, if a certificate has been given under subsection (2) of that section, and
(c) if every person who has made a remaining objection consents in the prescribed manner.

(3) If subsection (2) does not apply or if the confirming authority decides not to proceed under that subsection, it must either –

(a) cause a public local inquiry to be held, or
(b) give every person who has made a remaining objection an opportunity of appearing before and being heard by a person appointed by the confirming authority for the purpose.

(4) If a person who has made a remaining objection takes the opportunity to appear before a person appointed under subsection (3)(b) the confirming authority must give the acquiring authority and any other person it thinks appropriate the opportunity to be heard at the same time.

(5) The confirming authority may confirm the order with or without modifications if it has considered the objection and either –

(a) it has followed the written representations procedure, or
(b) in a case which falls within subsection (3), if an inquiry was held or a person was appointed under subsection (3)(b), it has considered the report of the person who held the inquiry or who was so appointed.

(6) The written representations procedure is such procedure as is prescribed for the purposes of this section including provision affording an opportunity to –

(a) every person who has made a remaining objection,
(b) the acquiring authority, and
(c) any other person the confirming authority thinks appropriate,

to make written representations as to whether the order should be confirmed.

(7) Relevant objection and disregarded must be construed in accordance with section 13.

**13B Written representations procedure: supplementary**

(1) This section applies where the confirming authority decides under section 13A to follow the written representations procedure.

(2) The confirming authority may make orders as to the costs of the parties to the written representations procedure, and as to which party must pay the costs.

(3) An order under subsection (2) may be made a rule of the High Court on the application of any party named in the order.

(4) The costs incurred by the confirming authority in connection with the written representations procedure must be paid by the acquiring authority, if the confirming authority so directs.

(5) The confirming authority may certify the amount of its costs, and any amount so certified and directed to be paid by the acquiring authority is recoverable summarily by the confirming authority as a civil debt.

(6) Section 42(2) of the Housing and Planning Act 1986 (recovery of Minister's costs in connection with inquiries) applies to the written representations procedure as if the procedure is an inquiry specified in section 42(1) of that Act.

(7) Regulations under section 13A(6) may make provision as to the giving of reasons for decisions taken in cases where the written representations procedure is followed.

**13C Confirmation in stages**

(1) The confirming authority may confirm an order (with or without modifications) so far as it relates to part of the land comprised in the order (the 'relevant part') if each of the conditions in subsection (2) is met.

(2) The conditions are –

   (a) the confirming authority is satisfied that the order ought to be confirmed so far as it relates to the relevant part but has not for the time being determined whether the order ought to be confirmed so far as it relates to the remaining part;

   (b) the confirming authority is satisfied that the notice requirements have been complied with.

(3) If there is a remaining objection in respect of the order, the confirming authority may only act under subsection (1) after complying with section 13A(2) or (3) (as the case may be).

(4) But it may act under subsection (1) without complying with those provisions if it is satisfied that all remaining objections relate solely to the remaining part of the land.

(5) If the confirming authority acts under subsection (1) –

   (a) it must give a direction postponing consideration of the order, so far as it relates to the remaining part, until such time as may be specified by or under the direction;

   (b) the order so far as it relates to each part of the land must be treated as a separate order.

(6) The notices to be published, affixed and served under section 15 must include a statement as to the effect of the direction given under subsection (5)(a).

(7) Notice requirements must be construed in accordance with section 13.

(8) Remaining objection must be construed in accordance with section 13A.'

(7) For section 15 there is substituted –

**'15 Notices after confirmation of order**

(1) After the order has been confirmed, the acquiring authority must –

(a)  serve a confirmation notice and a copy of the order as confirmed on each person on whom a notice was required to be served under section 12, and

(b)  affix a confirmation notice to a conspicuous object or objects on or near the land comprised in the order.

(2)  The notice under subsection (1)(b) must –

(a)  be addressed to persons occupying or having an interest in the land;

(b)  so far as practicable, be kept in place by the acquiring authority until the expiry of a period of six weeks beginning with the date when the order becomes operative.

(3)  The acquiring authority must also publish a confirmation notice in one or more local newspapers circulating in the locality in which the land comprised in the order is situated.

(4)  A confirmation notice is a notice –

(a)  describing the land;

(b)  stating that the order has been confirmed;

(c)  (except in the case of a notice under subsection (1)(a)) naming a place where a copy of the order as confirmed and of the map referred to there may be inspected at all reasonable hours;

(d)  that a person aggrieved by the order may apply to the High Court as mentioned in section 23.

(5)  A confirmation notice must be in the prescribed form.'

(8)  The amendments made by this section do not apply to orders of which notice under section 11 of the 1981 Act has been published before commencement of this section.

## 101  Procedure for authorisation by a Minister

(1)  Schedule 1 to the Acquisition of Land Act 1981 (c. 67) (the '1981 Act') is amended as follows.

(2)  In paragraph 2 (notices in newspapers), after sub-paragraph (2) there is added –

'(3)  In addition, the Minister shall affix a notice in the prescribed form to a conspicuous object or objects on or near the land comprised in the draft order.

(4)  The notice under sub-paragraph (3) must –

(a)  be addressed to persons occupying or having an interest in the land, and

(b)  set out each of the matters mentioned in sub-paragraph (2) (but reading the reference there to first publication of the notice as a reference to the day when the notice under sub-paragraph (3) is first affixed).'

(3)  In paragraph 3 (notices to owners, lessees and occupiers) –

(a)  in sub-paragraph (1), for the words from 'owner' to 'order' (where it first appears) there is substituted 'qualifying person';

(b)  for sub-paragraph (2) there is substituted –

'(2)  A person is a qualifying person, in relation to land comprised in a draft order, if –

(a)  he is an owner, lessee, tenant (whatever the tenancy period) or occupier of any such land, or

(b)  he falls within sub-paragraph (2A).

(2A)  A person falls within this sub-paragraph if he is –

(a)  a person to whom the Minister would, if proceeding under section 5(1) of the Compulsory Purchase Act 1965, be required to give a notice to treat, or

(b)  a person the Minister thinks is likely to be entitled to make a relevant claim if the order is made and the compulsory purchase takes place, so far as he is known to the Minister after making diligent inquiry.

(2B) A relevant claim is a claim for compensation under section 10 of the Compulsory Purchase Act 1965 (compensation for injurious affection).'

(4) For paragraph 4 there are substituted the following paragraphs –

'4   (1) The Minister may make a compulsory purchase order with or without modifications if he is satisfied –

   (a)  that the notice requirements have been complied with, and
   (b)  that one of the conditions in sub-paragraph (2) is satisfied.

(2) The conditions are –

   (a)  no relevant objection is made;
   (b)  every relevant objection made is either withdrawn or disregarded.

(3) The appropriate authority may require every person who makes a relevant objection to state the grounds of the objection in writing.

(4) If the appropriate authority is satisfied that an objection relates exclusively to matters which can be dealt with by the tribunal by whom the compensation is to be assessed it may disregard the objection.

(5) The notice requirements are the requirements under paragraphs 2 and 3 to publish, affix and serve notices in connection with the compulsory purchase order.

(6) A relevant objection is an objection by a person who is a qualifying person for the purposes of paragraph 3(2), but if such a person qualifies only by virtue of paragraph 3(2A)(b) and the Minister thinks that he is not likely to be entitled to make a relevant claim his objection is not a relevant objection.

(7) Disregarded means disregarded under sub-paragraph (4) or under any other power to disregard a relevant objection contained in the enactment providing for the compulsory purchase.

(8) The appropriate authority is –

   (a)  in the case of an order proposed to be made in the exercise of highway land acquisition powers, the Minister and the planning Minister acting jointly,
   (b)  in any other case, the Minister.

(9) Highway land acquisition powers must be construed in accordance with the Highways Act 1980.

(10) The planning Minister is the Secretary of State for the time being having general responsibility in planning matters.

4A   (1) This paragraph applies to the making of a compulsory purchase order if a relevant objection is made which is neither –

   (a)  withdrawn, nor
   (b)  disregarded,

   (a remaining objection).

(2) The appropriate authority may proceed under the written representations procedure –

   (a)  if the order is not subject to special parliamentary procedure;
   (b)  in the case of an order to which section 16 applies, if a certificate has been given under subsection (2) of that section, and
   (c)  if every person who has made a remaining objection consents in the prescribed manner.

(3) If sub-paragraph (2) does not apply or if the appropriate authority decides not to proceed under that sub-paragraph, it must either –

   (a)  cause a public local inquiry to be held, or

(b)    give every person who has made a remaining objection an opportunity of appearing before and being heard by a person appointed by the appropriate authority for the purpose.

(4)    If a person who has made a remaining objection takes the opportunity to appear before a person appointed under sub-paragraph (3)(b) the appropriate authority must give any other person it thinks appropriate the opportunity to be heard at the same time.

(5)    The Minister may make the order with or without modifications if –

(a)    the appropriate authority has considered the objection, and

(b)    one of the conditions in sub-paragraph (6) is satisfied.

(6)    The conditions are –

(a)    the appropriate authority has followed the written representations procedure;

(b)    in a case which falls within sub-paragraph (3), if an inquiry was held or a person was appointed under sub-paragraph (3)(b), the appropriate authority has considered the report of the person who held the inquiry or who was so appointed.

(7)    The written representations procedure is such procedure as is prescribed for the purposes of this paragraph including provision affording an opportunity to –

(a)    every person who has made a remaining objection, and

(b)    any other person the appropriate authority thinks appropriate,

to make written representations as to whether the order should be made.

(8)    Regulations under sub-paragraph (7) may make provision as to the giving of reasons for decisions taken in cases where the written representations procedure is followed.

(9)    Expressions used in this paragraph and in paragraph 4 must be construed in accordance with paragraph 4.

4B    (1)    The Minister may make an order (with or without modifications) so far as it relates to part of the land comprised in the draft order (the 'relevant part') if each of the conditions in sub-paragraph (2) is met.

(2)    The conditions are –

(a)    the Minister or, if there is a remaining objection in respect of the order, the appropriate authority is satisfied that the order ought to be made so far as it relates to the relevant part but has not for the time being determined whether the order ought to be made so far as it relates to the remaining part;

(b)    the Minister is satisfied that the notice requirements have been complied with.

(3)    If there is a remaining objection in respect of the order, the Minister may only act under sub-paragraph (1) after the appropriate authority has complied with paragraph 4A(2) or (3) (as the case may be).

(4)    But he may act under sub-paragraph (1) without the appropriate authority having complied with those provisions if he is satisfied that all remaining objections relate solely to the remaining part of the land.

(5)    If the Minister acts under sub-paragraph (1) –

(a)    he must give a direction postponing consideration of the order, so far as it relates to the remaining part, until such time as may be specified by or under the direction;

(b)    the order so far as it relates to each part of the land must be treated as a separate order.

(6)   The notices to be published, affixed and served under paragraph 6 must include a statement as to the effect of the direction given under sub-paragraph (5)(a).

(7)   Expressions used in this paragraph and in paragraph 4 or 4A must be construed in accordance with paragraph 4 or 4A (as the case may be).'

(5)   For paragraph 6 there is substituted –

'6   (1)   After the order has been made, the Minister must –

(a)   serve a making notice, and a copy of the order as made, on each person on whom a notice was required to be served under paragraph 3, and

(b)   affix a making notice to a conspicuous object or objects on or near the land comprised in the order.

(2)   The notice under sub-paragraph (1)(b) must –

(a)   be addressed to persons occupying or having an interest in the land;

(b)   so far as practicable, be kept in place by the acquiring authority until the expiry of a period of six weeks beginning with the date when the order becomes operative.

(3)   The Minister must also publish a making notice in one or more local newspapers circulating in the locality in which the land comprised in the order is situated.

(4)   A making notice is a notice –

(a)   describing the land;

(b)   stating that the order has been made;

(c)   (except in the case of a notice under sub-paragraph (1)(a)) naming a place where a copy of the order as made and of the map referred to there may be inspected at all reasonable hours;

(d)   that a person aggrieved by the order may apply to the High Court as mentioned in section 23.

(5)   A making notice must be in the prescribed form.'

(6)   The amendments made by this section do not apply to orders of which notice under paragraph 2 of Schedule 1 to the 1981 Act has been published before commencement of this section.

## 102   Confirmation by acquiring authority

(1)   The Acquisition of Land Act 1981 (c. 67) (the '1981 Act') is amended as follows.

(2)   After section 14 there is inserted –

### '14A   Confirmation by acquiring authority

(1)   The power to confirm an order may be exercised by the acquiring authority (instead of the confirming authority) if –

(a)   the confirming authority has notified the acquiring authority to that effect, and

(b)   the notice has not been revoked.

(2)   But this section does not apply to an order in respect of land –

(a)   falling within section 16(1) or paragraph 3(1) of Schedule 3, or

(b)   forming part of a common, open space or fuel or field garden allotment for the purposes of section 19.

(3)   The confirming authority may give notice under subsection (1) if it is satisfied –

(a)   that the notice requirements have been complied with,

(b)   that no objection has been made in relation to the proposed confirmation or that all objections have been withdrawn, and

    (c)   that the order is capable of being confirmed without modification.

(4) An objection is an objection made by any person (whether or not a person mentioned in section 12(2)), including an objection which is disregarded.

(5) The power to confirm an order under subsection (1) does not include any power –

    (a)   to confirm the order with modifications, or

    (b)   to confirm only a part of the order.

(6) The acquiring authority must notify the confirming authority as soon as reasonably practicable after it has determined whether or not to confirm the order.

(7) The confirming authority may revoke a notice given by it under subsection (1).

(8) But a notice may not be revoked if the determination has already been made and notified by the acquiring authority under subsection (6).

(9) An order confirmed by the acquiring authority under subsection (1) is to have the same effect as if it were confirmed by the confirming authority.

(10) Notices under this section must be in writing.

(11) Notice requirements and disregarded must be construed in accordance with section 13.'

(3)   The amendments made by this section do not apply to orders of which notice has been published under section 11 of the 1981 Act before commencement of this section.

## Valuation date

### 103  Assessment of compensation: valuation date

(1)   The Land Compensation Act 1961 (c. 33) is amended as follows.

(2)   After section 5 there is inserted –

#### '5A  Relevant valuation date

(1) If the value of land is to be assessed in accordance with rule (2) in section 5, the valuation must be made as at the relevant valuation date.

(2) No adjustment is to be made to the valuation in respect of anything which happens after the relevant valuation date.

(3) If the land is the subject of a notice to treat, the relevant valuation date is the earlier of –

    (a)   the date when the acquiring authority enters on and takes possession of the land, and

    (b)   the date when the assessment is made.

(4) If the land is the subject of a general vesting declaration, the relevant valuation date is the earlier of –

    (a)   the vesting date, and

    (b)   the date when the assessment is made,

and 'general vesting declaration' and 'vesting date' have the meanings given in section 2 of the Compulsory Purchase (Vesting Declarations) Act 1981.

(5) If the acquiring authority enters on and takes possession of part of the land –

    (a)   specified in a notice of entry, or

    (b)   in respect of which a payment into court has been made,

the authority is deemed, for the purposes of subsection (3)(a), to have entered on and taken possession of the whole of that land on that date.

(6) Subsection (5) also applies for the purposes of calculating interest under the following enactments –

(a)   section 11(1) of the Compulsory Purchase Act 1965;
(b)   paragraph 3 of Schedule 3 to that Act;
(c)   section 85 of the Lands Clauses Consolidation Act 1845;
(d)   section 52A of the Land Compensation Act 1973,

and references there to the date or time of entry are to be construed accordingly.

(7)   An assessment by the Lands Tribunal is treated as being made on the date certified by the Tribunal as –

(a)   the last hearing date before it makes its determination, or
(b)   in a case to be determined without an oral hearing, the last date for making written submissions before it makes its determination.

(8)   Nothing in this section affects –

(a)   any express provision in any other enactment which requires the valuation of land subject to compulsory acquisition to be made at a particular date;
(b)   the valuation of land for purposes other than the compulsory acquisition of that land (even if the valuation is to be made in accordance with the rules in section 5).

(9)   In this section –

(a)   a notice of entry is a notice under section 11(1) of the Compulsory Purchase Act 1965;
(b)   a payment into court is a payment into court under Schedule 3 to that Act or under section 85 of the Lands Clauses Consolidation Act 1845.'

## Advance payments

### 104   Compensation: advance payments to mortgagees

(1)   The Land Compensation Act 1973 is amended as follows.
(2)   In section 52 (right to advance payment of compensation) –

(a)   after subsection (1) there are inserted the following subsections –

'(1A) If the acquiring authority have taken possession of part of the land –

(a)   specified in a notice of entry, or
(b)   in respect of which a payment into court has been made,

the compensation mentioned in subsection (1) is the compensation payable for the compulsory acquisition of the interest in the whole of the land.

(1B) Notice of entry and payment into court must be construed in accordance with section 5A of the Land Compensation Act 1961.',

(b)   for subsection (6) there is substituted the following subsection –

'(6)   If the land is subject to a mortgage sections 52ZA and 52ZB apply.'

(3)   After section 52 of that Act there are inserted the following sections –

### '52ZA  Advance payments: land subject to mortgage

(1)   This section applies if –

(a)   an acquiring authority take possession of land,
(b)   a request is made in accordance with section 52(2) for an advance payment, and
(c)   the land is subject to a mortgage the principal of which does not exceed 90%; of the relevant amount.

(2)   The advance payment made to the claimant must be reduced by the amount the acquiring authority think will be required by them to secure the release of the interest of the mortgagee (or all the mortgagees if there is more than one).

(3)  The acquiring authority must pay to the mortgagee the amount the acquiring authority think will be required by them to secure the release of the mortgagee's interest, if –

(a)  the claimant so requests, and
(b)  the mortgagee consents to the making of the payment.

(4)  If there is more than one mortgagee –

(a)  subsection (3) applies to each mortgagee individually, but
(b)  payment must not be made to a mortgagee before the interest of each mortgagee whose interest has priority to his interest is released.

(5)  The amount of the advance payment made to the claimant under section 52 and the amount of the payments made to mortgagees under this section must not in aggregate exceed 90%; of the relevant amount.

(6)  Subsection (7) applies if –

(a)  the acquiring authority estimated the compensation,
(b)  it appears to the acquiring authority that their estimate was too low and they revise the estimate, and
(c)  a request is made by the claimant in accordance with section 52(2).

(7)  The provisions of subsections (2) to (5) must be re-applied on the basis of the revised estimate.

### 52ZB  Advance payments: land subject to mortgage exceeding 90%; threshold

(1)  This section applies if –

(a)  an acquiring authority take possession of land,
(b)  a request is made in accordance with section 52(2) for an advance payment, and
(c)  the land is subject to a mortgage the principal of which exceeds 90% of the relevant amount.

(2)  No advance payment is to be made to the claimant.

(3)  But the acquiring authority must pay to the mortgagee the amount found under subsection (4), if –

(a)  the claimant so requests, and
(b)  the mortgagee consents to the making of the payment.

(4)  The amount is whichever is the lesser of –

(a)  90% of the value of the land;
(b)  the principal of the mortgagee's mortgage.

(5)  The value of the land is the value –

(a)  agreed by the claimant and the acquiring authority, or (failing such agreement)
(b)  estimated by the acquiring authority.

(6)  For the purposes of subsection (5) the value of the land is to be calculated in accordance with rule 2 of section 5 of the Land Compensation Act 1961 (market value), whether or not compensation is or is likely to be assessed in due course in accordance with rule 5 of that section (equivalent re-instatement).

(7)  If there is more than one mortgagee, payment must not be made to a mortgagee until the interest of each mortgagee whose interest has priority to his interest is released.

(8)  But the total payments under subsection (3) must not in any event exceed 90% of the value of the land.

(9)  Subsection (10) applies if –

(a)    the acquiring authority estimated the compensation,

(b)    it appears to the acquiring authority that their estimate was too low and they revise the estimate,

(c)    the condition in section 52ZA(1)(b) would have been satisfied if the revised estimate had been used instead of their estimate, and

(d)    a request is made by the claimant in accordance with section 52(2).

(10) The provisions of section 52ZA(2) to (5) must be applied on the basis of the revised estimate.

(11) If –

(a)    the acquiring authority estimated the value of the land,

(b)    it appears to the acquiring authority that their estimate was too low and they revise the estimate, and

(c)    a request is made by the claimant in writing,

any balance found to be due to a mortgagee on the basis of the revised estimate is payable in accordance with this section.

### 52ZC  Land subject to mortgage: supplementary

(1)    This section applies for the purposes of sections 52ZA and 52ZB.

(2)    The claimant must provide the acquiring authority with such information as they may require to enable them to give effect to those sections.

(3)    A request under section 52ZA(3) or 52ZB(3) must be made in writing and must be accompanied by the written consent of the mortgagee.

(4)    Subsections (4) and (8) to (9) of section 52 apply to a payment which may be or is made under section 52ZA or 52ZB as they apply to a payment which may be or is made under section 52.

(5)    The relevant amount is the amount of the compensation agreed or estimated as mentioned in section 52(3).

(6)    If the land is subject to more than one mortgage, the reference in sections 52ZA(1)(c) and 52ZB(1)(c) to the principal is to the aggregate of the principals of all of the mortgagees.

(7)    A payment made to a mortgagee under section 52ZA or 52ZB –

(a)    must be applied by the mortgagee in or towards the discharge of the principal, interest and costs and any other money due under the mortgage;

(b)    must be taken to be a payment on account of compensation and treated for the purposes of section 52(10) as if it were an advance payment made under section 52;

(c)    must be taken, with effect from the date of the payment, to reduce by the amount of the payment the amount in respect of which interest accrues for the purposes of section 11(1) of the Compulsory Purchase Act 1965, any bond under Schedule 3 to that Act or section 85 of the Lands Clauses Compensation Act 1845;

(d)    must be taken into account for the purposes of determining any payments (or payments into court) which may be made for the purposes of sections 14 to 16 of the Compulsory Purchase Act 1965.

(8)    If the amount, or aggregate amount, of any payments under –

(a)    sections 52 and 52ZA, or

(b)    section 52ZB,

on the basis of the acquiring authority's estimate of the compensation exceed the compensation as finally determined or agreed, the excess must be repaid by the claimant.

(9)    No payment must be made to a mortgagee –

(a)   if any of the circumstances mentioned in subsection (10) applies, or

(b)   if the compulsory acquisition is only of a right over land.

(10) The circumstances are –

(a)   payment has been made under section 14(2) of the Compulsory Purchase Act 1965;

(b)   a notice under section 14(3) of that Act has been given;

(c)   there is an agreement under section 15(1) or 16(1) of that Act or the matter has been referred to the Lands Tribunal under that section.

(11) The claimant in relation to settled land for the purposes of the Settled Land Act 1925 is the persons entitled to give a discharge for capital money.'

(4)   In section 52A (right to interest where advance payment made) for subsection (2) there is substituted –

'(2)   If the authority make a payment under section 52(1) to any person on account of the compensation –

(a)   they must at the same time make a payment to that person of accrued interest, for the period beginning with the date of entry, on the amount of the compensation agreed or estimated under section 52(3) (the total amount), and

(b)   the difference between the paid amount and the total amount is an unpaid balance for the purposes of this section.

(2A) The paid amount is –

(a)   the amount of the payment under section 52(1), or

(b)   if the land is subject to a mortgage, the aggregate of that amount and the amount of any payment made under section 52ZA(3).'

## Information

### 105  Power to require information

(1)   The Acquisition of Land Act 1981 (c. 67) is amended as follows.

(2)   After section 5 (local inquiries) there is inserted –

#### '5A  Power to require information

(1)   This section applies to information about land in relation to which an acquiring authority is entitled to exercise a power of compulsory purchase.

(2)   The acquiring authority may serve a notice on a person mentioned in subsection (4) requiring him to give to the authority in writing the following information –

(a)   the name and address of any person he believes to be an owner, lessee, tenant (whatever the tenancy period) or occupier of the land;

(b)   the name and address of any person he believes to have an interest in the land.

(3)   The power in subsection (2) is exercisable for the purpose of enabling the acquiring authority to acquire the land.

(4)   The persons are –

(a)   the occupier of the land;

(b)   any person who has an interest in the land either as freeholder, mortgagee or lessee;

(c)   any person who directly or indirectly receives rent for the land;

(d)   any person who, in pursuance of an agreement between himself and a person interested in the land, is authorised to manage the land or to arrange for the letting of it.

(5)   The notice must specify the period within which the information must be given to the acquiring authority (being a period of not less than 14 days beginning with the day on which the notice is served).

(6)   The notice must also specify or describe –

    (a)   the land,

    (b)   the compulsory purchase power, and

    (c)   the enactment which confers the power.

(7)   The notice must be in writing.

(8)   Section 6(4) does not apply to notices to be served under this section.

### 5B  Offences relating to information

(1)   A person commits an offence if he fails without reasonable excuse to comply with a notice served on him under section 5A.

(2)   A person commits an offence if, in response to a notice served on him under section 5A –

    (a)   he gives information which is false in a material particular, and

    (b)   when he does so, he knows or ought reasonably to know that the information is false.

(3)   If an offence under this section committed by a body corporate is proved to have been committed with the consent or connivance of, or to be attributable to any neglect on the part of –

    (a)   a director, manager, secretary or other similar officer of the body corporate, or

    (b)   a person purporting to act in any such capacity,

he, as well as the body corporate, is guilty of that offence and liable to be proceeded against accordingly.

(4)   The reference in subsection (3) to a director must be construed in accordance with section 331(2) of the Town and Country Planning Act 1990.

(5)   A person guilty of an offence under this section is liable on summary conviction to a fine not exceeding level 5 on the standard scale.'

## Loss payments

### 106  Basic loss payment

(1)   After section 33 of the Land Compensation Act 1973 (c. 26) (home loss payments for certain caravan dwellers) there is inserted the following section –

## 'Other loss payments

### 33A  Basic loss payment

(1)   This section applies to a person –

    (a)   if he has a qualifying interest in land,

    (b)   if the interest is acquired compulsorily, and

    (c)   to the extent that he is not entitled to a home loss payment in respect of any part of the interest.

(2)   A person to whom this section applies is entitled to payment of whichever is the lower of the following amounts –

    (a)   7.5% of the value of his interest;

    (b)   £75,000.

(3)   A payment under this section must be made by the acquiring authority.

(4)  An interest in land is a qualifying interest if it is a freehold interest or an interest as tenant and (in either case) it subsists for a period of not less than one year ending with whichever is the earliest of –

   (a)  the date on which the acquiring authority takes possession of the land under section 11 of the Compulsory Purchase Act 1965 (entry to take possession of land);

   (b)  the date on which the acquiring authority enters the land if it proceeds under Schedule 3 to that Act;

   (c)  the vesting date (within the meaning of the Compulsory Purchase (Vesting Declarations) Act 1981) if a declaration is made under section 4 of that Act (general vesting declaration);

   (d)  the date on which compensation is agreed between the person and the acquiring authority;

   (e)  the date on which the amount of compensation is determined by the Lands Tribunal.

(5)  The compulsory acquisition of an interest in land includes acquisition of the interest in consequence of the service of –

   (a)  a purchase notice under section 137 of the Town and Country Planning Act 1990 (right to require purchase of certain interests);

   (b)  a notice under section 150 of that Act (purchase of blighted land).

(6)  The value of an interest is its value for the purpose of deciding the amount of compensation payable in respect of the acquisition; but this is subject to subsections (7) and (8).

(7)  If an interest consists partly of a dwelling in respect of which the person is entitled to a home loss payment the value of the interest is the value of the whole interest less the value of so much of the interest as is represented by the dwelling.

(8)  If rule (5) of section 5 of the Land Compensation Act 1961 (equivalent reinstatement) applies for the purpose of assessing the amount of compensation the value of the interest is nil.'

(2)  Section 33A of the Land Compensation Act 1973 (c. 26) (as inserted by subsection (1) above) does not apply in relation to a pre-commencement acquisition of an interest in land.

(3)  A pre-commencement acquisition of an interest in land is any of the following –

   (a)  acquisition by means of a compulsory purchase order if the order is made or made in draft before the commencement of this section;

   (b)  acquisition by means of an order made under section 1 or 3 of the Transport and Works Act 1992 (c. 42) (orders relating to certain transport works) if the application for the order was made to the Secretary of State before the commencement of this section;

   (c)  acquisition by means of an order under section 1 or 3 of that Act if the order is made in pursuance of section 7 of that Act (orders made without application) and the order is made in draft before the commencement of this section;

   (d)  acquisition by means of a power contained in an enactment (including a private or local Act) to acquire compulsorily specified land or a specified interest in land if the Bill providing for the power is introduced into Parliament before the commencement of this section.

## 107  Occupier's loss payment

(1)  After section 33A of the Land Compensation Act 1973 (inserted by section 106 of this Act) there are inserted the following sections –

'**33B Occupier's loss payment: agricultural land**

(1) This section applies to a person if –

    (a)   he has a qualifying interest in land for the purposes of section 33A,

    (b)   the land is agricultural land,

    (c)   the interest is acquired compulsorily, and

    (d)   he occupied the land for the period specified in section 33A(4).

(2) A person to whom this section applies is entitled to a payment of whichever is the greatest of the following amounts –

    (a)   2.5 % of the value of his interest;

    (b)   the land amount;

    (c)   the buildings amount.

(3) But the maximum amount which may be paid to a person under this section in respect of an interest in land is £25,000.

(4) A payment under this section must be made by the acquiring authority.

(5) The value of an interest is its value for the purpose of deciding the amount of compensation payable in respect of the acquisition; but this is subject to subsections (6) and (7).

(6) If an interest consists partly of a dwelling in respect of which the person is entitled to a home loss payment the value of the interest is the value of the whole interest less the value of so much of the interest as is represented by the dwelling.

(7) If rule (5) of section 5 of the Land Compensation Act 1961 (equivalent reinstatement) applies for the purpose of assessing the amount of compensation the value of the interest is nil.

(8) The land amount is the greater of £300 and the amount found in accordance with the following Table –

| Area of the land | Amount per hectare |
| --- | --- |
| Not exceeding 100 hectares | £100 per hectare or part of a hectare |
| Exceeding 100 hectares | (a) £100 per hectare for the first 100 hectares;<br>(b) £50 per hectare for the next 300 hectares or part of a hectare. |

(9) The buildings amount is £25 per square metre (or part of a square metre) of the gross floor space of any buildings on the land.

(10) The gross floor space must be measured externally.

## 33C Occupier's loss payment: other land

(1) This section applies to a person if –

    (a)   he has a qualifying interest in land for the purposes of section 33A,

    (b)   the land is not agricultural land,

    (c)   the interest is acquired compulsorily, and

    (d)   he occupied the land for the period specified in section 33A(4).

(2) A person to whom this section applies is entitled to a payment of whichever is the greatest of the following amounts –

    (a)   2.5 % of the value of his interest;

    (b)   the land amount;

    (c)   the buildings amount.

(3) But the maximum amount which may be paid to a person under this section in respect of an interest in land is £25,000.

(4) A payment under this section must be made by the acquiring authority.

(5) The value of an interest is its value for the purpose of deciding the amount of compensation payable in respect of the acquisition; but this is subject to subsections (6) and (7).

(6) If an interest consists partly of a dwelling in respect of which the person is entitled to a home loss payment the value of the interest is the value of the whole interest less the value of so much of the interest as is represented by the dwelling.

(7) If rule (5) of section 5 of the Land Compensation Act 1961 (equivalent reinstatement) applies for the purpose of assessing the amount of compensation the value of the interest is nil.

(8) The land amount is the greater of –

   (a)  £2,500;

   (b)  £2.50 per square metre (or part of a square metre) of the area of the land.

(9) But if only part of land in which a person has an interest is acquired, for the figure specified in subsection (8)(a) there is substituted £300.

(10) The buildings amount is £25 per square metre (or part of a square metre) of the gross floor space of any buildings on the land.

(11) The gross floor space must be measured externally.'

(2) Sections 33B and 33C of the Land Compensation Act 1973 (c. 26) (as inserted by subsection (1) above) do not apply in relation to a pre-commencement acquisition of an interest in land.

(3) A pre-commencement acquisition of an interest in land is any of the following –

   (a)  acquisition by means of a compulsory purchase order if the order is made or made in draft before the commencement of this section;

   (b)  acquisition by means of an order made under section 1 or 3 of the Transport and Works Act 1992 (c. 42) (orders relating to certain transport works) if the application for the order was made to the Secretary of State before the commencement of this section;

   (c)  acquisition by means of an order under section 1 or 3 of that Act if the order is made in pursuance of section 7 of that Act (orders made without application) and the order is made in draft before the commencement of this section;

   (d)  acquisition by means of a power contained in an enactment (including a private or local Act) to acquire compulsorily specified land or a specified interest in land if the Bill providing for the power is introduced into Parliament before the commencement of this section.

## 108 Loss payments: exclusions

(1) After section 33C of the Land Compensation Act 1973 (inserted by section 107 of this Act) there is inserted the following section –

### '33D Loss payments: exclusions

(1) This section applies to a person if –

   (a)  he is a person to whom section 33A, 33B or 33C applies,

   (b)  a notice falling within subsection (4) has been served on him in relation to the land mentioned in that section,

   (c)  at the relevant time the notice has effect or is operative, and

   (d)  he has failed to comply with any requirement of the notice.

(2) This section also applies to a person if –

   (a)  he is a person to whom section 33A, 33B or 33C applies,

   (b)  a copy of an order falling within subsection (5) has been served on him in relation to the land mentioned in that section, and

   (c)  the order has not been quashed on appeal.

(3)  No payment may be made under section 33A, 33B or 33C to a person to whom this section applies.

(4)  These are the notices –

    (a)  notice under section 215 of the Town and Country Planning Act 1990 (power to require proper maintenance of land);

    (b)  notice under section 189 of the Housing Act 1985 (requirement to repair dwelling etc. unfit for human habitation);

    (c)  notice under section 190 of that Act (requirement to repair dwelling etc. in state of disrepair);

    (d)  notice under section 48 of the Planning (Listed Buildings and Conservation Areas) Act 1990 (repairs notice prior to compulsory notice of acquisition of listed building).

(5)  These are the orders –

    (a)  an order under section 264 of the Housing Act 1985 (closure of dwelling etc. unfit for human habitation);

    (b)  an order under section 265 of that Act (demolition of dwelling etc. unfit for human habitation).

(6)  The relevant time is the time at which the compulsory purchase order in relation to the person's interest in the land –

    (a)  is confirmed, in the case of an order falling within section 2(2) of the Acquisition of Land Act 1981 (procedure for authorisation);

    (b)  is made, in the case of an order falling within section 2(3) of that Act.

(7)  The Secretary of State may by regulations amend subsections (4) and (5).'

(2)  Section 33D of the Land Compensation Act 1973 (c. 26) (as inserted by subsection (1) above) does not apply in relation to a notice or order specified in subsection (4) or (5) of that section if the notice or copy of the order was served on a person to whom that section applies before the commencement of this section.

## 109  Loss payments: supplementary

After section 33D of the Land Compensation Act 1973 (inserted by section 108 of this Act) there are inserted the following sections –

### '33E  Claims

(1)  This section applies for the purposes of sections 33A to 33C.

(2)  A claim for payment must be made in writing to the acquiring authority.

(3)  The claim must give such particulars as the authority may reasonably require for the purpose of deciding –

    (a)  whether a payment is to be made;

    (b)  the amount of any such payment.

(4)  For the purposes of the Limitation Act 1980 a person's right of action to recover a payment must be taken to have accrued –

    (a)  in the case of a claim under section 33A on the last day of the period specified in subsection (4) of that section;

    (b)  in the case of a claim under section 33B or 33C on the date of his displacement from the land.

### 33F  Insolvency

(1)  This section applies if a person is entitled to a payment under section 33A, 33B or 33C but before a claim is made under section 33E insolvency proceedings are started in relation to the person.

(2) Any of the following may make a claim instead of the person mentioned in subsection (1) –

    (a) a receiver, trustee in bankruptcy or the official receiver in the case of an individual;

    (b) an administrator, administrative receiver, liquidator or provisional liquidator or the official receiver in the case of a company or a partnership.

(3) Insolvency proceedings are –

    (a) proceedings in bankruptcy;

    (b) proceedings under the Insolvency Act 1986 for the winding up of a company or an unregistered company (including voluntary winding up of a company under Part 4 of that Act);

    (c) proceedings for the winding up of a partnership.

### 33G Death

(1) This section applies if a person is entitled to a payment under section 33A, 33B or 33C but before a claim is made under section 33E the person dies (the deceased).

(2) A claim may be made by a person who –

    (a) occupied the land for a period of not less than one year ending with the date on which the deceased is displaced from the land, and

    (b) is entitled to benefit on the death of the deceased by virtue of a ground mentioned in subsection (3).

(3) The grounds are –

    (a) a testamentary disposition;

    (b) the law of intestate succession;

    (c) the right of survivorship between joint tenants.

### 33H Agricultural land: dual entitlement

(1) This section applies if a person is entitled in respect of the same interest in agricultural land to a payment both –

    (a) under section 33B of this Act, and

    (b) by virtue of section 12(1) of the Agriculture (Miscellaneous Provisions) Act 1968 (additional payments in consequence of compulsory acquisition of agricultural holding).

(2) Payment may be made in respect of only one entitlement.

(3) If the person makes a claim under both provisions he must be paid in respect of the entitlement which produces the greater amount.

### 33I Payment

(1) Any dispute as to the amount of a payment to be made under section 33A, 33B or 33C must be determined by the Lands Tribunal.

(2) The acquiring authority must make any payment required by section 33A not later than whichever is the latest of the following dates –

    (a) the last day of the period specified in section 33A(4);

    (b) the last day of the period of three months beginning with the day the claim is made;

    (c) the day on which the amount of the payment is determined.

(3) The authority must make any payment required by section 33B or 33C not later than whichever is the latest of the following dates –

    (a)   the date the person is displaced from the land;

    (b)   the last day of the period of three months beginning with the day the claim is made;

    (c)   the day on which the amount of the payment is determined.

(4)  If paragraph (c) of subsection (2) or (3) applies the authority may at any time make a payment in advance to the person entitled to a payment (the claimant).

(5)  If when the value of the interest is agreed or determined the amount of a payment made under subsection (4) differs from the payment required by section 33A, 33B or 33C –

    (a)   the amount by which the advance payment exceeds the payment required must be repaid by the claimant to the authority;

    (b)   the amount by which the payment required exceeds the advance payment must be paid by the authority to the claimant.

(6)  The acquiring authority must pay interest on the amount required to be paid at the rate prescribed by regulations under section 32 of the Land Compensation Act 1961.

(7)  Interest accrues from the date specified in paragraph (a) of subsection (2) or (3) (as the case may be).

(8)  The authority may, at the request of the person entitled to the payment, make a payment on account of the interest mentioned in subsection (6).

### 33J  Acquisition by agreement

(1)  This section applies if –

    (a)   an interest in land which is a qualifying interest for the purpose of section 33A is acquired by agreement by an authority which has power to acquire the interest compulsorily, and

    (b)   the interest is acquired from a person who would be entitled to a payment under section 33A, 33B or 33C if the interest is acquired compulsorily.

(2)  The authority may make a payment to the person of an amount equal to the amount they would be required to pay if the interest is acquired compulsorily.

### 33K  Regulations

(1)  This section applies for the purposes of sections 33A to 33I.

(2)  The Secretary of State may by regulations substitute for any amount or percentage figure specified in these sections such other amount or percentage figure (as the case may be) as he thinks fit.

(3)  Except as provided in the following provisions of this section, a power to make regulations must be exercised by statutory instrument subject to annulment in pursuance of a resolution of either House of Parliament.

(4)  This subsection applies to regulations under subsection (2) which substitute –

    (a)   a percentage figure, or

    (b)   an amount, in a case where the change in value condition is not satisfied.

(5)  A statutory instrument containing regulations to which subsection (4) applies must not be made unless a draft of the regulations has been laid before and approved by resolution of each House of Parliament.

(6)  The change in value condition is satisfied if the Secretary of State thinks that in the case of the substitution of an amount it is expedient to make the substitution in consequence of changes in the value of money or land.

(7)  Regulations under subsection (2) may make different provision for different purposes.'

*Corresponding amendments of other enactments*

### 110  Corresponding amendments of other enactments

(1)  This section applies to any enactment passed or made before or in the same session as the passing of this Act (other than an enactment amended by this Part) which makes provision –

    (a)  in connection with the compulsory acquisition of an interest in land,

    (b)  creating a power which permits the interference with or affectation of any right in relation to land, or

    (c)  for the payment of any sum in connection with the acquisition, interference or affectation.

(2)  The Secretary of State may by order amend an enactment to which this section applies for the purpose of making provision which –

    (a)  corresponds to provision made by this Part, or

    (b)  applies any such provision or corresponding provision.

## PART 9  MISCELLANEOUS AND GENERAL

*Crown*

### 111  Crown

(1)  This Act (except Part 8) binds the Crown.

(2)  The amendment of an enactment by or by virtue of Part 8 applies to the Crown to the extent that the enactment amended so applies.

*Parliament*

### 112  Parliament

The planning Acts and this Act have effect despite any rule of law relating to Parliament or the law and practice of Parliament.

*Miscellaneous*

### 113  Validity of strategies, plans and documents

(1)  This section applies to –

    (a)  a revision of the regional spatial strategy;

    (b)  the Wales Spatial Plan;

    (c)  a development plan document;

    (d)  a local development plan;

    (e)  a revision of a document mentioned in paragraph (b), (c) or (d);

    (f)  the Mayor of London's spatial development strategy;

    (g)  an alteration or replacement of the spatial development strategy,

and anything falling within paragraphs (a) to (g) is referred to in this section as a relevant document.

(2)  A relevant document must not be questioned in any legal proceedings except in so far as is provided by the following provisions of this section.

(3)  A person aggrieved by a relevant document may make an application to the High Court on the ground that –

    (a)  the document is not within the appropriate power;

    (b)  a procedural requirement has not been complied with.

(4) But the application must be made not later than the end of the period of six weeks starting with the relevant date.

(5) The High Court may make an interim order suspending the operation of the relevant document –

    (a)  wholly or in part;

    (b)  generally or as it affects the property of the applicant.

(6) Subsection (7) applies if the High Court is satisfied –

    (a)  that a relevant document is to any extent outside the appropriate power;

    (b)  that the interests of the applicant have been substantially prejudiced by a failure to comply with a procedural requirement.

(7) The High Court may quash the relevant document –

    (a)  wholly or in part;

    (b)  generally or as it affects the property of the applicant.

(8) An interim order has effect until the proceedings are finally determined.

(9) The appropriate power is –

    (a)  Part 1 of this Act in the case of a revision of the regional spatial strategy;

    (b)  section 60 above in the case of the Wales Spatial Plan or any revision of it;

    (c)  Part 2 of this Act in the case of a development plan document or any revision of it;

    (d)  sections 62 to 78 above in the case of a local development plan or any revision of it;

    (e)  sections 334 to 343 of the Greater London Authority Act 1999 (c. 29) in the case of the spatial development strategy or any alteration or replacement of it.

(10) A procedural requirement is a requirement under the appropriate power or contained in regulations or an order made under that power which relates to the adoption, publication or approval of a relevant document.

(11) References to the relevant date must be construed as follows –

    (a)  for the purposes of a revision of the regional spatial strategy, the date when the Secretary of State publishes the revised strategy under section 9(6) above;

    (b)  for the purposes of the Wales Spatial Plan (or a revision of it), the date when it is approved by the National Assembly for Wales;

    (c)  for the purposes of a development plan document (or a revision of it), the date when it is adopted by the local planning authority or approved by the Secretary of State (as the case may be);

    (d)  for the purposes of a local development plan (or a revision of it), the date when it is adopted by a local planning authority in Wales or approved by the National Assembly for Wales (as the case may be);

    (e)  for the purposes of the spatial development strategy (or an alteration or replacement of it), the date when the Mayor of London publishes it.

## 114 Examinations

An examination of any document or plan for the purposes of Part 2 or Part 6 of this Act is a statutory inquiry within the meaning of the Tribunals and Inquiries Act 1992 (c. 53).

## 115 Grants for advice and assistance

In the principal Act after section 304 (grants for research and education) there is inserted the following section –

### '304A Grants for advice and assistance

    (1)  The appropriate authority may make grants for the purpose of assisting any person to provide advice and assistance in connection with any matter which is related to –

(a)   the planning Acts;

(b)   the Planning and Compulsory Purchase Act 2004;

(c)   the enactments mentioned in subsection (2).

(2)   The enactments are enactments which relate to planning contained in the following Acts –

(a)   the Planning and Compensation Act 1991;

(b)   the Transport and Works Act 1992;

(c)   the Environment Act 1995.

(3)   The appropriate authority may make a grant subject to such terms and conditions as it thinks appropriate.

(4)   Person includes a body whether or not incorporated.

(5)   The appropriate authority is –

(a)   the Secretary of State in relation to England;

(b)   the National Assembly for Wales in relation to Wales.'

## 116  Isles of Scilly

(1)   This Act applies to the Isles of Scilly subject to such exceptions, adaptations and modifications as the Secretary of State may by order direct.

(2)   An order may in particular provide for –

(a)   the Council of the Isles of Scilly to enter into arrangements in pursuance of section 4;

(b)   the exercise by the Council of the Isles of Scilly of any function exercisable by a local planning authority under Part 2.

(3)   But an order must not be made under this section unless the Secretary of State has consulted the Council of the Isles of Scilly.

## 117  Interpretation

(1)   Expressions used in this Act and in the principal Act have the same meaning in this Act as in that Act.

(2)   Expressions used in this Act and in the listed buildings Act have the same meaning in this Act as in that Act.

(3)   Expressions used in this Act and in the hazardous substances Act have the same meaning in this Act as in that Act.

(4)   The planning Acts are –

(a)   the principal Act;

(b)   the listed buildings Act;

(c)   the hazardous substances Act;

(d)   the Planning (Consequential Provisions) Act 1990 (c. 11).

(5)   The principal Act is the Town and Country Planning Act 1990 (c. 8).

(6)   The listed buildings Act is the Planning (Listed Buildings and Conservation Areas) Act 1990 (c. 9).

(7)   The hazardous substances Act is the Planning (Hazardous Substances) Act 1990 (c. 10).

(8)   The Scottish planning Acts are –

(a)   the Town and Country Planning (Scotland) Act 1997 (c. 8);

(b)   the Planning (Listed Buildings and Conservation Areas) (Scotland) Act 1997 (c. 9);

(c)   the Planning (Hazardous Substances) (Scotland) Act 1997 (c. 10); and

(d)   the Planning (Consequential Provisions) (Scotland) Act 1997 (c. 11).

## General

### 118  Amendments

(1)  Schedule 6 contains amendments of the planning Acts.

(2)  Schedule 7 contains amendments of other enactments.

(3)  A reference in Schedule 1 to the National Assembly for Wales (Transfer of Functions) Order 1999 to an enactment amended by this Act must be taken to be a reference to the enactment as so amended.

(4)  But subsection (3) does not affect such an enactment to the extent that the amendment makes express provision in connection with the exercise of a function in relation to Wales.

### 119  Transitionals

(1)  Schedule 8 contains transitional provisions relating to Parts 1 and 2.

(2)  The Scottish Ministers may by order make such transitional provision for Scotland, corresponding to the provisions of Schedule 4 and to section 30B of the hazardous substances Act (inserted by section 79(3)), as they consider necessary or expedient.

### 120  Repeals

Schedule 9 contains repeals.

### 121  Commencement

(1)  The preceding provisions of this Act (except section 115 and the provisions specified in subsections (4), (5) and (6)) come into force on such day as the Secretary of State may by order appoint.

(2)  But the Secretary of State must not make an order which relates to any of the following provisions unless he first consults the National Assembly for Wales –

(a)  Part 3;

(b)  Part 4, except sections 44 and 55;

(c)  Part 5;

(d)  in Part 7, Chapter 1;

(e)  Part 8;

(f)  in this Part sections 113, 114, 117, 118 and 120;

(g)  Schedules 3, 4, 6, 7 and 9.

(3)  And the Secretary of State must not make an order which relates to section 91 unless he first consults and has the agreement of the Scottish Ministers.

(4)  The following provisions come into force on such day as the Scottish Ministers may by order appoint –

(a)  sections 90 and 92 to 98;

(b)  Schedule 5;

(c)  section 117(8);

(d)  in so far as relating to the Town and Country Planning (Scotland) Act 1997, section 118(2) and Schedule 7;

(e)  section 119(2); and

(f)  in so far as relating to that Act, to the Planning (Listed Buildings and Conservation Areas) (Scotland) Act 1997 or to the Planning (Hazardous Substances) (Scotland) Act 1997, section 120 and Schedule 9.

(5)  Part 6 comes into force in accordance with provision made by the National Assembly for Wales by order.

(6)  In Schedule 7, paragraph 10(7) comes into force at the end of the period of two months starting on the day this Act is passed.

**122  Regulations and orders**

(1) A power to prescribe is (unless express provision is made to the contrary) a power to prescribe by regulations exercisable –

    (a)  by the Secretary of State in relation to England;

    (b)  by the National Assembly for Wales in relation to Wales.

(2) References in this section to subordinate legislation are to any order or regulations under this Act.

(3) Subordinate legislation –

    (a)  may make different provision for different purposes;

    (b)  may include such supplementary, incidental, consequential, saving or transitional provisions (including provision amending, repealing or revoking enactments) as the person making the subordinate legislation thinks necessary or expedient.

(4) A power to make subordinate legislation must be exercised by statutory instrument.

(5) A statutory instrument is subject to annulment in pursuance of a resolution of either House of Parliament unless it contains –

    (a)  regulations made by the Secretary of State under section 46;

    (b)  an order under section 98, 116(1) or 119(2);

    (c)  an order under section 110(2);

    (d)  an order under section 121(1) to which subsection (8) applies;

    (e)  an order under section 121(4);

    (f)  provision amending or repealing an enactment contained in an Act;

    (g)  subordinate legislation made by the National Assembly for Wales.

(6) A statutory instrument mentioned in subsection (5)(a), (c) or (f) must not be made unless a draft of the instrument has been laid before and approved by resolution of each House of Parliament.

(7) A statutory instrument containing an order under section 98 or 119(2) is subject to annulment in pursuance of a resolution of the Scottish Parliament.

(8) This subsection applies to an order which does not contain provision amending or repealing an enactment contained in an Act.

(9) A statutory instrument containing an order under section 121(4), if it includes provision amending or repealing an enactment contained in an Act, must not be made unless a draft of the instrument has been laid before and approved by resolution of the Scottish Parliament.

(10) In subsection (3), 'enactment' includes an enactment comprised in, or in an instrument made under, an Act of the Scottish Parliament and in subsections (8) and (9), 'Act' includes such an Act and 'enactment' includes an enactment comprised in such an Act.

**123  Finance**

(1) There is to be paid out of money provided by Parliament –

    (a)  any expenses of the Secretary of State in making grants in connection with the provision of advice and assistance in relation to the planning Acts;

    (b)  any increase attributable to this Act in the sums payable out of money so provided under any other enactment.

(2) There is to be paid into the Consolidated Fund any increase attributable to this Act in the sums so payable under any other enactment.

**124 Extent**

(1) Except as otherwise provided in this section, this Act extends to England and Wales only.

(2) Sections 111(1), 118(2), 120 to 122, this section and section 125 extend also to Scotland.

(3) Sections 90 to 98, 117(8) and 119(2) extend to Scotland only.

(4) The extent of any amendment, repeal or revocation made by this Act is the same as that of the enactment amended, repealed or revoked.

**125  Short Title**

This Act may be cited as the Planning and Compulsory Purchase Act 2004.

# SCHEDULES

## SCHEDULE 1    LOCAL DEVELOPMENT ORDERS: PROCEDURES

Section 40

In the principal Act after Schedule 4 (special provision as to land use in 1948) there is inserted the following Schedule –

### 'SCHEDULE 4A

### LOCAL DEVELOPMENT ORDERS: PROCEDURE

#### Preparation

1  (1)  A local development order must be prepared in accordance with such procedure as is prescribed by a development order.

 (2)  A development order may include provision as to –

   (a)  the preparation, submission, approval, adoption, revision, revocation and withdrawal of a local development order;

   (b)  notice, publicity, and inspection by the public;

   (c)  consultation with and consideration of views of such persons and for such purposes as are prescribed;

   (d)  the making and consideration of representations.

 (3)  Regulations under this paragraph may include provision as to the matters relating to a local development order to be included in the report to be made by a local planning authority under section 35 or 76 of the Planning and Compulsory Purchase Act 2004.

#### Revision

2  (1)  The local planning authority may at any time prepare a revision of a local development order.

 (2)  An authority in England must prepare a revision of a local development order –

   (a)  if the Secretary of State directs them to do so, and

   (b)  in accordance with such timetable as he directs.

 (3)  An authority in Wales must prepare a revision of a local development order –

   (a)  if the National Assembly for Wales directs them to do so, and

   (b)  in accordance with such timetable as it directs.

 (4)  If a development plan document mentioned in section 61A(1) is revised under section 26 of the Planning and Compulsory Purchase Act 2004 (revision of local planning documents) or revoked under section 25 of that Act (revocation by Secretary of State) a local development order made to implement the policies in the document must be revised accordingly.

 (5)  If a local development plan mentioned in section 61A(1) is revised under section 70 of the Planning and Compulsory Purchase Act 2004 (revision of

local development plan) or revoked under section 68 of that Act (revocation by National Assembly for Wales) a local development order made to implement the policies in the plan must be revised accordingly.

(6)    This Schedule applies to the revision of a local development order as it applies to the preparation of the order.

## Order to be adopted

3    A local development order is of no effect unless it is adopted by resolution of the local planning authority.

## Annual report

4    (1)    The report made under section 35 of the Planning and Compulsory Purchase Act 2004 must include a report as to the extent to which the local development order is achieving its purposes.

(2)    The Secretary of State may prescribe the form and content of the report as it relates to the local development order.

5    (1)    The report made under section 76 of the Planning and Compulsory Purchase Act 2004 must include a report as to the extent to which the local development order is achieving its purposes.

(2)    The National Assembly for Wales may prescribe the form and content of the report as it relates to the local development order.'

## SCHEDULE 2    TIMETABLE FOR DECISIONS                    Section 55

## Decisions

1    This Schedule applies to any decision which must be taken by the Secretary of State under –

(a)    section 77 of the principal Act (reference of applications to Secretary of State);

(b)    section 78 of the principal Act (right to appeal against planning decisions).

2    (1)    This Schedule also applies to a decision not mentioned in paragraph 1 if each of the following two conditions applies.

(2)    The first condition is that the Secretary of State thinks the decision is connected with a decision mentioned in paragraph 1.

(3)    The second condition is that –

(a)    the Secretary of State is required by virtue of any enactment to take the decision, or

(b)    (in any case to which paragraph (a) does not apply) the Secretary of State by virtue of a power under any enactment directs that the decision must be referred to him.

3    But the Secretary of State may by order specify decisions or descriptions of decisions to which a timetable is not to apply.

## Timetable

4    (1)    The Secretary of State must make one or more timetables for the purposes of decisions to which this Schedule applies.

(2)   A timetable may make different provision for different decisions or different descriptions of decision.

(3)   A timetable –

(a)   has effect from such time as the Secretary of State determines;

(b)   must set out the time within which the decision must be taken;

(c)   may set out the time within which any other step to be taken for the purposes of the decision must be taken.

(4)   A timetable made under this paragraph must be published in such form and manner as the Secretary of State thinks appropriate.

## Notice

5   (1)   The Secretary of State must notify the following persons as soon as practicable of the published timetable which applies to a decision –

(a)   the applicant or appellant (as the case may be) in relation to the decision;

(b)   the local planning authority for the area to which the decision relates;

(c)   any other person who requests such notification.

(2)   But the Secretary of State may direct that the timetable is subject to such variation as he specifies in the notice under sub-paragraph (1).

(3)   If the Secretary of State acts under sub-paragraph (2) the notice under sub-paragraph (1) must also specify the reasons for the variation.

(4)   The timetable notified under this paragraph is the applicable timetable.

## Variation

6   (1)   This paragraph applies if before the time at which any step must be taken in accordance with the applicable timetable the Secretary of State thinks that there are circumstances which are likely to prevent the taking of the step at that time.

(2)   The Secretary of State may vary the applicable timetable accordingly.

(3)   If the Secretary of State varies the applicable timetable under sub-paragraph (2) he must notify the persons mentioned in paragraph 5(1) of the variation and the reason for it.

## Written reasons

7   If the Secretary of State fails to take any step in accordance with the applicable timetable (or that timetable as varied under paragraph 6) he must give written reasons to the persons mentioned in paragraph 5(1).

## Annual report

8   (1)   The Secretary of State must lay before Parliament a report in respect of each year which –

(a)   reviews his performance under the provisions of this Schedule;

(b)   explains any failure to comply with a timetable.

(2)   The report must be published in such form and manner as the Secretary of State thinks appropriate.

# SCHEDULE 3   CROWN APPLICATION                    Section 79

## *Purchase notices*

1    After section 137 of the principal Act (circumstances in which a purchase notice may
     be served) there is inserted the following section –

### '137A  Purchase notices: Crown land

(1)  A purchase notice may be served in respect of Crown land only as mentioned in
     this section.

(2)  The owner of a private interest in Crown land must not serve a purchase notice
     unless –

    (a)  he first offers to dispose of his interest to the appropriate authority on
     equivalent terms, and

    (b)  the offer is refused by the appropriate authority.

(3)  The appropriate authority may serve a purchase notice in relation to the
     following land –

    (a)  land belonging to Her Majesty in right of Her private estates;

    (b)  land belonging to Her Majesty in right of the Duchy of Lancaster;

    (c)  land belonging to the Duchy of Cornwall;

    (d)  land which forms part of the Crown Estate.

(4)  An offer is made on equivalent terms if the price payable for the interest is equal
     to (and, in default of agreement, determined in the same manner as) the com-
     pensation which would be payable in respect of it if it were acquired in pur-
     suance of a purchase notice.

(5)  Expressions used in this section and in Part 13 must be construed in accordance
     with that Part.'

2    After section 32 of the listed buildings Act (circumstances in which a purchase notice
     may be served) there is inserted the following section –

### '32A  Purchase notices: Crown land

(1)  A listed building purchase notice may be served in respect of Crown land only as
     mentioned in this section.

(2)  The owner of a private interest in Crown land must not serve a listed building
     purchase notice unless –

    (a)  he first offers to dispose of his interest to the appropriate authority on
     equivalent terms, and

    (b)  the offer is refused by the appropriate authority.

(3)  The appropriate authority may serve a listed building purchase notice in relation
     to the following land –

    (a)  land belonging to Her Majesty in right of Her private estates;

    (b)  land belonging to Her Majesty in right of the Duchy of Lancaster;

    (c)  land belonging to the Duchy of Cornwall;

    (d)  land which forms part of the Crown Estate.

(4)  An offer is made on equivalent terms if the price payable for the interest is equal
     to (and, in default of agreement, determined in the same manner as) the
     compensation which would be payable in respect of it if it were acquired in
     pursuance of a listed building purchase notice.'

## Compulsory acquisition

3   (1)   Section 226 of the principal Act (compulsory acquisition of land for development and other planning purposes) is amended as follows.

(2)   After subsection (2) there is inserted the following subsection –

'(2A)   The Secretary of State must not authorise the acquisition of any interest in Crown land unless –

(a)   it is an interest which is for the time being held otherwise than by or on behalf of the Crown, and

(b)   the appropriate authority consents to the acquisition.'

(3)   After subsection (8) there is inserted the following subsection –

'(9)   Crown land must be construed in accordance with Part 13.'

4   (1)   Section 228 of the principal Act (compulsory acquisition of land by the Secretary of State) is amended as follows.

(2)   After subsection (1) there is inserted the following subsection –

'(1A)   But subsection (1) does not permit the acquisition of any interest in Crown land unless –

(a)   it is an interest which is for the time being held otherwise than by or on behalf of the Crown, and

(b)   the appropriate authority consents to the acquisition.'

(3)   After subsection (7) there is inserted the following subsection –

'(8)   Crown land must be construed in accordance with Part 13.'

5   (1)   Section 47 of the listed buildings Act (compulsory acquisition of listed building in need of repair) is amended as follows.

(2)   After subsection (6) there is inserted the following subsection –

'(6A)   This section does not permit the acquisition of any interest in Crown land unless –

(a)   it is an interest which is for the time being held otherwise than by or on behalf of the Crown, and

(b)   the appropriate authority (within the meaning of section 82C) consents to the acquisition.'

## Definitions

6   (1)   Section 293 of the principal Act (preliminary definitions) is amended as follows.

(2)   In subsection (1) for the definition of 'Crown interest' there is substituted the following definition –

'"Crown interest" means any of the following –

(a)   an interest belonging to Her Majesty in right of the Crown or in right of Her private estates;

(b)   an interest belonging to a government department or held in trust for Her Majesty for the purposes of a government department;

(c)   such other interest as the Secretary of State specifies by order;'.

(3)   In subsection (2) after paragraph (b) there is inserted the following paragraph –

'(ba) in relation to land belonging to Her Majesty in right of Her private estates means a person appointed by Her Majesty in writing under the Royal Sign Manual or, if no such appointment is made, the Secretary of State;'.

(4)  In subsection (2) after paragraph (e) there are inserted the following paragraphs –

> '(f)  in relation to Westminster Hall and the Chapel of St Mary Undercroft, means the Lord Great Chamberlain and the Speakers of the House of Lords and the House of Commons acting jointly;
> (g)  in relation to Her Majesty's Robing Room in the Palace of Westminster, the adjoining staircase and ante-room and the Royal Gallery, means the Lord Great Chamberlain.'

(5)  After subsection (2) there is inserted the following subsection –

> '(2A)  For the purposes of an application for planning permission made by or on behalf of the Crown in respect of land which does not belong to the Crown or in respect of which it has no interest a reference to the appropriate authority must be construed as a reference to the person who makes the application.'

(6)  After subsection (3) there are inserted the following subsections –

> '(3A)  References to Her Majesty's private estates must be construed in accordance with section 1 of the Crown Private Estates Act 1862.
> (3B)  In subsection (2A) the Crown includes –
>
> > (a)  the Duchy of Lancaster;
> > (b)  the Duchy of Cornwall;
> > (c)  a person who is an appropriate authority by virtue of subsection (2)(f) and (g).'

(7)  After subsection (4) there are inserted the following subsections –

> '(5)  An order made for the purposes of paragraph (c) of the definition of Crown interest in subsection (1) must be made by statutory instrument.
> (6)  But no such order may be made unless a draft of it has been laid before and approved by resolution of each House of Parliament.'

7    In the listed buildings Act after section 82B (inserted by section 83(1)) there is inserted the following section –

### '82C  Expressions relating to the Crown

(1)  In this Act, expressions relating to the Crown must be construed in accordance with this section.

(2)  Crown land is land in which there is a Crown interest or a Duchy interest.

(3)  A Crown interest is any of the following –

> (a)  an interest belonging to Her Majesty in right of the Crown or in right of Her private estates;
> (b)  an interest belonging to a government department or held in trust for Her Majesty for the purposes of a government department;
> (c)  such other interest as the Secretary of State specifies by order.

(4)  A Duchy interest is –

> (a)  an interest belonging to Her Majesty in right of the Duchy of Lancaster, or
> (b)  an interest belonging to the Duchy of Cornwall.

(5)  A private interest is an interest which is neither a Crown interest nor a Duchy interest.

(6)  The appropriate authority in relation to any land is –

> (a)  in the case of land belonging to Her Majesty in right of the Crown and forming part of the Crown Estate, the Crown Estate Commissioners;
> (b)  in relation to any other land belonging to Her Majesty in right of the Crown, the government department having the management of the land;

(c)   in relation to land belonging to Her Majesty in right of Her private estates, a person appointed by Her Majesty in writing under the Royal Sign Manual or, if no such appointment is made, the Secretary of State;

(d)   in relation to land belonging to Her Majesty in right of the Duchy of Lancaster, the Chancellor of the Duchy;

(e)   in relation to land belonging to the Duchy of Cornwall, such person as the Duke of Cornwall, or the possessor for the time being of the Duchy, appoints;

(f)   in the case of land belonging to a government department or held in trust for Her Majesty for the purposes of a government department, the department;

(g)   in relation to Westminster Hall and the Chapel of St Mary Undercroft, the Lord Great Chamberlain and the Speakers of the House of Lords and the House of Commons acting jointly;

(h)   in relation to Her Majesty's Robing Room in the Palace of Westminster, the adjoining staircase and ante-room and the Royal Gallery, the Lord Great Chamberlain.

(7) If any question arises as to what authority is the appropriate authority in relation to any land it must be referred to the Treasury, whose decision is final.

(8) For the purposes of an application for listed building consent made by or on behalf of the Crown in respect of land which does not belong to the Crown or in respect of which it has no interest a reference to the appropriate authority must be construed as a reference to the person who makes the application.

(9) For the purposes of subsection (8) the Crown includes –

(a)   the Duchy of Lancaster;

(b)   the Duchy of Cornwall;

(c)   a person who is an appropriate authority by virtue of subsection (6)(g) and (h).

(10) The reference to Her Majesty's private estates must be construed in accordance with section 1 of the Crown Private Estates Act 1862.

(11) An order made for the purposes of paragraph (c) of subsection (3) must be made by statutory instrument.

(12) But no such order may be made unless a draft of it has been laid before and approved by resolution of each House of Parliament.'

8      (1) Section 31 of the hazardous substances Act (exercise of powers in relation to Crown land) is amended as follows.

(2) Subsections (1) and (2) are omitted.

(3) In subsection (3) for the definition of 'Crown interest' there is substituted the following definition –

'"Crown interest" means any of the following –

(a)   an interest belonging to Her Majesty in right of the Crown or in right of Her private estates;

(b)   an interest belonging to a government department or held in trust for Her Majesty for the purposes of a government department;

(c)   such other interest as the Secretary of State specifies by order;'.

(4) In subsection (5) after paragraph (a) there is inserted the following paragraph –

'(aa) in relation to land belonging to Her Majesty in right of Her private estates means a person appointed by Her Majesty in writing under the Royal Sign Manual or, if no such appointment is made, the Secretary of State;'.

(5) In subsection (5) after paragraph (d) there are inserted the following paragraphs –

'(e)  in relation to Westminster Hall and the Chapel of St Mary Undercroft,
means the Lord Great Chamberlain and the Speakers of the House of Lords
and the House of Commons acting jointly;

(f)  in relation to Her Majesty's Robing Room in the Palace of Westminster, the
adjoining staircase and ante-room and the Royal Gallery, means the Lord
Great Chamberlain.'

(6)  After subsection (6) there are inserted the following subsections –

'(7)  References to Her Majesty's private estates must be construed in accordance
with section 1 of the Crown Private Estates Act 1862.

(8)  An order made for the purposes of paragraph (c) of the definition of Crown
interest in subsection (3) must be made by statutory instrument.

(9)  But no such order may be made unless a draft of it has been laid before and
approved by resolution of each House of Parliament.'

## Special enforcement notices

9  (1)  Sections 294 and 295 of the principal Act (control of development on Crown
land: special enforcement notices) are omitted.

(2)  But the repeal of sections 294 and 295 does not affect their operation in relation
to development carried out before the commencement of this paragraph.

## Applications for planning permission, etc.

10  (1)  After section 298 of the principal Act (supplementary provision as to Crown and
Duchy interests) there is inserted the following section –

### '298A  Applications for planning permission by Crown

(1)  This section applies to an application for planning permission or for a
certificate under section 192 made by or on behalf of the Crown.

(2)  The Secretary of State may by regulations modify or exclude any statutory
provision relating to the making and determination of such applications.

(3)  A statutory provision is a provision contained in or having effect under any
enactment.'

(2)  Section 299 of the principal Act is omitted.

(3)  The repeal of section 299 of the principal Act does not does not affect any
requirement made in pursuance of regulations made under subsection (5)(b) of
that section.

11  After section 82E of the listed buildings Act (inserted by section 84) there is inserted
the following section –

### '82F  Applications for listed building or conservation area consent by Crown

(1)  This section applies to an application for listed building consent or conservation
area consent made by or on behalf of the Crown.

(2)  The Secretary of State may by regulations modify or exclude any statutory
provision relating to the making and determination of such applications.

(3)  A statutory provision is a provision contained in or having effect under any
enactment.'

12  (1)  After section 31 of the hazardous substances Act (exercise of powers in relation
to Crown land) there is inserted the following section –

'31A  **Applications for hazardous substances consent by Crown**

(1)    This section applies to an application for hazardous substances consent made by or on behalf of the Crown.

(2)    The Secretary of State may by regulations modify or exclude any statutory provision relating to the making and determination of such applications.

(3)    A statutory provision is a provision contained in or having effect under any enactment.'

(2)  Section 32 of the hazardous substances Act is omitted.

## Rights of entry

13    After section 325 of the principal Act (supplementary provisions as to rights of entry) there is inserted the following section –

'325A  **Rights of entry: Crown land**

(1)  Section 324 applies to Crown land subject to the following modifications.

(2)  A person must not enter Crown land unless he has the relevant permission.

(3)  Relevant permission is the permission of –

(a)    a person appearing to the person seeking entry to the land to be entitled to give it, or

(b)    the appropriate authority.

(4)  In subsection (8) the words "Subject to section 325" must be ignored.

(5)  Section 325 does not apply to anything done by virtue of this section.

(6)  "Appropriate authority" must be construed in accordance with section 293(2).'

14    After section 88B of the listed buildings Act (rights of entry: supplementary provisions) there is inserted the following section –

'88C  **Rights of entry: Crown land**

(1)  Section 88 applies to Crown land subject to the following modifications.

(2)  A person must not enter Crown land unless he has the relevant permission.

(3)  Relevant permission is the permission of –

(a)    a person appearing to the person seeking entry to the land to be entitled to give it, or

(b)    the appropriate authority.

(4)  In subsection (6) the words "Subject to section 88B(8)" must be ignored.

(5)  Section 88B does not apply to anything done by virtue of this section.

(6)  "Appropriate authority" must be construed in accordance with section 82C(6).'

15    After section 36B of the hazardous substances Act (rights of entry: supplementary provisions) there is inserted the following section –

'36C  **Rights of entry: Crown land**

(1)  Section 36 applies to Crown land subject to the following modifications.

(2)  A person must not enter Crown land unless he has the relevant permission.

(3)  Relevant permission is the permission of –

(a)    a person appearing to the person seeking entry to the land to be entitled to give it, or

(b)    the appropriate authority.

(4)  Section 36B does not apply to anything done by virtue of this section.

(5)  "Appropriate authority" must be construed in accordance with section 31(5).'

## Service of notices

16   After section 329 of the principal Act (service of notices) there is inserted the following section –

### '329A  Service of notices on the Crown

(1)   Any notice or other document required under this Act to be served on the Crown must be served on the appropriate authority.

(2)   Section 329 does not apply for the purposes of the service of such a notice or document.

(3)   "Appropriate authority" must be construed in accordance with section 293(2).'

## Information as to interests in land

17   After section 330 of the principal Act (power to require information as to interests in land) there is inserted the following section –

### '330A  Information as to interests in Crown land

(1)   This section applies to an interest in Crown land which is not a private interest.

(2)   Section 330 does not apply to an interest to which this section applies.

(3)   For a purpose mentioned in section 330(1) the Secretary of State may request the appropriate authority to give him such information as to the matters mentioned in section 330(2) as he specifies in the request.

(4)   The appropriate authority must comply with a request under subsection (3) except to the extent –

(a)   that the matter is not within the knowledge of the authority, or

(b)   that to do so will disclose information as to any of the matters mentioned in section 321(4).

(5)   Expressions used in this section and in Part 13 must be construed in accordance with that Part.'

## Listed buildings and conservation areas

18   (1)   Sections 83 and 84 of the listed buildings Act (provisions relating to Crown land) are omitted.

(2)   The repeal of section 84 of the listed buildings Act does not affect any requirement made in pursuance of regulations made under subsection (4)(b) of that section.

19   (1)   Section 89(1) of the listed buildings Act (application of certain general provisions of principal Act) is amended as follows.

(2)   After the entry relating to section 329 there is inserted –

'section 329A(1) and (2) (service of notices on the Crown)'.

(3)   After the entry relating to section 330 there is inserted –

'section 330A(1) to (4) (information as to interests in Crown land)'.

## Hazardous substances

20   In section 17 of the hazardous substances Act (revocation of consent on change of control of land) after subsection (2) there is inserted the following subsection –

'(3)   This section does not apply if the control of land changes from one emanation of the Crown to another.'

21  (1)  Section 37(2) of the hazardous substances Act (application of certain general provisions of the principal Act) is amended as follows.

(2)  After the entry relating to section 329 there is inserted –

'section 329A(1) and (2) (service of notices on the Crown)'.

(3)  After the entry relating to section 330 there is inserted –

'section 330A(1) to (4) (information as to interests in Crown land)'.

## Miscellaneous

22  Section 293(4) of the principal Act (certain persons treated as having an interest in Crown land) is omitted.

23  Section 297 of the principal Act (agreements relating to Crown land) is omitted.

24  (1)  Section 298 of the principal Act (supplementary provisions as to Crown and Duchy interests) is amended as follows.

(2)  Subsections (1) and (2) are omitted.

(3)  In subsection (3) after 'in which there is' there is inserted 'a Crown interest or'.

25  Section 299A of the principal Act (Crown planning obligations) is omitted.

26  (1)  Section 300 of the principal Act (tree preservation orders in anticipation of disposal of Crown land) is omitted.

(2)  But the repeal of section 300 does not affect its operation in relation to a tree preservation order made by virtue of that section before the commencement of this paragraph.

27  (1)  Section 301 of the principal Act (requirement of planning permission for continuance of use instituted by the Crown) is omitted.

(2)  But the repeal of section 301 does not affect its operation in relation to an agreement made as mentioned in subsection (1) of that section before the commencement of this paragraph.

## SCHEDULE 4    TRANSITIONAL PROVISIONS: CROWN APPLICATION                                    Section 89

## PART 1

## THE PRINCIPAL ACT

### Introduction

1  This Part applies to a development if-

(a)  it is a development for which before the relevant date no planning permission is required,

(b)  it is not a development or of a description of development for which planning permission is granted by virtue of a development order, and

(c)  before the relevant date proposed development notice had been given to the local planning authority.

2  In this Part-

(a)  the relevant date is the date of commencement of section 79(1);

(b)  proposed development notice is notice of a proposal for development given by the developer in pursuance of arrangements made by the Secretary of State in relation to development by or on behalf of the Crown;

(c)  the developer is the Crown or a person acting on behalf of the Crown.

## *Acceptable development*

3    (1)    This paragraph applies if before the relevant date in pursuance of the arrangements either the local planning authority have or the Secretary of State has given notice to the developer that they or he (as the case may be) find the proposed development acceptable.

(2)    The notice must be treated as if it is planning permission granted under Part 3 of the principal Act.

(3)    If the notice is subject to conditions the conditions have effect as if they are conditions attached to the planning permission.

4    (1)    This paragraph applies if before the relevant date the local planning authority have in pursuance of the arrangements kept a register of proposed development notices.

(2)    The register must be treated as if it is part of the register kept by them in pursuance of section 69 of the principal Act.

## *Referred proposals*

5    (1)    This paragraph applies if –

(a)    before the relevant date the local planning authority have notified the developer in pursuance of the arrangements that they do not find the development acceptable, and

(b)    the matter has been referred to but not decided by the Secretary of State.

(2)    This paragraph also applies if –

(a)    before the relevant date the local planning authority have notified the developer in pursuance of the arrangements that they find the development acceptable subject to conditions, and

(b)    the matter has been referred to but not decided by the Secretary of State.

(3)    The Secretary of State must deal with the proposal as if it is an appeal by an applicant for planning permission under section 78 of the principal Act.

## *Pending proposals*

6    (1)    This paragraph applies if before the relevant date –

(a)    proposed development notice has been given, but

(b)    the local planning authority have not given notice to the developer as mentioned in paragraph 3 or 5.

(2)    The principal Act applies as if the proposal is an application for planning permission duly made under Part 3 of that Act.

## PART 2

## THE LISTED BUILDINGS ACT

## *Introduction*

7    This Part applies to works if –

(a)    they are works for which before the relevant date no listed building consent is required, and

(b)    before the relevant date proposed works notice had been given to the local planning authority.

8    In this Part –

    (a)   the relevant date is the date of commencement of section 79(1);

    (b)   proposed works notice is notice of a proposal for works given by the person pro-
posing to carry out the works (the developer) in pursuance of arrangements
made by the Secretary of State in relation to development by or on behalf of the
Crown;

    (c)   the developer is the Crown or a person acting on behalf of the Crown.

## Acceptable works

9    (1)   This paragraph applies if before the relevant date in pursuance of the arrangements either the local planning authority have or the Secretary of State has given
notice to the developer that they or he (as the case may be) find the proposed
works acceptable.

    (2)   The notice must be treated as if it is listed building consent granted under the
listed buildings Act.

    (3)   If the notice is subject to conditions the conditions have effect as if they are
conditions attached to the consent.

10    (1)   This paragraph applies if before the relevant date the local planning authority
have in pursuance of the arrangements kept a register of proposed works notices.

    (2)   The register must be treated as if it is part of the register kept by them in
pursuance of the listed buildings Act.

## Referred proposals

11    (1)   This paragraph applies if –

    (a)    before the relevant date the local planning authority have notified the
developer in pursuance of the arrangements that they do not find the works
acceptable, and

    (b)    the matter has been referred to but not decided by the Secretary of State.

    (2)   This paragraph also applies if –

    (a)    before the relevant date the local planning authority have notified the
developer in pursuance of the arrangements that they find the works
acceptable subject to conditions, and

    (b)    the matter has been referred to but not decided by the Secretary of State.

    (3)   The Secretary of State must deal with the proposal as if it is an appeal by an appli-
cant for listed building consent under section 20 of the listed buildings Act.

## Pending proposals

12    (1)   This paragraph applies if before the relevant date –

    (a)    proposed works notice has been given, but

    (b)    the local planning authority have not given notice to the developer as men-
tioned in paragraph 9 or 11.

    (2)   The listed buildings Act applies as if the proposal is an application for listed
building consent duly made under that Act.

## SCHEDULE 5    CROWN APPLICATION: SCOTLAND    Section 90

*****

## SCHEDULE 6    AMENDMENTS OF THE PLANNING ACTS    Section 118

### *Town and Country Planning Act 1990 (c. 8)*

1    The Town and Country Planning Act 1990 is amended as follows.

2    In section 55(2)(b) (meaning of development) the word 'local' is omitted.

3    For section 69 there is substituted the following section –

**'69    Register of applications etc**

(1)    The local planning authority must keep a register containing such information as is prescribed as to –

(a)    applications for planning permission;

(b)    requests for statements of development principles (within the meaning of section 61E);

(c)    local development orders;

(d)    simplified planning zone schemes.

(2)    The register must contain –

(a)    information as to the manner in which applications mentioned in subsection (1)(a) and requests mentioned in subsection (1)(b) have been dealt with;

(b)    such information as is prescribed with respect to any local development order or simplified planning zone scheme in relation to the authority's area.

(3)    A development order may require the register to be kept in two or more parts.

(4)    Each part must contain such information as is prescribed relating to the matters mentioned in subsection (1)(a) and (b).

(5)    A development order may also make provision –

(a)    for a specified part of the register to contain copies of applications or requests and of any other documents or material submitted with them;

(b)    for the entry relating to an application or request (and everything relating to it) to be removed from that part of the register when the application (including any appeal arising out of it) or the request (as the case may be) has been finally disposed of.

(6)    Provision made under subsection (5)(b) does not prevent the inclusion of a different entry relating to the application or request in another part of the register.

(7)    The register must be kept in such manner as is prescribed.

(8)    The register must be kept available for inspection by the public at all reasonable hours.

(9)    Anything prescribed under this section must be prescribed by development order.'

4    Section 76 (Duty to draw attention to certain provisions for benefit of disabled) is omitted.

5    Sections 106 to 106B (planning obligations) are omitted.

6    In section 108 (compensation for refusal of planning permission formerly granted by development order) after subsection (3) there is inserted the following subsection –

'(3A)    This section does not apply if –

(a) development authorised by planning permission granted by a development order or local development order is started before the permission is withdrawn, and

(b) the order includes provision in pursuance of section 61D permitting the development to be completed after the permission is withdrawn.'

7 (1) In section 245 (modification of incorporated enactments), subsections (2) and (3) are omitted.

 (2) The amendments made by sub-paragraph (1) do not apply to compulsory purchase orders of which notice under section 11 of or, as the case may be, paragraph 2 of Schedule 1 to the Acquisition of Land Act 1981 (c. 67) is published before commencement of this paragraph.

8 In section 284(1) (restriction on challenge to validity of certain documents), paragraph (a) is omitted.

9 (1) Section 287 (procedure for questioning the validity of certain matters) is amended as follows.

 (2) For subsections (1) to (3) there are substituted the following subsections –

'(1) This section applies to –

(a) a simplified planning zone scheme or an alteration of such a scheme;

(b) an order under section 247, 248, 249, 251, 257, 258 or 277,

and anything falling within paragraphs (a) and (b) is referred to in this section as a relevant document.

(2) A person aggrieved by a relevant document may make an application to the High Court on the ground that –

(a) it is not within the appropriate power, or

(b) a procedural requirement has not been complied with.

(3) The High Court may make an interim order suspending the operation of the relevant document –

(a) wholly or in part;

(b) generally or as it affects the property of the applicant.

(3A) Subsection (3B) applies if the High Court is satisfied –

(a) that a relevant document is to any extent outside the appropriate power;

(b) that the interests of the applicant have been substantially prejudiced by a failure to comply with a procedural requirement.

(3B) The High Court may quash the relevant document –

(a) wholly or in part;

(b) generally or as it affects the property of the applicant.

(3C) An interim order has effect until the proceedings are finally determined.

(3D) The appropriate power is –

(a) in the case of a simplified planning zone scheme or an alteration of the scheme, Part III;

(b) in the case of an order under section 247, 248, 249, 251, 257, 258 or 277, the section under which the order is made.'

 (3) In subsection (5) –

(a) paragraph (a) is omitted;

(b) in each of paragraphs (b) to (e) the words 'by virtue of subsection (3)' are omitted.

 (4) Subsection (6) is omitted.

10 (1) Section 296 (exercise of powers in relation to Crown land) is amended as follows.

 (2) In subsection (1) for paragraph (a) there is substituted the following paragraph –

'(a)   a document, plan or strategy specified in subsection (1A) may include proposals relating to the use of Crown land;'.

(3)   After subsection (1) there is inserted the following subsection –

'(1A) These are the documents, plans and strategies –

(a)   the regional spatial strategy (or a revision of it) within the meaning of Part 1 of the Planning and Compulsory Purchase Act 2004;

(b)   a local development document (or a revision of it) adopted or approved under Part 2 of that Act;

(c)   a local development plan (or a revision of it) adopted or approved under Part 6 of that Act;

(d)   the Mayor of London's spatial development strategy (or any alteration or replacement of it) published in pursuance of section 337 of the Greater London Authority Act 1999.'

11   (1)   Section 303A (recovery of costs of certain inquiries) is amended as follows.

(2)   For subsection (1) there are substituted the following subsections –

'(1)   This section applies if the appropriate authority appoints a person to carry out or hold a qualifying procedure.

(1A)  A qualifying procedure is –

(a)   an independent examination under section 20 or 64 of the Planning and Compulsory Purchase Act 2004;

(b)   a local inquiry or other hearing under paragraph 8(1)(a) of Schedule 7;

(c)   the consideration of objections under paragraph 8(1)(b) of that Schedule.

(1B)  The appropriate authority is –

(a)   the Secretary of State if the local planning authority causing the procedure to be carried out or held is in England;

(b)   the National Assembly for Wales if the local planning authority causing the procedure to be carried out or held is in Wales.'

(3)   In each of subsections (2) to (6) and (10)(a) in each place where it occurs –

(a)   for 'Secretary of State' there is substituted 'appropriate authority';

(b)   for 'him' there is substituted 'it';

(c)   for 'he' there is substituted 'it'.

(4)   In each of subsections (2), (4), (5) and (6) in each place where it occurs for 'inquiry' there is substituted 'procedure'.

(5)   In subsection (5) each of the following is omitted –

(a)   'or appointed as one of the persons who are to hold it';

(b)   '(in addition to what may be recovered by virtue of the appointment of any other person)';

(c)   in paragraph (c), '(or, in a case where that person is appointed as one of the persons who are to hold the qualifying inquiry, an appropriate proportion of any costs attributable to the appointment of an assessor to assist those persons)'.

(6)   Subsections (7) to (9) are omitted.

(7)   Before subsection (10) there is inserted the following subsection –

'(9A) References to a local planning authority causing a qualifying inquiry to be held include references to a requirement under the Planning and Compulsory Purchase Act 2004 on the authority to submit a plan to the appropriate authority for independent examination.'

12    In section 306(2) (local authorities and statutory undertakers may contribute to certain costs of local planning authorities) for paragraph (a) there are substituted the following paragraphs –

'(a)    any expenses incurred by a local planning authority for the purposes of carrying out a review under section 13 or 61 of the Planning and Compulsory Purchase Act 2004 (duty of local planning authority to keep under review certain matters affecting development);

(ab)    any expenses incurred by a county council for the purposes of carrying out a review under section 14 of that Act (duty of county council to keep under review certain matters affecting development);'

13    In section 324(1) (rights of entry) for paragraph (a) there is substituted the following paragraph –

'(a)    the preparation, revision, adoption or approval of a local development document under Part 2 of the Planning and Compulsory Purchase Act 2004 or a local development plan under Part 6 of that Act;'

14    (1)    Section 333 (provision about regulations and orders) is amended as follows.

(2)    After subsection (2) there is inserted the following subsection –

'(2A) Regulations may make different provision for different purposes.'

15    In section 336(1) (interpretation) for the definition of development plan there is substituted –

'"development plan" must be construed in accordance with section 38 of the Planning and Compulsory Purchase Act 2004;'.

16    (1)    Schedule 1 (distribution of functions of local planning authorities) is amended as follows.

(2)    Paragraph 2 is omitted.

(3)    In paragraph 3(7) the words 'but paragraph 4 shall apply to such applications instead' are omitted.

(4)    For paragraph 7 there is substituted the following paragraph –

'7    (1)    A local planning authority must not determine an application for planning permission to which the consultation requirements apply unless it complies with sub-paragraph (7).

(2)    The consultation requirements are –

(a)    consultation with the RPB for the region in which the authority's area is situated if the development is one to which sub-paragraph (3) applies;

(b)    consultation by a district planning authority with the county planning authority for their area if the development is one to which sub-paragraph (4) applies.

(3)    This sub-paragraph applies to –

(a)    a development which would by reason of its scale or nature or the location of the land be of major importance for the implementation of the RSS or a relevant regional policy, or

(b)    a development of a description in relation to which the RPB has given notice in writing to the local planning authority that it wishes to be consulted.

(4)    This sub-paragraph applies to –

(a)    a development which would materially conflict with or prejudice the implementation of a relevant county policy,

(b)    a development in an area in relation to which the county planning authority have given notice in writing to the district planning authority that development is likely to affect or be affected by the winning and working of minerals, other than coal,

(c)   a development of land in respect of which the county planning authority have given notice in writing to the district planning authority that they propose to carry out development,

(d)   a development which would prejudice a proposed development mentioned in paragraph (c) in respect of which notice has been given as so mentioned,

(e)   a development of land in relation to which the county planning authority have given notice in writing to the district planning authority that it is proposed to use the land for waste disposal, or

(f)   a development which would prejudice a proposed use mentioned in paragraph (e) in respect of which notice has been given as so mentioned.

(5)  The consultation requirements do not apply –

(a)   in respect of a development to which sub-paragraph (3) applies if the RPB gives a direction authorising the determination of the application without compliance with the requirements;

(b)   in respect of a development to which sub-paragraph (4) applies if the county planning authority gives a direction authorising the determination of the application without compliance with the requirements.

(6)  A direction under sub-paragraph (5) may be given in respect of a particular application or a description of application.

(7)  If the consultation requirements apply the local planning authority –

(a)   must give notice to the RPB or county planning authority (as the case may be) (the consulted body) that they propose to consider the application,

(b)   must send a copy of the application to the consulted body, and

(c)   must not determine the application until the end of such period as is prescribed by development order beginning with the date of the giving of notice under paragraph (a).

(8)  Sub-paragraph (7)(c) does not apply if before the end of the period mentioned in that sub-paragraph –

(a)   the local planning authority have received representations concerning the application from the consulted body, or

(b)   the consulted body gives notice that it does not intend to make representations.

(9)  A relevant regional policy is –

(a)   a policy contained in a draft revision of the RSS which has been submitted to the Secretary of State in pursuance of section 5(8) of the 2004 Act, or

(b)   a policy contained in a structure plan which has effect by virtue of paragraph 1 of Schedule 8 to the 2004 Act.

(10)  A relevant county policy is –

(a)   a policy contained in a local development document which has been prepared in accordance with a minerals and waste scheme and submitted to the Secretary of State in pursuance of section 20(1) of the 2004 Act or adopted by the county planning authority in pursuance of section 23 of that Act, or

   (b) a policy contained in a structure plan which has effect by virtue of paragraph 1 of Schedule 8 to the 2004 Act.

  (11) RPB and RSS must be construed in accordance with Part 1 of the 2004 Act.

  (12) The 2004 Act is the Planning and Compulsory Purchase Act 2004.'

17 In Schedule 2 (transitional provisions relating to development plans) Parts 1, 2 and 3 are omitted.

18 (1) Schedule 13 (blighted land) is amended as follows.

  (2) Paragraphs 1 to 4 are omitted.

  (3) The following paragraph is inserted as paragraph 1A –

  '1A Land which is identified for the purposes of relevant public functions by a development plan document for the area in which the land is situated.

### Notes

  (1) Relevant public functions are-

   (a) the functions of a government department, local authority, National Park authority or statutory undertakers;

   (b) the establishment or running by a public telecommunications operator of a telecommunication system.

  (2) For the purposes of this paragraph a development plan document is –

   (a) a development plan document which is adopted or approved for the purposes of Part 2 of the Planning and Compulsory Purchase Act 2004 (in this paragraph, the 2004 Act);

   (b) a revision of such a document in pursuance of section 26 of the 2004 Act which is adopted or approved for the purposes of Part 2 of the 2004 Act;

   (c) a development plan document which has been submitted to the Secretary of State for independent examination under section 20(1) of the 2004 Act;

   (d) a revision of a development plan document in pursuance of section 26 of the 2004 Act if the document has been submitted to the Secretary of State for independent examination under section 20(1) of that Act.

  (3) But Note (2)(c) and (d) does not apply if the document is withdrawn under section 22 of the 2004 Act at any time after it has been submitted for independent examination.

  (4) In Note (2)(c) and (d) the submission of a development plan document to the Secretary of State for independent examination is to be taken to include the holding of an independent examination by the Secretary of State under section 21 or section 27 of the 2004 Act.'

 (4) In paragraph 5 for 'any such functions as are mentioned in paragraph 1(a)(i) or (ii)' there is substituted 'relevant public functions (within the meaning of paragraph 1A)'.

 (5) In paragraph 6 for 'any such functions as are mentioned in paragraph 5' there is substituted 'relevant public functions (within the meaning of paragraph 1A)'.

 (6) In paragraph 13, for 'paragraphs 1, 2, 3 and 4' there is substituted 'paragraph 1A'.

## Planning (Listed Buildings and Conservation Areas) Act 1990 (c. 9)

19   The Planning (Listed Buildings and Conservation Areas) Act 1990 is amended as follows.

20   In section 10(3) (regulations relating to applications for listed building consent) –

(a)   for paragraph (b) and the word 'and' following it there is substituted the following paragraph-

'(b)   requirements as to publicity in relation to such applications;';

(b)   after paragraph (c) there are inserted the following paragraphs –

'(d)   requirements as to consultation in relation to such applications;

(e)   prohibiting the determination of such applications during such period as is prescribed;

(f)   requirements on the local planning authority to take account of responses from persons consulted.'

21   In section 23(2) (matters to which regard is to be had by local planning authority in exercising function of revoking or modifying consent) for 'the development plan and to any other' there is substituted 'any'.

22   In section 26(2) (matters to which regard is to be had by the Secretary of State in exercising function of revoking or modifying consent) for 'the development plan and to any other' there is substituted 'any'.

23   In section 67 (publicity for applications affecting the setting of listed buildings) for subsections (1) to (7) there is substituted the following subsection –

'(1)   The Secretary of State may prescribe requirements as to publicity for applications for planning permission in cases where the local planning authority think that the development of land would affect the setting of a listed building.'

24   In section 73 (publicity for applications affecting conservation areas) for subsection (1) there is substituted the following subsection –

'(1)   The Secretary of State may prescribe requirements as to publicity for applications for planning permission in cases where the local planning authority think that the development of land would affect the character or appearance of a conservation area.'

25   In section 91(2) (interpretation) 'development plan' is omitted.

26   In section 93 (provision about regulations and orders) after subsection (6) there are inserted the following subsections –

'(6A)   Regulations and orders may make different provision for different purposes.

(6B) The powers to make regulations under sections 10(3)(b), 67(1) and 73(1) must be taken to be powers mentioned in section 100(2) of the Local Government Act 2003 (powers exercisable in relation to descriptions of certain local authorities which fall into particular categories for the purposes of section 99 of that Act).'

## Planning (Hazardous Substances) Act 1990 (c. 10)

27   In section 40 of the Planning (Hazardous Substances) Act 1990 (provision about regulations) after subsection (3) there is inserted the following subsection –

'(4)   Regulations may make different provision for different purposes.'

## SCHEDULE 7    AMENDMENTS OF OTHER ENACTMENTS

Section 118

### Gas Act 1965 (c. 36)

1    In paragraph 7(2) of Schedule 3 of the Gas Act 1965 after 'development order' there is inserted 'or local development order'.

### Finance Act 1969 (c. 32)

2    In section 58(4) of the Finance Act 1969 (disclosure of information for statistical purposes), in the Table in the entry relating to local planning authorities –

   (a)  in the first column for 'the Town and Country Planning Act 1990' there is substituted 'Part 2 or 6 of the Planning and Compulsory Purchase Act 2004';

   (b)  In the second column for 'Part II of the Town and Country Planning Act 1990' there is substituted 'Part 2 or 6 of the Planning and Compulsory Purchase Act 2004'.

### Leasehold Reform Act 1967 (c. 88)

3    In section 28(6)(a) of the Leasehold Reform Act 1967 (development for certain public purposes) for 'Town and Country Planning Act 1990' there is substituted 'Planning and Compulsory Purchase Act 2004'.

### Agriculture (Miscellaneous Provisions) Act 1968 (c. 34)

4    In section 12 of the Agriculture (Miscellaneous Provisions) Act 1968 after subsection (3) there is inserted the following subsection –

   '(4)  If a person is entitled in respect of the same interest in land to a payment both –

   (a)  by virtue of subsection (1), and

   (b)  under section 33B of the Land Compensation Act 1973 (additional loss payment for agricultural land),

   section 33H of that Act (only one payment to be made if a person has dual entitlement) applies.'

### Countryside Act 1968 (c. 41)

5    (1)  Paragraph 3 of Schedule 2 to the Countryside Act 1968 is amended as follows.

   (2)  In sub-paragraph (2), after 'published' there is inserted ', affixed'.

   (3)  In sub-paragraph (4)(a), after 'published' there is inserted ', affixed'.

   (4)  The amendments made by this paragraph do not apply to compulsory purchase orders of which notice under section 11 of the Acquisition of Land Act 1981 (c. 67) is published before commencement of this paragraph.

### Greater London Council (General Powers) Act 1969 (c lii)

6    In section 13 of the Greater London Council (General Powers) Act 1969 (exercise of powers relating to walkways), in the proviso for the words from 'any local plan' to 'Schedule 1 to that Act)' there is substituted 'a local development document (within the meaning of Part 2 of the Planning and Compulsory Purchase Act 2004)'.

## Land Compensation Act 1973 (c. 26)

7  (1)  The Land Compensation Act 1973 is amended as follows.

   (2)  In section 29 (home loss payments) after subsection (3A) there is inserted the following subsection –

   '(3B) For the purposes of this section a person must not be treated as displaced from a dwelling in consequence only of the compulsory acquisition of part of a garden or yard or of an outhouse or appurtenance belonging to or usually enjoyed with the building which is occupied or is intended to be occupied as the dwelling.'

   (3)  Sections 34 to 36 are omitted.

   (4)  In section 87(1) (general interpretation) in the definition of 'dwelling' '(except in section 29)' is omitted.

   (5)  But the amendments made by this paragraph do not have effect in relation to a compulsory purchase order made or made in draft before the commencement of this paragraph.

## Greater London Council (General Powers) Act 1973 (c xxx)

8  In section 24(4) of the Greater London Council (General Powers) Act 1973 (definitions for the purpose or provision relating to parking place agreements) –

   (a)  in the definition of appropriate provision for 'the Greater London' there is substituted 'their';

   (b)  in the second place where it occurs 'Greater London development plan' is omitted.

## Welsh Development Agency Act 1975 (c. 70)

9  (1)  Schedule 4 to the Welsh Development Agency Act 1975 is amended as follows.

   (2)  Paragraph 2 is omitted.

   (3)  In paragraph 3, in sub-paragraph (1)(c), for 'section 13 of that Act to objections made by an owner, lessee or occupier' there is substituted 'sections 13 and 13A of that Act to relevant objections'.

   (4)  The amendments made by this paragraph do not apply to compulsory purchase orders of which notice under section 11 of the Acquisition of Land Act 1981 (c. 67) is published before commencement of this paragraph.

## Local Government, Planning and Land Act 1980 (c. 65)

10  (1)  The Local Government, Planning and Land Act 1980 is amended as follows.

   (2)  In section 142 (acquisition by corporation), in subsection (2A), '(subject to section 144(2))' is omitted.

   (3)  In section 143 (acquisition by local highway authority), in subsection (3A), '(subject to section 144(2))' is omitted.

   (4)  In section 144, in subsection (2), 'the 1981 Act and' is omitted.

   (5)  In Schedule 28, in paragraph 1, 'The 1981 Act and' and the words from 'and in paragraph 2' to the end are omitted.

   (6)  The amendments made by this paragraph do not apply to compulsory purchase orders of which notice under section 11 of or, as the case may be, paragraph 2 of Schedule 1 to the Acquisition of Land Act 1981 is published before commencement of this paragraph.

   (7)  In Schedule 26 (Urban Development Corporations), after paragraph 14 there are inserted the following paragraphs –

## 'Delegation of planning functions

14A (1)  This paragraph applies in relation to any function conferred on the corporation by virtue of an order under section 149 above.

(2)  The corporation may appoint committees and such committees may appoint sub-committees.

(3)  Anything which is authorised or required to be done by the corporation –

   (a)  may be done by any member of the corporation or of its staff who is authorised for the purpose either generally or specifically;

   (b)  may be done by a committee or sub-committee which is so authorised.

(4)  The corporation may –

   (a)  determine the quorum of a committee or sub-committee;

   (b)  make such arrangements as it thinks appropriate relating to the meetings and procedure of a committee or sub-committee.

(5)  Anything done for the purposes of sub-paragraph (4) is subject to directions given by the Secretary of State.

(6)  The validity of anything done by a committee or sub-committee is not affected by –

   (a)  any vacancy among its members;

   (b)  any defect in the appointment of any of its members.

(7)  This paragraph does not extend to Scotland.

14B (1)  This paragraph has effect in relation to the membership of committees and sub-committees appointed under paragraph 14A.

(2)  A committee may consist of –

   (a)  such members of the corporation as it appoints;

   (b)  such other persons as the corporation (with the consent of the Secretary of State) appoints.

(3)  A sub-committee of a committee may consist of –

   (a)  such members of the committee as it appoints;

   (b)  such persons who are members of another committee of the corporation (whether or not they are members of the corporation) as the committee appoints;

   (c)  such other persons as the corporation (with the consent of the Secretary of State) appoints.

(4)  The membership of a committee or sub-committee –

   (a)  must always include at least one person who is a member of the corporation;

   (b)  must not include any person who is a member of the staff of the corporation.'

## Highways Act 1980 (c. 66)

11  (1)  The Highways Act 1980 is amended as follows.

(2)  In section 232(8) after '1990' there is inserted 'and Parts 2 and 6 of the Planning and Compulsory Purchase Act 2004'.

(3)  In section 232(9) for the definition of development plan there is substituted –

'"development plan" must be construed in accordance with section 38 of the Planning and Compulsory Purchase Act 2004;

"local authority" has the same meaning as in the Town and Country Planning Act 1990.'

(4) Section 259 (power to confirm, etc, compulsory purchase order in part) is omitted.

(5) The amendment made by sub-paragraph (4) does not apply to a compulsory purchase order of which notice under section 11 of or, as the case may be, paragraph 2 of Schedule 1 to the Acquisition of Land Act 1981 is published before the commencement of that sub-paragraph.

## Acquisition of Land Act 1981 (c. 67)

12    In section 29(5) of the Acquisition of Land Act 1981 for the words 'any reference to any owner, lessee or occupier' there are substituted the words 'the reference to a qualifying person for the purposes of section 12(2)'.

## Housing Act 1985 (c. 68)

13    (1) In section 578A of the Housing Act 1985 (modification of compulsory purchase order in case of acquisition of land for clearance), in subsection (2), for 'section 13' there is substituted 'sections 13 to 13C'.

(2) The amendment made by sub-paragraph (1) does not apply to compulsory purchase orders of which notice under section 11 of the Acquisition of Land Act 1981 is published before commencement of this paragraph.

## Education Reform Act 1988 (c. 40)

14    (1) The Education Reform Act 1988 is amended as follows.

(2) In section 190 (wrongful contracts or disposals), in subsection (6) for the words from 'references' to the end there is substituted 'the reference in section 12 of that Act to an owner of the land included reference to the London Residuary Body'.

(3) In section 201 (wrongful disposals), in subsection (6), for the words from 'references' to the end there is substituted 'the reference in section 12 of that Act to an owner of the land included reference to the local education authority concerned'.

(4) The amendments made by this paragraph do not apply to compulsory purchase orders of which notice under section 11 of the Acquisition of Land Act 1981 (c. 67) is published before commencement of this paragraph.

## Housing Act 1988 (c. 50)

15    (1) Paragraph 2 of Schedule 10 to the Housing Act 1988 (modifications of Acquisition of Land Act 1981) is omitted.

(2) The amendment made by sub-paragraph (1) does not apply to compulsory purchase orders of which notice under section 11 of or, as the case may be, paragraph 2 of Schedule 1 to the Acquisition of Land Act 1981 is published before commencement of this paragraph.

## Planning and Compensation Act 1991 (c. 34)

16    In Schedule 4 to the Planning and Compensation Act 1991 Part 3 is omitted.

## Local Government Act 1992 (c. 19)

17   In section 14(5) of the Local Government Act 1992 (structural changes which may be recommended by the Electoral Commission), paragraph (d) is omitted.

## Leasehold Reform, Housing and Urban Development Act 1993 (c. 28)

18   (1)   Schedule 20 to the Leasehold Reform, Housing and Urban Development Act 1993 (modification of Acquisition of Land Act 1981) is amended as follows.
     (2)   In paragraph 1, for 'modifications specified in paragraphs 2 and' there is substituted 'modification specified in paragraph'.
     (3)   Paragraph 2 is omitted.
     (4)   The amendments made by this paragraph do not apply to compulsory purchase orders of which notice under section 11 of or, as the case may be, paragraph 2 of Schedule 1 to the Acquisition of Land Act 1981 (c. 67) is published before commencement of this paragraph.

## Environment Act 1995 (c. 25)

19   (1)   The Environment Act 1995 is amended as follows.
     (2)   In section 67 (which makes provision for a National Park authority to be the local planning authority) subsections (2) to (4) are omitted.
     (3)   In Schedule 14 (periodic review of mineral planning permissions) in paragraph 2(1), in the definition of 'first review date', for 'paragraph 5' there is substituted 'paragraphs 3A and 5'.
     (4)   In Schedule 14 after paragraph 3 there is inserted the following paragraph –

'3A   (1)   The Secretary of State may by order specify a first review date different from the first review date found in pursuance of paragraph 3(1) or (2).
      (2)   Sub-paragraph (3) applies if no first review date is found in pursuance of paragraph 3(1) or (2).
      (3)   The Secretary of State may by order specify a first review date.
      (4)   An order under sub-paragraph (3) may make different provision for different cases or different classes of case.
      (5)   An order under this paragraph must be made by statutory instrument subject to annulment in pursuance of a resolution of either House of Parliament.'

## Town and Country Planning (Scotland) Act 1997 (c. 8)

*******

## Regional Development Agencies Act 1998 (c. 45)

21   (1)   Paragraph 1 of Schedule 5 to the Regional Development Agencies Act 1998 (modifications of Acquisition of Land Act 1981) is omitted.
     (2)   The amendment made by sub-paragraph (1) does not apply to compulsory purchase orders of which notice has been published under section 11 of or, as the case may be, paragraph 2 of Schedule 1 to the Acquisition of Land Act 1981 (c. 67) before commencement of this paragraph.

## *Greater London Authority Act 1999 (c. 29)*

22   (1)   The Greater London Authority Act 1999 is amended as follows.

   (2)   In section 337 (publication) –

   (a)   for 'relevant regional planning guidance' there is substituted 'the regional spatial strategy for a region which adjoins Greater London';

   (b)   subsection (10) is omitted.

   (3)   In section 342(1) (matters to which Mayor is to have regard) for paragraph (a) there is substituted the following –

   '(a)   the regional spatial strategy for a region which adjoins Greater London;'.

   (4)   In section 346(b) (Mayor to monitor plans) for 'unitary development plan' there is substituted 'local development documents (within the meaning of Part 2 of the Planning and Compulsory Purchase Act 2004)'.

## *Countryside and Rights of Way Act 2000 (c. 37)*

23   In section 86(4) of the Countryside and Rights of Way Act 2000–

   (a)   'II,' is omitted;

   (b)   at the end there is inserted 'or under Part 2 or 6 of the Planning and Compulsory Purchase Act 2004'.

## SCHEDULE 8   TRANSITIONAL PROVISIONS:
## PARTS 1 AND 2                              Section 119

## *Development plan*

1   (1)   During the transitional period a reference in an enactment mentioned in section 38(7) above to the development plan for an area in England is a reference to –

   (a)   the RSS for the region in which the area is situated or the spatial development strategy for an area in Greater London, and

   (b)   the development plan for the area for the purposes of section 27 or 54 of the principal Act.

   (2)   The transitional period is the period starting with the commencement of section 38 and ending on whichever is the earlier of –

   (a)   the end of the period of three years;

   (b)   the day when in relation to an old policy, a new policy which expressly replaces it is published, adopted or approved.

   (3)   But the Secretary of State may direct that for the purposes of such policies as are specified in the direction sub-paragraph (2)(a) does not apply.

   (4)   An old policy is a policy which (immediately before the commencement of section 38) forms part of a development plan for the purposes of section 27 or 54 of the principal Act.

   (5)   A new policy is a policy which is contained in –

   (a)   a revision of an RSS;

   (b)   an alteration or replacement of the spatial development strategy;

   (c)   a development plan document.

   (6)   But –

   (a)   an old policy contained in a structure plan is replaced only by a new policy contained in a revision to an RSS;

(b)    an old policy contained in a waste local plan or a minerals local plan is replaced in relation to any area of a county council for which there is a district council only by a new policy contained in a development plan document which is prepared in accordance with a minerals and waste development scheme.

(7) A new policy is published if it is contained in –

(a)    a revision of an RSS published by the Secretary of State under section 9(6);

(b)    an alteration or replacement of the Mayor of London's spatial development strategy published in pursuance of section 337 of the Greater London Authority Act 1999 (c. 29).

(8) A new policy is adopted or approved if it is contained in a development plan document which is adopted or approved for the purposes of Part 2.

(9) A minerals and waste development scheme is a scheme prepared in accordance with section 16.

(10) The development plan mentioned in sub-paragraph (1)(b) does not include a street authorisation map which continued to be treated as having been adopted as a local plan by virtue of paragraph 4 of Part 3 of Schedule 2 to the principal Act.

## Structure plans

2      (1) This paragraph applies to proposals for the alteration or replacement of a structure plan for the area of a local planning authority.

(2) If before the commencement of Part 1 of this Act the authority have complied with section 33(2) of the principal Act (making copies of proposals and the explanatory memorandum available for inspection) the provisions of Chapter 2 of Part 2 of the principal Act continue to have effect in relation to the proposals.

(3) In any other case –

(a)    the authority must take no further step in relation to the proposals;

(b)    the proposals have no effect.

(4) If the proposals are adopted or approved by virtue of sub-paragraph (2) above, paragraph 1 of this Schedule applies to the policies contained in the proposals as if –

(a)    they were policies contained in a development plan within the meaning of section 54 of the principal Act;

(b)    the date of commencement of section 38 is the date when the proposals are adopted or approved (as the case may be).

## Unitary development plan

3      (1) This paragraph applies to proposals for the alteration or replacement of a unitary development plan for the area of a local planning authority.

(2) If before the relevant date the authority have not complied with section 13(2) of the principal Act (making copies of the proposals available for inspection) –

(a)    they must take no further step in relation to the proposals;

(b)    the proposals have no effect.

(3) In any other case paragraph 4 or 5 below applies.

4      (1) This paragraph applies if –

(a)    before the relevant date the local planning authority is not required to cause an inquiry or other hearing to be held by virtue of section 16(1) of the principal Act (inquiry must be held if objections made), or

(b)    before the commencement of Part 2 of this Act a person is appointed under that section to hold an inquiry or other hearing.

(2)    If this paragraph applies the provisions of Chapter 1 of Part 2 of the principal Act continue to have effect in relation to the proposals.

(3)    The relevant date is whichever is the later of –

(a)    the end of any period prescribed by regulations under section 26 of the principal Act for the making of objections to the proposals;

(b)    the commencement of Part 2 of this Act.

5    (1)    If paragraph 4 does not apply the provisions of Chapter 1 of Part 2 of the principal Act continue to have effect in relation to the proposals subject to the modifications in sub-paragraphs (2) to (5) below.

(2)    If before the commencement of Part 2 of this Act the local planning authority have not published revised proposals in pursuance of regulations under section 26 of the principal Act –

(a)    any provision of the regulations relating to publication of revised proposals must be ignored,

(b)    the authority must comply again with section 13(2) of the principal Act.

(3)    If before the commencement of Part 2 of this Act the local planning authority have published revised proposals in pursuance of regulations under section 26 of the principal Act the authority must comply again with section 13(2) of that Act.

(4)    Any provision of regulations under section 26 of the principal Act which permits the local planning authority to modify proposals after an inquiry or other hearing has been held under section 16 of that Act must be ignored.

(5)    If such an inquiry or other hearing is held the authority must adopt the proposals in accordance with the recommendations of the person appointed to hold the inquiry or other hearing.

6    If proposals are adopted or approved in pursuance of paragraph 4 or 5 above paragraph 1 of this Schedule applies to the policies contained in the proposals as if –

(a)    they were policies contained in a development plan for the purposes of section 27 of the principal Act;

(b)    the date of commencement of section 38 is the date when the proposals are adopted or approved.

7    (1)    This paragraph applies if at the date of commencement of Part 1 a local planning authority have not prepared a unitary development plan in pursuance of section 12 of the principal Act.

(2)    References in paragraphs 3 to 6 to proposals for the alteration or replacement of a plan must be construed as references to the plan.

## Local plan

8    (1)    This paragraph applies to proposals for the alteration or replacement of a local plan for the area of a local planning authority.

(2)    If before the commencement of Part 2 of this Act the authority have not complied with section 40(2) of the principal Act (making copies of the proposals available for inspection) –

(a)    they must take no further step in relation to the proposals;

(b)    the proposals have no effect.

(3)    In any other case paragraph 9 or 10 below applies.

9    (1)    This paragraph applies if –

    (a)    before the relevant date the local planning authority is not required to cause an inquiry or other hearing to be held by virtue of section 42(1) of the principal Act (inquiry must be held if objections made), or

    (b)    before the commencement of Part 2 of this Act a person is appointed under that section to hold an inquiry or other hearing.

(2)    If this paragraph applies the provisions of Chapter 2 of Part 2 of the principal Act continue to have effect in relation to the proposals.

(3)    The relevant date is whichever is the later of –

    (a)    the end of any period prescribed by regulations under section 53 of the principal Act for the making of objections to the proposals;

    (b)    the commencement of Part 2 of this Act.

10    (1)    If paragraph 9 does not apply the provisions of Chapter 2 of Part 2 of the principal Act continue to have effect in relation to the proposals subject to the modifications in sub-paragraphs (2) to (5) below.

(2)    If before the commencement of Part 2 of this Act the local planning authority have not published revised proposals in pursuance of regulations under section 53 of the principal Act –

    (a)    any provision of the regulations relating to publication of revised proposals must be ignored,

    (b)    the authority must comply again with section 40(2) of the principal Act.

(3)    If before the commencement of Part 2 of this Act the local planning authority have published revised proposals in pursuance of regulations under section 53 of the principal Act the authority must comply again with section 40(2) of that Act.

(4)    Any provision of regulations under section 53 of the principal Act which permits the local planning authority to modify proposals after an inquiry or other hearing has been held under section 42 of that Act must be ignored.

(5)    If such an inquiry or other hearing is held the authority must adopt the proposals in accordance with the recommendations of the person appointed to hold the inquiry or other hearing.

11    (1)    This paragraph applies if the Secretary of State thinks –

    (a)    that the conformity requirement is likely to give rise to inconsistency between the proposals and relevant policies or guidance, and

    (b)    that it is necessary or expedient to avoid such inconsistency.

(2)    The Secretary of State may direct that to the extent specified in the direction the conformity requirement must be ignored.

(3)    The Secretary of State must give reasons for the direction.

(4)    The conformity requirement is –

    (a)    the requirement under section 36(4) of the principal Act that the local plan is to be in general conformity with the structure plan;

    (b)    the prohibition under section 43(3) of the principal Act on the adoption of proposals for a local plan or for its alteration or replacement which do not conform generally with the structure plan.

(5)    Relevant policies and guidance are –

    (a)    national policies;

    (b)    advice contained in guidance;

    (c)    policies in the RSS.

12    If proposals are adopted or approved in pursuance of paragraphs 9 to 11 above paragraph 1 of this Schedule applies to the policies contained in the proposals as if –

(a)    they were policies contained in a development plan for the purposes of section 54 of the principal Act;

(b)    the date of commencement of section 38 is the date when the proposals are adopted or approved.

13    (1)    This paragraph applies if at the date of commencement of Part 1 a local planning authority have not prepared a local plan in pursuance of section 36 of the principal Act.

(2)    References in paragraphs 8 to 12 to proposals for the alteration or replacement of a plan must be construed as references to the plan.

## Minerals and waste local plans

14    Paragraphs 8 to 13 above apply to a minerals local plan and a waste local plan as they apply to a local plan and references in those paragraphs to a local planning authority must be construed as including references to a mineral planning authority and an authority who are entitled to prepare a waste local plan.

## Schemes

15    (1)    This paragraph applies to –

(a)    the local development scheme which a local planning authority are required to prepare and maintain under section 15 of this Act;

(b)    the minerals and waste development scheme which a county council are required to prepare and maintain for any part of their area for which there is a district council.

(2)    During the transitional period the local planning authority or county council (as the case may be) must include in the scheme as a development plan document –

(a)    any plan or document which relates to an old policy (for the purposes of paragraph 1 above) which has not been replaced by a new policy;

(b)    any proposals adopted or approved by virtue of paragraphs 3 to 12 above.

## Savings

16    (1)    The repeal by this Act of paragraphs 1 to 4 of Schedule 13 to the principal Act does not affect anything which is required or permitted to be done for the purposes of Chapter 2 of Part 6 of the principal Act during any time when a plan mentioned in any of those paragraphs continues to form part of the development plan by virtue of –

(a)    paragraph 1 of this Schedule, or

(b)    that paragraph as applied by any other provision of this Schedule.

(2)    References to a plan mentioned in any of paragraphs 1 to 4 include any proposal for the alteration or replacement of the plan.

(3)    The development plan is the development plan for the purposes of section 27 or 54 of the principal Act.

## Regulations and orders

17    (1)    The Secretary of State may by regulations make provision for giving full effect to this Schedule.

(2)    The regulations may, in particular –

    (a)   make such provision as he thinks is necessary in consequence of this Schedule;

    (b)   make provision to supplement any modifications of the principal Act required by this Schedule.

(3)  The Secretary of State may by order make such provision as he thinks is necessary in consequence of anything done under or by virtue of this Schedule.

(4)  Provision under sub-paragraph (3) includes provisions corresponding to that which could be made by order under Schedule 2 of the principal Act.

18   The Secretary of State may by regulations make provision –

    (a)   for treating anything done or purported to have been done for the purposes of Part 2 before the commencement of that Part as having been done after that commencement;

    (b)   for disregarding any requirement of section 19 in respect of anything done or purported to have been done for the purposes of any other provision of Part 2.

## Interpretation

19  (1)  References to section 27 of the principal Act must be construed subject to section 28(3)(a) and (c) of that Act.

    (2)  RSS must be construed in accordance with Part 1 of this Act.

    (3)  Development plan document must be construed in accordance with Part 2 of this Act.

## SCHEDULE 9    REPEALS

Section 120

| Short title and chapter | Extent of repeal |
|---|---|
| Land Compensation Act 1973 (c. 26) | Sections 34 to 36.<br>In section 87(1), in the definition of 'dwelling', '(except in section 29)'. |
| Greater London Council (General Powers) Act 1973 (c. xxx) | In section 24(4), the second 'Greater London development plan'. |
| Welsh Development Agency Act 1975 (c. 70) | In Schedule 4, paragraph 2. |
| Local Government, Planning and Land Act 1980 (c. 65) | In section 142(2A), '(subject to section 144(2))'.<br>In section 143(3A), '(subject to section 144(2))'.<br>In section 144(2), 'the 1981Act and'.<br>In Schedule 28, in paragraph 1, 'The 1981Act and' and the words from 'and in paragraph 2' to the end. |
| Highways Act 1980 (c. 66) | Section 259. |
| Housing Act 1988 (c. 50) | In Schedule 10, paragraph 2. |
| Town and Country Planning Act 1990 (c. 8) | Part 2.<br>In section 55(2)(b), the word 'local'.<br>Section 73(3).<br>Section 76.<br>Section 83(1).<br>Sections 106 to 106B.<br>In section 220(3), the expression '62'.<br>In section 226, in subsection (1) the first 'which' and subsection (2).<br>Section 245(2) and (3).<br>In section 284(1), paragraph (a).<br>In section 287, in subsection (5), paragraph (a) and in each of paragraphs (b) to (e) the words 'by virtue of subsection (3)' and subsection (6).<br>Section 293(4).<br>Sections 294 to 297.<br>Section 298(1) and (2).<br>Sections 299 to 301.<br>Section 303(6).<br>In section 303A, in subsection (5) the words 'or appointed as one of the persons who are to hold it', the words '(in addition to what may be recovered by virtue of the appointment of any other person)' and in paragraph (c) the words '(or, in a case where that person is appointed as one of the persons who are to hold the qualifying inquiry, an appropriate proportion of any costs attributable to the appointment of an |

| Short title and chapter | Extent of repeal |
|---|---|
| | assessor to assist those persons)' and subsections (7) to (9). In Schedule 1, paragraph 2, in para graph 3(7) the words 'but paragraph 4 shall apply to such applications instead'. In Schedule 2, Parts 1, 2 and 3. In Schedule 7, paragraphs 3 and 4. In Schedule 13, paragraphs 1 to 4. |
| Planning (Listed Buildings and Conservation Areas) Act 1990 (c. 9) | In section 10, in subsection (2) the words 'shall be made in such form as the authority may require and' and in sub-section (3) the word 'and' after paragraph (b). Section 67(2) to (7). Sections 83 and 84. In section 91(2), ''development plan''. In section 92(2)(a), '83, 84,'. |
| Planning (Hazardous Substances) Act 1990 (c. 10) | Section 31(1) and (2). Section 32. |
| Planning and Compensation Act 1991 (c. 34) | Section 17(1). In Schedule 4, Part 3. In Schedule 18, Part 2 in the entry relating to the Land Compensation Act 1973, 'section 36(6) (farm loss payment),'. |
| Local Government Act 1992 (c. 19) | In section 14(5), paragraph (d). |
| Leasehold Reform, Housing and Urban Development Act 1993 (c. 28) | In Schedule 20, paragraph 2. |
| Environment Act 1995 (c. 25) | In section 67, subsections (2) to (4). |
| Town and Country Planning (Scotland) Act 1997 (c. 8) | Section 242(4). Sections 243 to 250. |
| Planning (Listed Buildings and Conservation Areas) (Scotland) Act 1997 (c. 9) | Sections 74 and 75. |
| Planning (Hazardous Substances) (Scotland) Act 1997 (c. 10) | Section 31(1) and (2). Section 32. |
| Regional Development Agencies Act 1998 (c. 45) | In Schedule 5, paragraph 1. |
| Countryside and Rights of Way Act 2000 (c. 37) | In section 86(4), 'II,'. |

Note:  The repeal of sections 34 to 36 of the Land Compensation Act 1973 does not have effect in relation to a compulsory purchase order made or made in draft before the commencement of paragraph 7(3) of Schedule 7.

## Appendix 2
# SUBSEQUENT AND RELATED REGULATIONS

2004 NO. 1633

ENVIRONMENTAL PROTECTION

**The Environmental Assessment of Plans and Programmes Regulations 2004**

Made 28th June 2004
Laid before Parliament 29th June 2004
Coming into force 20th July 2004

### ARRANGEMENT OF REGULATIONS

#### PART 1    INTRODUCTORY PROVISIONS

#### PART 2    ENVIRONMENTAL ASSESSMENT FOR PLANS AND PROGRAMMES

## PART 3    ENVIRONMENTAL REPORTS AND CONSULTATION PROCEDURES

12.    Preparation of environmental report
13.    Consultation procedures
14.    Transboundary consultations
15.    Plans and programmes of other Member States

## PART 4    POST-ADOPTION PROCEDURES

16.    Information as to adoption of plan or programme
17.    Monitoring of implementation of plans and programmes

## SCHEDULES

1.    Criteria for determining the likely significance of effects on the environment
2.    Information for environmental reports

The Secretary of State, being a designated Minister for the purposes of section 2(2) of the European Communities Act 1972 in relation to matters relating to the assessment of the effects of certain plans and programmes on the environment, in exercise of the powers conferred by that section 2, and of all other powers enabling him in that behalf, hereby makes the following Regulations:

## PART 1    INTRODUCTORY PROVISIONS

**Citation and commencement**

1.    These Regulations may be cited as the Environmental Assessment of Plans and Programmes Regulations 2004 and shall come into force on 20th July 2004.

**Interpretation**

2.    (1)    In these Regulations –

'consultation body' has the meaning given by regulation 4;
'England' includes the territorial waters of the United Kingdom that are not part of Northern Ireland, Scotland or Wales, and waters in any area for the time being designated under section 17(1) of the Continental Shelf Act 1964;
'the Environmental Assessment of Plans and Programmes Directive' means Directive 2001/42/EC of the European Parliament and of the Council on the assessment of the effects of certain plans and programmes on the environment;
'the Habitats Directive' means Council Directive 92/43/EEC on the conservation of natural habitats and of wild flora and fauna, as last amended by Council Directive 97/62/EC;
'Northern Ireland' has the meaning given by section 98 of the Northern Ireland Act 1998;
'plans and programmes' means plans and programmes, including those co-financed by the European Community, as well as any modifications to them, which –

(a)    are subject to preparation or adoption by an authority at national, regional or local level; or

    (b)    are prepared by an authority for adoption, through a legislative procedure by Parliament or Government; and, in either case,

    (c)    are required by legislative, regulatory or administrative provisions; and

'responsible authority', in relation to a plan or programme, means –

    (a)    the authority by which or on whose behalf it is prepared; and

    (b)    where, at any particular time, that authority ceases to be responsible, or solely responsible, for taking steps in relation to the plan or programme, the person who, at that time, is responsible (solely or jointly with the authority) for taking those steps;

'Scotland' has the meaning given by section 126 of the Scotland Act 1998; and 'Wales' has the meaning given by section 155 of the Government of Wales Act 1998.

(2)    Other expressions used both in these Regulations and in the Environmental Assessment of Plans and Programmes Directive have the same meaning in these Regulations as they have in that Directive.

### Application of Regulations

3.    (1)    With the exception of regulations 14 and 15, these Regulations apply as follows.

    (2)    These Regulations apply to a plan or programme relating –

    (a)    solely to the whole or any part of England; or

    (b)    to England (whether as to the whole or part) and any other part of the United Kingdom.

    (3)    These Regulations apply to a plan or programme relating (whether wholly or in part) to the Isles of Scilly as if the Isles were a county in England.

    (4)    These Regulations do not apply to a plan or programme relating solely –

    (a)    to the whole or any part of Northern Ireland;

    (b)    to the whole or any part of Scotland; or

    (c)    to the whole or any part of Wales.

### Consultation bodies

4.    (1)    Subject to paragraph (5), in relation to every plan or programme to which these Regulations apply, each of the following bodies shall be a consultation body –

    (a)    the Countryside Agency;

    (b)    the Historic Buildings and Monuments Commission for England (English Heritage);

    (c)    English Nature; and

    (d)    the Environment Agency,

but where paragraph (2), (3) or (4) applies, the functions of those bodies under these Regulations shall be exercisable only in relation to so much of the plan or programme as relates to England.

    (2)    In relation to such part of a plan or programme to which these Regulations apply as relates to Northern Ireland, the Department of the Environment for Northern Ireland shall be a consultation body for the purposes of these Regulations.

    (3)    In relation to such part of a plan or programme to which these Regulations apply as relates to Scotland, each of the following shall be a consultation body for the purposes of these Regulations –

    (a)    the Scottish Ministers;

    (b)    the Scottish Environment Protection Agency; and

    (c)    Scottish Natural Heritage.

(4)  In relation to such part of a plan or programme to which these Regulations apply as relates to Wales, each of the following shall be a consultation body for the purposes of these Regulations –

(a)   the National Assembly for Wales; and

(b)   the Countryside Council for Wales.

(5)  Where a body mentioned in paragraph (1) is at any time the responsible authority as regards a plan or programme, it shall not at that time exercise the functions under these Regulations of a consultation body in relation to that plan or programme; and references to the consultation bodies in the following provisions of these Regulations shall be construed accordingly.

## PART 2    ENVIRONMENTAL ASSESSMENT FOR PLANS AND PROGRAMMES

**Environmental assessment for plans and programmes: first formal preparatory act on or after 21st July 2004**

5.    (1)  Subject to paragraphs (5) and (6) and regulation 7, where –

(a)   the first formal preparatory act of a plan or programme is on or after 21st July 2004; and

(b)   the plan or programme is of the description set out in either paragraph (2) or paragraph (3),

the responsible authority shall carry out, or secure the carrying out of, an environmental assessment, in accordance with Part 3 of these Regulations, during the preparation of that plan or programme and before its adoption or submission to the legislative procedure.

(2)  The description is a plan or programme which –

(a)   is prepared for agriculture, forestry, fisheries, energy, industry, transport, waste management, water management, telecommunications, tourism, town and country planning or land use, and

(b)   sets the framework for future development consent of projects listed in Annex I or II to Council Directive 85/337/EEC on the assessment of the effects of certain public and private projects on the environment, as amended by Council Directive 97/11/EC.

(3)  The description is a plan or programme which, in view of the likely effect on sites, has been determined to require an assessment pursuant to Article 6 or 7 of the Habitats Directive.

(4)  Subject to paragraph (5) and regulation 7, where –

(a)   the first formal preparatory act of a plan or programme, other than a plan or programme of the description set out in paragraph (2) or (3), is on or after 21st July 2004;

(b)   the plan or programme sets the framework for future development consent of projects; and

(c)   the plan or programme is the subject of a determination under regulation 9(1) or a direction under regulation 10(3) that it is likely to have significant environmental effects,

the responsible authority shall carry out, or secure the carrying out of, an environmental assessment, in accordance with Part 3 of these Regulations, during the preparation of that plan or programme and before its adoption or submission to the legislative procedure.

(5)  Nothing in paragraph (1) or (4) requires the carrying out of an environmental assessment for –

(a)  a plan or programme the sole purpose of which is to serve national defence or civil emergency;

(b)  a financial or budget plan or programme; or

(c)  a plan or programme co-financed under –

(i)  the 2000–2006 programming period for Council Regulation (EC) No. 1260/1999; or

(ii)  the 2000–2006 or 2000–2007 programming period for Council Regulation (EC) No. 1257/1999.

(6)  An environmental assessment need not be carried out –

(a)  for a plan or programme of the description set out in paragraph (2) or (3) which determines the use of a small area at local level; or

(b)  for a minor modification to a plan or programme of the description set out in either of those paragraphs,

unless it has been determined under regulation 9(1) that the plan, programme or modification, as the case may be, is likely to have significant environmental effects, or it is the subject of a direction under regulation 10(3).

### Environmental assessment for plans and programmes: first formal preparatory act before 21st July 2004

6.  (1)  Subject to paragraph (2) and regulation 7, where –

(a)  a plan or programme of which the first formal preparatory act is before 21st July 2004 has not been adopted or submitted to the legislative procedure for adoption before 22nd July 2006; and

(b)  the plan or programme is such that, had the first act in its preparation occurred on 21st July 2004, the plan or programme would have required an environmental assessment by virtue of regulation 5(1); or

(c)  the responsible authority is of the opinion that, if a determination under regulation 9(1) in respect of the plan or programme had been made on 21st July 2004, it would have determined that the plan or programme was likely to have significant environmental effects,

the responsible authority shall carry out, or secure the carrying out of, an environmental assessment, in accordance with Part 3 of these Regulations, during the preparation of that plan or programme and before its adoption or submission to the legislative procedure.

(2)  Nothing in paragraph (1) shall require the environmental assessment of a particular plan or programme if the responsible authority –

(a)  decides that such assessment is not feasible; and

(b)  informs the public of its decision.

### Environmental assessment for plans and programmes co-financed by the European Community

7.  The environmental assessment required by any provision of this Part for a plan or programme co-financed by the European Community shall be carried out by the responsible authority in conformity with the specific provisions in relevant Community legislation.

### Restriction on adoption or submission of plans, programmes and modifications

8.  (1)  A plan, programme or modification in respect of which a determination under regulation 9(1) is required shall not be adopted or submitted to the legislative procedure for the purpose of its adoption –

(a) where an environmental assessment is required in consequence of the determination or of a direction under regulation 10(3), before the requirements of paragraph (3) below have been met;

(b) in any other case, before the determination has been made under regulation 9(1).

(2) A plan or programme for which an environmental assessment is required by any provision of this Part shall not be adopted or submitted to the legislative procedure for the purpose of its adoption before –

(a) if it is a plan or programme co-financed by the European Community, the environmental assessment has been carried out as mentioned in regulation 7;

(b) in any other case, the requirements of paragraph (3) below, and such requirements of Part 3 as apply in relation to the plan or programme, have been met.

(3) The requirements of this paragraph are that account shall be taken of –

(a) the environmental report for the plan or programme;

(b) opinions expressed in response to the invitation referred to in regulation 13(2)(d);

(c) opinions expressed in response to action taken by the responsible authority in accordance with regulation 13(4); and

(d) the outcome of any consultations under regulation 14(4).

### Determinations of the responsible authority

9. (1) The responsible authority shall determine whether or not a plan, programme or modification of a description referred to in –

(a) paragraph (4)(a) and (b) of regulation 5;

(b) paragraph (6)(a) of that regulation; or

(c) paragraph (6)(b) of that regulation,

is likely to have significant environmental effects.

(2) Before making a determination under paragraph (1) the responsible authority shall –

(a) take into account the criteria specified in Schedule 1 to these Regulations; and

(b) consult the consultation bodies.

(3) Where the responsible authority determines that the plan, programme or modification is unlikely to have significant environmental effects (and, accordingly, does not require an environmental assessment), it shall prepare a statement of its reasons for the determination.

### Powers of the Secretary of State

10. (1) The Secretary of State may at any time require the responsible authority to send him a copy of –

(a) any determination under paragraph (1) of regulation 9 with respect to the plan, programme or modification;

(b) the plan, programme or modification to which the determination relates; and

(c) where paragraph (3) of that regulation applies, the statement prepared in accordance with that paragraph.

(2) The responsible authority shall comply with a requirement under paragraph (1) within 7 days.

(3) The Secretary of State may direct that a plan, programme or modification is likely to have significant environmental effects (whether or not a copy of it has been sent to him in response to a requirement under paragraph (1)).

(4) Before giving a direction under paragraph (3) the Secretary of State shall –

    (a)   take into account the criteria specified in Schedule 1 to these Regulations; and

    (b)   consult the consultation bodies.

(5) The Secretary of State shall, as soon as reasonably practicable after the giving of the direction, send to the responsible authority and to each consultation body –

    (a)   a copy of the direction; and

    (b)   a statement of his reasons for giving the direction.

(6) In relation to a plan, programme or modification in respect of which a direction has been given –

    (a)   any determination under regulation 9(1) with respect to the plan, programme or modification shall cease to have effect on the giving of the direction; and.

    (b)   if no determination has been made under regulation 9(1) with respect to the plan, programme or modification, the responsible authority shall cease to be under any duty imposed by that regulation.

### Publicity for determinations and directions

11. (1) Within 28 days of making a determination under regulation 9(1), the responsible authority shall send to each consultation body –

    (a)   a copy of the determination; and

    (b)   where the responsible authority has determined that the plan or programme does not require an environmental assessment, a statement of its reasons for the determination.

(2) The responsible authority shall –

    (a)   keep a copy of the determination, and any accompanying statement of reasons, available at its principal office for inspection by the public at all reasonable times and free of charge; and

    (b)   within 28 days of the making of the determination, take such steps as it considers appropriate to bring to the attention of the public –

        (i)   the title of the plan, programme or modification to which the determination relates;

        (ii)   that the responsible authority has determined that the plan, programme or modification is or is not likely to have significant environmental effects (as the case may be) and, accordingly, that an environmental assessment is or is not required in respect of the plan, programme or modification; and

        (iii)   the address (which may include a website) at which a copy of the determination and any accompanying statement of reasons may be inspected or from which a copy may be obtained.

(3) Where the responsible authority receives a direction under regulation 10(3), it shall –

    (a)   keep a copy of the direction and of the Secretary of State's statement of his reasons for giving it available at its principal office for inspection by the public at all reasonable times and free of charge; and

    (b)   within 28 days of the receipt of such a direction, take such steps as it considers appropriate to bring to the attention of the public –

(i)   the title of the plan, programme or modification to which the direction relates;

(ii)  that the Secretary of State has directed that the plan, programme or modification is likely to have significant environmental effects and, accordingly, that an environmental assessment is required in respect of the plan, programme or modification; and

(iii) the address (which may include a website) at which a copy of the direction and of the Secretary of State's statement of his reasons for giving it may be inspected or from which a copy may be obtained.

(4)   The responsible authority shall provide a copy of any document referred to in paragraph (2)(b)(iii) or (3)(b)(iii) free of charge.

## PART 3   ENVIRONMENTAL REPORTS AND CONSULTATION PROCEDURES

### Preparation of environmental report

12. (1)  Where an environmental assessment is required by any provision of Part 2 of these Regulations, the responsible authority shall prepare, or secure the preparation of, an environmental report in accordance with paragraphs (2) and (3) of this regulation.

(2)  The report shall identify, describe and evaluate the likely significant effects on the environment of –

(a)   implementing the plan or programme; and

(b)   reasonable alternatives taking into account the objectives and the geographical scope of the plan or programme.

(3)  The report shall include such of the information referred to in Schedule 2 to these Regulations as may reasonably be required, taking account of –

(a)   current knowledge and methods of assessment;

(b)   the contents and level of detail in the plan or programme;

(c)   the stage of the plan or programme in the decision-making process; and

(d)   the extent to which certain matters are more appropriately assessed at different levels in that process in order to avoid duplication of the assessment.

(4)  Information referred to in Schedule 2 may be provided by reference to relevant information obtained at other levels of decision-making or through other Community legislation.

(5)  When deciding on the scope and level of detail of the information that must be included in the report, the responsible authority shall consult the consultation bodies.

(6)  Where a consultation body wishes to respond to a consultation under paragraph (5), it shall do so within the period of 5 weeks beginning with the date on which it receives the responsible authority's invitation to engage in the consultation.

### Consultation procedures

13. (1)  Every draft plan or programme for which an environmental report has been prepared in accordance with regulation 12 and its accompanying environmental report ('the relevant documents') shall be made available for the purposes of consultation in accordance with the following provisions of this regulation.

(2)  As soon as reasonably practicable after the preparation of the relevant documents, the responsible authority shall –

(a)   send a copy of those documents to each consultation body;

(b)   take such steps as it considers appropriate to bring the preparation of the relevant documents to the attention of the persons who, in the authority's opinion, are affected or likely to be affected by, or have an interest in the decisions involved in the assessment and adoption of the plan or programme concerned, required under the Environmental Assessment of Plans and Programmes Directive ('the public consultees');

(c)   inform the public consultees of the address (which may include a website) at which a copy of the relevant documents may be viewed, or from which a copy may be obtained; and

(d)   invite the consultation bodies and the public consultees to express their opinion on the relevant documents, specifying the address to which, and the period within which, opinions must be sent.

(3)   The period referred to in paragraph (2)(d) must be of such length as will ensure that the consultation bodies and the public consultees are given an effective opportunity to express their opinion on the relevant documents.

(4)   The responsible authority shall keep a copy of the relevant documents available at its principal office for inspection by the public at all reasonable times and free of charge.

(5)   Nothing in paragraph (2)(c) shall require the responsible authority to provide copies free of charge; but where a charge is made, it shall be of a reasonable amount.

### Transboundary consultations

14. (1)   Where a responsible authority, other than the Secretary of State, is of the opinion that a plan or programme for which it is the responsible authority is likely to have significant effects on the environment of another Member State, it shall, as soon as reasonably practicable after forming that opinion –

(a)   notify the Secretary of State of its opinion and of the reasons for it; and

(b)   supply the Secretary of State with a copy of the plan or programme concerned, and of the accompanying environmental report.

(2)   Where the Secretary of State has been notified under paragraph (1)(a), the responsible authority shall, within such period as the Secretary of State may specify by notice in writing to the authority, provide the Secretary of State with such other information about the plan or programme or its accompanying environmental report as he may reasonably require.

(3)   Where –

(a)   the Secretary of State, whether in consequence of a notice under paragraph (1)(a) or otherwise, considers that the implementation of a plan or programme in any part of the United Kingdom is likely to have significant effects on the environment of another Member State); or

(b)   a Member State that is likely to be significantly affected by the implementation of a plan or programme so requests,

the Secretary of State shall, before the adoption of the plan or programme or its submission to the legislative procedure for adoption, forward a copy of it and of its accompanying environmental report to the Member State concerned.

(4)   Where the Secretary of State receives from a Member State an indication that it wishes to enter into consultations before the adoption, or submission to the legislative procedure for adoption, of a plan or programme forwarded to it in accordance with paragraph (3), the Secretary of State shall –

(a)  agree with the Member State –

   (i)  detailed arrangements to ensure that the authorities referred to in paragraph 3 of Article 6 of the Environmental Assessment of Plans and Programmes Directive and the public referred to in paragraph 4 of that Article in the Member State likely to be significantly affected are informed and given an opportunity to forward their opinion within a reasonable time; and

   (ii)  a reasonable time for the duration of the consultations;

(b)  enter into consultations with the Member State concerning –

   (i)  the likely transboundary environmental effects of implementing the plan or programme; and

   (ii)  the measures envisaged to reduce or eliminate such effects; and

(c)  where he is not the responsible authority, direct the responsible authority that it shall not adopt the plan or programme, or submit it to the legislative procedure for adoption, until the consultations with the Member State have been concluded.

(5)  Where consultations take place pursuant to paragraph (4), the Secretary of State shall –

(a)  as soon as reasonably practicable after those consultations begin, notify the consultation bodies of that fact; and

(b)  notify the consultation bodies and, where he is not the responsible authority, the responsible authority, of the outcome of the consultations.

### Plans and programmes of other Member States

15.  (1)  This regulation applies where the Secretary of State receives from a Member State (whether or not in response to a request made by the United Kingdom in that behalf under the Environmental Assessment of Plans and Programmes Directive) a copy of a draft plan or programme –

(a)  that is being prepared in relation to any part of that Member State; and

(b)  whose implementation is likely to have significant effects on the environment of any part of the United Kingdom.

(2)  The Secretary of State shall indicate to the Member State whether, before the adoption of the plan or programme or its submission to the legislative procedure for adoption, the United Kingdom wishes to enter into consultations in respect of that plan or programme concerning –

(a)  the likely transboundary environmental effects of implementing the plan or programme; and

(b)  the measures envisaged to reduce or eliminate such effects.

(3)  Where the Secretary of State so indicates, he shall agree with the Member State concerned –

(a)  detailed arrangements to ensure that the consultation bodies and the public in the United Kingdom or, as the case may be, the part of the United Kingdom that is likely to be significantly affected by the implementation of the plan or programme, are informed and given an opportunity to forward their opinion within a reasonable time; and

(b)  a reasonable time for the duration of the consultations.

(4)  Where such consultations take place under this regulation, the Secretary of State shall –

(a)  inform the consultation bodies of the receipt of the draft plan or programme;

(b)  provide them with a copy of the draft plan or programme and the relevant environmental report provided under Article 7.1 of the Environmental Assessment of Plans and Programmes Directive or specify the address (which may include a website) at which those documents may be inspected;

(c)  take such steps as he considers appropriate to bring the receipt of the draft plan or programme to the attention of such persons as, in his opinion, are affected or likely to be affected by, or have an interest in the decisions involved in the assessment and adoption of the plan or programme concerned, required under the Environmental Assessment of Plans and Programmes Directive ('the transboundary consultees');

(d)  inform the transboundary consultees of the address (which may include a website) at which a copy of the draft plan or programme and the relevant environmental report provided under Article 7.1 of the Environmental Assessment of Plans and Programmes Directive may be inspected, or from which a copy may be obtained; and

(e)  invite the consultation bodies and the transboundary consultees to forward to him their opinions within such period as he may specify.

(5)  The period specified under paragraph (4)(e) shall end not later than 28 days before the end of the period that the Secretary of State has agreed with the Member State concerned, pursuant to paragraph (3)(b), as reasonable for the duration of their consultations.

(6)  Nothing in paragraph (4)(d) shall require the Secretary of State to provide copies free of charge; but where a charge is made, it shall be of a reasonable amount.

## PART 4    POST-ADOPTION PROCEDURES

### Information as to adoption of plan or programme

16.  (1)  As soon as reasonably practicable after the adoption of a plan or programme for which an environmental assessment has been carried out under these Regulations, the responsible authority shall –

(a)  make a copy of the plan or programme and its accompanying environmental report available at its principal office for inspection by the public at all reasonable times and free of charge; and

(b)  take such steps as it considers appropriate to bring to the attention of the public –

(i)   the title of the plan or programme;

(ii)  the date on which it was adopted;

(iii) the address (which may include a website) at which a copy of it and of its accompanying environmental report, and of a statement containing the particulars specified in paragraph (4), may be viewed or from which a copy may be obtained;

(iv)  the times at which inspection may be made; and

(v)   that inspection may be made free of charge.

(2)  As soon as reasonably practicable after the adoption of a plan or programme –

(a)  the responsible authority shall inform –

(i)   the consultation bodies;

(ii)  the persons who, in relation to the plan or programme, were public consultees for the purposes of regulation 13; and

(iii) where the responsible authority is not the Secretary of State, the Secretary of State; and

   (b)    the Secretary of State shall inform the Member State with which consul-
          tations in relation to the plan or programme have taken place under
          regulation 14(4),

of the matters referred to in paragraph (3).

(3)  The matters are –

   (a)    that the plan or programme has been adopted;
   (b)    the date on which it was adopted; and
   (c)    the address (which may include a website) at which a copy of –

       (i)     the plan or programme, as adopted,
       (ii)    its accompanying environmental report, and
       (iii)   a statement containing the particulars specified in paragraph (4),

may be viewed, or from which a copy may be obtained.

(4)  The particulars referred to in paragraphs (1)(b)(iii) and (3)(c)(iii) are –

   (a)    how environmental considerations have been integrated into the plan or
          programme;
   (b)    how the environmental report has been taken into account;
   (c)    how opinions expressed in response to –

       (i)     the invitation referred to in regulation 13(2)(d);
       (ii)    action taken by the responsible authority in accordance with regulation
               13(4),

       have been taken into account;
   (d)    how the results of any consultations entered into under regulation 14(4)
          have been taken into account;
   (e)    the reasons for choosing the plan or programme as adopted, in the light of
          the other reasonable alternatives dealt with; and
   (f)    the measures that are to be taken to monitor the significant environmental
          effects of the implementation of the plan or programme.

## Monitoring of implementation of plans and programmes

17.  (1)  The responsible authority shall monitor the significant environmental effects of
          the implementation of each plan or programme with the purpose of identifying
          unforeseen adverse effects at an early stage and being able to undertake
          appropriate remedial action.
     (2)  The responsible authority's monitoring arrangements may comprise or include
          arrangements established otherwise than for the express purpose of complying
          with paragraph (1).

## SCHEDULE 1    CRITERIA FOR DETERMINING THE LIKELY SIGNIFICANCE OF EFFECTS ON THE ENVIRONMENT                Regulations 9(2)(a) and 10(4)(a)

1.  The characteristics of plans and programmes, having regard, in particular, to –

    (a) the degree to which the plan or programme sets a framework for projects and other activities, either with regard to the location, nature, size and operating conditions or by allocating resources;

    (b) the degree to which the plan or programme influences other plans and programmes including those in a hierarchy;

    (c) the relevance of the plan or programme for the integration of environmental considerations in particular with a view to promoting sustainable development;

    (d) environmental problems relevant to the plan or programme; and

    (e) the relevance of the plan or programme for the implementation of Community legislation on the environment (for example, plans and programmes linked to waste management or water protection).

2.  Characteristics of the effects and of the area likely to be affected, having regard, in particular, to –

    (a) the probability, duration, frequency and reversibility of the effects;

    (b) the cumulative nature of the effects;

    (c) the transboundary nature of the effects;

    (d) the risks to human health or the environment (for example, due to accidents);

    (e) the magnitude and spatial extent of the effects (geographical area and size of the population likely to be affected);

    (f) the value and vulnerability of the area likely to be affected due to –

        (i)   special natural characteristics or cultural heritage;

        (ii)  exceeded environmental quality standards or limit values; or

        (iii) intensive land-use; and

    (g) the effects on areas or landscapes which have a recognised national, Community or international protection status.

## SCHEDULE 2    INFORMATION FOR ENVIRONMENTAL REPORTS                                    Regulation 12(3)

1.  An outline of the contents and main objectives of the plan or programme, and of its relationship with other relevant plans and programmes.

2.  The relevant aspects of the current state of the environment and the likely evolution thereof without implementation of the plan or programme.

3.  The environmental characteristics of areas likely to be significantly affected.

4.  Any existing environmental problems which are relevant to the plan or programme including, in particular, those relating to any areas of a particular environmental importance, such as areas designated pursuant to Council Directive 79/409/EEC on the conservation of wild birds and the Habitats Directive.

5.  The environmental protection objectives, established at international, Community or Member State level, which are relevant to the plan or programme and the way those objectives and any environmental considerations have been taken into account during its preparation.

6.  The likely significant effects on the environment, including short, medium and long-term effects, permanent and temporary effects, positive and negative effects, and secondary, cumulative and synergistic effects, on issues such as –

(a)  biodiversity;
(b)  population;
(c)  human health;
(d)  fauna;
(e)  flora;
(f)   soil;
(g)  water;
(h)  air;
(i)   climatic factors;
(j)   material assets;
(k)  cultural heritage, including architectural and archaeological heritage;
(l)   landscape; and
(m)  the inter-relationship between the issues referred to in sub-paragraphs (a) to (l).

7.  The measures envisaged to prevent, reduce and as fully as possible offset any significant adverse effects on the environment of implementing the plan or programme.

8.  An outline of the reasons for selecting the alternatives dealt with, and a description of how the assessment was undertaken including any difficulties (such as technical deficiencies or lack of know-how) encountered in compiling the required information.

9.  A description of the measures envisaged concerning monitoring in accordance with regulation 17.

10.  A non-technical summary of the information provided under paragraphs 1 to 9.

2004 NO. 2097 (C. 89)

## TOWN AND COUNTRY PLANNING ACQUISITION OF LAND

## The Planning and Compulsory Purchase Act 2004 (Commencement No.1) Order 2004

### Made 4th August 2004

The First Secretary of State in exercise of the powers conferred on him by section 121(1) to (3) of the Planning and Compulsory Purchase Act 2004 and all other powers enabling him in that behalf, with the agreement of the Scottish Ministers and after consultation with the National Assembly for Wales, hereby makes the following Order:

### Citation and interpretation

1.  (1) This Order may be cited as the Planning and Compulsory Purchase Act 2004 (Commencement No 1) Order 2004.
    (2) In this Order 'the 2004 Act' means the Planning and Compulsory Purchase Act 2004.

### Provisions coming into force for certain purposes on 6th August 2004

2.  So much of the following provisions of the 2004 Act as confers on the Secretary of State, the Lord Chancellor, the National Assembly for Wales or the Scottish Ministers a power or imposes a duty to make or to make provision by rules, regulations, development order or other order or to give directions, or make provision with respect to the exercise of any such power or performance of such duty, shall come into force on 6th August 2004:

> sections 1 to 3;
> section 5;
> section 8;
> sections 10 to 15;
> section 16;
> section 17;
> sections 19 to 22;
> sections 24 to 26;
> sections 28 and 29;
> section 31;
> sections 35 and 36;
> sections 40 to 42;
> section 44;
> sections 46 to 50;
> sections 52 to 54;
> section 57;
> section 59;
> sections 79 to 83;
> section 88;
> section 91;
> sections 100 and 101;
> section 116;
> section 117(1) to (7);

section 118 except subsection (2) in so far as it relates to the Town and Country Planning (Scotland) Act 1997;

section 119(1);section 120 except in so far as it relates to the Town and Country Planning (Scotland) Act 1997, to the Planning (Hazardous Substances) (Scotland) Act 1997 or to the Planning (Listed Buildings and Conservation Areas) (Scotland) Act 1997;

Schedule 1;

Schedule 2 paragraph 3;

Schedule 3 paragraphs 6 to 8 and 10 to 12;

Schedule 6 paragraphs 1, 3, 14, 16, 19, 20, 23, 24, 26, and 27;

Schedule 7 paragraph 19 and

Schedule 8 paragraphs 4, 9, 17 and 18.

2004 NO. 2203

TOWN AND COUNTRY PLANNING, ENGLAND

The Town and Country Planning (Regional Planning) (England)
Regulations 2004

Made 26th August 2004
Laid before Parliament 7th September 2004
Coming into force 28th September 2004

## PART 1    ARRANGEMENT OF REGULATIONS

### GENERAL

## PART 2    CRITERIA FOR RECOGNITION OF REGIONAL PLANNING BODIES, ANNUAL MONITORING REPORTS AND REGIONAL PARTICIPATION STATEMENTS

## PART 3    FORM AND CONTENT OF DRAFT REVISION OF REGIONAL SPATIAL STRATEGY

## PART 4    PROCEDURE FOR THE PREPARATION OF A REVISION OF THE REGIONAL SPATIAL STRATEGY

15.    Report of examination in public
16.    Proposed changes
17.    Publication of a revision of the regional spatial strategy
18.    Withdrawal of draft revision

## PART 5    AVAILABILITY OF DOCUMENTS

19.    Availability of direction made by the Secretary of State under section 10(1)
20.    Availability of other documents: general
21.    Availability of the Regional Spatial Strategy
22.    Duty to provide copies of documents

## PART 6    PREPARATION BY SECRETARY OF STATE OF DRAFT REVISION OF REGIONAL SPATIAL STRATEGY

23.    Preparation of a draft revision by the Secretary of State

The First Secretary of State, in exercise of the powers conferred upon him by sections 2(2), 3(5), 5(3)(g), 5(7)(b) and (c) and 11 of the Planning and Compulsory Purchase Act 2004, and of all other powers enabling him in that behalf, hereby makes the following Regulations:

## PART 1    GENERAL

**Citation and commencement**
1.    (1)    These Regulations may be cited as the Town and Country Planning (Regional Planning) (England) Regulations 2004 and shall come into force on 28th September 2004.
       (2)    These Regulations apply in relation to England only.

**Interpretation**
2.    (1)    In these Regulations –
              'the Act' means the Planning and Compulsory Purchase Act 2004;
              'address', in relation to electronic communications, means any number or address used for the purposes of such communications;
              'disabled person' has the same meaning as in section 1(2) of the Disability Discrimination Act 1995;
              'draft revision' means a draft revision of the regional spatial strategy ('RSS') prepared by a regional planning body ('RPB') or the Secretary of State (as the case may be) in accordance with Part 1 of the Act;
              'draft revision documents' means –

              (a)    the draft revision,
              (b)    the sustainability appraisal report,
              (c)    the pre-submission consultation statement, and
              (d)    such supporting documents as in the opinion of the RPB are relevant to the preparation of the draft revision;

              'draft revision matters' means –

              (a)    the subject matter and area covered by the draft revision,

(b)    where the Secretary of State is of the opinion that the draft revision constitutes a minor amendment to the RSS, a statement to that effect,

(c)    the period within which representations on the draft revision must be made in accordance with regulation 13(4)(a),

(d)    the address to which and where appropriate the person to whom –

      (i)    written representations, and
      (ii)    representations by electronic communications,

    must be sent in accordance with regulation 13(4)(b),

(e)    a statement that any representations made may be accompanied by a request to be notified at a specified address of the publication of any changes the Secretary of State proposes to make to the draft revision of the RSS under section 9(3) and of the publication of the revision to the RSS,

(f)    an explanation of the procedure under Part 1 of the Act for considering representations on a draft revision and publishing a revision of the RSS, and

(g)    if the Secretary of State were to decide to hold an examination in public –

      (i)    the likely place the examination will be held,
      (ii)    the likely date the examination will start, and
      (iii)    the name of the person likely to be appointed by the Secretary of State for the purposes of section 8(2);

'electronic communication' has the same meaning as in section 15(1) of the Electronic Communications Act 2000;

'electronic communications apparatus' has the same meaning as in paragraph 1(1) of the electronic communications code;

'electronic communications code' has the same meaning as in section 106(1) of the Communications Act 2003;

'general consultation bodies' means the following bodies –

(a)    voluntary bodies some or all of whose activities benefit any part of the region,

(b)    bodies which represent the interests of different racial, ethnic or national groups in the region,

(c)    bodies which represent the interests of different religious groups in the region,

(d)    bodies which represent the interests of disabled persons in the region,

(e)    bodies which represent the interests of persons carrying on business in the region;

'inspection' means inspection by the public;

'local planning authority' means –

(a)    a district council,
(b)    a London borough council,
(c)    a metropolitan district council,
(d)    a county council in relation to any area in England for which there is no district council,
(e)    the Broads Authority,
(f)    a National Park authority.

'pre-submission consultation statement' means the statement prepared under regulation 11(2);

'pre-submission consultees' means those bodies which the RPB consults in accordance with regulation 11(1);

'proposed changes matters' means –

(a)    the period within which representations on the changes mentioned in section 9(3) must be made in accordance with regulation 16(3)(a);

(b)    the address to which and where appropriate the person to whom –

    (i)    written representations, and

    (ii)    representations by electronic communications,

must be sent in accordance with regulation 16(3)(b); and

(c)    a statement that any representations made may be accompanied by a request to be notified at a specified address of the publication of the revision to the RSS;

'publication statement' means a statement of –

(a)    the date a revision to the RSS is published,

(b)    that any person aggrieved by the revision may make an application to the High Court under section 113 and –

    (i)    the grounds on which such an application can be made,

    (ii)    the time within which such an application must be made;

'specific consultation bodies' means the following bodies –

(a)    a local planning authority any part of whose area is in or adjoins the RPB's region,

(b)    a county council referred to in section 16(1) any part of whose area is in or adjoins the RPB's region,

(c)    a parish council any part of whose area is in or adjoins the RPB's region,

(d)    the RPB for each adjoining region,

(e)    the Countryside Agency,

(f)    the Historic Buildings and Monuments Commission for England,

(g)    English Nature,

(h)    the Environment Agency,

(i)    the Strategic Rail Authority,

(j)    a Regional Development Agency whose area is in or adjoins the RPB's region,

(k)    the Council of the Isles of Scilly,

(l)    any person –

    (i)    to whom the electronic communications code applies by virtue of a direction given under section 106(3)(a) of the Communications Act 2003, and

    (ii)    who owns or controls electronic communications apparatus situated in any part of the region;

(m)    any –

    (i)    Strategic Health Authority,

    (ii)    person to whom a licence has been granted under section 6(1)(b) or (c) of the Electricity Act 1989,

    (iii)    person to whom a licence has been granted under section 7(2) of the Gas Act 1986,

    (iv)    sewerage undertaker,

    (v)    water undertaker,

exercising functions in any part of the region;

'submission consultees' means any person to whom regulation 13(1)(c) applies;

'sustainability appraisal report' means the report prepared pursuant to section 5(4)(b); and

'website' in relation to the Secretary of State means a website which he maintains for the purpose of publishing information about a region which is relevant to Part 1 of the Act.

(2)  In these Regulations any reference to a section is a reference to a section of the Act unless otherwise stated.

### Electronic communications

3.   (1)  Where any provision of these Regulations requires a person –

   (a)   to send a notice, any other document or a copy of a document to another person, or notify another person of any matter; and

   (b)   that other person has an address for the purposes of electronic communications;

   the notice, document, copy or notification may be sent or made by way of electronic communications.

   (2)  Where under any provision of these Regulations or Part 1 of the Act a person may make representations on any document or matter, those representations may be made –

   (a)   in writing, or

   (b)   by way of electronic communications.

   (3)  Where –

   (a)   an electronic communication is used as mentioned in paragraphs (1) and (2), and

   (b)   the communication is received by the recipient outside his office hours, it shall be taken to have been received on the next working day,

   and in this paragraph 'working day' means a day which is not a Saturday, Sunday, Bank Holiday or other public holiday.

## PART 2   CRITERIA FOR RECOGNITION OF REGIONAL PLANNING BODIES, ANNUAL MONITORING REPORTS AND REGIONAL PARTICIPATION STATEMENTS

### Criteria for recognition of regional planning bodies

4.   (1)  The criteria prescribed for the purposes of section 2(2) are that –

   (a)   at least 30% of the members of the RPB are not also members of a relevant authority;

   (b)   all the members of the RPB are entitled to vote when any decision relating to the exercise by the RPB of its functions under the Act is taken by the RPB; and

   (c)   the membership of the RPB includes at least one member from each type of relevant authority, if such an authority exists within the region concerned.

   (2)  In paragraph 1(a) and (c) 'relevant authority' means –

   (a)   a district council,

   (b)   a county council,

   (c)   a metropolitan district council,

   (d)   a National Park authority,

   (e)   the Broads Authority,

   (f)   the Council of the Isles of Scilly.

### Annual monitoring reports

5.   (1)  The period in respect of which reports must be prepared under section 3(4) is the period of twelve months commencing on 1st April in each year and ending on 31st March in the following year.

(2)  The date prescribed for the purposes of section 3(5)(c) is 28th February in the year following that in respect of which the report under section 3(4) is prepared.

(3)  A report under section 3(4) must contain the following information –

(a)  a statement identifying any policy in the RSS which in the opinion of the RPB is not being implemented;

(b)  where a policy is identified as mentioned in paragraph (a), a statement of –

(i)  the reasons why the RPB is of the opinion that the policy is not being implemented; and

(ii)  the measures that the RPB intends to take to secure that the policy is implemented including, in particular, whether the RPB intends to prepare a draft revision of the RSS which will amend the policy;

(c)  in a case to which paragraph (4) applies, a statement as to the number of dwellings built in the part of the region in question –

(i)  during the period of the report, and

(ii)  since the policy concerned was first published by the Secretary of State.

(4)  This paragraph applies where the RSS contains a policy which specifies, whether by reference to a year or any other period, the number of dwellings to be built in any part of the region.

(5)  At the time an RPB submits a report to the Secretary of State under section 3(5)(c) it must publish the report on its website.

### Regional participation statement

6.  In complying with the duty imposed by section 6(1) (preparation and publication of statement of policies as to involvement of persons interested in exercise of RPB's functions under section 5), an RPB must –

(a)  include in that statement policies in particular about –

(i)  how and when persons who appear to the RPB to have an interest in the revision of the RSS will be involved in its revision, and

(ii)  the identification and involvement of other persons to work with the RPB in the revision of the RSS;

(b)  make the statement available for inspection during office hours at its principal office and at such other places within the region as the RPB considers appropriate; and

(c)  publish on its website –

(i)  the statement;

(ii)  confirmation that the statement is available for inspection; and

(iii)  details of the times and places at which the statement may be inspected.

## PART 3   FORM AND CONTENT OF DRAFT REVISION OF REGIONAL SPATIAL STRATEGY

### Content of draft revision of Regional Spatial Strategy

7.  (1)  A draft revision must contain new or amended policies to the RSS and amendments to the diagrams mentioned in regulation 9 as the RPB is of the opinion are appropriate.

(2)  A draft revision must contain a reasoned justification of the policies contained in it.

(3) Those parts of a draft revision which comprise the policies of the revision and those parts which comprise the reasoned justification required by paragraph (2) must be clearly identified.

### Different provision for different parts of region

8.  (1) Where the RPB decides to make different provision for different parts of the region under section 5(5) –

  (a) it must notify the authorities referred to in section 4(4) of its decision; and
  (b) it may give to those authorities information about how the detailed proposals for that different provision are to be made.

  (2) The information referred to in paragraph (1) may indicate –

  (a) the geographical area to be covered by the detailed proposals;
  (b) the broad subject matter of the detailed proposals;
  (c) other bodies that the RPB considers should work with the authorities in making the detailed proposals; and
  (d) which of the authorities the RPB considers should lead in making the detailed proposals.

  (3) The authorities referred to in section 4(4) must make the detailed proposals for the different provision within twelve weeks of being notified by the RPB under paragraph (1).

### Diagrams in a draft revision of the Regional Spatial Strategy

9.  (1) A draft revision must contain a diagram, called a key diagram, illustrating the policies contained in the draft revision.

  (2) A draft revision may also contain a diagram, called an inset diagram, which –

  (a) is drawn to a larger scale than the key diagram, and
  (b) illustrates the application of the policies to part of the area covered by the revision.

  (3) Where a draft revision contains an inset diagram –

  (a) the area covered by the inset diagram must be identified on the key diagram, and
  (b) the application of the policies to that area must be illustrated on the inset diagram only.

  (4) Key diagrams and inset diagrams must –

  (a) set out the title of the draft revision, and
  (b) include an explanation of any symbol or other notation that appears on them, and
  (c) be prepared otherwise than on a map base.

### Regard to be had to certain matters

10.  (1) Matters prescribed for the purposes of section 5(3) (in addition to those specified in paragraphs (a) to (f) of that subsection) are –

  (a) the strategy prepared for the region under section 7 of the Regional Development Agencies Act 1998;
  (b) the objectives of preventing major accidents and limiting the consequences of such accidents;
  (c) the need, in the long term, to maintain appropriate distances between establishments and residential areas, buildings and areas of public use, major transport routes as far as possible, recreational areas and areas of particular natural sensitivity or interest;

(d)    where the region or part of the region for which the draft revision is being prepared adjoins Scotland, the National Planning Framework for Scotland, published by the Scottish Executive in April 2004.

(2)  Expressions appearing both in paragraph (1) and in Council Directive 96/82/EC on the control of major accident hazards involving dangerous substances (as amended by Council Directive 2003/105/EC) have the same meaning as in that Directive.

## PART 4    PROCEDURE FOR THE PREPARATION OF A REVISION OF THE REGIONAL SPATIAL STRATEGY

### Pre-submission consultation

11.  (1)  Without prejudice to section 4(1) (RPB's duty to seek advice from certain author-ities), before submitting a draft revision to the Secretary of State under section 5(8)(b), an RPB must consult –

(a)    such of the specific consultation bodies as are, in the opinion of the RPB, likely to be affected by the draft revision;

(b)    such of the general consultation bodies as the RPB considers appropriate.

(2)  The RPB must prepare a statement setting out –

(a)    which of the specific and general consultation bodies the RPB have consulted;

(b)    how those bodies, and any other persons whom the RPB have consulted, were consulted;

(c)    a summary of the main issues raised in those consultations; and

(d)    how those main issues have been addressed in the draft revision.

### Submission to the Secretary of State

12.  When an RPB complies with section 5(8)(b), it must also send the draft revision documents to the Secretary of State in electronic form.

### Submission consultation

13.  (1)  When the RPB complies with section 5(8)(a) it must –

(a)    make copies of the draft revision documents and a statement of the draft revision matters available for inspection –

(i)    at its principal office during office hours, and

(ii)   at such other places within the region as the RPB considers appropriate;

(b)    publish on its website –

(i)    the draft revision documents,

(ii)   the draft revision matters, and

(iii)  a statement that the draft revision documents are available for inspec-tion and particulars of the places and times at which they can be inspected;

(c)    send to the pre-submission consultees, and to such other persons who in the opinion of the RPB may wish to make representations on the draft revision –

(i)    the draft revision,

(ii)   the sustainability appraisal report,

(iii)  the pre-submission consultation statement,

(iv)   such of the supporting documents as in the RPB's opinion are relevant to the person to whom the documents are being sent,

        (v)   notice of the draft revision matters, and

        (vi)  the statement referred to in paragraph (b)(iii).

(2) Subject to paragraph (3), when the RPB complies with section 5(8)(a) –

    (a)   each local planning authority within the region, and

    (b)   any county council within the region whose area includes an area for which there is a district council,

must make copies of the draft revision documents and draft revision matters available for inspection at their principal offices during office hours.

(3) Paragraph (2) does not apply to an authority or council unless the draft revision relates to any part of its area.

(4) Representations on a draft revision must be –

    (a)   made within the period, and

    (b)   sent to the address and where appropriate the person,

specified pursuant to paragraph (1).

(5) The period referred to in paragraph (4)(a) –

    (a)   where the Secretary of State has informed the RPB that, in his opinion, a draft revision constitutes a minor amendment to the RSS, must not be less than 6 weeks;

    (b)   in any other case, must not be less than 12 weeks;

starting on the day the RPB complies with section 5(8)(a).

(6) The Secretary of State is not required to have regard to a representation on a draft revision unless that representation is made in accordance with paragraph (4).

### Examination in public

14. (1) Where the Secretary of State decides that an examination in public is to be held –

    (a)   as soon as reasonably practicable after so deciding the Secretary of State must publish on his website –

        (i)   a statement of that decision,

        (ii)  the address of the place where the examination in public will take place,

        (iii) the date when the examination will start,

        (iv) the name of person appointed by the Secretary of State for the purposes of section 8(2);

    (b)   where particulars of any of the matters published in accordance with paragraph (a)(ii) to (iv) differ in a material respect from the information in paragraph (g) of the definition of 'draft revisions matters' in regulation 2(1) supplied by the RPB in complying with regulation 13(1) –

        (i)   the Secretary of State must notify –

            (aa)  the submission consultees, and

            (bb)  any other person who has made representations on the draft revision in accordance with regulation 13(4) and not withdrawn those representations,

        of those changes;

        (ii)  the RPB must publish on its website particulars of the matters referred to in paragraph (a) and indicate the material respects in which those particulars differ from the particulars supplied in complying with regulation 13(1); and

        (iii) each authority or council to which regulation 13(2) applies must make available for inspection during office hours at their principal office the information provided pursuant to paragraph (ii).

(2)   Where the Secretary of State decides that an examination in public is not to be held –

    (a)   as soon as reasonably practicable after so deciding the Secretary of State must –

        (i)   notify –

            (aa)   the submission consultees,

            (bb)   any other person who has made representations on the draft revision in accordance with regulation 13(4) and not withdrawn those representations,

        of that decision;

        (ii)   publish a statement of that decision on his website; and

    (b)   the RPB must publish a statement of that decision on its website.

### Report of examination in public

15.   (1)   Where an examination in public has been held pursuant to section 7(3), the Secretary of State must –

    (a)   as soon as reasonably practicable after receipt of the report of the person appointed to hold the examination, publish the report on his website;

    (b)   publish on his website a statement that the report is available for inspection and of the places and times at which it can be inspected;

    (c)   send to any person who requested to be notified of the publication by the Secretary of State of the report a copy of the statement referred to in paragraph (b).

(2)   As soon as reasonably practicable after the Secretary of State complies with paragraph (1), the RPB must –

    (a)   publish on its website the report of the person appointed to hold the examination;

    (b)   make the report available for inspection during office hours at the places at which draft revision documents were made available under regulation 13(1);

    (c)   publish on its website a statement that the report is available for inspection and of the places and times it can be inspected.

(3)   As soon as reasonably practicable after the Secretary of State complies with paragraph (1), each authority or council to which regulation 13(2) applies must make available for inspection during office hours at their principal office the report of the person appointed to hold the examination.

### Proposed changes

16.   (1)   Where, in accordance with section 9(3), the Secretary of State publishes proposed changes to the draft revision, he must –

    (a)   send to the submission consultees, and to any other person who has made representations on the draft revision in accordance with regulation 13(4) and not withdrawn those representations –

        (i)   copies of the proposed changes and a statement of his reasons for proposing them, and

        (ii)   notice of the proposed changes matters; and

    (b)   publish on his website –

        (i)   the proposed changes and statement of reasons,

        (ii)   the proposed changes matters, and

        (iii)   a statement that the changes and statement of reasons are available for inspection and of the places and times at which they can be inspected; and

(c)  send to any person who requested to be notified of the publication by the Secretary of State of any proposed changes –

    (i)  a notice of the proposed changes matters, and

    (ii)  a statement that the changes and statement of reasons are available for inspection and of the places and times at which they can be inspected.

(2)  When the Secretary of State has complied with paragraph (1) –

  (a)  the RPB must –

    (i)  make copies of the changes and statement of reasons and the proposed changes matters available for inspection during office hours at the places at which the draft revision documents were made available under regulation 13(1); and

    (ii)  publish on its website –

      (aa)  the proposed changes and statement of reasons,

      (bb)  the proposed changes matters, and

      (cc)  a statement that the proposed changes and statement of reasons are available for inspection in accordance with paragraph (a) and of the places and times at which they can be inspected; and

  (b)  each authority or council to which regulation 13(2) applies must make available for inspection during office hours at their principal office –

    (i)  copies of the proposed changes and statement of reasons, and

    (ii)  the proposed changes matters.

(3)  Representations on the proposed changes must be –

  (a)  made within the period, and

  (b)  sent to the address and , where appropriate, the person,

specified pursuant to paragraph (1).

(4)  The period referred to in paragraph (3)(a) must not be less than 8 weeks starting on the day the Secretary of State publishes his proposed changes under section 9(3).

(5)  The Secretary of State is not required to have regard to a representation on a draft revision unless that representation is made in accordance with paragraph (3).

### Publication of a revision of the regional spatial strategy

17.  As soon as reasonably practicable after the Secretary of State publishes a revision of the RSS under section 9(6) –

  (a)  the RPB must –

    (i)  make available for inspection at the places at which the draft revision documents were made available under regulation 13(1) –

      (aa)  a publication statement, and

      (bb)  a copy of the revision; and

    (ii)  publish on its website –

      (aa)  the publication statement, and

      (bb)  a statement that a copy of the revision is available for inspection in accordance with paragraph (i), and of the places and times at which the copy can be inspected;

  (b)  the Secretary of State must –

    (i)  publish on his website –

      (aa)  the documents referred to in paragraph (a)(i),

      (bb)  a statement that a copy of the revision is available for inspection, and of the places and times at which the copy can be inspected; and

(ii)    send a copy of the publication statement to any person who has asked to be notified of the publication of the revision;

(c)    each authority or council to which regulation 13(2) applies must make a copy of the revision available for inspection during office hours at their principal office.

### Withdrawal of draft revision

18. (1)    As soon as reasonably practicable after a draft revision is withdrawn under section 5(9) (withdrawal by RPB), the RPB must –

(a)    publish on its website a statement that it has withdrawn its draft revision and its reasons for doing so; and

(b)    notify any person with whom it has corresponded (whether in writing or by electronic communications) about the draft revision, of those matters.

(2)    As soon as reasonably practicable after a draft revision is withdrawn under section 9(7) (withdrawal by Secretary of State) –

(a)    the RPB must –

(i)    publish on its website a statement that the Secretary of State has withdrawn the draft revision; and

(ii)    remove all copies, documents, matters or statements made available or published under regulations 13(1)(a) and (b), 14(1)(b)(ii) and (2)(b) and 16(2)(a), or published under section 5(8)(a);

(b)    each authority or council to which regulation 13(2) applies must remove any copies, document or matters made available under that regulation and regulations 14(1)(b)(iii) and 16(2)(b); and

(c)    the Secretary of State must –

(i)    publish on his website a statement that he has withdrawn the draft revision,

(ii)    notify –

(aa)    the submission consultees, and

(bb)    any other person who has made representations in accordance with regulation 13(4) or 16(3) and not withdrawn those representations,

that he has withdrawn the draft revision, and

(iii)    remove all documents, matters or statements published under regulations 14(1)(a), (2)(a)(ii) and 16(1)(b) or under section 9(3).

## PART 5    AVAILABILITY OF DOCUMENTS

### Availability of direction made by the Secretary of State under section 10(1)

19.    Where the Secretary of State issues a direction under section 10(1), the RPB to which the direction is issued must –

(a)    make that direction available for public inspection at its principal office during office hours, and

(b)    publish that direction on its website.

### Availability of other documents: general

20. (1)    This regulation does not apply to a document made available or published under regulation 21.

(2)    Copies, documents, directions, matters, or statements which under these Regulations are –

(a)    made available for inspection, or

(b)    published on a website,

may be removed at the end of the period of six weeks referred to in section 113(4) (period for challenging the validity of certain strategies, plans and documents) that applies as regards the strategy, plan or document concerned.

(3)    Paragraph (2) does not apply if a challenge is made as mentioned in that paragraph and shall not apply until any challenge proceedings are finally determined.

### Availability of the Regional Spatial Strategy

21.    (1)    An RPB must –

(a)    make a copy of the RSS for its region available for inspection at its principal office during office hours, and

(b)    publish the RSS on its website.

(2)    Where the Secretary of State revokes an RSS in its entirety the RPB for the region concerned must cease to make it available for inspection (whether on its website or at its principal office).

### Duty to provide copies of documents

22.    (1)    Where –

(a)    a person makes a document available for inspection under these Regulations,

(b)    that document is not published as required by or under Part 1 of the Act, and

(c)    the person is asked by another person for a copy of that document,

the person first mentioned must provide a copy of the document to that other person as soon as reasonably practicable after receipt of that other person's request.

(2)    A person who provides a copy –

(a)    under paragraph (1), or

(b)    of a document published as required by or under Part 1 of the Act,

may make a reasonable charge for the copy.

## PART 6    PREPARATION BY SECRETARY OF STATE OF DRAFT REVISION OF REGIONAL SPATIAL STRATEGY

### Preparation of a draft revision by the Secretary of State

23.    If the Secretary of State prepares a draft revision under section 10(3), regulations 7, 9 to 11, 13 to 17, 18 (ignoring paragraph (1)) and 20 apply so far as practicable and with any necessary modifications.

**2004 NO. 2204**

**TOWN AND COUNTRY PLANNING, ENGLAND**

The Town and Country Planning (Local Development) (England)
Regulations 2004

Made 26th August 2004
Laid before Parliament 7th September 2004
Coming into force 28th September 2004

## ARRANGEMENT OF REGULATIONS

### PART 1    GENERAL

### PART 2    SURVEY OF AREA

### PART 3    LOCAL DEVELOPMENT SCHEMES AND DOCUMENTS WHICH MUST BE DEVELOPMENT PLAN DOCUMENTS

### PART 4    FORM AND CONTENT OF LOCAL DEVELOPMENT DOCUMENTS AND REGARD TO BE HAD TO CERTAIN MATTERS

## PART 5    SUPPLEMENTARY PLANNING DOCUMENTS

## PART 6    DEVELOPMENT PLAN DOCUMENTS

## PART 7    CORRESPONDING DOCUMENTS AND CORRESPONDING SCHEMES

## PART 8    ANNUAL MONITORING REPORT

## PART 9    AVAILABILITY OF DOCUMENTS

49.    Availability of documents: general
50.    Availability of adopted or approved local development documents
51.    Copies of documents

The First Secretary of State, in exercise of the powers conferred upon him by sections 13(2)(f), 14(3) and (5), 15(2)(g), (3) and (7), 17(1)(a) and (7), 19(2)(j), 20(3), 24(3), 28(9) and (11), 31(6) and (7), 35(2) and (3) and 36 of the Planning and Compulsory Purchase Act 2004 and paragraph 4(2) of Schedule 4A to the Town and Country Planning Act 1990 and of all other powers enabling him in that behalf, hereby makes the following Regulations:

## PART 1    GENERAL

**Citation, commencement and application**

1.    (1)    These Regulations may be cited as the Town and Country Planning (Local Development) (England) Regulations 2004 and shall come into force on 28th September 2004.
       (2)    These Regulations apply in relation to England only.

**Interpretation**

2.    (1)    In these Regulations –

           'the Act' means the Planning and Compulsory Purchase Act 2004;
           'DPD' means development plan document;
           'LDD' means local development document;
           'SPD' means supplementary planning document;
           'address' in relation to electronic communications means any number or address used for the purposes of such communications;
           'adopted proposals map' means a document of the description referred to in regulation 6(6);
           'by local advertisement' means by publication on at least one occasion in a local newspaper circulating in the whole of the area of the local planning authority;
           'core strategy' means a document of the description referred to in regulation 6(3);
           'disabled person' has the same meaning as in section 1(2) of the Disability Discrimination Act 1995;
           'electronic communication' has the same meaning as in section 15(1) of the Electronic Communications Act 2000;
           'electronic communications apparatus' has the same meaning as in paragraph 1(1) of the electronic communications code;
           'electronic communications code' has the same meaning as in section 106(1) of the Communications Act 2003;
           'general consultation bodies' means the following bodies –

               (a)    voluntary bodies some or all of whose activities benefit any part of the authority's area,
               (b)    bodies which represent the interests of different racial, ethnic or national groups in the authority's area,
               (c)    bodies which represent the interests of different religious groups in the authority's area,

(d)   bodies which represent the interests of disabled persons in the authority's area,

(e)   bodies which represent the interests of persons carrying on business in the authority's area;

'inspection' means inspection by the public;

'national waste strategy' means any statement which contains the Secretary of State's policies in relation to the recovery and disposal of waste in England, and which is made under section 44A of the Environmental Protection Act 1990, or pending the publication of the first such statement, any relevant waste disposal plan prepared under section 50 of that Act;

'Ordnance Survey map' means a map produced by Ordnance Survey or a map on a similar base at a registered scale;

'person appointed' means a person appointed by the Secretary of State under section 20(4) to carry out an independent examination;

'regional planning body' is a body that meets the requirements of section 2;

'relevant authority' means –

(a)   a local planning authority,

(b)   a county council referred to in section 16(1),

(c)   a parish council;

'site allocation policy' means a policy which allocates a site for a particular use or development;

'specific consultation bodies' –

(a)   in relation to a local planning authority whose area is in a region other than London, means the regional planning body and the bodies specified or described in sub-paragraphs (i) to (x);

(i)     the Countryside Agency,

(ii)    the Environment Agency,

(iii)   the Historic Buildings and Monuments Commission for England,

(iv)    English Nature,

(v)     the Strategic Rail Authority,

(vi)    the Highways Agency,

(vii)   a relevant authority any part of whose area is in or adjoins the area of the local planning authority,

(viii)  a Regional Development Agency whose area is in or adjoins the area of the local planning authority,

(ix)    any person –

(aa)  to whom the electronic communications code applies by virtue of a direction given under section 106(3)(a) of the Communications Act 2003, and

(bb)  who owns or controls electronic communications apparatus situated in any part of the area of the local planning authority,

(x)     if it exercises functions in any part of the local planning authority's area

(aa)  a Strategic Health Authority,

(bb)  a person to whom a licence has been granted under section 6(1)(b) or (c) of the Electricity Act 1989,

(cc)  a person to whom a licence has been granted under section 7(2) of the Gas Act 1986,

(dd)  a sewerage undertaker,

(ee)  a water undertaker;

(b)    if the authority are a London borough council, means the Mayor of London and the bodies specified or described in paragraph (a)(i) to (x);

'submission proposals map' means a document of the description referred to in regulation 6(5);

'sustainability appraisal report' means the report prepared pursuant to section 19(5)(b); and

'supplementary planning document' means an LDD which is not a DPD, but does not include the local planning authority's statement of community involvement.

(2)    In these Regulations any reference to a section is a reference to a section of the Act unless otherwise stated.

### Scope of Regulations

3.    (1)    Subject to paragraph (2), these Regulations have effect in relation to –

  (a)    the revision of an LDD as they apply to the preparation of an LDD;

  (b)    a minerals and waste development scheme as they have effect in relation to a local development scheme and for that purpose –

  (i)    references to a local development scheme include references to a minerals and waste development scheme, and

  (ii)    references to a local planning authority include references to a county council within the meaning of section 16(1).

  (2)    Regulations 5, 12(3) and 47 have no effect in relation to minerals and waste development schemes.

### Electronic communications

4.    (1)    Where within these Regulations –

  (a)    a person is required to –

  (i)    send a document, a copy of a document or any notice to another person,

  (ii)    notify another person of any matter; and

  (b)    that other person has an address for the purposes of electronic communications;

  the document, copy, notice or notification may be sent or made by way of electronic communications.

  (2)    Where within these Regulations a person may make representations on any matter or document, those representations may be made –

  (a)    in writing, or

  (b)    by way of electronic communications.

  (3)    Where –

  (a)    an electronic communication is used as mentioned in paragraphs (1) and (2), and

  (b)    the communication is received by the recipient outside his office hours, it shall be taken to have been received on the next working day, and in this regulation 'working day' means a day which is not a Saturday, Sunday, Bank Holiday or other public holiday.

## PART 2   SURVEY OF AREA

**Survey of area: county councils**

5.   (1)   Each county council shall keep under review, in relation to that part of their area for which there is a district council, the following matters –

    (a)   the principal physical, economic, social and environmental characteristics of the authority;

    (b)   the size, composition and distribution of the population of the area;

    (c)   the communications, transport system and traffic of the area;

    (d)   any other considerations which may be expected to affect those matters.

    (2)   The persons prescribed for the purposes of section 14(5) are –

    (a)   any local planning authority any part of whose area lies within the area of the county council; and

    (b)   if the regional planning body within whose area the area of the county council lies requests a copy of the results of the review under section 14(3), that body.

## PART 3   LOCAL DEVELOPMENT SCHEMES AND DOCUMENTS WHICH MUST BE DEVELOPMENT PLAN DOCUMENTS

**Documents to be specified in local development schemes as local development documents**

6.   (1)   The descriptions of document prescribed for the purposes of section 17(1)(a) which must be specified as LDDs in a local development scheme are –

    (a)   any document containing statements of –

      (i)   the development and use of land which the local planning authority wish to encourage during any specified period;

      (ii)   objectives relating to design and access which the local planning authority wish to encourage during any specified period;

      (iii)   any environmental, social and economic objectives which are relevant to the attainment of the development and use of land mentioned in paragraph (i);

      (iv)   the authority's general policies in respect of the matters referred to in paragraphs (i) to (iii); and

    (b)   where a document of the description mentioned in paragraph (a) contains policies applying to sites or areas by reference to an Ordnance Survey map, an LDD which accompanies a DPD and shows how the adopted proposals map is to be amended as a result of the submission of that DPD to the Secretary of State under regulation 28.

    (2)   The descriptions of other documents prescribed for the purposes of section 17(1)(a) which, if prepared, must be specified as LDDs in a local development scheme are –

    (a)   any document which –

      (i)   relates to part of the area of the local planning authority;

      (ii)   identifies that area as an area of significant change or special conservation; and

      (iii)   contains the authority's policies relevant to areas of significant change or special conservation; and

    (b)   any other document which includes a site allocation policy.

(3)  A document of the description in paragraph (1)(a) is referred to in the following provisions of these Regulations as a core strategy.

(4)  A document of the description in paragraph (2)(a) is referred to in the following provisions of these Regulations as an area action plan.

(5)  A document of the description in paragraph (1)(b) is referred to in the following provisions of these Regulations as a submission proposals map.

(6)  In paragraph (1)(b) 'the adopted proposals map' means a document which –

(a)  when first adopted shows the matters specified in regulation 14(4),

(b)  is revised in the manner specified in regulation 9, and

(c)  consists of text and maps, of which the text prevails if the map and text conflict.

### Documents which must be development plan documents

7.  Documents which must be DPDs are –

(a)  core strategies,

(b)  area action plans, and

(c)  any other document which includes a site allocation policy.

### Additional matters to be specified in local development schemes and revisions of such schemes

8.  The matters (in addition to those mentioned in section 15(2)) to be specified in a local development scheme or any revision of such a scheme are –

(a)  in relation to each document to be specified in the scheme or revision as an LDD –

(i)  its proposed title,

(ii)  its proposed subject matter, and

(iii)  the area proposed to be covered by the document;

(b)  in relation to each document to be specified in the scheme or revision as an SPD, the month and year in which the local planning authority or county council (as the case may be) intends to –

(i)  comply with regulation 17,

(ii)  adopt the document;

(c)  in relation to each document to be specified in the scheme or revision as a DPD and the local planning authority's statement of community involvement, the date on which the local planning authority intends to comply with –

(i)  regulation 26,

(ii)  section 20(1); and

(d)  in relation to proposals to which any of paragraphs 4, 5, 9 and 10 of Schedule 8 to the Act applies –

(i)  the timetable for the preparation of the proposals, including the month and year in which the local planning authority intends to adopt the proposals, and

(ii)  where the proposals are for the alteration of a plan, the area and subject matter of the proposals.

### Other requirements for the preparation of local development schemes

9.  When a local development scheme is prepared it must specify that the adopted proposals map will be revised –

(a)  at the same time as any DPD is adopted,

(b)  so as to illustrate geographically the application of the policies in the DPD or revision.

**Submission of local development schemes to the Secretary of State**

10. (1) The time prescribed for the purposes of section 15(3)(b) is 6 months after the commencement of Part 2 of the Act.

(2) A local development scheme shall be submitted to the Secretary of State by –

   (a) sending it to him electronically; and
   (b) sending to him 4 copies of the scheme in paper form.

**Bringing local development schemes and revisions of such schemes into effect**

11. (1) For the purpose of bringing a local development scheme or any revision of such a scheme into effect –

   (a) the requirements of one of paragraphs (2) to (5) shall be met; and
   (b) the local planning authority shall –

      (i) resolve that the scheme shall have effect; and
      (ii) shall specify in that resolution the date from which the scheme shall have effect.

(2) The requirement of this paragraph is that, before the end of the relevant period, the local planning authority has received from the Secretary of State notice that he does not intend to give them a direction under section 15(4).

(3) The requirements of this paragraph are that the relevant period has ended and the local planning authority have not received any of the following –

   (a) notice that the Secretary of State does not intend to give them a direction under section 15(4),
   (b) a direction under section 15(4), or
   (c) notice that the Secretary of State requires more time to consider the scheme.

(4) The requirements of this paragraph are that the local planning authority have received a direction under section 15(4) and have either –

   (a) complied with the direction, or
   (b) received notice that it has been withdrawn.

(5) The requirements of this paragraph are that the local planning authority have received notice that the Secretary of State requires more time to consider the scheme, and either –

   (a) they have subsequently received notice that the Secretary of State does not intend to give them a direction under section 15(4), or
   (b) the requirements of paragraph (4) are satisfied.

(6) In this regulation 'relevant period' means the period of 4 weeks starting on the day on which the authority submit the scheme to the Secretary of State under section 15(3)(b).

**Availability of a local development scheme**

12. (1) Where a local development scheme takes effect in accordance with regulation 11, a local planning authority must –

   (a) make a copy of the scheme available for inspection at their principal office during normal office hours, and
   (b) publish the scheme on their website.

(2) Where a revision to a local development scheme takes effect under regulation 11, within 2 weeks a local planning authority must incorporate the revision into the scheme made available for inspection and published under paragraph (1).

(3) Where paragraph (1) or (2) applies to a minerals and waste development scheme, within 2 weeks the county council must send a copy of –

(a)    the scheme, or

(b)    the scheme incorporating the revision,

to any local planning authority any part of whose area is within so much of the area of the county council as is mentioned in section 16(1).

## PART 4    FORM AND CONTENT OF LOCAL DEVELOPMENT DOCUMENTS AND REGARD TO BE HAD TO CERTAIN MATTERS

### Form and content of local development documents: general

13.    (1) Subject to paragraph (9), an LDD must contain a reasoned justification of the policies contained in it.

(2) Subject to paragraph (9), those parts of an LDD which comprise the policies of the LDD and those parts which comprise the reasoned justification required by paragraph (1) must be clearly identified.

(3) An LDD must contain –

   (a)    a title which must –

   (i)    name the local planning authority by which the LDD is prepared, and

   (ii)    indicate whether the document is a DPD or a SPD; and

   (b)    a sub-title which must indicate –

   (i)    the subject matter of the document, and

   (ii)    the date on which the document is adopted.

(4) Subject to paragraph (9), and only if it includes a site allocation policy, a DPD must include a submission proposals map showing the changes which will result to the adopted proposals map if the DPD is adopted.

(5) Where a DPD contains a policy that is intended to supersede another policy, it must state that fact and identify the superceded policy.

(6) Subject to paragraphs (7), (9) and (10), the policies contained in a DPD must be in conformity with either –

   (a)    where a core strategy has been adopted, the policies in the core strategy, or

   (b)    in any other case, the policies in the development plan as referred to in paragraph 1(1)(b) of Schedule 8 to the Act.

(7) Paragraph (6) does not apply in a case falling within paragraph (b) of that paragraph where the policies in the DPD are intended to supersede an old policy as defined in paragraph 1(4) of Schedule 8 to the Act.

(8) The policies in an SPD must be in conformity with –

   (a)    the policies in the core strategy,

   (b)    the policies in any other DPD, or

   (c)    if neither paragraph (a) nor (b) applies, an old policy.

(9) Paragraphs (1), (2), (4) and (6) do not apply to the submission proposals map or the adopted proposals map.

(10) Paragraph (6) does not apply to the core strategy.

### Form and content of local development documents: specific

14.    (1) The adopted proposals map must be comprised of or contain a map of the local planning authority's area which must –

   (a)    be reproduced from, or based on, an Ordnance Survey map;

   (b)    show National Grid lines and reference numbers; and

   (c)    include an explanation of any symbol or notation which it uses.

(2) The adopted proposals map may contain a map, called an inset map, which must –

  (a) comply with the requirements in paragraph 1(a) to (c);
  (b) be drawn to a larger scale than the map referred to in paragraph (1); and
  (c) show the application of the local planning authority's policies to part of the authority's area.

(3) Where the adopted proposals map includes an inset map –

  (a) the area covered by the inset map must be identified on the map referred to in paragraph (2), and
  (b) the application of the local planning authority's policies to that area must be shown on the inset map only.

(4) When the adopted proposals map is first adopted it must illustrate geographically the application of –

  (a) the policies in any DPD adopted at the same time, and
  (b) an old policy which applies at that time.

### Local development documents: additional matters to which regard to be had

15. (1) The matters (additional to those specified in section 19(2)(a) to (i)) prescribed for the purposes of section 19(2) are –

  (a) the strategy prepared under section 7 of the Regional Development Agencies Act 1998 for the region in which the area of the local planning authority is situated;
  (b) any local transport plan, the policies of which affect any part of the local planning authority's area;
  (c) any other policies prepared under section 108(1) and (2) of the Transport Act 2000 which affect any part of the local planning authority's area;
  (d) the objectives of preventing major accidents and limiting the consequences of such accidents;
  (e) the need –

    (i) in the long term, to maintain appropriate distances between establishments and residential areas, buildings and areas of public use, major transport routes as far as possible, recreational areas and areas of particular natural sensitivity or interest, and
    (ii) in the case of existing establishments, for additional technical measures in accordance with Article 5 of Council Directive 96/82/EC on the control of major accident hazards involving dangerous substances so as not to increase the risks to people

  (f) the national waste strategy;
  (g) where a local planning authority's area or part of the area adjoins Scotland, the National Planning Framework for Scotland, published by the Scottish Executive in April 2004.

(2) Expressions appearing both in paragraph (1) and in Council Directive 96/82/EC (as amended by Council Directive 2003/105/EC) have the same meaning as in that Directive.

(3) In paragraph 1(b) 'local transport plan' has the same meaning as in section 108(3) of the Transport Act 2000.

## PART 5    SUPPLEMENTARY PLANNING DOCUMENTS

### Application and interpretation of Part 5

16. (1)  This Part applies to SPDs only.

   (2)  In this Part –

      'adoption statement' means a document that specifies –

         (a)  the date on which an SPD is adopted, and

         (b)  that any person aggrieved by the SPD may apply to the High Court for permission to apply for judicial review of the decision to adopt the SPD; and

         (c)  that any such application for leave must be made promptly and in any event not later than 3 months after the date on which the SPD was adopted;

      'consultation statement' means the statement prepared under regulation 17(1);

      'SPD documents' means –

         (a)  the SPD,

         (b)  the sustainability appraisal report,

         (c)  the consultation statement, and

         (d)  such supporting documents as in the opinion of the authority are relevant to the preparation of the SPD; and

      'SPD matters' means –

         (a)  the title of the SPD,

         (b)  the subject matter of, and the area covered by, the SPD,

         (c)  the period within which representations about the SPD must be made in accordance with regulation 18(2)(a),

         (d)  the address to which and, where appropriate, the person to whom representations (whether made by way of electronic communications or otherwise) must be sent in accordance with regulation 18(2)(b),

         (e)  a statement that any representations may be accompanied by a request to be notified at a specified address of the adoption of the SPD.

### Public participation

17. (1)  Before a local planning authority adopt an SPD they must –

      (a)  make copies of the SPD documents and a statement of the SPD matters available for inspection during normal office hours –

         (i)   at their principal office, and

         (ii)  at such other places within their area as the authority consider appropriate; and

      (b)  prepare a statement setting out –

         (i)   the names of any persons whom the authority consulted in connection with the preparation of the SPD,

         (ii)  how those persons were consulted,

         (iii) a summary of the main issues raised in those consultations,

         (iv)  how those issues have been addressed in the SPD.

   (2)  At the time the authority comply with paragraph (1)(a) they must –

      (a)  publish on their website –

         (i)   the SPD documents,

         (ii)  the SPD matters, and

         (iii) a statement of the fact that the SPD documents are available for inspection and of the places and times at which they can be inspected;

(b)   send to the bodies specified in paragraph (3) –

    (i)   the SPD,

    (ii)   the sustainability appraisal report,

    (iii)   the consultation statement,

    (iv)   such of the supporting documents as are relevant to the body to which the documents are being sent,

    (v)   notice of the SPD matters, and

    (vi)   the statement referred to in paragraph (a)(iii);

(c)   give notice by local advertisement of –

    (i)   the SPD matters,

    (ii)   the fact that the SPD documents are available for inspection and the places and times at which they can be inspected; and

(d)   make a request under section 24(2)(b) or (4)(b) (conformity with regional strategy).

(3)   The bodies referred to in paragraph (2)(b) are –

(a)   each of the specific consultation bodies to the extent that the local planning authority thinks that the SPD affects the body; and

(b)   such of the general consultation bodies as the local planning authority consider appropriate.

## Representations on supplementary planning documents

18.   (1)   Any person may make representations about an SPD.

    (2)   Any such representations must be –

(a)   made within the period, and

(b)   sent to the address and, where appropriate, the person, specified pursuant to regulation 17(2).

    (3)   The period referred to in paragraph (2)(a) must be a period of not less than 4 weeks or more than 6 weeks starting on the day on which the local planning authority complies with regulation 17(1).

    (4)   A local planning authority shall not adopt an SPD until –

(a)   they have considered any representations made in accordance with paragraph (2); and

(b)   have prepared a statement setting out –

    (i)   a summary of the main issues raised in these representations, and

    (ii)   how these main issues have been addressed in the SPD which they intend to adopt.

## Adoption of supplementary planning documents

19.   As soon as reasonably practicable after the local planning authority adopt an SPD they must –

(a)   make available for inspection during normal office hours at the places at which the SPD was made available under regulation 17(1)(a) –

    (i)   the statement in regulation 18(4)(b),

    (ii)   an adoption statement, and

    (iii)   the SPD;

(b)   publish on their website –

    (i)   the statement referred to in regulation 18(4)(b), and

    (ii)   the adoption statement; and

(c)   send the adoption statement to any person who has asked to be notified of the adoption of the SPD.

### Withdrawal of a supplementary planning document

20. If an SPD is withdrawn the local planning authority must –
    (a) publish a statement of that fact on their website;
    (b) notify –
        (i) any body to which notification was given and to whom documents were sent under regulation 17(2)(b),
        (ii) any person who has made a representation in accordance with regulation 18(2),
        of that fact; and
    (c) remove any copies, documents, matters and statements made available or published under regulation 17(1)(a) and (2)(a).

### Revocation of a supplementary planning document

21. A local planning authority may revoke an SPD if –
    (a) it ceases to comply with regulation 13(8); or
    (b) it contains policies relating to the development of a site specified in the SPD, and that development has been completed.

### Direction not to adopt a supplementary planning document

22. (1) The Secretary of State may at any time direct a local planning authority –
        (a) not to adopt an SPD until he has decided whether to give a direction under section 21(1); and
        (b) to send to him a copy of the SPD made available under regulation 17(1)(a).
    (2) If the Secretary of State issues the first-mentioned direction in paragraph (1), the authority must –
        (a) if the direction is made before they have complied with regulation 17, at the time they comply with that regulation –
            (i) publish the direction and make it available for inspection during normal office hours –
                (aa) at their principal office, and
                (bb) at such other places within their area as the authority consider appropriate; and
            (ii) send a copy of the SPD to the Secretary of State;
        (b) if the direction is made after they have complied with regulation 17–
            (i) make the direction available for inspection during normal office hours at the places at which the SPD was made available under regulation 17(1)(a),
            (ii) publish the direction on their website.
    (3) The first-mentioned direction in paragraph (1) shall be treated as withdrawn on the date on which the authority receive –
        (a) notice that the Secretary of State does not intend to give a direction under section 21(1); or
        (b) the Secretary of State's direction under section 21(1).

### Direction to modify a supplementary planning document

23. If the Secretary of State gives a direction under section 21(1) in respect of an SPD, the local planning authority must –
    (a) make the direction available for inspection during normal office hours at the places at which the SPD was made available under regulation 17(1)(a);
    (b) publish the direction on their website; and

(c)   at the time they comply with regulation 19 –

(i)   make available for inspection during normal office hours at the places at which the SPD was made available under regulation 17(1)(a); and

(ii)   publish on their website,

(aa)   a statement that the Secretary of State has withdrawn the direction, or

(bb)   the Secretary of State's notice under section 21(2)(b).

## PART 6   DEVELOPMENT PLAN DOCUMENTS

### Application and interpretation of Part 6

24.   (1)   This Part applies to a local planning authority's statement of community involvement as it applies to a DPD; and accordingly, unless otherwise indicated, any reference in this Part to a DPD includes a reference to a statement of community involvement.

(2)   This Part applies to a submission proposals map as it applies to a DPD; and accordingly, with the exception of regulations 25 and 26, any reference in this Part to a DPD includes a reference to a submission proposals map.

(3)   With the exception of regulation 45(b), regulations 40 to 44 apply to any part of a DPD as they apply to the whole of a DPD.

(4)   In this Part –

'adoption statement' means a statement –

(a)   of the date on which a DPD is adopted;

(b)   that a person aggrieved by the DPD may make an application to the High Court under section 113;

(c)   of the grounds on which, and the time within which, such an application may be made;

(d)   that a person aggrieved by a statement of community involvement may apply to the High Court for permission to apply for judicial review of the decision to adopt the statement; and

(e)   that any such application must be made promptly and in any event not later than 3 months after the day on which the statement was adopted;

'decision statement' means –

(a)   a statement that the Secretary of State has decided to approve, approve subject to modifications, or reject a DPD (as the case may be),

(b)   where the Secretary of State decides to approve a DPD, or to approve a DPD subject to modifications, a statement –

(i)   of the date on which the DPD is adopted,

(ii)   that a person aggrieved by the DPD may make an application to the High Court under section 113, and

(iii)   of the grounds on which, and the time within which, such an application may be made;

'DPD bodies' means the bodies consulted by a local planning authority under regulation 25;

'DPD documents' means the following documents –

(a)   the DPD,

(b)   the sustainability appraisal report,

(c)   the pre-submission consultation statement,

(d)   such supporting documents as in the opinion of the authority are relevant to the preparation of the DPD;

'DPD matters' means the following matters –

(a)    the title of the DPD,
(b)    the subject matter of , and the area covered by, the DPD,
(c)    the period within which representations about the DPD must be made in accordance with regulation 29(1),
(d)    the address to which and, where appropriate, the person to whom representations (whether made by way of electronic communications or otherwise) must be sent in accordance with regulation 29(1),
(e)    a statement that representations may be accompanied by a request to be notified at a specified address of the publication of the recommendations of the person appointed to carry out an examination under section 20 or the adoption of the DPD or both;

'pre-submission consultation statement' means the statement prepared pursuant to regulation 28(1)(c);

'pre-submission proposals documents' means the authority's proposals for the DPD and such supporting documents as in the opinion of the authority are relevant to those proposals;

'proposals matters' means the following matters –

(a)    the proposed title of the DPD,
(b)    the proposed subject matter and area of the DPD,
(c)    the period within which representations on the proposals may be made in accordance with regulation 27(2)(a),
(d)    the address to which and, where appropriate, the person to whom representations (whether made by way of electronic communications or otherwise) must be sent in accordance with regulation 27(2)(b),
(e)    a statement that any representations may be accompanied by a request to be notified at a specified address that the DPD has been submitted to the Secretary of State for independent examination under section 20 and of the adoption of the DPD; and

'site allocation representation' means any representation which seeks to change a DPD by –

(a)    adding a site allocation policy to the DPD, or
(b)    altering any site allocation policy in the DPD.

## Pre-submission consultation

25.  (1)  Subject to paragraph (2), before a local planning authority comply with regulation 26 they must consult –

(a)    each of the specific consultation bodies to the extent that the local planning authority thinks that the proposed subject matter of the DPD affects the body; and
(b)    such of the general consultation bodies as the local planning authority consider appropriate.

(2)  If the document is the local planning authority's statement of community involvement, the requirement referred to in paragraph (1)(a) is satisfied –

(a)    by an authority whose area is in a region other than London, if the authority consult –

(i)    the regional planning body;
(ii)    each relevant authority any part of whose area is in or adjoins the area of the local planning authority; and
(iii)    the Highways Agency;

(b)    by a London borough council, if they consult –

(i)    the Mayor of London;

(ii)    each relevant authority any part of whose area is in or adjoins the area of the local planning authority; and

(iii)   the Highways Agency.

### Pre-submission public participation

26.  Before a local planning authority prepare and submit a DPD to the Secretary of State they must –

(a)  make copies of the pre-submission proposals documents and a statement of the proposals matters available for inspection during normal office hours –

(i)    at their principal office, and

(ii)   at such other places within their area as the authority consider appropriate;

(b)  publish on their website –

(i)    the pre-submission proposals documents,

(ii)   the proposals matters,

(iii)  a statement of the fact that the pre-submission proposals documents are available for inspection and the places and times at which they can be inspected;

(c)  send to the DPD bodies –

(i)    the authority's proposals for a DPD,

(ii)   such supporting documents as are relevant to the body to which the documents are being sent,

(iii)  notice of the proposals matters,

(iv)   the statement in paragraph (b)(iii); and

(d)  give notice by local advertisement of –

(i)    the proposals matters,

(ii)   the fact that the pre-submission proposals documents are available for inspection and the places and times at which they can be inspected.

### Representations on proposals for a development plan document

27.  (1)  Any person may make representations about a local planning authority's proposals for a DPD.

(2)  Any such representations must be –

(a)  made within a period of 6 weeks starting on the day the local planning authority comply with regulation 26(a), and

(b)  sent to the address and, where appropriate, the person specified pursuant to regulation 26(b) to (d).

(3)  A local planning authority shall not prepare and submit the DPD to the Secretary of State until they have considered any representations made in accordance with paragraph (2).

### Submission of documents and information to the Secretary of State

28.  (1)  The documents prescribed for the purposes of section 20(3) are –

(a)  the sustainability appraisal report;

(b)  if the authority have adopted their statement of community involvement, that statement;

(c)  a statement setting out –

(i)    which of the bodies they have consulted pursuant to regulation 25(1),

(ii)   how these bodies, and any other persons whom the authority have consulted, were consulted,

(iii)  a summary of the main issues raised in those consultations, and

(iv)   how those main issues have been addressed in the DPD;

   (d)   a statement setting out –

      (i)   if representations were made under regulation 27(2) –

         (aa)   the number of representations made,
         (bb)   a summary of the main issues raised in those representations, and
         (cc)   how those main issues have been addressed in the DPD; or

      (ii)   that no such representations were made;

   (e)   such supporting documents as in the opinion of the authority are relevant to the preparation of the DPD.

(2) Of the documents and statements mentioned or referred to in paragraph (1) –

   (a)   4 copies of each shall be sent in paper form,
   (b)   1 copy of those mentioned or referred to in paragraphs (1)(a) to (d) and, if practicable, of those referred to in paragraph (1)(e), shall be sent electronically.

(3) As soon as reasonably practicable after the authority submit a DPD to the Secretary of State they must –

   (a)   make copies of the DPD documents and a statement of the DPD matters available for inspection during normal office hours at the places at which the pre-submission proposals documents were made available under regulation 26(a);

   (b)   publish on their website –

      (i)   the DPD documents,
      (ii)   the DPD matters, and
      (iii)   a statement of the fact that the DPD documents are available for inspection and of the places and times at which they can be inspected;

   (c)   send to each of the DPD bodies copies of –

      (i)   the DPD,
      (ii)   the sustainability appraisal report,
      (iii)   the pre-submission consultation statement,
      (iv)   such of the supporting documents sent to the Secretary of State pursuant to paragraph (1)(e) as are relevant to that body,
      (v)   notice of the DPD matters, and
      (vi)   the statement referred to in paragraph (b)(iii);

   (d)   give notice by local advertisement of –

      (i)   the DPD matters, and
      (ii)   the fact that the DPD documents are available for inspection and of the places and times at which they can be inspected; and

   (e)   give notice to those persons who requested to be notified of the submission of the DPD to the Secretary of State that it has been so submitted.

**Representations on development plan documents**

29. (1) Subject to paragraph (3), a person may make representations about a DPD by sending them to the address and, where appropriate, the person specified pursuant to regulation 28(3) within the period of 6 weeks starting on the date on which the DPD is submitted to the Secretary of State under section 20(1).

   (2) Before the person appointed to carry out the examination complies with section 20(7) he must consider any representations made in accordance with paragraph (1).

(3)  Paragraph (1) does not apply to representations taken to have been made as mentioned in section 24(6) or (7) (non-conformity opinions of RPBs and the Mayor of London).

## Conformity with regional strategy

30.  (1)  A local planning authority must make a request under section 24(2)(a) or (4)(a) on the same day that they submit a DPD to the Secretary of State.
(2)  The period prescribed for the purposes of section 24(3) is 6 weeks starting on the day the request under section 24(2)(a) or (4)(a) is made.

## Handling of representations: general

31.  (1)  This regulation does not apply to a site allocation representation.
(2)  As soon as reasonably practicable after a local planning authority have received a representation on a DPD under regulation 29(1) they must –

(a)  make a copy of the representation available at the places at which the pre-submission proposals documents were made available under regulation 26(a),
(b)  where practicable, publish the representation on their website,
(c)  send to the Secretary of State –

(i)  a statement of the total number of representations made,
(ii)  copies of the representations,
(iii)  a summary of the main issues raised in the representations, or
(iv)  a statement that no representation has been made.

(3)  A local planning authority need not comply with paragraph 2(a) to (c)(iii) if the representation is made after the period specified in regulation 29(1).
(4)  The documents mentioned in paragraph (2)(c) shall be submitted to the Secretary of State by sending –

(a)  4 copies of each in paper form; and
(b)  1 copy electronically.

## Handling of representations: site allocation representations

32.  (1)  This regulation applies to a site allocation representation.
(2)  As soon as reasonably practicable after the period in regulation 29(1) the local planning authority must –

(a)  make a site allocation representation and a statement of the matters in paragraph (3) available for inspection during normal office hours at the places at which the pre-submission proposals documents were made available under regulation 26(a);
(b)  publish on their website –

(i)  where practicable, the site allocation representation,
(ii)  the matters in paragraph (3),
(iii)  a statement of the fact that the site allocation representation is available for inspection and the places and times at which it can be inspected;
(c)  send to the DPD bodies –

(i)  the address of the site to which the site allocation representation relates,
(ii)  notice of the matters in paragraph (3),
(iii)  a statement of the fact that the site allocation representation is available for inspection and the places and times at which it can be inspected; and

(d)  give notice by local advertisement of –

  (i)   the matters in paragraph (3),
  (ii)  the fact that the site allocation representation is available for inspection and the places and times at which it can be inspected.

(3)  The matters referred to in paragraph (2) are –

(a)  the period within which representations on the site allocation representation must be made;
(b)  the address to which and, where appropriate, the person to whom –

  (i)   written representations, and
  (ii)  representations by way of electronic communications,

  must be sent.

### Representations on a site allocation representation

33. (1)  Any person may make representations on a site allocation representation by sending them to the address and, where appropriate, the person specified pursuant to regulation 32(2) within the period of 6 weeks starting on the day the local planning authority comply with regulation 32(2).

(2)  As soon as reasonably practicable after the authority has received a representation on a site allocation representation the local planning authority must send to the Secretary of State –

(a)  a statement of the number of representations made,
(b)  copies of all the representations,
(c)  a summary of the main issues raised in those representations, or
(d)  a statement that no such representations have been made.

(3)  The documents mentioned in paragraph (2) shall be submitted to the Secretary of State by sending –

(a)  4 copies of each in paper form; and
(b)  1 copy electronically.

(4)  Before the person appointed to carry out the examination complies with section 20(7) he must consider any representations made in accordance with paragraph (1).

### Independent examination

34. (1)  This regulation applies where a person requests the opportunity to appear before and be heard by the person carrying out the examination under section 20.

(2)  At least 6 weeks before the opening of an independent examination the local planning authority must –

(a)  publish the matters mentioned in paragraph (3) on their website;
(b)  notify any person who has made a representation in accordance with regulation 29(1) or 33(1), and not withdrawn that representation, of those matters; and
(c)  give notice by local advertisement of those matters.

(3)  The matters referred to in paragraph (2) are –

(a)  the time and place at which the examination is to be held, and
(b)  the name of the person appointed to carry out the examination.

### Publication of the recommendations of the person appointed

35. (1)  The local planning authority must comply with section 20(8) –

(a)  as soon as reasonably practicable after the day on which the DPD is adopted, or

(b)   if the Secretary of State gives a direction under section 21(1) or (4) after the person appointed has complied with section 20(7), as soon as reasonably practicable after receipt of the direction.

(2)   When the local planning authority comply with section 20(8) they must –

(a)   make the recommendations of the person appointed and his reasons for those recommendations available for inspection during normal office hours at the places at which the pre-submission proposals documents were made available under regulation 26(a);

(b)   publish the recommendations and reasons on their website; and

(c)   give notice to those persons who requested to be notified of the publication of the recommendations of the person appointed that they have been so published.

### Adoption of a development plan document

36.   As soon as reasonably practicable after the local planning authority adopt a DPD they must –

(a)   make available for inspection during normal office hours at the places at which the pre-submission proposals documents were made available under regulation 26(a) –

(i)   the DPD,

(ii)   an adoption statement, and

(iii)   the sustainability appraisal report;

(b)   publish the adoption statement on their website;

(c)   give notice by local advertisement of –

(i)   the adoption statement,

(ii)   the fact that the DPD is available for inspection and the places and times at which the document can be inspected,

(d)   send the adoption statement to any person who has asked to be notified of the adoption of the DPD; and

(e)   send the DPD and the adoption statement to the Secretary of State.

### Withdrawal of a development plan document

37.   (1)   As soon as reasonably practicable after a DPD is withdrawn under section 22(1) the local planning authority must –

(a)   publish a statement of that fact on their website;

(b)   give notice of that fact by local advertisement;

(c)   notify any body to which notification was given under regulation 26(c) of that fact;

(d)   remove any copies, documents, matters and statements made available or published under regulation 26(a) and (b).

(2)   As soon as reasonably practicable after a DPD is withdrawn under section 22(2) the local planning authority must comply with paragraph (1)(a) to (d) and in addition must –

(a)   notify any person who has made a representation in accordance with regulation 29(1) or 33(1), and not withdrawn that representation, of this fact; and

(b)   remove any copies, documents, representations, matters and statements made available or published under regulation 28(3)(a) and (b), 31(2), 32(2)(a) and (b) and 34(2)(a).

### Direction not to adopt a development plan document

38. (1) Where, in relation to a DPD, the person appointed to carry out an examination under section 20 has complied with subsection (7) of that section, the Secretary of State may at any time direct the local planning authority not to adopt that DPD until he has decided whether to give a direction under section 21(1) or (4).

    (2) If the Secretary of State gives such a direction the authority must –

    (a) make the direction available for inspection during normal office hours at the places at which the pre-submission proposals documents were made available under regulation 26(a),

    (b) publish the direction on their website,

    (c) not adopt the DPD until the Secretary of State has notified them of his decision under paragraph (1).

### Direction to modify a development plan document

39. If the Secretary of State gives a direction under section 21(1) in respect of a DPD, the local planning authority must –

    (a) make the direction available for inspection during normal office hours at the places at which the pre-submission proposals documents were made available under regulation 26(a);

    (b) publish the direction on their website; and

    (c) at the time they comply with regulation 36 publish and make available for inspection in accordance with that regulation –

        (i) a statement that the Secretary of State has withdrawn the direction, or

        (ii) the Secretary of State's notice under section 21(2)(b).

### Section 21(4) directions (call-in): supplementary

40. (1) This regulation and regulations 41 to 44 apply where the Secretary of State gives a direction under section 21(4).

    (2) If the direction is given before the local planning authority submit to the Secretary of State the DPD to which the direction relates –

    (a) the Secretary of State must –

        (i) carry out an appraisal of the sustainability of the proposals in the DPD or, where his direction relates to part only of the DPD, the proposals in that part and prepare a report of the findings of the appraisal, and

        (ii) comply with regulation 30 as if references in that regulation to the local planning authority were references to the Secretary of State; and

    (b) the local planning authority must –

        (i) if the direction is given before they comply with regulation 26, publish the direction and make it available for inspection –

            (aa) when they comply with that regulation, and

            (bb) in accordance with that regulation,

        (ii) if the direction is given after the authority have complied with regulation 26–

            (aa) make the direction available for inspection during normal office hours at the places at which the pre-submission proposals documents were made available under regulation 26(a), and

            (bb) publish the direction on their website; and

        (iii) subject to any necessary modifications, comply with the regulations in paragraph (3) as if they were preparing the DPD;

    (3) The regulations referred to in paragraph (2)(b)(iii) are regulations 26 to 34 (with the exception of regulation 30) and regulation 37 (ignoring paragraph (1)).

(4) Nothing in paragraph (2)(b)(iii) requires a local planning authority to take again any step taken before receipt of the direction.

## Changes proposed by the Secretary of State to development plan documents (call-in)

41. (1) If the Secretary of State proposes to depart from the recommendations of the person appointed to carry out an examination under section 20, he must publish –

    (a) the changes he proposes to make, and

    (b) his reasons for doing so.

  (2) As soon as reasonably practicable after the Secretary of State complies with paragraph (1) the local planning authority must –

    (a) make copies of the changes and reasons and a statement of the matters in paragraph (3) available for inspection during normal office hours at the places at which the pre-submission proposals documents were made available under regulation 26(a);

    (b) publish on their website –

        (i) the changes and reasons,

        (ii) the matters in paragraph (3),

        (iii) a statement of the fact that the changes and reasons are available for inspection and the places and times at which they can be inspected;

    (c) send copies of the changes and reasons to the bodies in paragraph (4) and notify these bodies of the matters in paragraph (3); and

    (d) give notice by local advertisement of –

        (i) the matters in paragraph (3),

        (ii) the fact that the changes and reasons are available for inspection and the places and times at which they can be inspected.

  (3) The matters referred to in paragraph (2) are –

    (a) the period within which representations on the changes must be made;

    (b) the address to which and, where appropriate, the person to whom representations (whether made by way of electronic communications or otherwise) must be sent; and

    (c) a statement that any representations made may be accompanied by a request to be notified at a specified address of the Secretary of State's decision under section 21(9)(a).

  (4) The bodies referred to in paragraph (2)(c) are –

    (a) each of the specific consultation bodies to the extent that the Secretary of State thinks the changes affect the body; and

    (b) such of the general consultation bodies as the Secretary of State considers appropriate.

## Representations on proposed changes (call-in)

42. (1) Any person may make representations on the changes the Secretary of State proposes to make by sending them to the address and, where appropriate, the person specified pursuant to regulation 41(2) within the period of 6 weeks starting on the day on which the Secretary of State complies with regulation 41(1).

  (2) Before the Secretary of State complies with section 21(9)(a) he must consider any representations made in accordance with paragraph (1).

**Publication of the recommendations of the person appointed to carry out the independent examination (call-in)**

43. As soon as reasonably practicable after the Secretary of State complies with section 21(6), the local planning authority must –

    (a) make the recommendations and reasons of the person appointed to carry out the examination available for inspection during normal office hours at the places at which the pre-submission proposals documents were made available under regulation 26(a), and

    (b) publish the recommendations and reasons on their website.

**Secretary of State's decision after section 21(4) direction (call-in)**

44. As soon as reasonably practicable after the Secretary of State approves, approves subject to modifications or rejects a DPD or part of it (as the case may be) in accordance with section 21(9)(a), the local planning authority must –

    (a) make available for inspection during normal office hours at the places at which the pre-submission proposals documents were made available under regulation 26(a) –

        (i) the DPD and the reasons given by the Secretary of State pursuant to section 21(9)(b),

        (ii) a decision statement,

    (b) publish the decision statement on their website,

    (c) give notice by local advertisement of –

        (i) the decision statement,

        (ii) the fact that the DPD and the Secretary of State's reasons are available for inspection and the places where and times when the document and reasons can be inspected, and

    (d) send the decision statement to any person who has asked to be notified of the Secretary of State's decision under section 21(9)(a).

**Secretary of State's default power**

45. Where the Secretary of State prepares or revises a DPD under section 27–

    (a) he must comply with such provisions of Part 2 of the Act and such provisions of these Regulations –

        (i) as are relevant to the preparation of the DPD or revision, and

        (ii) as if references in those provisions to the local planning authority were references to the Secretary of State;

    (b) regulations 41 to 44 apply, subject to any necessary modifications and as if references to a local planning authority were references to the Secretary of State.

## PART 7    CORRESPONDING DOCUMENTS AND CORRESPONDING SCHEMES

**Joint local development documents: corresponding documents**

46. (1) In relation to an agreement mentioned in section 28(1), the period prescribed for the purposes of section 28(9) is 3 months starting on the day on which any local planning authority which is a party to the agreement withdraws from it.

    (2) A corresponding document for the purposes of section 28(7) is a document which –

(a) does not relate to any part of the area of the authority that has withdrawn from the agreement; and

(b) with respect to the areas of the local planning authorities which prepared it, has substantially the same effect as the original joint document.

(3) In paragraph (2)(b) 'original joint document' means a joint LDD prepared pursuant to the agreement mentioned in paragraph (1).

### Joint committees: corresponding documents and corresponding schemes

47. (1) The period prescribed for the purposes of section 31(6) is 3 months starting on the day on which the Secretary of State revokes under section 31(2) an order under section 29 (joint committees).

(2) Subject to paragraph (5), for the purposes of section 31(3) and (6) a corresponding document is a document which –

(a) does not relate to any part of the area of the constituent authority which requested the revocation of the order; and

(b) with respect to the area of the successor authority, has substantially the same effect as the original LDD.

(3) For the purposes of section 31(3), a corresponding scheme is a scheme of a successor authority which –

(a) specifies a document that is a corresponding document for the purposes of section 31(3), but

(b) does not specify the original LDD,

as a document which is to be an LDD.

(4) In paragraph (3)(b) 'original LDD' means an LDD prepared by the joint committee constituted by the order under section 29.

(5) Paragraph (2)(a) does not apply where the constituent authority is a county council for which there is also a district council.

## PART 8    ANNUAL MONITORING REPORT

### Annual monitoring report

48. (1) The period prescribed for the purposes of section 35(3)(a) is the period of twelve months commencing on 1st April in each year and ending on 31st March in the following year.

(2) The time prescribed for the purposes of section 35(3)(b) is 9 months after the end of the period in respect of which the report is made.

(3) An annual report must contain the following information –

(a) the title of the documents specified in the authority's local development scheme;

(b) in relation to each of those documents –

(i) the timetable specified in the authority's scheme for the document's preparation,

(ii) the information referred to in regulation 8(b)(i) and (ii) or (c)(ii) (as the case may be),

(iii) where, within the period in respect of which the report is made, the first step has been taken in the preparation of the document –

(aa) the stage the document has reached in its preparation,

(bb) if the document's preparation is behind the timetable mentioned in paragraph (i) the reasons for this, and

(cc) a timetable relating to the further steps that are likely to be taken for the preparation of the document;

    (c)    where any document specified in the authority's local development scheme has been adopted or approved within the period in respect of which the report is made, a statement of that fact and of the date of adoption or approval;

    (d)    the title of any local development order adopted by the authority under section 61A of the Town and Country Planning Act 1990;

    (e)    in relation to any such order –

        (i)    a statement of the authority's reasons for making the order,

        (ii)    a statement about the effect of the order and a comparison of that with the reasons given in the statement to be provided pursuant to paragraph (e)(i);

    (f)    where the authority have revoked any local development order, a statement of the title of the order and the authority's reasons for revoking it.

(4)    Where an authority are not implementing a policy specified in a DPD or an old policy as defined in paragraph 1(4) of Schedule 8 to the Act, the annual report must identify that policy.

(5)    Where an annual report identifies a policy pursuant to paragraph (4) the report must include a statement of –

    (a)    the reasons why the authority are not implementing the policy;

    (b)    the steps (if any) that the authority intend to take to secure that the policy is implemented; and

    (c)    whether the authority intend to prepare a DPD or a revision of the DPD (as the case may be) to replace or amend the policy.

(6)    Paragraph (7) applies where a policy specified in a DPD or an old policy specifies –

    (a)    an annual number, or

    (b)    a number relating to any other period specified in –

        (i)    the DPD, or

        (ii)    the development plan for the purposes of paragraph 1(1) of Schedule 8 to the Act,

    of net additional dwellings in any part of the area of the authority.

(7)    Where this paragraph applies, the annual report must specify the number of dwellings built in the part of the authority's area concerned –

    (a)    in the period in respect of which the report is made, and

    (b)    since the policy referred to in paragraph (6) was first published, adopted or approved.

(8)    As soon as reasonably practicable after an authority make an annual report to the Secretary of State they must publish the report on their website.

## PART 9    AVAILABILITY OF DOCUMENTS

### Availability of documents: general

49.  (1)    This regulation does not apply to a document or revision which is made available or published under regulation 50.

    (2)    Copies, documents, representations, directions, matters, notices or statements which under these Regulations are –

    (a)    made available for inspection, or

    (b)    published on a website,

    may be removed at the time specified in paragraph (3).

(3)   The time mentioned in paragraph (2) –

    (a)   where the copies, documents, representations, directions, matters, notices or statements relate to an SPD or to the local planning authority's statement of community involvement, is 3 months after the day on which the SPD or statement of community involvement is adopted;

    (b)   where the copies, documents, representations, directions, matters, notices or statements relate to a DPD, is the end of the period of 6 weeks referred to in section 113(4) (period for challenging the validity of relevant documents) that applies as regards the DPD concerned.

### Availability of adopted or approved local development documents

50.   (1)   Paragraph (2) applies where a local planning authority adopt, or the Secretary of State approves, an LDD.

    (2)   As soon as reasonably practicable after the document is adopted or approved the authority must –

        (a)   make a copy of the LDD available for inspection at their principal office during normal office hours;

        (b)   publish the LDD on their website.

    (3)   Paragraph (4) applies where a local planning authority adopt, or the Secretary of State approves, a revision of an LDD.

    (4)   As soon as reasonably practicable after the revision is adopted or approved the authority must incorporate the revision into the LDD made available for inspection and published under paragraph (2).

    (5)   Where the Secretary of State or a local planning authority revoke an LDD, within 2 weeks of the date on which the LDD was revoked the authority must –

        (a)   publish a statement of that fact on their website;

        (b)   remove the copy of the LDD made available for inspection and published under paragraph (2);

        (c)   take such other steps as they consider necessary to draw the revocation of the LDD to the attention of persons living or working in their area; and

        (d)   if the document is a DPD, give notice of the revocation of the LDD by local advertisement.

### Copies of documents

51.   (1)   Where –

    (a)   a person makes a document available for inspection under these Regulations,

    (b)   that document is not published pursuant to a requirement of Part 2 of the Act, and

    (c)   the person is asked by another person for a copy of that document,

the person first-mentioned must provide a copy of the document to that other person as soon as reasonably practicable after receipt of that other person's request.

    (2)   Any person who provides a copy –

    (a)   under paragraph (1), or

    (b)   of a document published as required by or under Part 2 of the Act,

may make a reasonable charge for the copy.

## 2004 NO. 2205

## TOWN AND COUNTRY PLANNING, ENGLAND

## The Town and Country Planning (Transitional Arrangements) (England) Regulations 2004

Made 26th August 2004
Laid before Parliament 7th September 2004
Coming into force 28th September 2004

The First Secretary of State, in exercise of the powers conferred upon him by paragraphs 17(1) and (2) and 18 of Schedule 8 to the Planning and Compulsory Purchase Act 2004, and of all other powers enabling him in that behalf, hereby makes the following Regulations:

#### Citation, commencement and application

1.  (1)  These Regulations may be cited as the Town and Country Planning (Transitional Arrangements) (England) Regulations 2004 and shall come into force on 28th September 2004.

    (2)  These Regulations apply in relation to England only.

#### Interpretation

2.  In these Regulations –

    'the 2004 Act' means the Planning and Compulsory Purchase Act 2004;
    'the 1999 Regulations' mean the Town and Country Planning (Development Plan) (England) Regulations 1999;
    'Chapter 1' means Chapter 1 of Part 2 of the Town and Country Planning Act 1990;
    'Chapter 2' means Chapter 2 of Part 2 of the Town and Country Planning Act 1990; and
    'Schedule 8' means Schedule 8 to the 2004 Act.

#### Structure plans

3.  Subject to the amendments set out in the Schedule to these Regulations, the 1999 Regulations shall continue to apply to proposals to which paragraph 2 of Schedule 8 applies.

#### Unitary development plans

4.  (1)  The 1999 Regulations shall continue to apply as regards proposals in relation to which the provisions of Chapter 1 continue to have effect by virtue of paragraph 4 of Schedule 8.

    (2)  Subject to the amendments set out in the Schedule to these Regulations, the 1999 Regulations shall continue to apply as regards proposals in relation to which the provisions of Chapter 1 continue to have effect by virtue of paragraph 5 of Schedule 8.

#### Local plans

5.  (1)  The 1999 Regulations shall continue to apply as regards proposals in relation to which the provisions of Chapter 2 continue to have effect by virtue of paragraph 9 of Schedule 8.

(2) Subject to the amendments set out in the Schedule to these Regulations, the 1999 Regulations shall continue to apply as regards proposals in relation to which the provisions of Chapter 2 continue to have effect by virtue of paragraph 10 of Schedule 8.

### Local development documents prepared before commencement

6.  (1) Subject to paragraph (2), any step taken or purportedly taken for the purposes of Part 2 of the 2004 Act before the date on which these Regulations come into force shall be treated, on and after that date, as having been taken after that date.

(2) Subject to paragraph (3), the local planning authority by which the step was taken or purportedly taken must –

(a) prepare –

(i) as described in regulation 17(1) of the Town and Country Planning (Local Development) (England) Regulations 2004, a statement about the participation of the public in the preparation of a local development document (referred to in those Regulations as a supplementary planning document); and

(ii) as described in regulation 18(4)(b) of those Regulations, a statement about representations made on a supplementary planning document;

(b) make the statements mentioned in sub-paragraph (a) available for inspection and arrange for their publication, as described in such other provisions of regulations 17 to 19 of those Regulations as they relate to supplementary planning documents;

(c) prepare –

(i) as described in regulation 28(1)(c) of those Regulations, a statement about pre-submission consultation matters required for the preparation of a local development document (referred to in those Regulations as a development plan document); and

(ii) as described in regulation 28(1)(d) of those Regulations, a statement about representations made on proposals for a development plan document;

(d) take, as regards the statements referred to in sub-paragraph (c), such other steps as are required by regulation 28 of those Regulations to be taken as regards development plan documents.

(3) Nothing in paragraph (2) requires the authority to satisfy the requirements of section 19(1) of the 2004 Act.

SCHEDULE   AMENDMENT TO THE TOWN AND COUNTRY
PLANNING (DEVELOPMENT PLAN) (ENGLAND)
REGULATIONS 1999                Regulations 3, 4(2) and 5(2)

1.   In regulation 2(1) (interpretation), insert in the appropriate places –

"'the 2004 Act" means the Planning and Compulsory Purchase Act 2004;', and
"'RSS" has the same meaning as in Part 1 of the 2004 Act;'

2.   (1)  Subject to sub-paragraph (2), omit regulation 24 (deposit of revised proposals).
     (2)  Sub-paragraph (1) does not apply if –
         (a)   before the coming into force of these Regulations a local planning authority
               have complied with regulation 24(2), and
         (b)   on the coming into force of these Regulations the period referred to in
               regulation 24(8)(a) has not ended.

3.   After regulation 24 (deposit of revised proposals) insert –

     'Further deposit of proposals

     24A.(1)  This regulation applies where a local planning authority have complied
              with any of paragraphs 5(2)(b), 5(3), 10(2)(b) and 10(3) of Schedule 8 to
              the 2004 Act.
          (2)  The local planning authority may revise –
              (a)   the plan or proposals; or
              (b)   where the authority have complied with regulation 24, the revised
                    plan or revised proposals.
          (3)  The local planning authority shall –
              (a)   make the plan or proposals available for inspection at those places at
                    which the plan or proposals were made available under regulation
                    22(1)(a);
              (b)   give notice by advertisement of the following matters –
                   (i)    the title of the plan or proposals;
                   (ii)   the fact that the plan or proposals were made available under
                          regulation 22 or, as the case may be, that the revised plan or
                          revised proposals were made available under regulation 24 and,
                          in either case, the date on which they were first made available;
                   (iii)  if it be the case, that the plan or proposals have been revised
                          under paragraph (2), that fact;
                   (iv)   that copies of the plan or proposals are available for inspection
                          and the places and times at which they can be inspected;
                   (v)    the period set out in paragraph (9) and the address to which,
                          and, where appropriate, the person to whom, representations
                          on the plan or proposals must be made;
                   (vi)   that any such representations may be accompanied by a request
                          to be notified at a specified address of the adoption of the plan
                          or proposals; and
                   (vii)  where paragraph (4) applies, that if no objections are received
                          during the period for receipt of representations, the authority
                          intend to adopt the plan or proposals 28 days after the expiry
                          of that period; and
              (c)   notify in writing –
                   (i)    the persons referred to in paragraph (5); and
                   (ii)   such other persons as the authority think fit,

of the matters referred to in paragraph (3)(b)(i), (ii), (iv) and (v) and, if applicable, those referred to in paragraph (3)(b)(iii) and (vii).

(4) This paragraph applies if –

    (a)   at the time the local planning authority comply with this regulation –

        (i)   no objections in accordance with these Regulations have been made in respect of the plan or proposals, or

        (ii)   if such objections have been made, they have been withdrawn; or

    (b)   the local planning authority comply with paragraph (2) and those parts of it in respect of which objections have been made and not subsequently withdrawn no longer form part of the plan or proposals.

(5) The persons referred to in paragraph (3)(c) are any person who, in accordance with these Regulations, has objected to, or made a representation in respect of the plan or proposals (whether or not that person has subsequently withdrawn that objection or representation).

(6) The plan or proposals made available under paragraph (3)(a) shall –

    (a)   comprise the full text of the plan or proposals; and

    (b)   in the case of a plan or proposal revised under paragraph (2), indicate clearly the revisions that have been made.

(7) Where revisions have been made under paragraph (2), the plan or proposals made available –

    (a)   shall be accompanied by a list of the revisions made;

    (b)   need not contain a revised version of the map required by section 12(4)(b) or 36(6)(a) provided –

        (i)   the plan or proposals contain that map, and

        (ii)   such diagrams and maps as are necessary to indicate the revisions are annexed to that map.

(8) The authority shall send –

    (a)   four copies of the documents made available for inspection to the Secretary of State; and

    (b)   one copy of those documents to –

        (i)   each of the bodies listed in regulation 10(1)(c) to (f), and

        (ii)   any other local authority any part of whose area is covered by the plan or proposals.

(9) An objection or representation is made in accordance with this regulation if it is made –

    (a)   within six weeks beginning with the date on which the local planning authority complies with paragraph (3)(b),

    (b)   in writing and sent to the address, and, where appropriate, the person, specified under paragraph (3)(b)(v).

(10) In addition to the requirement to consider objections imposed by section 13(6) or 40(7) (as the case may be) the local planning authority shall also consider any representations made in accordance with this regulation.

(11) A representation –

    (a)   that matters relating to the development and use of land not included in the plan or proposals ought to have been so included; or

    (b)   made by the Secretary of State that the plan or proposals should be modified to accord with current national policies or policies in an RSS;

shall, if it is made in accordance with this regulation, be treated as an objection made to the plan or proposals in accordance with these Regulations for the purpose of regulations 26 and 28 and sections 16 and 42.'.

4.  Omit regulation 25 (withdrawal of proposals).
5.  In regulation 26 –

    (a) at the beginning of paragraph (2) insert 'Where, by virtue of paragraph 4 or 9 of Schedule 8 to the 2004 Act, Chapter 1 or Chapter 2 of Part 2 of this Act continue to have effect in relation to proposals,';

    (b) after paragraph (2) insert –

'(2A) Where paragraphs 5 or 10 of Schedule 8 to the 2004 Act apply to proposals, on the date specified in paragraph (2B) the local planning authority shall make the report of the person holding an inquiry or other hearing to which this regulation applies available for inspection at those places at which the proposals were made available under regulation 22(1)(a).

(2B) The date referred to in paragraph (2A) is –

    (a) the date the authority adopt the plan or proposals, or

    (b) if –

        (i) the Secretary of State issues a direction under section 17(1), 18(1), 43(4) or 44(1) (as the case may be), and

        (ii) that direction is issued after the local planning authority have received the report of the person holding the inquiry or other hearing,

    as soon as practicable after that direction is issued.'.

6.  Omit regulation 27 (consideration of proposals following a local inquiry or other hearng) except in so far as that regulation is applied by regulation 28(2) (consideration of objections without a local inquiry or hearing).
7.  Omit regulation 29 (modification of proposals) except in so far as that regulation is applied by regulation 28(2).
8.  For regulation 30 substitute –

**'Notice of intention to adopt**

30.  Where the authority have given notice of their intention to adopt in accordance with regulation 24A(3)(b)(vii) or in Form 9 or Form 10, a plan or proposals to which regulation 22 applies shall not be adopted by the authority until the period specified by the authority in that notice has expired.'

9.  In regulation 31 (adoption) –

    (a) for paragraph (1) substitute –

'(1) Where a local planning authority adopt a plan or proposals to which regulation 22 refers they shall –

    (a) give notice by advertisement of the following matters –

        (i) the title of the plan or proposals;

        (ii) that the plan or proposals have been adopted and the date of adoption;

        (iii) if the Secretary of State issued a direction under sections 17(1) or 43(4) of the 1990 Act that –

            (aa) the Secretary of State withdrew that direction, or

            (bb) he was satisfied that the necessary modifications to the plan or proposals had been made to comply with that direction;

        (iv) that copies of the adopted plan or proposals and, where relevant, copies of the Secretary of State's notification of the matters specified in paragraph (iii)(aa) or (bb) are available for inspection and the places and times at which they can be inspected;

(v)   that copies of the adopted plan can be obtained on request and on payment of a reasonable charge;

(vi)   that any person aggrieved by the adopted plan or proposals may make an application to the High Court under section 287 of the 1990 Act and –

(aa)   the grounds on which such an application may be made,

(bb)   the time within which such an application must be made;

(b)   notify any person who has asked to be notified of the adoption of the plan or proposals of the matters specified in sub-paragraph (a)(i), (ii) and (iv) to (vi) and, if applicable, in sub-paragraph (a)(iii); and

(c)   publish the plan, the plan as altered, or the replacement plan as the case may be on their website.'; and

(b)   in paragraph (3) for 'four copies' substitute 'one copy'.

10.   (1)   Subject to paragraph (2), in regulation 33 (direction to modify proposals) for paragraph (1) substitute –

'(1)   Where the Secretary of State directs a local planning authority to modify their proposals under section 17(1), 35(2) or 43(4), the authority shall make a copy of the direction available for inspection at each place at which the plan or proposals were made available for inspection under regulation 22(1)(a).'

(2)   Paragraph (1) does not apply to a plan or proposals to which regulation 28 applies.

11.   In regulation 35 (called-in proposals) –

(a)   for paragraph (1)(b) substitute –

'(b)   give notice by advertisement of the following matters –

(i)   the title of the statutory plan proposals;

(ii)   the name of the local planning authority;

(iii)   that the proposals have been submitted to the Secretary of State for his approval and the date when this occurred;

(iv)   that the Secretary of State proposes to modify the proposals;

(v)   that copies of the proposals and lists of the proposed modifications are available for inspection and the places and times at which they can be inspected;

(vi)   the period within which and the address to which representations on the proposed modifications must be made;

(vii)   that any representations made may be accompanied by a request to be notified at a specified address of the approval or rejection of the statutory plan proposals;'

(b)   for paragraph (7)(a) substitute –

'(a)   give notice by advertisement of the following matters –

(i)   the title of the statutory plan proposals;

(ii)   the name of the local planning authority;

(iii)   that the statutory plan proposals have been submitted to the Secretary of State for his approval and the date when this occurred;

(iv)   whether the Secretary of State has approved or rejected the proposals and, if he has approved the proposals, whether he has done so in whole or in part and with or without modifications or reservations;

(v)   that copies of the Secretary of State's letter notifying his decision are available for inspection and the places and times at which they can be inspected;

(vi)   if the Secretary of State has approved any part of the proposals –

(aa)    that any person aggrieved by the approved proposals may make an application to the High Court under section 287 of the 1990 Act,

(bb)    the grounds on which such an application may be made, and

(cc)    the time within which such an application must be made;'.

12.  After regulation 45 insert –

'Electronic communications

46.  (1)    Where any provision of these Regulations –

(a)    requires a person to send a document, a copy of a document or any notice to another person, or

(b)    requires a person to notify another person of any matter; and

(c)    that other person has an address for the purposes of electronic communications,

the document, copy, notice or notification may be sent or made by way of electronic communications.

(2)    Where any provision of these Regulations enables a person to make representations on any matter or document, those representations may be made –

(a)    in writing, or

(b)    by way of electronic communications.

(3)    Where –

(a)    electronic communications are used as mentioned in paragraph (1) or (2), and

(b)    the communication is received by the recipient outside their office hours,

it shall be taken to have been received on the next working day, and in this subsection "working day" means a day which is not a Saturday, Sunday, Bank Holiday or other public holiday.'

13.  In the Schedule to the 1999 Regulations, omit Forms 7, 11, 12 and 13.

14.  In the Schedule to the 1999 Regulations, for Form 10 substitute the following form –

'FORM 10

**Regulation 29**

NOTICE OF INTENTION TO ADOPT AND OF PROPOSED MODIFICATIONS TO A UNITARY DEVELOPMENT PLAN, LOCAL PLAN, MINERALS LOCAL PLAN OR WASTE LOCAL PLAN, OR PROPOSALS FOR THE ALTERATION OR REPLACEMENT OF SUCH A PLAN

Town and Country Planning Act 1990

**Notice of intention to adopt and of proposed modifications to [proposals for the [alteration] [replacement] of] a [Unitary Development Plan] [Local Plan] [Minerals Local Plan] [Waste Local Plan]**

(Title of plan)

[The [local inquiry] [hearing] into [this plan] [these proposals] has been held and the report of the person holding the [inquiry] [hearing] has been considered by (1).] [(1) has considered the objections and representations made to [this plan] [these proposals].]

(1)    propose to make [further] modifications to [this plan] [these proposals].

A list of the proposed modifications (other than modifications which the authority are satisfied will not materially affect the content of the [plan] [proposals]), with the authority's reasons for proposing them, are available for inspection at (2) on (3). Also available for inspection are:

copies of the [plan] [proposals];

[a direction from the Secretary of State directing the authority to modify the [plan] [proposals];]

[the report of the person who held the [local inquiry] [hearing] and the authority's statement of reasons and decisions in the light of the report;]

[the authority's statement of reasons and decisions as respects objections to the [plan] [proposals].]

[The authority do not intend to accept all of the recommendations in the report. A list of the recommendations which the authority do not intend to accept is available for inspection with the above documents.]

Objections to, and representations in respect of, the proposed modifications [and the intention not to modify the [plan] [proposals] in accordance with certain of the recommendations in the report] should be sent in writing to (4) before (5). Objections and representations should specify the matters to which they relate and the grounds on which they are made. They may be accompanied by a request to be notified at a specified address of the withdrawal, adoption, approval or rejection of the [plan] [proposals].

### Notice of Intention to Adopt Proposals

If no objections are received during the period given for making objections [and the Secretary of State is satisfied that the modifications proposed conform with his direction or the direction is withdrawn], (1) intend to adopt the [plan] [proposals] on the expiry of that period.

Notes

a)   Omit any expression within square brackets which is inappropriate.
b)   The first sentence of the first paragraph and the third indent of the third paragraph apply where there has been no inquiry or hearing.
c)   Insert at:
   (1)   the name of the local planning authority;
   (2)   the address of the local planning authority's principal office and any other place at which the documents are available for inspection;
   (3)   the days on which, and the hours between which, the documents are available for inspection;
   (4)   the name or title of the officer to whom objections and representations should be sent and the address to which they are to be sent;
   (5)   the date (six weeks from the date on which the notice is first published in a local newspaper) by which objections and representations should be received.'

## 2004 NO. 2206

## TOWN AND COUNTRY PLANNING, ENGLAND

## The Town and Country Planning (Initial Regional Spatial Strategy) (England) Regulations 2004

Made 26th August 2004
Laid before Parliament 7th September 2004
Coming into force 28th September 2004

The First Secretary of State, in exercise of the powers conferred upon him by section 1(5) of the Planning and Compulsory Purchase Act 2004, hereby makes the following Regulations:

### Citation, commencement and application

1.  (1)  These Regulations may be cited as the Town and Country Planning (Initial Regional Spatial Strategy)(England) Regulations 2004 and shall come into force on 28th September 2004.
    (2)  These Regulations apply in relation to England only.

### Initial Regional Spatial Strategies

2.  The regional planning guidance set out in the first column of the Schedule to these Regulations is prescribed as the regional spatial strategy for the corresponding region in the second column of that Schedule.

## SCHEDULE
Regulation 2

| Regional planning guidance | Region |
|---|---|
| Regional Planning Guidance for the North East to 2016 (RPG1, November 2002) | North East |
| Regional Planning Guidance for East Anglia to 2016 (RPG6, November 2000) and such part of the Regional Planning Guidance for the South East (RPG 9 March 2001) as relates to Hertfordshire, Bedfordshire and Essex. | East of England |
| Regional Planning Guidance for the East Midlands to 2021 (RPG8, January 2002) | East Midlands |
| Regional Planning Guidance for the South East (RPG9, March 2001) as revised in July 2004 by the Regional Transport Strategy (Chapter 9) and the Ashford Growth Area (Chapter 12) and excluding such part as relates to Greater London, Hertfordshire, Bedfordshire and Essex | South East |
| Regional Planning Guidance for the South West (RPG10, September 2001) | South West |
| Regional Planning Guidance for the West Midlands (RPG11, June 2004) | West Midlands |
| Regional Planning Guidance for Yorkshire and the Humber to 2016 (RPG12, October 2001) | Yorkshire and the Humber |
| Regional Planning Guidance for the North West (RPG13, March 2003) | North West |

2004 NO. 2208

TOWN AND COUNTRY PLANNING, ENGLAND

## The Town and Country Planning (Regional Planning Guidance as Revision of Regional Spatial Strategy) Order 2004

Made 26th August 2004
Laid before Parliament 7th September 2004
Coming into force 28th September 2004

The First Secretary of State, thinking that steps taken in connection with the preparation of parts of regional planning guidance correspond to steps which must be taken under Part 1 of the Planning and Compulsory Purchase Act 2004 in connection with the preparation and publication of revisions of regional spatial strategies, in exercise of the powers conferred upon him by section 10(8) of the Act, hereby makes the following Order:

### Citation, commencement and application

1. (1) This Order may be cited as the Town and Country Planning (Regional Planning Guidance as Revision of Regional Spatial Strategy) Order 2004 and shall come into force on 28th September 2004.
   (2) This Order applies in relation to England only.

### Steps having effect as revisions of Regional Spatial Strategies

2. The part of the regional planning guidance set out in the first column of the Schedule to this Order shall have effect as a revision of the regional spatial strategy specified in the corresponding entry in the second column of that Schedule.

## SCHEDULE

### Article 2

| *Part of the Regional Planning Guidance* | *Steps Taken in the Preparation of a Revision of the Regional Spatial Strategy having effect as a Revision of the Regional Spatial Strategy (References to sections are references to sections of the Planning and Compulsory Purchase Act 2004.)* |
|---|---|
| Development of initial detailed proposals, including different provisions for different parts of the region, for the revision of Regional Planning Guidance for the North East to 2016 (RPG 1, November 2002) | Preparation of a draft revision of the RSS for the North East Region, which once prepared must be published and submitted to the Secretary of State in accordance with section 5(8). |
| Publication by the Secretary of State of proposed changes to the draft selective revision of Regional Planning Guidance for the East Midlands to 2021 (RPG8, January 2002) (excluding such part of the Milton Keynes and South Midlands Sub-Regional Strategy that applies to the region) contained in the 'Revised Regional Planning Guidance for the East Midlands to 2021 Draft Proposed Changes. Public Consultation Draft, July 2004' and accompanied by a statement of reasons | Publication by the Secretary of State of his proposed changes to the draft revision of the RSS for the East Midland Region and of his reasons (section 9(3)). |
| Secretary of State consideration of the Panel report of the public examination into the draft revisions of such parts of the following regional planning guidance as are affected by the Milton Keynes and South Midlands Sub-Regional Strategy and any representations not considered by the Panel: <br><br> – Regional Planning Guidance for the East Midlands to 2021 (RPG8, January 2002) <br> – Regional Planning Guidance for the South East (RPG9, March 2001) as revised in July 2004 by the Regional Transport Strategy (Chapter 9) and the Ashford Growth Area (Chapter 12) and excluding such part as relates to Greater London, Hertfordshire, Bedfordshire and Essex <br> – Regional Planning Guidance 14 for the East of England Draft Strategy, February 2004 which are contained in the 'Milton Keynes and South Midlands Sub Regional Strategy. Public Examination March/April 2004. Report of the Panel, August 2004'. | Consideration by the Secretary of State of the report by the person appointed to hold an examination of the draft revision of the RSS for the following regions and of representations not considered by the person appointed to hold the examination (section 9(2)) <br><br> – East Midlands <br> – South East <br> – East of England. |
| Decision by the Secretary of State to hold a public examination after the submission of the draft revision of the minerals and waste policies of Regional Planning Guidance for the South East (RPG9, March 2001), as revised in July 2004 by the Regional Transport Strategy (Chapter 9) and the Ashford Growth Area (Chapter 12) and excluding such part as relates to Greater London, Hertfordshire, Bedfordshire and Essex, which is contained in the 'Proposed Alterations to Regional Planning Guidance, South East – Regional Waste Management Strategy, March 2004' and the 'Proposed Alterations to Regional Planning Guidance, South East – Regional Minerals Strategy, March 2004'. | Decision by the Secretary of State to hold an examination in public of the draft revision of the RSS for the South East Region (section 7(3)). |

| Part of the Regional Planning Guidance | Steps Taken in the Preparation of a Revision of the Regional Spatial Strategy having effect as a Revision of the Regional Spatial Strategy (References to sections are references to sections of the Planning and Compulsory Purchase Act 2004.) |
|---|---|
| Publication by the Secretary of State of proposed changes to the draft revision of Regional Planning Guidance for the South East (RPG9, March 2001) in relation to energy efficiency and renewable energy, tourism and related sport and recreation, which are contained in the 'Proposed Changes to Regional Planning Guidance for the South East (RPG9). Energy Efficiency and Renewable Energy, Tourism and Related Sport and Recreation. Public Consultation July 2004' and accompanied by a statement of reasons. | Publication by the Secretary of State of his proposed changes to the draft revision of the RSS for the South East Region and of his reasons (section 9(3)). |
| Preparation of a draft revision of Regional Planning Guidance for the South East (RPG9, March 2001) (including such part of the Milton Keynes and South Midlands Sub-Regional Strategy that applies in the region) and notification of the Secretary of State of intention to do so by the regional assembly. | Preparation of a draft revision of the RSS for the South East Region and notification to the Secretary of State of the regional planning body's intention to do so (section 5(1) and (2)). |
| Preparation of a draft revision of Regional Planning Guidance for the South West (RPG10, September 2001) and notification of the Secretary of State of intention to do so by the regional assembly. | Preparation of a draft revision of the RSS for the South West Region and notification to the Secretary of State of the regional planning body's intention to do so (section 5(1) and (2)). |
| Publication by the Secretary of State of the proposed changes to the draft selective revision of Regional Planning Guidance for Yorkshire and the Humber to 2016 (RPG12, October 2001), which is contained in the 'Proposed Changes to Draft Revised Regional Planning Guidance (RPG12) for Yorkshire and the Humber. Public Consultation Draft, July 2004' and accompanied by a statement of reasons. | Publication by the Secretary of State of his proposed changes to the draft revision of the RSS for the region of Yorkshire and the Humber and of his reasons (section 9(3)). |
| Preparation of a draft full revision of Regional Planning Guidance for Yorkshire and the Humber to 2016 (RPG12, October 2001) and notification to the Secretary of State of the intention to do so by the regional assembly. | Preparation of a draft revision of the RSS for the region of Yorkshire and the Humber and notification to the Secretary of State of the regional planning body's intention to do so (section 5(1) and (2)). |
| Decision by the Secretary of State to hold a public examination after the submission of the draft partial revision of Regional Planning Guidance for the North West (RPG13, March 2003), which are contained in the 'Partial Review of Regional Planning Guidance for the North West (RPG13). Submitted Draft Revised RPG, March 2004'. | Decision by the Secretary of State to hold an examination in public of the draft revision of the RSS for the North West Region (section 8(1)). |
| Development of the initial detailed proposals, including different provisions for different parts of the region, for the revision of Regional Planning Guidance (RPG14) for the East of England Draft Strategy (excluding such part of the Milton Keynes and South Midlands Sub-Regional Strategy that applies to the region). | Preparation of a draft revision of the RSS for the East of England Region (for publication and submission to the Secretary of State under section 5(8)). |

## 2004 NO. 204 (C.8)

## TOWN AND COUNTRY PLANNING, ENGLAND

## The Planning and Compulsory Purchase Act 2004 (Commencement No.4 and Savings) Order 2005

### Made 3rd February 2005

The Secretary of State, in exercise of the powers conferred upon him by section 121(1) and (2) and section 122(3) of the Planning and Compulsory Purchase Act 2004, and after consultation with the National Assembly for Wales, hereby makes the following Order:

#### Citation and interpretation

1.    (1)    This Order may be cited as the Planning and Compulsory Purchase Act 2004 (Commencement No. 4 and Savings) Order 2005.
      (2)    In this Order 'the Act' means the Planning and Compulsory Purchase Act 2004.

#### Provisions coming into force on 7th March 2005 in relation to England

2.    To the extent to which they are not already in force, sections 52 and 53 of the Act shall come into force in relation to England on 7th March 2005.

#### Provisions coming into force on 1st April 2005 in relation to England

3.    Subject to article 4 and to the extent to which they are not already in force, section 55 of, and Schedule 2 to, the Act shall come into force in relation to England on 1st April 2005.

#### Savings

4.    (1)    This paragraph applies to a decision mentioned in paragraph (1) or (2) of Schedule 2 to the Act which is to be taken on or after 1st April 2005 following the holding of an inquiry or hearing which closed before that date.
      (2)    This paragraph applies to a decision mentioned in paragraph (1) or (2) of Schedule 2 to the Act which is to be taken on or after 1st April 2005 where –
            (a)    the decision relates to an appeal which is to be disposed of on the basis of written representations following a visit to the site which is the subject of the appeal; and
            (b)    that visit took place before that date.
      (3)    Schedule 2 to the Act shall have no effect in relation to a decision to which paragraph (1) or (2) above applies.

# INDEX

# Business Tenancies

## A Guide to the New Law

### *Jason Hunter*

Part II of the Landlord and Tenant Act 1954 was amended by a Regulatory Reform Order implemented on 1 June 2004. This book gives a clear explanation of the changes and, crucially, places each change in the context of the position prior to implementation.

Useful appendices include:

- the Regulatory Reform Order (Business Tenancies) (England and Wales) 2003
- the 'Keeling Schedule' from the Office of the Deputy Prime Minister (giving a quick reference to the changes)
- the Landlord and Tenant Act 1954, Part 2 (Notices) Regulations 2004.

Also included are worked examples to illustrate how the changes might take effect in practice.

**Jason Hunter** is a partner and head of Russell-Cooke's Contentious Property department where he specialises in commercial and residential property disputes.

Available from Marston Book Services:
Tel. 01235 465 656.

1 85328 956 6
200 pages
£39.95
June 2004

The Law Society

# Conveyancing Handbook

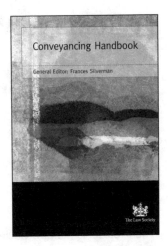

## 12th Edition

*General Editor:*
*Frances Silverman*

The most reliable, accurate, and up-to-date source of information and guidance on all aspects of conveyancing practice, this book has been specifically designed to give busy practitioners the answers to their everyday questions.

The Handbook collects all the relevant guidance from a multitude of sources so practitioners never have to search far for an answer or authority.

Specific elements new to the 12th edition include:

- a new chapter on Licensing
- the Stamp Duty Land Tax guidance and rates
- the Solicitors' Practice (Conveyancing) Amendment Rules 2005
- revisions to Part 1 of the CML Lenders' Handbook
- an outline of the Land Registry's plans for e-conveyancing
- an introduction to Home Information Packs.

Available from Marston Book Services:
Tel. 01235 465 656.

1 85328 928 0
Approx: 1312 pages
£79.95
Due Autumn 2005

The Law Society

# A Guide to the National Conveyancing Protocol

## 5th Edition

*The Law Society*

The Protocol is the Law Society's definitive guide to best practice in domestic transactions of freehold and leasehold property. This edition has been revised to cover changes to the legal framework, including commonhold, Stamp Duty Land Tax, Money Laundering Regulations 2003 and the Land Registration Act 2002.

This concise, user-friendly reference guide contains copies of all the latest editions of the TransAction forms:

- Seller's Property Information Form (fourth edition)
- Seller's Leasehold Information Form (third edition)
- Fixtures, Fittings and Contents (fourth edition)
- Completion Information and Requisitions on Title (second edition)
- Seller's Commonhold Information Form (first edition)

Written by the Law Society's TransAction Working Party, it is essential reading for practitioners.

Available from Marston Book Services:
Tel. 01235 465 656.

1 85328 997 3
144 pages
£19.95
April 2005

The Law Society